GLOBALIZATION AND NEOLIBERALISM

GLOBALIZATION AND NEOLIBERALISM

The Caribbean Context

Edited by Thomas Klak

ROWMAN & LITTLEFIELD PUBLISHERS, INC.
Lanham • Boulder • New York • Oxford

ROWMAN & LITTLEFIELD PUBLISHERS, INC.

Published in the United States of America
by Rowman & Littlefield Publishers, Inc.
4720 Boston Way, Lanham, Maryland 20706

12 Hid's Copse Road
Cummor Hill, Oxford OX2 9JJ, England

British Library Cataloguing in Publication Information Available

Library of Congress Cataloging-in-Publication Data
Globalization and neoliberalism : the Caribbean context / [edited by] Thomas
Klak.
    p.   cm.
    Includes bibliographical references and index.
    ISBN 0-8476-8536-5 (alk. paper).—ISBN 0-8476-8537-3 (pbk. : alk. paper)
    1. Caribbean Area—Economic conditions—1945– . 2. Caribbean
Area—Economic policy.   I. Klak, Thomas, 1957– .
HC151.G58   1998
338.9729—dc21   97-30698
                                                                      CIP

ISBN 0-8476-8536-5 (cloth : alk. paper)
ISBN 0-8476-8537-3 (pbk. : alk. paper)

Printed in the United States of America

On 6 March 1997 two Caribbean champions of social justice and self-determination—Jamaica's Michael Manley and Guyana's Cheddi Jagan—died. Although forced in recent years to relax their campaigns for democratic socialism by the combined pressures of imperialist intervention, trade deterioration, foreign debt, and domestic backlash, both remained philosophically committed. This book is dedicated to them and their ideals.

Contents

Figures

Tables

Acronyms

ABC	Aruba, Bonaire, and Curaçao (Dutch islands)
ACP	African-Caribbean-Pacific countries, seventy in all, that are former colonies of European Union member states and signatories to the Lomé Convention
BLP	Barbados Labor Party
CARDI	Caribbean Agricultural Research and Development Institute: a CARICOM subsidiary organization that conducts and disseminates the results of agricultural research in the region
CARIBCAN	Caribbean-Canadian trade agreement
CARICOM	Caribbean Community and Common Market: the primary organization oriented toward achieving higher levels of integration within the English-speaking Caribbean, and now extending to incorporate other countries of the region
CARIFTA	Caribbean Free Trade Agreement
CBI	Caribbean Basin Initiative: trade agreement with the United States
CMEA	Council for Mutual Economic Assistance: former trading alliance among state socialist countries, including the Soviet Union, its allies, and Cuba; also abbreviated COMECON
CTO	Caribbean Tourism Organization: an international organization that promotes tourism cooperatively among Caribbean member states; it also serves as a source of tourism-related data
DLP	Democratic Labor Party (Barbados)
EC	European Community (now the European Union [or EU])
ECU	European Currency Unit
EPNDP	Export Processing within Neoliberal Development Policy
EPZ	Export Processing Zone
EU	European Union: a group of fifteen (as of 1997) Western European countries pursuing a high level of economic integration
FAO	Food and Agriculture Organization: a United Nations subsidiary responsible for monitoring global food supplies and for conducting and disseminating research on agriculture and food-production issues

FDI	Foreign Direct Investment: investment in operations; contrasts with portfolio investment in stocks, bonds, bank deposits, and other relatively liquid assets
FTAA	Free Trade Association of the Americas
GATT	General Agreement on Tariffs and Trade: one of the Bretton Woods institutions created to shape the post-World War II world economy, the GATT has given way to the WTO in the 1990s
GSP	Generalized System of Preferences
INS	Immigration and Naturalization Service, U.S. government
JAMPRO	Jamaica's Investment Promotion Agency
JLP	Jamaican Labour Party
JUCEPLAN	Former central planning body of the Cuban government
MERCOSUR	Southern Common Market, the trade alliance of Brazil, Uruguay, Paraguay, and Argentina, with Chile joining in 1997
NGO	Nongovernmental Organization
NIC	Newly Industrialized Countries (of East Asia)
NTAE	Nontraditional Agricultural Exports
OAS	Organization of American States
OECD	Organization for Economic Cooperation and Development, trade forum and economic research body of wealthy capitalist countries
OECS	Organization of Eastern Caribbean States: an organization aimed at pooling the limited resources and enhancing economic, political, cultural, and social integration among the member states of Antigua and Barbuda, Dominica, Grenada, Montserrat, St. Kitts and Nevis, St. Lucia, and St. Vincent and the Grenadines
PNC	People's National Congress (Guyana)
PNM	People's National Movement (Trinidad and Tobago)
PNP	People's National Party (Jamaica)
PPP	People's Progressive Party (Guyana)
PRG	People's Revolutionary Government (Grenada)
SIECA	Secretariat for Central American Integration
T&T	Trinidad and Tobago
TNC	Transnational Corporation
TOJ	Telecommunications of Jamaica
UBPC	Basic Units of Cooperative Production, Cuba
WI	West Indies
WIBDECO	Windward Islands Banana Development Corporation: founded in 1995, it is an umbrella agency for the banana-marketing boards of Dominica, Grenada, St. Lucia, and St. Vincent; together with Fyffes, Ltd., it purchased Geest, Ltd.'s banana operations in the eastern Caribbean
WTO	World Trade Organization: created in 1994 as a result of the Uruguay round of GATT negotiations, it replaces the GATT and has stronger enforcement powers to liberalize world trade

Preface

The idea for this book originated with seven paper sessions on Caribbean development that I organized with Dennis Conway for the Association of American Geographers (AAG) annual meeting in Charlotte, North Carolina, in April 1996. All of the papers were completed specifically for the purpose of this book and have not been previously published.

The three maps and two tables are designed to provide a geographical and statistical overview of the Caribbean region. All Caribbean place-names mentioned in the book are located on one of the three maps that portray different parts of the Caribbean region. Each chapter is followed by three suggested further readings. Additional reading suggestions can be obtained from the editor (email: tcklak@miamiu.muohio.edu). The book's collected bibliography contains many of the seminal works of Caribbean scholarship, as well as key works in the recent literature on Caribbean development, globalization, and political economy. The bibliography should serve as a useful compilation of references for anyone interested in pursuing research and study on contemporary Caribbean development.

Acknowledgments

I would like to thank several people for providing crucial elements of this book project. Janice Glenn formatted and edited most chapters and most tables in the chapters, obtained some data for the project, and did copying, letters, and mailings. She also decoded my bad penmanship to make editorial changes to most chapters. Debbi White assisted me with making editorial changes to chapters, copying, and collating. Mark Killian helped put the tables in final format. He also made corrections to a chapter on diskette. Pam Martin took primary responsibility for the maps and tables that appear prior to chapter 1. Mike Walczak compiled a list of the place-names and the collected bibliography. Mike Hollingsworth of Indiana University's geography department produced map 1. Kevin Young kindly offered some guidance during the map production. Peter Claggett deftly compiled the index. For comments on chapter 1 I wish to thank Tony Bebbington, Jessica Byron, Raju Das, Alex Dupuy, Jeanne Hey, Cristóbal Kay, Pam Martin, Beverley Mullings, Emilio Pantojas-García, Sarah Ratcliffe, and Bon Richardson. The result is my responsibility alone.

Finally I wish to thank Jeanne and Jackson for being tolerant and understanding of my late night absences while completing the book. I promise to work at keeping a more reasonable schedule in the future.

I close on a somber note. One contributing author, Aaron Segal, died 17 April 1997. A week later, I asked another Latin American studies scholar, Bud Kenworthy, if he had known Segal. Indeed he had. Twenty-five years before, when the two were on the political science faculty at Cornell, Aaron's generosity shined through. When a personal tragedy occurred in Bud's life, Aaron stepped forward to take over teaching his course on Latin American politics. Over his long career, Aaron was tenaciously devoted to Caribbean research and to the betterment of Caribbean people.

Maps

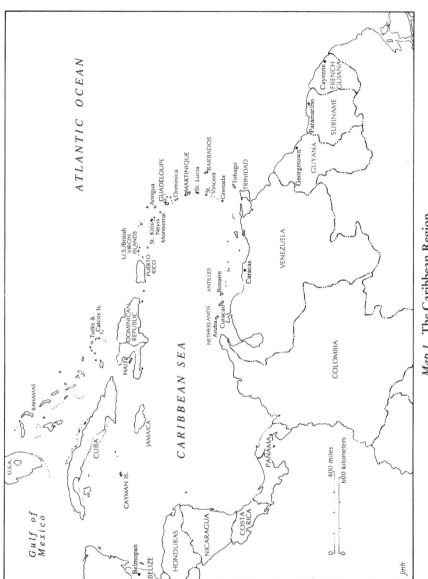

Map 1. The Caribbean Region

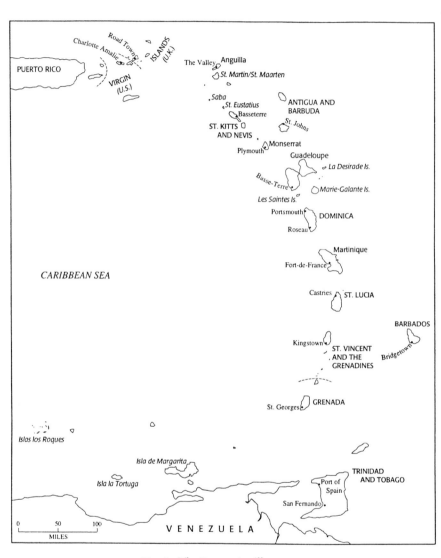

Map 2. The Lesser Antilles

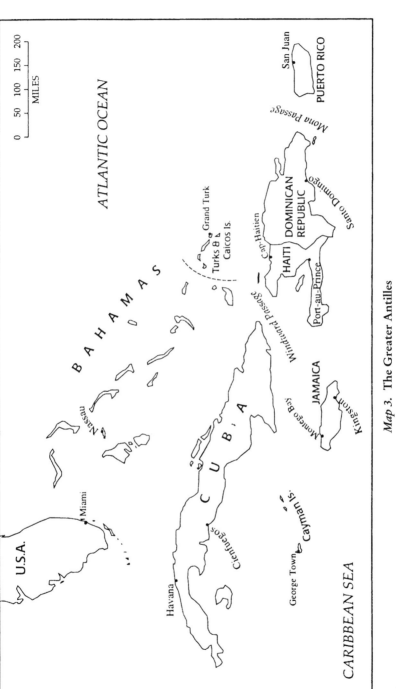

Map 3. The Greater Antilles

Introductory Tables

TABLE 1
Countries and Territories of the Caribbean

	Political Status	Capital	Area (sq mi)
Anguilla	British Colony	The Valley	35
Antigua and Barbuda	Independent 1981	St. John's	171
Aruba	Non-metropolitan territory of the Netherlands	Oranjestad	75
Bahamas	Independent 1973	Nassau	5382
Barbados	Independent 1966	Bridgetown	166
Belize	Independent 1981	Belmopan	8867
British Virgin Islands	British Colony	Road Town	59
Cayman Islands	British Colony	George Town	102
Cuba	Independent 1902	Havana	42804
Dominica	Independent 1978	Roseau	290
Dominican Republic	Independent 1844	Santo Domingo	18704
French Guiana	Overseas Department of France	Cayenne	33399
Grenada	Independent 1974	St. George's	133
Guadeloupe	Overseas Department of France	Basse-Terre	687
Guyana	Independent 1966	Georgetown	83000
Haiti	Independent 1804	Port-au-Prince	10597
Jamaica	Independent 1962	Kingston	4244
Martinique	Overseas Department of France	Fort-de-France	421
Montserrat	British Colony	Plymouth	40
Netherlands Antilles	Non-metropolitan territory of the Netherlands	Willemstad	308
Puerto Rico	US Commonwealth	San Juan	3515
St. Kitts and Nevis	Independent 1983	Basseterre	104
St. Lucia	Independent 1979	Castries	238
St. Vincent and the Grenadines	Independent 1979	Kingstown	150
Suriname	Independent 1975	Paramaribo	63251
Trinidad and Tobago	Independent 1962	Port of Spain	1978
Turks and Caicos Islands	British Colony	Cockburn Town	193
US Virgin Islands	US Territory	Charlotte Amalie	136

Source: Richardson 1992

TABLE 2
Caribbean Social and Economic Indicators

	Pop.	IMR	PCGDP (year)	Debt-US$ (year)	Industries
Anguilla	10	23.0	7600 (94)	NA	tourism, boats, offshore finance
Antigua and Barbuda	66	17.2	6600 (94)	377 (95)	tourism, construction, light manufacturing
Aruba	68	8.2	18000 (94)	669 (95)	tourism, transshipment, oil
Bahamas	259	23.3	18700 (95)	408 (94)	tourism, banking, cement
Barbados	257	18.7	9800 (95)	408 (95)	tourism, sugar, light manufacturing
Belize	219	33.9	2750 (94)	168 (92)	garments, food, tourism
British Virgin Is.	13	19.1	10600 (91)	5 (85)	tourism, light industry, construction
Cayman Is.	35	8.4	22500 (94)	15 (86)	tourism, banking, insurance & finance
Cuba	10951	9.0	1300 (95)	9100 (95) 20000 (95)*	sugar, petroleum, food
Dominica	83	9.6	2450 (95)	92.8 (92)	soap, coconut oil, tourism
Dominican Republic	8089	47.7	3400 (95)	4600 (94)	tourism, sugar, ferronickel & gold
French Guiana	151	14.6	6000 (93)	1200 (88)	construction, shrimp, forestry
Grenada	95	11.9	3000 (95)	89 (95)	food, textiles, light assembly
Guadeloupe	408	8.3	9200 (95)	NA	construction, cement, rum
Guyana	712	51.4	2200 (95)	2200 (94)	bauxite, sugar, rice
Haiti	6732	103.8	1000 (95)	827 (95)	sugar, flour, textiles
Jamaica	2595	15.6	3200 (95)	3600 (94)	bauxite, tourism, textiles
Martinique	399	7.1	10000 (95)	180 (94)	construction, rum, cememt
Monserrat	13	11.8	4500 (94)	10 (94)	tourism, rum, electronics
Netherlands Antilles	209	8.9	10400 (94)	1950 (95)	tourism, petroleum, light manufacturing
Puerto Rico	3819	12.4	7800 (95)	NA	pharmaceuticals, electronics, apparel
St. Kitts and Nevis	41	18.9	5380 (95)	45 (94)	sugar, tourism, cotton
St. Lucia	158	20.0	4080 (95)	223 (95)	clothing, electronics, beverages
St. Vincent & the Grenadines	118	16.8	2060 (95)	75 (93)	food, cement, furniture
Suriname	436	29.3	2950 (95)	180 (93)	bauxite, lumber, food
Trinidad and Tobago	1272	18.2	12100 (95)	2000 (94)	petroleum, chemicals, tourism
Turks and Caicos Is.	14	12.6	6000 (92)	NA	fishing, tourism, offshore finance
US Virgin Is.	97	12.5	12500 (87)	NA	tourism, petroleum, watches

Notes: Population figures are for 1996 and measured in thousands; IMR (infant mortality rate) figures are for 1996; External Debt is measured in millions.
*Russian Debt
Source: The World Factbook 1997, http://odci.gov/cia/publications/nsolo/factbook/global.htm

I

INTRODUCTION

1

Thirteen Theses on Globalization and Neoliberalism

Thomas Klak

Two of the most common terms used to characterize current and emerging trends on the international scene are *globalization* and *neoliberalism*. The conventional understanding of globalization views it as a process of international integration that defines the present and future economic reality. Neoliberal policy represents a country's ticket or passport to the globalizing economy. Using the analytical lens of political economy, this chapter offers a critical assessment of the globalization thesis, especially as it applies to the Caribbean region. By extension, the chapter also evaluates globalization's policy affiliate, neoliberalism. This is accomplished through an analytical framework for globalization and neoliberalism in the form of thirteen theses.

In this book *the Caribbean* refers to the island territories of the Caribbean Sea, plus the four mainland territories of Belize, Guyana, Suriname, and French Guiana, which are historically and culturally linked to the islands (see map 1; chap. 10 provides reasons behind this geographical definition). Many of the book's themes are also highly relevant to the small countries of neighboring Central America and to the many others across the global periphery that now pursue export-oriented economic development (Henke and Boxill 1998). This chapter raises a number of broad conceptual issues that both frame and summarize the more detailed investigations of globalization and neoliberalism in the Caribbean context in subsequent chapters.

Although *globalization* has become a common term in corporate and political circles, neither the mass media nor scholars define it, much less interrogate it against evidence. In fact, *globalization* is perhaps the most overused, abused, and (as I will argue below) dangerous euphemism for the current restructuring of international capitalism. Most contemporary discourse takes it for granted that globalization is now occurring. Indeed, globalization is more than just an assumed occurrence; it is elevated to the level of a powerful worldwide force. So the first point to be stressed is that detailed empirical documentation of globalization trends is severely lacking in comparison with a burgeoning literature whose use of the term evokes a range of meanings. This chapter therefore also asks, What does globalization mean, in what sense are we globalizing, and what are the implications for peripheral regions such as the Caribbean?

Judging from the contexts in which a globalization thesis is invoked, it is possible to discern some of the meanings and messages behind this highly equivocal term. The literature can be classified in terms of whether globalization trends are interpreted as *positive or negative* with respect to global and national distributions of power, wealth, and development, and political and economic struggles over resources. This is my classification of the literature, although not all writers accept it. Some mainstream writers deny that globalization trends have any impact at all on political power and struggle, or even that differential power and struggle is a central feature of the capitalist world. Such a view often portrays economic trends simply as "natural" results of "efficiency" and "progress." However, the assumed progress associated with capitalist economic trends in mainstream views connects it with interpretations of globalization implying that it is a positive force. Robert Cox (1996, 23) suggests this connection when he observes that "globalization began to be represented as a finality, as the logical and inevitable culmination of the powerful tendencies of the market at work. The dominance of economic forces was regarded as both necessary and beneficial."

Connections between mainstream schools of thought can be taken one step further. It is important to note the intellectual affinity among (1) conventional views of economic progress and globalization, (2) upwardly progressive views of development emanating from modernization theory and Walt Rostow in the 1950s, and (3) today's neoliberal economic thought that speaks of unleashing global market forces from the dampening effects of states (Kay 1989; Cubitt 1995; Corbridge 1995; Green 1995; Leyshon 1997). It is in part a response to these interrelated sets of ideas, and in particular the mainstream neglect of power and struggle, that this chapter develops a political economy perspective on globalization and neoliberalism. Because mainstream views often deny the reality of power and struggle, they are status quo reinforcing and therefore serve to perpetuate the highly unequal power distributions at the national and international levels. In other words, imbedded in the mainstream assumption of economic "progress" is an uncritical acceptance of socially constructed systems of inequality, scarcity, and poverty (Sachs 1992; Yapa 1996).

Those making negative assessments of globalization tend to see it as both an ideological force (i.e., a conceptualization of the world) and a material force (i.e., real transnational movements of capital and commodities). From this perspective globalization serves as a tool for investors to extract concessions from states, and for investors and states to extract concessions from workers and other citizens. These critical ideas are developed later in the chapter. First I want to explore the more positive spins on globalization. Many (but certainly not all) of the usages of the term *globalization* in the academic literature can be encompassed by a "global village" concept. By the idea of a global village I refer to the often optimistic, and at times even celebratory (e.g., Reich 1991), notions of what is now taking place in the international political economy, and the implications of these newly emerging trends for peripheral countries such as those in the Caribbean and for their peoples.

Global village ideas suggest that (1) the world is "shrinking" as a result of greater international connectivity, (2) traditional distinctions between core and peripheral regions of the world are blurring, (3) foreign investment, trade, and opportunities for development are more widely distributed across world regions and nation-states, (4) there is convergence into one world economy, to which all places and people can, and generally do, find export market "niches," (5) media and cultural influences are more widespread and multilateral, and (6) people themselves are more integrated through immigration and communications. To varying degrees and in various ways, all these global village components suggest that the world is coming together and balancing out, and they can be viewed as inherently positive about trends in the international political economy. Let's examine the six theses on globalization and neoliberalism listed above. My critique of "global village" components is followed by seven other theses about globalization and neoliberalism that draw more heavily from the critical literature. Throughout the discussion I will discern the relevance of these ideas for understanding the contemporary Caribbean.

Thesis 1: Some globalization writers argue that the world is "shrinking"; this socially and spatially uneven trend is nothing new to Caribbean people. By "shrinking world" I refer to those uses of the term *globalization* that depict growing integration and compression of the world's peoples, places, and nation-states, as well as a blurring of their territorial boundaries. This notion is the essence of the World Bank's 1995 annual report subtitled "Workers in an Integrating World." Similar arguments pervade social science. Giddens (1990, 64) in his book on modernity, for instance, defines globalization as an "intensification of worldwide social relations which link distant localities in such a way that local happenings are shaped by events occurring many miles away and vice versa." Watts (1996, 64–65) similarly declares that "places are now global sites," meaning that places are now products of networks "linking the local to global spaces."

Such emerging global linkages come as no news to people of the Caribbean, which historically is perhaps the most globalized of world regions. Since the 1500s the Caribbean has been controlled by outside powers, based economically on imported labor, cleared to create monocrop landscapes (especially for bananas and sugar cane exported for refining into sugar in Europe), and reliant on the import of virtually everything else needed to sustain local populations. Caribbean sugar cane processing was industrialized before European production was. Because all dimensions of Caribbean society were exogenously constructed and transplanted there, the culture of Afro-Caribbean people from the outset has been detached from its historical and geographical roots, and therefore modern and global. It has blended a wide range of African regional traditions, Asian traditions, West Indian adaptations, and many foreign influences introduced by Europeans or picked up during circular migration for work in other parts of the hemisphere and Europe (Richardson 1992; Mintz 1996).

The Caribbean's historical global integration, modernization, and industrialization, as outlined above, underlie the region's abject dependency, which continues to the present. The Caribbean region is now largely independent from Europe politically but is still reeling under the historical legacies of dependency on outside authorities, suppliers, markets, and geopolitical agendas. Now that the entire world has entered the present era of (U.S.-dominated) globalization, the Caribbean offers a chronicle of the impact produced by exposure to many previous rounds of transformations of global capitalism. As in the past, the world is now "shrinking" very unevenly in spatial and social terms, a point explored further below. For the Caribbean, the present era of globalization needs to be analyzed in terms of a region that has previously needed to adapt to many rounds of it. But first the concept of globalization needs to be unpacked further. There is also a need to distinguish trends attributed to globalization that have empirical support in particular world regions and those that do not, and specify the impacts on the Caribbean.

Thesis 2: Contrary to what some globalization writers suggest, core-periphery relations remain highly relevant for understanding the Caribbean. It is increasingly popular to claim that the traditional division between core and peripheral regions of the world is no more. As Kearney (1995, 548) puts it, "Globalization implies a decay in [the] distinction" between core and periphery. McMichael (1996, 41) states that " 'core' and 'periphery' lose their salience" in favor of "chains of commodity production and exchange." Clifford argues that "the old localizing strategies—bounded by community, by organic culture, by region, by center and periphery . . . obscure as much as they reveal" (Clifford 1994, 303). A related theme in the globalization literature, noted by Hirst and Thompson (1996, 1), is that "national cultures, national economies, and national borders are dissolving."

As always, the trends that scholars highlight cannot be divorced from the analytical methods contemporaneously in vogue (Giddens 1990). Few scholars since the early 1980s have dared to admit any residual intellectual affinity with dependency theory and its component concept of core/periphery relations (see Evans 1985). A conceptualization of a world system integrated by commodity chains is among the ways in which dependency theory has been supplanted (Gereffi and Korzeniewicz 1994).

Commodity chains for certain products such as textiles are unquestionably relevant to the contemporary political economy of the Caribbean, and so in the narrow sense of "core" (i.e., manufacturing) and "periphery" (i.e., primary products) things have indeed changed (Dicken 1992). But the deeper meaning of these terms refers to power, authority, and the accumulation of wealth (Broad 1995). The more important question is whether the fact that production (of certain items) is more geographically dispersed across nation-states indicates an accompanying fundamental redistribution of control over and benefits from production. A few countries, primarily in East Asia, have rapidly raised their income above Third World levels.

But for the vast majority of countries of the South, the gap with respect to global core countries has grown wider over recent decades (UN 1996). The richest of the Caribbean states with more than a quarter of a million people, Trinidad and Tobago, has a per capita income of less than half that of the poorest U.S. state, Mississippi. Garment workers in most Caribbean countries are paid one dollar per hour (or less) compared to the $11 per hour earnings of their U.S. counterparts (NLC 1997). Subcontractors pay Haitian workers less than sixty cents an hour to make clothing with Disney logos. On the other end of the corporate hierarchy, Disney is so profitable that shareholders recently were able to approve CEO Michael Eisner's new contract, purportedly worth $400 million over ten years (about $9,700 per hour). These gaps have little to do with differences in the price of necessities. The cost of living in the Caribbean, which imports much of what it consumes from the United States, is comparable to that of the United States.

The gaps have all to do with (1) class-based exploitation and control over the means of and output from production and (2) the contributions made to these inequities by state policies in core and peripheral countries and by the barriers that nation-states pose to working class mobility.

Core/periphery relations should not be understood as homogeneous regions exploiting other regions (Frank 1966), but as class exploitation that is shaped by political geography through differences in national conditions and the application of state power. Workers in the United States have been able to struggle for a larger share of the surplus value from production, higher wages and better living standards by international standards. In the Caribbean workers have been much less successful on these fronts, owing in large part to states that more heavily favor capital. Since 1959 Cuba has been the major exception to this Caribbean rule, and one result is social indicators that parallel those found in wealthy industrial countries (Eckstein 1994). What Cuba has not escaped is the imposed constraints on development and living standards by the core state to the north. A U.S. State Department white paper a few years ago, for example, estimated that the U.S. economic embargo had lowered Cuban living standards by a third of the level they would be if there were open bilateral relations. For the rest of the Caribbean, U.S. policies have suppressed regimes that favor the working class, and have regularly supported many others that do not allow for collective organizing. They have imposed bilateral trade rules with very unequal consequences (Thomas 1988; Deere et al. 1990; Kenworthy 1995; Dupuy 1997).

In short, the constraints imposed on Caribbean workers by their own capitalist classes and states, and the constraints imposed on Caribbean countries by core states, especially the regional hegemon, the United States, produce vast international gaps in income and living standards. The notion of core-periphery relations is therefore still highly relevant to an understanding of U.S.–Caribbean relations. While some researchers may have grown tired of conceptualizing core/periphery relations, they have not lost their salience for Caribbean states and peoples.

Thesis 3: The benefits of economic "globalization" are concentrated in the core triad, while the so-called lagging countries constitute the vast majority of the world. The notion that foreign investment, trade, and the associated developmental opportunities are becoming more widely distributed across world regions and nation-states is often argued, especially by those working for the World Bank and kindred institutions. Zia Qureshi (1996, 31), a principal economist in the World Bank's Latin American and Caribbean office, characterizes this perspective as follows: "The global economic environment is favorable to continued integration of developing countries into the world economy." Qureshi supports this assessment by noting a recent dramatic increase in the share of direct foreign investment *flows* to developing countries. That share grew from 23 percent in 1985–97 to 40 percent in 1992–94.

But the details suggest less opportunity and optimism. Fully 50 percent of the approximately one-half trillion dollars of flows to developing countries in 1991–94 went to just three—China, Mexico, and Argentina. A total of twelve so-called developing countries received 89 percent of these same investment flows, and the list includes South Korea, Portugal, Hungary, and Turkey. So another way to interpret the global economy's "favorable" circumstances for poor countries is to say that the favorability is highly selective of those generally already better-off.

Other evidence even suggests that the global economy has become *less* economically integrated, particularly for the worse-off countries and regions. Hirst and Thompson (1996), for example, document that for most countries of Western Europe and North America, international trade relative to GDP was greater around a century ago than in recent years. Relatedly, of the world *stock* of direct foreign investment, 81 percent was located in the core triad—the European Union, North America, and Japan as of 1991, up from 69 percent in 1967 (Koechlin 1995, 98). Thus what Qureshi (1996) refers to as the "lagging countries" in fact constitutes the vast majority of the world, including the Caribbean. Most have recently made large sacrifices under the IMF- and World Bank–directed neoliberal transformation, but have few economic gains to show for that effort. There is indeed a global integration apace with regard to the basic ideas about development and neoliberal policy, but the material rewards are enormously unequal.

Thesis 4: Enthusiasm for the "export market niches" availed by globalization and neoliberalism should be tempered by noting the parallels to the "historical and geographical crevices" allotted to Caribbean people. The era of globalization is said to feature a world economy made up of a community of economically open nation-states, each contributing competitively to the whole by filling "market niches" (McMichael 1996). Leyshon (1997) has witnessed this sort of reasoning in Britain, where Thatcherites have cultivated the myth that globalization and neoliberalism are "a 'natural' consequence of the free-market progress." But for peripheral regions such as the Caribbean, market niches are narrow, highly competitive, and fraught with obstacles. They are largely outlets for selling nontraditional goods and services (i.e., fruits, vegetables, flowers, garments, electronic products, processed data, and tourism) to wealthy Western consumers. Such market niches have an uncanny structural resemblance to the more aptly termed "historical and geographical *crevices*" allotted to Afro-Caribbean people under colonialism. Historical crevices were the multiyear periods when preoccupied Europe temporarily eased its pressure on slave economies to produce export crops, which therefore opened limited opportunities for slaves to pursue other cultural and economic agendas. Geographical crevices were marginal gully and mountainous lands, unsuited for plantation crops, that masters allowed slaves to cultivate. These lands contributed to slave autonomy while reducing masters' food bills (Olwig 1993).

Both crevices then and niches now offer Caribbean people very narrow windows of opportunity for advancement within an international political economy dominated by outside powers. Countries around the world are now under pressure to find such market niches, as chapter 5 on neoliberal export-oriented development policy describes. However, the Caribbean has thus far seen only modest success in developing new export market niches, as chapters 6–8 document, and that success is overwhelmed by losses from traditional exports, industries, jobs, and social services. Despite such attempts by the peripheral regions to find new markets in core countries, fully 80 percent of all world trade is within the core triad, although it is less than 20 percent of world population (Dicken 1992; Hirst and Thompson 1996).

Thesis 5: Global media and cultural influences do not approach the balance between core and peripheral countries that some writers suggest. Globalization is said to mean that media and cultural influences are more widespread and multilateral. This thesis was recently advanced by one of the Caribbean's best known and most respected cultural commentators, the Jamaican-born Harvard professor of sociology Orlando Patterson. While acknowledging that relations between the United States and the Caribbean have not reached a point of balance, he declares that a "West Atlantic regional cosmos," stretching across international borders from New York City to Port-of-Spain, has emerged in which "people, wealth, ideas, and cultural patterns move in both directions, influencing both the metropolitan center as well as the peripheral areas, although asymmetrically" (Patterson 1994, 108). He further argues that "culturally, the periphery is greatly influenced by the society of the center, but the reverse is also the case, as the example of reggae demonstrates" (Patterson 1994, 109). This argument suggests a trend toward bilateral balance, or an evening out of influences across rich and poor nation-states. Summarizing the literature in anthropology, Kearney (1995, 555) goes a step beyond regional bilateralism to suggest that "reverse cultural imperialism" is an apt catchphrase for recent trends. He reports that "the distinction between centers and peripheries has largely dissolved with respect to media production and consumption."

It is a stretch, however, to compare the northward influence of such artifacts as reggae music to the multitude of cultural impacts in the opposite direction. To use St. Lucia as an example, about 95 percent of television programming comes from the United States (Laird and Hall 1993). Regarding the print media, although each island has one or more local newspapers (often allied with a particular political party), none has a regional following. The most widely read paper in the Caribbean is *The Miami Herald*. The mass media presents Caribbean people with more information about the United States than about their own societies, and what is shown about the Caribbean itself is often filtered through the priority system of the corporate-controlled U.S. mass media. U.S. affluence and opportunity, often romanticized, is especially well-known, deeply ingrained, and alluring to the Caribbean (see how this is manifested in Trinidad in chap. 11; Richardson 1992). Caribbean people are prone to set their living standard goals in accordance with what the U.S. media ascribe to the United States. And the imbalance in media flows is increasing with the Caribbean's economic crisis and neoliberalism, as local media have been slashed. Even in Brazil, with Latin America's largest, best-established, and globally influential film industry, movie output is now one-fifth the level it was a decade ago (*Latin America Press* 1996). Cuban filmmaking, too, has been decimated in recent years, despite all the governmental efforts since the revolution to make a homegrown film industry a vibrant and vital part of socialist society.

The imbalance in the flows of influence between the United States and the Caribbean is greater for economic and geopolitical issues than for cultural ones. In the United States, the repercussions of its policy vicissitudes on economically peripheral places are often unappreciated, much less given full hearing (Richardson 1992). Few people in the United States have ever heard of an "807 firm," for example, although they probably wear clothes assembled by one. In the Caribbean, however, people understand that 807 firms and the associated jobs exist only because of U.S. tariff codes (e.g., *The Jamaican Weekly Gleaner* 1986). Lastly and relatedly, despite a globalization of the messages of consumer culture, which should be understood as essentially core firms advertising worldwide (Leslie 1995), 80 percent of the world lives outside of that culture with regard to actual consumption (Barnet and Cavanagh 1994, 383). The Caribbean is better off on this score than many peripheral countries, although aspirations for U.S.-style consumption remain widely unfulfilled.

Thesis 6: Increasing international flows of people and information should not obscure the region- and class-specific motives for and access to emigration and communication. The people of the world themselves are said to be more integrated through immigration and communications. Evidence includes the fact that a record 100 million people are now living outside the nation-state in which they were born (Kearney 1995, 557). But that leaves the other approximately 98 percent of the world's population living in the country of origin. Further, such pronouncements of global trends are much clearer when regionally specified.

Depending on the level of affluence of their natal country, people experience very different levels of global access through telephones, computers, faxes, the Internet, and other electronic media (Demko and Wood 1994). Opportunities for international mobility and communication correlate strongly with a country's wealth, but in this sense the Caribbean people are unique. In pursuit of opportunities for economic development and also for social and cultural expression, people of the Caribbean have engaged in more twentieth century emigration than those of any other region, leading to a "deterritorialization of Afro-Caribbean communities" (Olwig 1993, 206). An understanding of the Caribbean in the global era must include the coping mechanisms of a disadvantaged and dispersed people who emigrate from and circulate back to highly permeable societies. The societal porousness and citizens' coping strategies are not global phenomena, but are particular to the historical and geographical context of the Caribbean region and its inhabitants (as chap. 11 illustrates; Simmons and Guengant 1992).

Thesis 7: Trends towards economic globalization and neoliberalism in the Caribbean have been accompanied paradoxically by the region's economic and political marginalization. Contrary to the universalistic notion of a "global village" described above, in which the world is in various ways coming together, synthesizing, and balancing out, the Caribbean may be better depicted as a region that is increasingly irrelevant in economic and geopolitical terms. At one level, this is an ironic statement. Indeed, Caribbean *people* are more internationally integrated than ever before, thanks to the unprecedented scale of the Caribbean diaspora in North Atlantic countries and the associated remittances (see chaps. 10–11). But the massive scale of contemporary emigration and remittances is the result of growing marginalization and pessimism about the economic prospects back home. The Caribbean is economically stagnant, having few realistic options by which countries and most people can escape. It is witnessing an exodus of what was only a modest level of foreign investment in the first place, and there are growing gaps between rich and poor (Klak 1995). The Caribbean has become more geopolitically irrelevant. Its deep and irreversible neoliberal reforms, policy concessions to the United States, and aggressive pursuit of continuity of Lomé market access to the European Union and NAFTA parity have largely fallen on deaf North Atlantic ears (chap. 4 reviews Caribbean integration efforts). Its cultural influences abroad (e.g., music, cuisine) notwithstanding, the Caribbean is more unilaterally inundated by the consumerism and geopolitical priorities of the North Atlantic region, especially the United States. And while they are far from simply helpless and passive victims of exogenous forces beyond their control, Caribbean people and states are nonetheless under tremendous pressure to respond, adjust, and cope as the region undergoes a rapid and profound transformation of a variety of norms governing society as a whole and making a living within it.

Aside from the empirically questionable and excessively optimistic global village notions discussed thus far in this chapter, there are a few other aspects of the contemporary globalization argument that do indeed capture distinctive features of the world economy and the Caribbean's role within it. Hirst and Thompson (1996), while dispelling most of the myths of economic globalization, find empirical substantiation for the internationalization, particularly since the 1970s, of certain manufacturing and service sectors and major financial markets. From a political economy perspective, a commonality uniting these trends is the pressure they place on governments worldwide to conform to the emerging neoliberal order.

One source of pressure toward conformity extends from the growing importance of global commodity chains for certain industries (Dicken 1992; Gereffi and Korzeniewicz 1994). With traditional exports and domestic industries in ruin, playing a role in the international division of labor and production for such commodities as garments, electronics, and data processing has become a major item on the policy agenda of Caribbean governments (such policies are described in chaps. 5, 7 and 8). In addition, lucrative international financial speculation has diverted investment away from fixed assets (Hirst and Thompson 1996, 27) and creates additional pressure towards policy conformity. Caribbean governments are under pressure to conform to international standards of currency convertibility and maintain vigilance regarding neoliberal reforms (McMichael 1996, 28; McGowan 1997). The increased international fluidity of finance capital can expose those countries that are not sufficiently committed to the neoliberal order. As a U.S. State Department spokesperson aptly noted at the December 1994 Summit of the Americas, from which only Cuba was excluded, what Castro needed to do was "get with the program" (Vanderbush and Klak 1996). This financial pressure is enhanced when Caribbean countries seek to attract mobile capital to their nascent offshore finance sectors (see chap. 12).

In short, little evidence bears out the positive interpretations of globalization and neoliberalism, at least for peripheral regions such as the Caribbean, and especially for their working classes. In fact, a depiction contrary to the global village thesis perhaps gets closer to an accurate portrayal of the current situation in the world. To this effect Gill (1992) summons the metaphor of "global apartheid" to capture the increasing polarization between rich and poor worldwide (UN 1996). But, ironically, even the limited political and economic integration of apartheid suggests that it is perhaps an overly optimistic analogy. Under apartheid, black African labor from the homelands and townships was crucial to upholding the high living standards of white South Africans. Now blacks have a voice within a racially unified South African state. Peripheral regions such as the Caribbean play no such central economic role with respect to the living standards of core countries. Nor can they make political-territorial claims for unity with North Atlantic countries.

Thesis 8: Widespread uncritical absorption of the "global village" notion is attributable to the power and influence of mainstream development economics. As the discussion thus far implies, how relations between economic and political processes are conceptualized in this book contrasts with that of mainstream development economics. The latter represents the dominant view in social science and, as Escobar (1995, 18) notes, is "the single most influential force shaping the development field." Mainstream economics has also been absorbed into popular discourse by the news media. The news is replete with such staples of mainstream economics (and, not coincidentally, such capitalist concerns) as investment, growth rates, interest rates, competitiveness, stock-market trends, profit, and relations between unemployment, wages, and inflation (Leyshon 1997). The news includes more about economic health than human or ecological health. Owing to the reflexive (i.e., dialectical) relationship between concepts and everyday life, commonly used concepts absorbed from mainstream economics shape our understanding of the world and our behaviors within it (Giddens 1990, 36–45). Amid this discourse, societies have been conceptually transformed from *having* economies to *being* economies. "Development" is becoming the "master concept" of the social sciences, politics, and everyday life (Sachs 1992; McMichael 1996). This language establishes parameters for discussing development options and excludes ideas that are not steeped in the discourse (Pantojas-García 1990; Leyshon 1997).

In contrast to such thinking that emanates from mainstream economics, this book works from a political economy perspective. We follow Sayer (1995, ix) when he defines political economy as "approaches which view the economy as socially and politically embedded and as structured by power relations." Unlike mainstream economics, our approach does not premise economic processes on supply-and-demand relations, nor on equilibrium solutions. Instead, economic processes are examined in relation to the principles of capitalism, politics and culture (e.g., Marshall 1996; Kopinak 1996; Peck 1996). Revealingly, when neoliberal-favoring economists engage in political analysis, it is usually in pursuit of understanding the country-specific *obstacles* to neoliberal transformation (e.g., Williamson 1990; Grindle and Thoumi 1993; Haggard and Webb 1994). Further, the approach advocated here does not reduce the political to elections, as sometimes occurs in mainstream political science and its Caribbean applications.

To these distinctions should be added that a political economy approach is deeply concerned with history and, increasingly, with discourse (Pantojas-García 1990). As chapter 2 by Conway exemplifies, political economy also situates contemporary analysis in the historical trajectory leading to current arrangements. With regard to discourse, as Barnes (1995, 427) explains, "the kind of institutional political economy that is emerging from this criticism [of the methods of neoclassical economics and positivism] is one that is sensitive to language, discourse, power and practice." Discourse analysis has been widely deployed to extract the meaning and the message beneath the language and symbols of contemporary development (O Tuathail and Luke 1994; Dalby 1994; Vanderbush and Klak 1996).

This and subsequent chapters seek to demonstrate the fallacy of framing contemporary problems in narrow and economistic terms. A political economy perspective is more multidimensional than mainstream economics, e.g., it takes seriously impact on the poor, women, the environment, and the distribution of resources and wealth. It is also more nuanced than the current neoliberal dogmatism, and is therefore more capable of appraising the impacts of the current round of global capitalism on the Caribbean. The chapters seek to highlight both more promising trends (e.g., how international exposure has begun to dislodge some of the stifling effects of entrenched merchant capital and other privileged interests) and more negative consequences (e.g., the hyper-exploitation of young female workers in the new export industries). The result is a sophisticated picture of the direction that global capitalism and neoliberalism are leading the Caribbean. In the process we also address the question of the extent to which the region is following, reformulating, and/or resisting these powerful trends that tend to sweep economically weak countries along with them.

Thesis 9: Globalization and neoliberalism have reduced the sovereignty of the state relative to capital. Note that in the analytical approach outlined above the economic and the political are not on equal footing. The political must be understood as subservient to the economic (Alavi 1982), especially in the contemporary Caribbean during the present era of globalization and neoliberalism. This subservience owes to investors' "veto power" to withdraw capital from activities and locations on which the state relies for revenues and the working class relies for income. The state and the working class, while capable of expressing their interests and demands in a variety of ways, have no powers of comparable significance to capital's control over production processes and its mobility. Gill (1992) characterizes the recent trend as "the internationalization of political authority" (i.e., away from states), while McMichael (1996, 39) depicts it as one whereby "states lose capacity as sovereign rule makers." Hirst and Thompson, too, stress that national economic policy making has become circumscribed, especially outside the core triad:

> States are less autonomous, they have less exclusive control over the economic and social processes within their territories, and they are less able to maintain national distinctiveness and cultural homogeneity. (Hirst and Thompson 1996, 177)

This increasing geographical imbalance in the distribution of power between states and multinational firms is especially important for understanding the local impact of globalization. What does it mean for the Caribbean, which historically has had markedly little sovereignty over development priorities? For Caribbean islands, state sovereignty is additionally constrained to territories that are relatively small and generally resource poor (the implications of which are explored in chap. 3) and were developed historically by colonial powers to produce only a few plantation exports. The working class, despite Herculean efforts historically to use international migration as a survival strategy (as chaps. 10–11 recount), nonetheless is not in capital's league regarding negotiating power and mobility. Capital is especially fickle in the Caribbean because it is only weakly engaged in production. For its part, domestic capital has always been wary of productive investments and preferential to mercantile (e.g., the import/export business) or rentier (e.g., real estate, landlordism) ones. International capital has long viewed Caribbean contexts with great skepticism in regard to their productivity and stability (Klak 1995). The interests of capital are rightly considered universal, since failing to serve them will mean a quick withdrawal of the investments on which all others depend within the hegemonic system now in effect. The interests of the state, the working class, nature, etc., to the extent that they differ from those of capital, are labeled as narrow, obstructionist, or unconducive to a healthy business environment (chap. 5 expounds on this development discourse).

During the neoliberal transformation, the state is as usual caught in an unenviable position at the intersection of class relations (Alavi 1982). But the current arrangement pushes the Caribbean state further into an awkward and contradictory role of both championing and resisting globalization and neoliberalism. The collapse of traditional exports, mounting foreign debt, and "free market" messages from core elite, especially the United States, have left Caribbean political leaders with few choices. Either they zealously join the crusade or they risk being branded and isolated as anticapitalist renegades. After all, the exogenous and immutable forces of globalization and neoliberalism are also handy scapegoats for explaining to working class constituencies why further belt tightening and reduced expectations for wages, benefits, and social services are required.

At the same time, however, state systems, especially the prodigiously developed ones found in the Caribbean, are not easily dismantled under the aegis of fiscal conservatism and privatization. Nor are state actors keen on posting their own termination notices, especially when dictated from abroad. Public officials resist dismantling the state even as they champion and orchestrate that cause, especially in the international arena. They and their private-sector allies also give neoliberal policies their own home grown spin, creating a "Caribbean creolized form" (Pantojas-García and Dietz 1996, 49). Caribbean political and economic leaders are not simply passive mouthpieces for international capital and core interests. Some are firm believers, while others are pragmatically repositioning themselves to make the best of dire international conditions. As might be expected, creolized neoliberalism contains some reactionary elements that reflect the historically undynamic and dampening qualities of many regional elites. But there are also some creative signs, for example, producers who take advantage of new, narrow export opportunities in tourism, banking, consumer goods, foods, flowers, and crafts (chaps. 4 and 8 offers prominent examples of these).

Thesis 10: Neoliberal policy is presently hegemonic, but it is also dogmatically imposed, normatively flawed, and therefore unsustainable. Examined from a political-economy perspective, mainstream economics and neoliberalism can be seen to share paradigmatic foundations and some conceptual shortcomings. With reference to regions of the global periphery such as the Caribbean, the label "neoliberal" is usually applied to several mutually reinforcing phenomena, including liberal (mainstream) economic thought, the prevailing ideology of development, the main features of current government policy, and the technocrats carrying out that policy. In essence, neoliberalism is a movement toward a more laissez-faire capitalism in the global periphery (Bresser Pereira et al. 1993). Wealthy capitalist countries too, in order to appear more attractive to mobile international capital, have needed to adopt structural adjustment policies that are parallel but far less "savage" in terms of their human impacts (Anderson and Witter 1992). Similar to transformations in the global periphery under neoliberalism, policies in the core are associated with such trends as the shrinkage of state regulation and protections, privatization, and antiwelfare movements. The "one size fits all" nature of the neoliberal movement is one of its weaknesses. Whether it is in its scholarly, ideological, or policy forms, economic liberalism is narrow because it tends to treat economic issues ahistorically and detached from their political and social contexts. As noted earlier, context seems to matter only in that it can pose an obstacle in the way of (the ideology of) neoliberalism.

The dogmatism of IMF and World Bank economists and allied "intellectuals of statecraft" (O Tuathail and Luke 1994) is revealed by their treatment of empirical evidence. Favorable results are held up as validation of the neoliberal policy prescriptions. Unfavorable results are interpreted as evidence of the state's timid implementation of the neoliberal model, as well as its unwillingness to make the difficult choices and reductions in traditional privilege and waste. If only the state were more serious about reform, neoliberalism's universal benefits would be forthcoming. Negative impacts are also seen as normal and inevitable short-term consequences of the profligacy of the past. In the conveniently unspecified long term, there will eventually be positive results (Danaher 1994; Caufield 1996; McGowan 1997).

Besides the problems of universalism and dogmatism, neoliberal policy is vulnerable to other normative criticisms. All social science that extends from a theoretical or paradigmatic foundation has built into it, implicitly if not explicitly, normative goals for society. Given its aim of unleashing the private sector, neoliberal-favoring work implies the normative goal of prioritizing the interests of capital. In contrast, this book's concluding chapter outlines alternative goals for the Caribbean region premised on humane, ecologically sound, and sustainable policies. Against the criticism of class bias, neoliberal-favoring authors are likely to draw on some version of the "whatever's good for corporations is good for the nation" argument. There is precedence for such a position in such famous statements as "what's good for GM is good for America" by that auto maker's CEO, or Calvin Coolidge's "The business of America is business." Neoliberal advocates are also likely to suggest that "in the long run" it is in everyone's best interest.

These points are partially true in two respects. The first one, that capital has veto power, was mentioned earlier. A second element of truth relates to some of the more universally despised societal problems that neoliberalism seeks to address. Many oppressive, exploitative, unfair, wasteful and unproductive practices, in both public and private sectors, and in the Caribbean and elsewhere, could be ameliorated through changing the role of the state. The neoliberal position also has problems, however. First, no singular and simple solution such as the neoliberal notion of unleashing the private sector can effectively address the range of problems and needs found in specific societal contexts. Second, while there are undoubtedly many problems in the private and state sectors of the Caribbean as the following chapters document, neoliberalism is but one of a variety of ways in which they could be addressed. Third, the a priori universal judgment as to the merits of one set of interests (i.e., capital's) over others in neoliberal research and policy is at best intellectually and empirically stifling.

The political-economy approach being advocated here is more open to evidence and to a range of policy responses. It seeks to understand why conditions lead to particular practices on the part of capital, the state, the working class, and other interests. Such an approach avoids neoliberals' branding of capital as rational and branding of others as obstructionist. It also establishes a more informed grasp of current Caribbean conditions from which inclusive and workable policies can extend.

Mainstream/neoliberal critics might counter with the claim that this argument is at least as class-favoring as liberal economics' procapitalist one in that it prioritizes the interests of the working class. But that sort of reaction reflects the hegemonic status of capital-favoring ideas. Any considerations that do not accept that the interests of capital should prevail are systematically degraded. Such views have been labeled as engaging in "class warfare," as has occurred recently in the United States when worker interests are broached. Alternatively they are branded as creating "a bad business climate," as when environmental or human impacts of development are entertained. Real working-class prioritizing, however, would involve issues of turning over control to the productive forces (Thomas 1988). Rather than pursuing that normative goal, the assessment in this book is grounded in what is possible within the foreseeable time frame. It accepts the inevitability of the continued neoliberal transformation of the Caribbean, including Cuba (chap. 9), and the wider world for the foreseeable future. It then asks to what extent trends serve the interests of the various social groups, as well as how neoliberal policies might be steered toward more inclusively benefitting (however unequally) those social groups while at the same time taking account of long-term environmental conditions.

Thesis 11: Economic globalization and neoliberalism undermine important components of political liberalism. Neoliberalism and globalization are twin processes, at both the ideological and the empirical levels. That is, they strongly overlap in terms of intellectual roots and the patterns that emerge in the roles of governments and the nature of international economic activity. Harvey (1995, 16) captures this point when he depicts the Zapatista struggle as one against "neoliberal capitalism through globalization." Hirst and Thompson (1996) similarly describe the political rhetoric associated with globalization as an "antipolitical" liberalism: states should withdraw to the function of ensuring "the protection of the world free trading system." Neoliberalism is, in essence, about shifting power and resources away from the state and the working class and toward capitalists, as Marshall (1996, 447) explains, "to ensure the unfettered circulation of goods and services globally." It also has major redistributive consequences in terms of world regions, as predictions concerning the beneficiaries of the Uruguay Round of GATT attest: exports are expected to correlate highly with level of development (World Bank 1995). It is therefore more than coincidence that those states and firms leading such legal revision toward "free trade" are those with preexisting capacities to benefit most from the liberalization. This follows the historical patterns for the more advanced capitalist countries. They have practiced protectionism or have advocated open trade according to what suits their interests at any point in time. The international political power of First World countries also allows them the option of resurrecting tariff barriers should the manufacturing or even agricultural exports of peripheral countries become domestically damaging (Hirst and Thompson 1996, 119), as the United States has done to Mexican products such as citrus, tomatoes, and brooms.

Thesis 12: Economic globalization is as much an ideological force as a material one. Another window on the current popularity of globalization themes is offered by considering the power of elite discourse (see also chap. 5). As Leyshon explains,

> Although the globalization thesis may well be flawed and based upon a mixture of poor social science, hyperbole, exaggeration and corporate desire, it works as a discourse because it has a highly receptive audience with the offices and boardrooms of the international business community. It is in this sense a self-affirming and self-propagating discourse. (Leyshon 1997)

But why would globalization have such corporate appeal? The current prominence of "globalization" in the lexicon is partly because it is a discursive tool used by the economic elite to extract political concessions, and by both the political and economic elites to discipline and coopt the working class and its allies (Harvey 1995; K. Cox 1997). Elites often place the power and responsibility over trends negatively affecting people's lives in the hands of an exogenous, intractable, and inevitable process of "globalization" and the emergence of a "global economy" (R. Cox 1996). States can thereby shield themselves against blame as they dismantle welfare systems in the name of "reducing dependency" or "getting people off the dole" and as they facilitate the export of capital and jobs in the name of "competitiveness" and "efficiency" (McMichael 1996). In this elite discourse, political and economic leaders present themselves not as the actors behind economic polarization, deindustrialization and the dismantling of the social welfare system, but rather as a stabilizing force working in everyone's best interest given the dizzying changes happening all around. But such usage of the term *globalization*, however, obscures the distinctive empirical features of the present international political economy.

If domestic elites present "globalization" and "the new global economy" as a seemingly intractable and irreversible force to which the working class must respond with belt tightening and lower expectations for remuneration and services, similar patterns occur at the international level. The World Bank disciplines countries by spreading fears about being excluded from the globalization bandwagon. The advice is to follow the neoliberal prescription or suffer at your own peril. As the World Bank's Zia Qureshi (1996, 31–33) warns, "Lagging countries risk being left farther behind. . . . For economies that remain inward-looking, the risk of becoming marginalized is greater than ever." The threat of being excluded from global commodity chains and trade is in itself a powerful ideological force serving to discipline governments into granting business concessions and lowering remuneration standards in order to reduce the expectations of the working class (K. Cox 1997).

Globalization is therefore in part a tool of class power. It is important that users of the term *globalization* specify its meaning in particular contexts, as we attempt to do in this book. Otherwise there is a danger of simply reinforcing ideological globalization while further mystifying its empirical referents. In this sense the discourse of even progressive-minded observers can inadvertently play a reactionary role. Harvey (1995, 12) suggests that we jettison "globalization" and replace it with the "uneven spatio-temporal development of capitalism." That is a mouthful, but it points in the right direction. Political economists should employ a lexicon that gets as close as possible to the processes of concern, and avoid reiterating (and reifying) the language of power and oppression.

Thesis 13: Despite the globally homogenizing pressures in favor of neoliberal reforms, states and peoples respond to and resist them in myriad ways. The book is organized around the relationships between top-down development policies and bottom-up reactions. The basic point is that the powerful homogenizing forces operating in the global political economy today by no means annihilate regional, national, and local expressions of interests. In other words, the contemporary world economy is imposing a new order and a homogenized set of rules through the commonalities of neoliberalism, global production chains, trade agreements, consumerism, and the mass media. At the same time, however, such homogenizing influences do not replace local forms of production, consumption, media, and problem conceptualization. In fact, in most cases they engender distinctive localized interpretations and new oppositional forms to them. Foreign ideas and pressures to change inevitably mix with local ways, both established and novel, at the institutional and popular levels. Even the IMF appreciates this point at one level. When the IMF tracks neoliberal reforms, it allows for the fact that structural adjustment agreements are seldom implemented according to the plan and its macro-economic parameters (Hey and Klak 1997).

This conceptual dichotomy between global and local processes should not suggest that the two sides are independent of one another. To the contrary, it is their dialectical or iterative relationship that produces the global trends and their expression in a particular place. In this way rigorous studies of globalization and neoliberalism in regional contexts such as the Caribbean shed light on the operation of widespread processes affecting all corners of the globe. Among the wide range of "local responses" to globalization and neoliberalism now occurring in the Caribbean, the subsequent chapters focus primarily on two types: those associated with state policies, and those of Caribbean people themselves. This two-fold division of responses corresponds with the emphasis in the book on development policies, including those at the national and the regional level through Caricom, and on international migration and circulation, one of the many ways that Caribbean people have responded historically and presently to economic and political adversity. The themes of state and popular actions, resistance and adjustment carry through to varying degrees in most chapters.

SUGGESTIONS FOR FURTHER READING

Corbridge, Stuart. *Development Studies: A Reader*. London: Edward Arnold, 1995. This is a compilation of both classics and some recent important statements that represent major debates in Third World development research. Work in both development economics and sociological approaches is represented. Emphasis is on developmental problems rather than state policies or popular responses. It provides an essential foundation for anyone seeking a broad overview of this diverse field over recent decades.

Hirst, P., and G. Thompson. *Globalization in Question: The International Economy and the Possibilities of Governance*. Cambridge: Polity, 1996. This is the most thorough and careful interrogation of the ideas and evidence behind economic globalization to date. It refutes many truisms about globalization and offers empirical evidence to document the extent and the precise ways in which global economic integration is actually occurring.

Sachs, Wolfgang, ed. *The Development Dictionary: A Guide to Knowledge as Power*. Atlantic Highlands, N.J.: Zed Books, 1992. This collection provides a critical etymology and ecopolitical interrogation of the principal concepts used in the discourse of Third World development. The book aims to break open for careful historical and contemporary examination the major concepts and ideas associated with the theory and practice of Third World development. Representing a "south-centric" perspective on development, it is essential reading for anyone who resists the intellectual blinders of mainstream development economics.

II

DEVELOPMENT MODELS AND NEOLIBERAL POLICIES

Part II reviews how Caribbean states pursue "development" and sets the contemporary policy context for the more empirically and sectorally focused chapters that follow. The main issues are (1) the variety of ways that Caribbean countries have approached development over recent decades, (2) the daunting constraints and unique opportunities afforded to small, trade-dependent countries by globalization and neoliberalism, (3) the recent efforts of Caribbean leaders to respond to NAFTA and other international trends, including responses through Caricom, and (4) the ways that states market their countries and people globally as neoliberal sites ripe for investment, and the extent to which the contexts of those countries contrasts with their marketing images.

More specifically, in chapter 2 Dennis Conway reviews Caribbean development trends during the postindependence era (since the 1960s when most countries have achieved independence; table A). For each of the last four decades, he describes the range of paths tried across the region pursuing elusive "development." The policies tried divide geopolitically into two categories, each with distinctive risks. One set has pursued development through socialistic routes (emphasizing redistribution and equity, social welfare, prioritization of working class needs). This route has purposefully turned away from the historical dependence on (and therefore has alienated and angered) elite interests in North Atlantic countries, especially the United States. Cuba, Guyana, Jamaica, and Grenada have tried variants on this approach. The essential challenge for socialistic policies has been to run a peripheral economy against the tide of global capitalism and U.S. hegemony. Inevitably such departures raise broad questions: How can the Caribbean pursue a noncapitalist path without the trade, capital, and blessing of the United States and the rest of the largely capitalist world? and How can internal resources be progressively redistributed when there are few to go around, and when societies are poor and unequal and therefore prone to internal divisions and patronage systems? This is clearly a tall order, and Conway shows that it has encountered many obstacles.

A second contrary and more common policy tack has reinforced and extended ties with the North Atlantic region. It is represented by Puerto Rico's Operation Bootstrap, the Caribbean Basin Initiative, and the present neoliberal transformation. This path avoids U.S. hostility and instead aims to exploit opportunities availed by strong trade and policy ties to advanced capitalist countries. The risk is that the results will replicate history whereby the Caribbean has gained relatively little from its subordinate relationship with the core.

In chapter 3 Conway fleshes out the pros and cons of Caribbean countries' status as "micro states in a macro world." Such small countries are characterized as unstable (Harden 1985) and dismissed as unviable in the global era. Former UN Secretary-General Boutros Boutros-Ghali, for example, warned that recent worldwide trends towards balkanization could yield "400 economically crippled mini-states" (Cole 1996, 9). Conway acknowledges the legacy of vulnerability resulting from the colonial creation of tiny, often spatially fragmented, resource-depleted, underindustrialized, and trade-dependent states. But he also notes that Caribbean smallness has positive features such as community and political transparency, transportation and communication accessibility, and a history of adaptability to exogenous changes. The challenge for Caribbean countries is to exploit these positive features as developmental advantages in the neoliberal era.

In chapter 4 Dennis Gayle describes the many international trade agreements forged across the Americas since the 1980s, noting their implications for Caribbean countries. He documents how neoliberalism is being operationalized in the region's main trade organization, Caricom, and in the hemisphere's other trade groups. He explains how NAFTA has increased the Caribbean's economic isolation and how Caricom has reacted by pressing the United States for trade concessions. Caricom's most urgent recent aim is parity with Mexico within NAFTA, so that the Caribbean will no longer be comparatively disadvantaged as an export-platform. Gayle documents that Mexico's foreign investment and exports have indeed grown relative to the Caribbean since 1994. The U.S. government has offered much rhetoric claiming its interest in deeper economic ties with the Caribbean and regional cooperation toward mutual and complementary development. The main result thus far, however, is the United States's large and growing export surplus with the Caribbean, which along with Latin America, is the only world region to which the United States now exports more than it imports. Thus it is difficult not to conclude that Washington's policy toward the Caribbean—if such scattered actions and mostly inactions deserves to be called "policy"—is self-serving, narrow, and shortsighted.

The hegemony of the globalization and neoliberalism discourse is apparent as Caricom and most member countries expend their energies lobbying hard for integration with NAFTA. They do this despite all the hardship in Mexico over its first three years (Anderson et al. 1994; Schrieberg 1997) and despite the many factors Gayle lists that make them ill prepared for and uncompetitive in such a venture. Caribbean countries will have comparative advantage in NAFTA for little more than low-wage labor. This suggests that the Caribbean continues to engage in a "race to the bottom" that characterizes the majority of the world's countries that have seen little payoff from globalization and neoliberalism (Green 1996). Besides assessing hemispheric integration, Gayle's chapter also identifies the most dynamic economic sectors and firms in the Caribbean. This helps to sort out sectors and firms that are likely to survive and even prosper as neoliberal reforms press forward.

In chapter 5 Thomas Klak and Garth Myers reveal the main features of current Caribbean development policy at the country level and under the neoliberal banner. They examine investment-promotion materials from Caribbean countries at different levels of industrialization and development, from Barbados to Jamaica, St. Lucia, and Haiti. The chapter reveals that policy makers, through promises of a proinvestor climate, images of scientific production, and avoidance of the reality of social discontent in their investment promotional materials, are constructing "neoliberal mediascapes." They signal that the country is a signatory to the neoliberal world order and is ripe for investment in manufacturing, tourism, and other nontraditional exports. The investment materials demonstrate considerable homogeneity regarding discursive tactics, messages, and promises to capital. An advertising package typically combines *neoliberal and contextual depiction* (pledges of subsidies, an open economy, and cheap and unorganized labor; tropical paradise and friendly natives), *science fiction* (dreams of high technology, sophisticated exports, telecommunications, and informatics), and *strategic omission* (exclusion of strife, resistance, hardship, and societal degradation). The homogeneity of generous incentive packages across countries causes them to cancel each other out, thereby further increasing the public costs necessary to lure fastidious investors. Homogenization through mediascapes is not total, however. The invitations to international capital must ultimately deliver the ground level reality to which they refer in the guidebooks, a reality inevitably more multifarious than the guidebooks suggest. Investors discover either through the guidebooks or on site that local history and struggle preclude an unproblematic absorption and implementation of the neoliberal project.

2

Misguided Directions, Mismanaged Models, or Missed Paths?

Dennis Conway

The Caribbean is a region of small states, many of them dismissed disparagingly as unviable in the global era. Their maritime accessibility contributed to their incorporation into the Western world's earliest mercantile empires in the sixteenth century. Their insular character exposed them to external forces, external patterns of interaction, and flows of capital, people, and goods. The Caribbean peoples' post–World War II experience reflects both a continuation of five hundred years of externally dominated incorporation into a succession of metropolitan empires and a widely differing record of contemporary changes in social, economic, and political systems in specific locales, be they island states, island clusters, or Caribbean mainland enclave societies (see map 1). Environmental diversity adds to the regional character, but it is primarily external influences that have contributed to regional heterogeneity, through introduced cultural and societal diversity (Boswell and Conway 1992).

The externally dominated and colonial/metropolitan-propelled agendas of Caribbean economies were locally challenged in the early decades of the twentieth century, driven by the peoples' desperate state of impoverishment and destitution that was exacerbated by colonial office neglect. Of course, there were the innumerable colonial commissions reporting the deplorable situations, recommending local action, and arguing that colonial powers were responsible for addressing the peoples' plight. After World War II, the time for concerted action and the need for "development" and self-determination for Caribbean people arrived. Their political action brought about the decolonization of many territories, though some fifteen microstates remain to this day as metropolitan dependencies. Once reluctant dependencies, many of these colonial outposts (e.g., Bermuda, the Cayman Islands, Turks and Caicos Islands, and Mont-

serrat) are now more confident of their external dependency because recent trends in service-sector growth—especially offshore banking,
tourism, and industrial diversification—have favored them (Connell 1993;
Roberts 1994; McElroy and de Albuquerque 1996). The majority of the
British West Indies, after the demise of the well-intentioned but flawed
experiment of a West Indies Federation in 1961, sought political independence as a supposed pathway to economic self-reliance and development
(Lewis 1976, 1985).

European hegemony gradually gave way to U.S. hegemony, completing
the transfer of this "backyard Mediterranean Sea" region to the external
domination of the United States. This geopolitical maneuver was invoked
when the Monroe Doctrine ruled the hemisphere's sea routes in the nineteenth century, gained currency with the acquisition of the Caribbean
dependent territories of Puerto Rico and the U.S. Virgin Islands, and assumed a neocolonial garb, as Britain finally relinquished its Caribbean
colonial responsibilities and acquiesced to North American (Canadian
and U.S.) geopolitical leadership in its excolonial domains (Thorndike
1988). We should be reminded, lest one of the region's significant historical events is not awarded due merit, that Haitian "independence" in 1804
preceded U.S. hegemonic overtures. France, on the other hand, retains its
Departements D'Outre Mer, Martinique, French Guiana, and Guadeloupe and dependencies. The Netherlands has not formally relinquished
its colonial ties with Aruba, Bonaire, Curacao, and St. Maarten. British
sovereignty still persists over Anguilla, Bermuda, the British Virgins, the
Cayman Islands, Montserrat, and the Turks and Caicos. Other politically
independent countries such as the Dominican Republic and Haiti, Jamaica, and Trinidad and Tobago saw their incorporation into the U.S.
geopolitical sphere become the prevailing reality of their interdependent
status: politically, economically, even culturally.

The 1980s brought a world recession and massive indebtedness. The
optimistic development plans of many of the region's politically independent states were stymied. The international financial community sought
succor in IMF and World Bank–imposed "conditionalities," burdening
the relatively powerless Third World debtors with the costs and the pain.
The ensuing restructuring of the global capitalist project saw the ascendence of international corporate capital as the neoliberal hegemon of the
Americas: overseeing U.S. "national" capital interests' dominance while
relying on its allegiance. Globalization begot neoliberalism in U.S. relations with its hemisphere, and Caribbean affairs, and political economic
relations, were often subordinated to wider hemispheric and global issues.
In essence, the Caribbean small states became even smaller geopolitical
players in this globalizing world (Aponte Garcia and Gautier Mayoral
1995; Bakan, Cox, and Leys 1993). Yet the people of the region struggled

to adjust to this new dependent condition and this new dominance, as they have to other external regimes.

The region's migration traditions are another factor in its longstanding incorporation into external mercantile empires, colonial and neocolonial spheres of core dominance, and the continuation of these deepseated dependent relations to this day (Conway 1989; Marshall 1982; Patterson 1987; Richardson 1983, 1992; Thomas-Hope 1992). Migration colonized the region's islands and colonial enclaves. Convict deportations, the forced mass intercontinental transfers of the slave trade, and recruitment via indentured contracts ensured a transoceanic supply of plantation labor and brought a global cultural and ethnic plurality into the region. Migrants (men and women) sought better opportunities "off the island" (Crane 1971; Thomas-Hope 1992). Sometimes such migration was at the behest of international capital, but just as often it was stimulated by declining circumstances in the islands, and primed by the skillful exhortations of overseas recruiters located within the region, in the American hemisphere, or in European "mother countries" (Richardson 1985; Conway 1989). Today, emigration and repetitive circulation are widely held strategies among all classes of Caribbean people. Both Caribbean source and extraregional receiving communities in host metropoles such as England, France, the Netherlands, Canada, and the United States are linked in social and familial networks of mutual support, wherein the maintenance and sustenance of such networks enable Caribbean people to live, survive, and even prosper as they exist "between two worlds" (Conway 1988, 1994; Grasmuck and Pessar 1991; Palmer 1995).

This introduction to the region's political economy leads to many questions. How have these microstates fared in the thirty-plus years of searches for self-reliant paths and progress, development and "modernization," industrial diversification, and the fulfillment of peoples' aspirations and improved well-being? What paths have these island states taken? How limiting have the domestic circumstances been? How constraining the international and external forces? How successful (or unsuccessful) have regional trade agreements, like Caricom, and bilateral arrangements, like CARIBCAN and CBI, been? There again, how are such regional plans constrained under today's neoliberal regime, with NAFTA legitimizing greater hemispherical openness, centralizing U.S. dominance, and placing the Caribbean microstates in no-man's land? Though diverse colonial and postcolonial experiences characterize the island societies, common threads can also be traced and common experiences and planning strategies can be assessed.

A few unique cases cannot be given sufficient treatment if included in this general overview. Cuba's ongoing revolutionary struggle with nine U.S. administrations, its neocolonial dependency relations with the Soviet

Union and CMEA countries, and the particulars of the transformations undertaken by its socialist regime are the focus of chapter 9. Haiti's chronically desperate economic situation, entailing deprivation, eternal hardship, and societal crisis for its people, also sets it apart from others in the region (see chaps. 5, 12; Dupuy 1997). French Guiana, though a French *Departement D'Outre Mer*, displays all the dual characters of a relic tropical plantation society surrounding a truly enclave European colony: the launching station for Europe's space projects and rockets, in an expenal colony of Devil's Island and Papillon fame. Suriname, once Dutch Guiana, does not receive comparative treatment in this chapter, and the rebuilding of Guyana in the 1990s after President Forbes Burnham's disastrous "reign of error" is not afforded its due either. Omission, or minimal treatment, of the comparative development experiences of the four Caribbean mainland "enclave" territories—Belize, Guyana, Suriname and French Guiana—is deliberate, allowing this chapter to focus more sharply on Caribbean island development experiences.

CARIBBEAN DEVELOPMENT MODELS: MANY PATHS, SOME PROGRESS, STYMIED BY MACRO EVENTS

The 1960s: Decade of Caribbean National Independence Movements

Certain aspects of colonial plantation exploitation fostered the growth of independence movements in the post-World War II era. Sugar and merchant capital allied to continue to dominate island economies. "Reconstituted peasantries" emerged as a small farming class always at the margins of agrarian society where plantation work still offered proletarian wages. Then there was the growth of a working class (helped by international socialist movements and cemented in the experiences of the two world wars). The professional middle class joined with the masses to struggle for constitutional reform and a widened franchise, thereby fomenting another societal transformation of note. Some would argue that this alliance undermined prospects for real progressive societal transformation even as it successfully fought for and won political independence (Beckles 1990; Sunshine 1988).

The region's economy remained distorted and "peripheral," with two characteristics prevailing. One was the island economies' reliance on resource extractive economic sectors, especially agriculture and mining. The other was their reliance on imported industrial and commercial goods and heavy dependence on foreign capital and expertise to feed people, service industry, and finance internal capital expansion. The region's societal woes were equally severe. There was widespread poverty, high levels of malnutrition, inadequate and unhealthy housing stocks, little to no social

welfare services, and a general lack of educational and occupational opportunities for the masses. The region's depressed state was an accumulation of decades of hardship, declining fortunes in the plantations, not-so-
benign neglect, and the structural limitations of many an island's once
profitable but now economically stagnating and too small plantation-
mercantile economy. The Caribbean's monocrop plantation systems
might seek to diversify their export staple crop—for example, substituting
bananas for sugar, bananas for arrowroot, bananas for cocoa, coffee for
cocoa, or citrus for sugar—but such limited adjustments of the island's
agrarian production did not bring back the profitable days of the previous
centuries (Richardson 1992).

The various colonial office responses to the plight of their Caribbean
outposts were similar: pessimism reigned. They perceived their territories
as geographical problem areas, with overpopulation and small arable land
areas making an untenable equation, with a racialist view that denied industrialization as an option, and with views on geographical determinism
that suggested development in such tropical climates was virtually impossible (Kuznets 1960). They conducted commissions of enquiry, largely as
a response to growing social unrest and mass political agitation. Island
governors and administrations had the additional goal of empowering
their colonial offices in order to substantiate their petitions for more revenue to distribute. The colonial office administrators also found the infrastructural facilities inadequate, and so they planned extensive road and
power networks and they envisaged growth and territorial coverage of
public utilities. They viewed these development initiatives as state enticements, and the state as "facilitator" of private enterprise initiatives regarding utilities.

Most uniform was the colonial offices' practice of coordinating and
directing the inflow of foreign capital through their offices. The level of
development attained would be directly attributable to the amount of foreign capital invested and directed to projects within each office's domain
(Benedict 1967). The assessment of viable projects was determined by colonial office permission and was funded by grants or state-facilitated private ventures. Often such projects were merely adequate, scarcely ever
forward-looking or expansive. For example, some of the smallest Windward Islands were not deemed "developable" and airport facilities with
only the most meager and limited capabilities were finally built, often
reluctantly. The same was argued with respect to upgrading port facilities,
upgrading communications networks, and developing health-care facilities. Simply providing the most basic facility with the most limited technological equipment was considered "more than adequate" (O'Loughlin
1962).

The postcolonial path was therefore hard, with the new political leaders suffering from Fanon's (1967, 1968) "postcolonial mentalities." The nationalist model(s) of economic development were more often than not outgrowths of the postwar colonial development strategies. They were constrained by the limiting vision that they inherited from their colonial mother administrations, development advisers, foreign engineers, agricultural extension offices, teachers, doctors, health practitioners, legal experts, and metropolitan commercial interests.

There was, however, some progress in this struggle for independence. The main pressures against the injustice of the old colonial regimes came from the popular masses—workers, peasantry, and unemployed. Mass mobilization brought political responses as never before. A broader franchise brought more local autonomy, better pay and better working conditions, better prices for agricultural goods, and a more secure living standard. Unfortunately, the very allegiance between the new professional class and the masses, which had enlarged and enlivened the mass movements that posed a real challenge to the old elite structures and colonial authorities, proved to be the movement's Achilles' heel. Time and time again, the new leaders of the independence movements, who either came from the intermediate professional classes or betrayed their class roots once in power, chose to *depoliticize* the masses, rather than building on their support and reversing the neocolonial ordering of institutional power and authority (Beckles 1990; Thomas 1988).

Sir Arthur Lewis' developmental solution that islands in the region should embrace industrialization as an essential economic transformation was, in its full theoretical formulation, a thoughtful and progressive model to follow (Lewis 1950). Unfortunately, in practice the derivative "industry-by-invitation" policies that were followed did not fully implement Lewis' broader agenda of sectoral diversification, substantial investment in human capital development, and diversification of agriculture (Bernal et al. 1984).

The 1970s: A Disastrous Decade for Regime Experimentation

By the beginning of the 1970s, the nationalist agendas for economic development and social progress were in conflict, and the promises were unfulfilled. Yet there was a plethora of paths to follow, from Cuba's socialist experiment to Puerto Rico's industrialization strategy, which sought "modernization at all costs" by embracing an externally directed capitalization of the island's economy (Pantojas-García 1990). The political regimes varied, and the genesis of each was invariably due to a combination of internal and external factors, including regional influences. As it turned out, the 1970s was not an era in which peripheral capitalist or socialist models of development were given time to mature, evolve, and become refined or restructured according to each regime's longer term objectives or goals.

International macrostructural events interceded to such an extent that the countries of the Caribbean region faced an economic development "crisis," which was part of a growing "debt crisis." It was partially due to regime fallibilities, partially dependency related, and partially an outcome of the region's continuing peripheral and marginal relations with metropoles. The Bretton Woods Agreement unraveled when President Nixon took the U.S. dollar off the gold standard and Eurodollar markets grew. The two OPEC oil price shocks of 1973–74 and 1978–79 posed energy cost burdens that threw many Caribbean accounts into default. The ensuing heavy indebtedness heralded the intrusion of the IMF in the fiscal affairs of many Caribbean countries, Jamaica especially. Cuba, isolated by U.S. administrative fiat, sought neocolonial support from the Soviet Union to avoid its own version of the 1970s crisis. Puerto Rico's industrialization progress faltered, but its peoples' answer was high levels of migration and circulation to the U.S. mainland, as well as greater reliance on the federally mandated social welfare net. The Dominican Republic's openness to multinational corporate involvement (Wiarda and Kryzanek 1992), did not spare it from structural malaise and downturns in national performance. These also prompted the beginning of a large scale exodus to the United States, primarily New York City, often by way of neighboring Puerto Rico (Hendricks 1974; Morrison and Sinkin 1982; Rohter 1997). For the remaining politically independent nations such as Jamaica, Trinidad and Tobago, Guyana, Barbados, Antigua, and the Eastern Caribbean small islands, nationalist experiments foundered in the 1970s. These are the stories, in brief.

Radical Options

New national development models were posed as "alternative paths" to peripheral capitalism, U.S. core hegemony, and international corporate dominance and subordination. These noncapitalist experiments in state-led, postcolonial transformation were driven by popular desire and political support for more local ownership of the economy, more self-reliance, and more local decision making. Political independence was expected to lead to economic and societal independence. Guyana, Jamaica, and Grenada are discussed here; the fourth candidate, Cuba, is not. Cuba is bypassed because it was the archetypal model. Its dependent relations with the Soviet Union, the uniqueness of Fidel Castro's regime, and the Cuban experience of over thirty years at odds with U.S. administrations from Kennedy to Clinton make easy summarization impossible (see chap. 9 for an analysis of Cuba's current situation).

Guyana's "cooperative socialism" came into being in 1970, four years after political independence, promoted by Forbes Burnham's People's National Congress (PNC) government on a wave of militant, anticolonial popular support. Long-held traditions of trade unionism and anticolonial fervor were common among both the Indo- and Afro-Guyanese populations, so the PNC adopted a political platform that espoused popular socialist rhetoric while the party and its clients pursued the more self-serving agenda of legitimizing the state's (their) ascendence to become a national bourgeois class (Thomas 1983). The principles of cooperative socialism were quite explicit and straightforward, including (1) a trisector national economy under private, state, and cooperative control, with the cooperative sector eventually becoming the dominant sector; (2) an expansion of state ownership through the nationalization of foreign assets; (3) a strategy of national development that implemented a program to feed, clothe, and house the nation; and (4) the ruling PNC possessing ultimate authority, even over the state.

PNC pursuit of these principles was often more rhetorical than effective. The bauxite industry was the first to be nationalized in 1972, with Reynolds Aluminum and Alcan affected. Indeed, it was bauxite nationalization that prompted Forbes Burnham's sudden change of political ideologies and his initial declaration on behalf of the PNC to follow a cooperative socialist path. In 1976 the state nationalized the sugar industry, appropriating the sector from Booker McConnell Ltd., which owned over 90 percent of the sugar plantation assets. But the PNC's national development program delivered more political propaganda than basic goods. The Burnham regime's record of corruption, clientelism, nepotism, excessive patronage, and gratuitous diversions of state revenues became legendary in the region. The regime became the butt of regional cartoonists and was widely disrespected by the region's political leaders.

There was a gradual and accumulating deterioration of most public services, as PNC patronage favored areas of PNC support, while neglecting others, especially those identified as strongholds of support for the opposition party, the PPP. All aspects of the public infrastructure, including drinking water supply, electricity provision, postal services, telephone service, and public transport, suffered neglect. All major social services and welfare nets deteriorated as the PNC withdrew revenues, neglected maintenance provisions, and assaulted (by mandated freezes and the like) the pay scales of professionals in these service institutions. Few people built new houses, though President Burnham and his "PNC-troika" maintained opulent mansions. Guyana's education system, once the envy of Commonwealth neighbors, was treated shabbily but it struggled on despite the regime's shortsightedness. The University of Guyana was treated likewise, probably because faculty and students criticized the corruption and malfeasance of the Burnham regime. Between 1976 and 1980 real per capita income declined 15 percent. Unemployment rose precipitously, and a 1980 estimate that 40 percent of the labor force was seeking work demonstrates the severity of the economic stagnation. Inflation rose to double digits by 1979, compounded by the government's decision to simply print more money and to extend the external debt burden (Thomas 1983).

Through the 1980s Guyana continued to stagnate and regress. The PNC continued its authoritarian practices, effectively disenfranchising the masses, and the IMF's structural adjustment did not improve the situation. Forbes Burnham's death in 1985 brought Guyana's "shame" to an abrupt end. Desmond Hoyte led a more conciliatory PNC government. Finally, 1992 heralded the end of nearly twenty-eight years of PNC rule. The triumphant opposition party, the PPP, brought back normalcy, democracy, civility, and national self-respect, both at home and abroad.

Another "alternative path" was Jamaica's "democratic socialism," devised by Michael Manley in his party, the People's National Party (PNP). Manley's (1974) book *The Politics of Change* was the blueprint for social transformation. He advanced some of C. L. R. James's (1969) ideas for participatory democracy. Manley believed in the necessity for a "politics of popular participation" and generally adopted Nyerere's (1969) critical position toward colonialism, capitalism, and imperialism. The argument is that attitudes and psychological barriers need to be overcome and self-confidence and national pride need to be instilled before there will be success in productive enterprise, local independence, or progressive development. Like the Guyanese premier, Michael Manley took on the foreign bauxite corporations, though he did not attempt the outright nationalization of their assets. Instead, Manley's government introduced a production levy set at 7.5 percent of the selling price of alumina, replacing the previous method, which strongly favored the mining companies. In November 1975, the PNP pronounced its "thirteen principals of democratic socialism," which encapsulated the new government's stance in socialist rhetoric. It promoted people power, socialism, and cooperation along with more reasoned assessments of Jamaican reality such as a continued respect for property ownership, private sector autonomy, and the promotion of a mixed economy (part state-owned and part private, allowing some foreign ownership while promoting domestic ownership). Manley articulated five main aims in another of his literary challenges, *Jamaica: Struggle in the Periphery*: (1) to reduce the dependence of the Jamaican economy; (2) to create a mixed economy with the commanding heights under state control; (3) to reduce social inequalities; (4) to deepen political democracy; and (5) to forge an independent foreign policy (Manley 1982).

Michael Manley stepped onto the world stage as a spokesperson for the "new international economic order" in the Nonaligned Movement and Socialist International, and on behalf of the Third World in general, propelled by the bauxite levy controversy, international exposure and acclaim, and his personal eloquence. Fidel Castro and Michael Manley spoke on behalf of Caribbean and Latin American oppressed peoples. The PNC's willingness to entertain closer political and economic ties with Cuba evoked suspicion and hostility from the U.S. State Department. The United States worked to destabilize Manley's Jamaica through CIA activities, media reports on the dangers of tourism, and loan denials (Thomas 1988). Although there were economic repercussions and an escalation in social tensions, the Jamaican people returned Manley to power with a landslide vote in 1976, with the charismatic leader even securing "Rasta" support. But 1977 was to see the prime minister's demise.

After confronting the IMF's draconian conditionality package with his "we are not for sale" declaration, within three months Manley had to reverse his polemic stance by accepting an IMF credit line of $74 million, along with the humiliating conditions of the IMF structural adjustment program: begin a program of antilabor measures, hold wages constant, agree to a 40 percent devaluation of the Jamaican dollar, and undertake a series of cutbacks in public spending. For the next two years, Manley and the PNP abandoned their populist agenda, attempted to regain the political high ground via pragmatism, and generally lost credibility among the electorate. It came as no surprise when Edward Seaga and the opposition Jamaican Labor Party were swept into power on a electoral landslide in 1980 (Ambursely 1983).

A third "alternative path" was attempted by the New Jewel Movement in Grenada whose accession to power in 1979 in a bloodless coup started their "Revo" and gave this small (45 persons) group of intellectuals and radical leaders an opportunity to chart a "noncapitalist" development path (Jacobs and Jacobs 1980). The socialist program of the Peoples Revolutionary Government (PRG) was optimistic as well as idealistic. Several objectives were framed to thoroughly redevelop the island's economy: (1) construct the Point Salins international airport to handle wide-bodied jets and invest in the infrastructure necessary for a restructured, locally owned tourism industry; (2) encourage growth of a mixed economy with three major institutional bases—state, cooperative, and private—with the state playing the leading role; (3) improve the standard of living through a comprehensive program aimed at upgrading social services and ensuring basic needs; and (4) diversifying overseas trade and diversifying the portfolio of foreign aid and assistance, particularly courting assistance and linkages with CMEA countries, including Cuba, and improving South-South cooperation (Thomas 1988).

Bernard Coard as finance minister diversified the PRG's assistance portfolio. Maurice Bishop, prime minister, befriended Fidel Castro, and Cuban aid was very evident in revolutionary Grenada. Unfortunately, the international acclaim that Bishop garnered, championing the antiimperialist cause on behalf of the Nonaligned Movement, was often made at the expense of the Reagan administration. Bishop's rhetoric, like Michael Manley's, was answered by U.S. state department reaction and displeasure. Bishop's principled stances were championed by the U.S. Congressional Black Caucus, but the Republican administration was not amused. In the end, the "Revo" lasted only four years. Strife within the PRG, culminating in a military coup and the assassination of Maurice Bishop and other followers, provided an opportunity for the U.S. military and the Reagan administration to coordinate the invasion and occupation of that Windward "Spice Isle" (for details of this "gunboat action" see Conway 1983b, c). Grenada was gradually admitted back into the fold, the airport was finished, tourist facilities were opened to foreign finance, and the national economy was to be open, export-oriented, and dominated by foreign capital. A conservative path was the road to the future, and the nationalist fervor of the "Revo" was suppressed and/or put aside by the majority on the island.

Conventional Options

There were Caribbean development models that embraced currently favored economic views in regard to national planning and industrialization. A favored model came from one of the region's favorite sons, Nobel Laureate Sir Arthur Lewis. Puerto Rican development took its great step forward with Operation Bootstrap and the attempt to attract footloose industries. "Industry by invitation" was the more derogatory label applied by radical economists at the University of the West Indies (the New World Group) to efforts encouraging international corporate penetration. Puerto Rico provided a regional showcase for this model, but, as argued below, its experience was not one to be emulated. Trinidad and Tobago attempted a variant on this industrialization model. Trinidad was blessed with oil and gas resources, both on- and offshore, and so the politicians spent thoughtlessly. Its own "alterative path" was labeled "state capitalism" or what Prime Minister Eric Williams termed a "middle path for development" (Conway 1984; Sandoval 1983).

Using OPEC-derived windfall gains from oil and gas, Eric Williams's People's National Movement (PNM) party embarked on a massive restructuring scheme to literally purchase most foreign-owned assets, and industrialize and modernize the Trinidadian economy. This state capitalist model had five components: (1) state utilization of oil revenues to create large-scale, resource-intensive export industries, especially energy-intensive ones such as fertilizers and iron and steel; (2) negotiation of state and TNC joint ventures; (3) development of import-substituting manufacturing and assembly plant operations with export and domestic market capabilities; (4) use of the oil boom surpluses to upgrade basic infrastructure; and (5) dispersion of government revenues into welfare funds, plus massive yearly transfers and subsidies to bolster unprofitable state-owned industries, though they had largely patronage-fueled payrolls. By the end of the oil bonanza in 1983, Trinidad's economic engine had overheated, the glut of revenues had not realized the diversification, and the exchequer was once again reliant on foreign debt (Conway 1984; Ryan 1991; St. Cyr 1993; Thomas 1988).

The development path taken by Barbados since independence in 1966 is best characterized as "conservative and pragmatic." Five dimensions characterized the island's progress, which some suggest may be the region's leading success story (Blackman 1982, 1991; Worrell 1987). First, both major parties, the Barbados Labor Party (BLP) and the Democratic Labor Party (DLP), have ruled as residing governments in this parliamentary democracy, exchanging positions as "opposition" and "ruling" party in accordance with the popular vote. Both hold to parliamentary codes of civility, both view the promotion of political and social stability as a vital necessity, and both agree on high standards of democratic tolerance. Both are committed to maintaining law and order and respect for the judiciary and the police force, and both hold to traditions of "social democratic" ideals that are built on British and European Fabianism and on models of the welfare state.

Second, the economic policies of successive governments since independence are relatively nonideological. Instead they are technocratic, pragmatic, and rational. Barbadian economic policy making is not framed in confrontational posturing, and its conservatism has never been flaunted.

Third, every government, BLP or DLP, whether led by Sir Grantley Adams, Tom Adams, Erskine Sandiford, Errol Barrow, or Owen Arthur, has by and large accepted the colonial mandate and early postindependence strategies of outward orientation and heavy reliance on foreign capital. Each government's goal has been to maintain continuity and make inherited programs more effective. Three major developments can be identified in this respect: (1) sound management for economic development and fiscal planning; (2) systematic development of institutions that improve laborers' skills at all levels; and (3) cultivation of an outlook and a management style that tries to anticipate global economic changes, particularly in North American and European markets, which the country can exploit through tourism, export processing, and offshore financial services (see chap. 5).

Fourth, measures have been taken to facilitate the inflow of foreign capital and to work closely with the Central Bank. As part of this open economy policy, successive governments have encouraged local industry to be export oriented, particularly within the regional Caricom market.

Fifth, all governments have been committed to upgrading the island's physical infrastructure, improving basic services, investing in education, health, and welfare services, respecting and defending the island's national heritage, and using the most applicable forms of institutional control and comprehensive planned use of the island's physical landscape, coastal zone environment, and human and natural resources. In essence, the agenda is to maintain and enhance the island's quality of life (Thomas 1988).

The national record supports the view that the island's development has been a success. While per capita GDP in 1970 was estimated to be approximately $678, by 1975 it had risen to $1,504, and by 1985 stood at $4,400. There were, however, some not-so-healthy indicators accompanying this national accounting. Unemployment has remained high, especially among young males. Governments have reluctantly accepted this structural and endemic feature as unsurmountable in the near, if not the long term. The reliance on tourism and export-oriented producer service sectors as the island's major sources of hard currency leaves policy makers concerned about the sustainability of the island's economic progress. The goal of economic diversification still has not been attained. But Bajan pragmatism prevails to this day.

Like Barbados, Antigua embraced mass tourism as its development core, deliberately turning away from plantation sugar production. However, despite the completeness of Antigua's structural realignment, the recurring excesses of the Bird patriarchy, including a scarcely disputed record of corruption, clientelism, and nepotism, have stifled development (Lorah 1995). Other small islands, such as St. Lucia, St. Vincent and the Grenadines, Dominica, St. Kitts and Nevis, hung on to bilateral agreements with Britain (and the E.U.) which favored their plantation exports, attempted to enlarge their tourist sectors, and sought offshore export-oriented assembly manufacturing (see chapter 5). Some of the smallest British colonies, such as the Cayman Islands, Turks and Caicos, and Bermuda, looked to offshore international finance as their salvation (Roberts 1994; McElroy and de Albuquerque 1996). For all Caribbean islands, tourism provided national accounts with some revenues, but the performances in other sectors did not improve. For these small islands, the 1980s were to merge with the early 1990s as a period of stagnation or little expansion, and without promising signs that their development paths would be easier to chart.

Neocolonial Options

Although most Caribbean island nations sought political independence, colonial ties and neocolonialism persisted. The neocolonial situations are only summarized here, since they are models to be compared with the alternatives, not to be advocated. For parsimony, treatment of every Caribbean territory under neocolonialism is not attempted. Notably, Haiti is mentioned only briefly (but see Fass 1990; Lundahl 1979, 1983, 1992; Dupuy 1997).

Puerto Rico's Operation Bootstrap began in 1947 when U.S. corporations were invited to open their factories on the island with a package of stimuli to subsidize their investments, including tax-free repatriation of profits, freedom from U.S. income taxes, and promises of low-wage, non-union labor. In its earlier years, the industrialization experience was declared an "economic miracle," with average annual growth rates of GDP of 6 percent in the 1950s, of 5 percent in the 1960s, and 4 percent in the 1970s. Foreign investment, mostly from U.S. sources, increased from $1.4 billion in 1970 to $24 billion in 1979. Puerto Rico had the highest per capita level of imports from the United States and 34 percent of total U.S. foreign direct investment. After an earlier enticement of labor-intensive light industrial enterprises, like shoes, glassware, and clothing (many leaving after their fifteen years of tax-sheltered status expired), petroleum refining and petrochemical production came to predominate. After 1973, the refining sector slumped, but pharmaceutical stayed on, exacting a severe price in terms of pollution and offshore environmental degradation (Meyn 1996). In addition, such rapid industrialization came with its geopolitical price: greater dependency on foreign capital and greater dependency on U.S. subsidies and welfare assistance. Paralleling the successive waves of invited industry have been excesses in nuclear power plant siting, with toxic spillages and the poisoning of land and water eventually igniting popular local resistance. Mass circulation between island and mainland has been the human response to this rapid and destructive pattern of industrialization. The high structural unemployment that still haunts the island is a constant reminder of Operation Bootstrap's myopic vision (Sunshine 1988).

Modernization of infrastructure and the leading sectors of the economic bases of the French *Departements D'Outre Mer* have benefited tremendously from metropolitan subsidies, as well as from preferential access of their tropical produce to the European market. The Dominican Republic, however, its sugar industry dominated by Gulf and Western, missed the longer-term returns that would translate into domestic sector growth and expansion. In 1978, when Gulf and Western abruptly pulled out and sold its considerable holdings, it became evident that the Balaguer government's attempts to replicate its own version of Brazil's economic miracle had foundered. Export revenues declined, debt obligations increased, and civil unrest mounted (Wiarda and Kryzanek 1992). Haiti, long exhausted by the exploitative and autocratic regimes of the Duvaliers and their elite clients, found U.S. aid fomenting and entrenching greater dependency (Fass 1990). Migration, environmental degradation of arable land resources, forest cover, and river basin systems, as well as widespread corruption and authoritarian inhumanity, characterized Haitians' lives and struggles for survival.

Cuba's growing dependence on trade, commerce, and financial support from the Soviet Union and Eastern Europe's CMEA countries also reflected the country's plight under a neocolonial regime. Cuba, in distinct contrast to the experience of the rest of the incorporated Caribbean peripheral states, saw sound transformations that were considerable and deep, including equitably administered social welfare services and impressive microbrigade housing performances. Cuban fortunes seemed to be at variance with the rest of the region's (Mathey 1997; see chap. 9).

The 1980s: Global Recession, Debt, and IMF/World Bank Restructuring

In 1978–79 many Caribbean economies registered peak performances, but this boom merely heralded a bust and a recessional slide that reverberated through the region, the hemisphere, and the world. Led by the Reagan administration's counterinflationary strategies, imposed to bring the U.S. domestic economy into order with draconian supply-side policies and fiscal measures, the Caribbean was dragged into a global recession. And although the 1980–83 period was referenced as the official trough, in which market clearing took place and the economies of the world were "rationalized," for many Caribbean, Latin American, and African economies, the depression was a decade-long experience of continuing hardship, global indebtedness, and externally imposed restructuring imperatives. Economic accounting of the dramatic declines of six Caribbean countries for the 1980–83 period demonstrates enough of the dramatic change of fortunes occurring in the 1980s. By the end of 1983, Barbados, Dominican Republic, Guyana, Haiti, Jamaica, and Trinidad and Tobago averaged approximately − 17.0 percent in real GDP at 1980 factor prices, with Jamaica suffering the most at − 27.3 percent (Bakan, Cox, and Leys 1993).

In addition to the external shocks that rained down on Caribbean economies, there were long-standing internal diseconomies that made them doubly vulnerable to growing imbalances in their national accounts. Distortions include a reliance on external financing for excessively high import bills,[1] weak economic management in public and private sectors, and the high costs of maintaining the social-welfare net. But it was the peripheral vulnerability of these economies to the world recession that were most significant. The second oil shock (1978–79) dramatically increased energy costs, while export commodity demand and prices fell. Strictures on discretionary monies in North America and Europe reduced tourist volumes, shrank tourist spending, and forced bankruptcy among fledgling tourism entrepreneurs in the Caribbean. Global foreign direct investment was in retreat during the 1980–83 recession, and the Caribbean peripheral economies ranked as low priorities for the shrinking pool of international capital.

The remainder of the 1980s painted a picture only slightly rosier than the 1980–83 recessionary trough. The global competitiveness of Caribbean export staples and mineral resources continued to decline in relation to other regions of the South (i.e., the "restructuring" competitors in Latin America, Africa, and Asia). There was increased protectionism on the part of northern countries, especially the United States. Bilaterally negotiated quotas for Caribbean commodities were reduced, while renegotiations for increases in foreign market shares in East and Southeast Asia disadvantaged Caribbean commodities such as coffee. The "debt trap," as some critics have labeled the IMF/World Bank "conditionalities," scarcely provided a lending hand to the struggling Caribbean states and their people (Latin American Bureau 1983).

McAfee (1991) depicts the plight as a "hemorrhage of dollars," with debt repayments far exceeding the inflow of aid, loans, and grants. For example, in June 1990, Guyana (the nation with the most depressed economy) paid off debt bills of $237 million, yet it had to take on more than $276 million of new debt (McAfee 1991, 13–14). With its debt burden at punitive levels, Caribbean indebtedness is higher than elsewhere in the hemisphere. In 1988, regional debt as a percentage of the Caribbean's combined GNP/GDP was 79 percent, as compared to 44.2 percent for Latin America. Caribbean debt to foreign governments hover around 40 percent of the region's total debt, whereas the rest of Latin America's indebtedness to foreign governments is only 11.5 percent. Perhaps illustrative of the powerless position of many Caribbean financial managers is the continuing reality that while the Canadian government has agreed to forgive a proportion of the unrepayable loan owed them by several Commonwealth Caribbean countries, the United States government has not been so philanthropic (McAfee 1991). The crisis facing Caribbean finance ministries, economists, development planners, industrial development corporations, even the region's multinational corporations, is deeply structural, deeply global, and highly problematic. It has always been so for these ministates, ever since their incorporation into the earliest imperialist domain in the fifteenth and sixteenth centuries. And it is in the 1990s.

FROM THE WEST INDIES FEDERATION TO CARIFTA/CARICOM AND CBI: THE ONGOING SAGA OF REGIONAL INTEGRATION

How can these island societies overcome the limitations of their essential smallness, islandness, underdevelopment, and limited resource bases? One long-standing idea or "seminal truth," according to Gordon Lewis (1968), was for Caribbean countries to join in a federation and seek economic and political integration. Certainly such configurations were suggested under colonial auspices: the 1897 British Royal Commission proposed a federation between Barbados and the Windward Islands, and the 1938 Caribbean Labour Congress supported integration that included the Bahamas, Belize, and British Guiana. The Royal 1938 Moyne Commission, on the other hand, viewed such an integration as a distant ideal (Thomas 1983).

The British government made the first serious attempt at such a regional grouping with its coordination of the West Indian Federation, which comprised ten of their colonial island territories (1958). Though it lasted less than four years (Sir Alexander Bustemante's nationalist message in favor of Jamaica's independence and the people's referendum doomed it), the West Indies Federation left its legacy. Regionalism was viewed sympathetically. Eminent regional economists such as William Demas argued long and consistently on behalf of the advantages of regional integration for small, disadvantaged territories (Chernick 1978; Demas 1965). Despite the success of 1960s national movements, the federation's major players, namely Jamaica, Trinidad and Tobago, Guyana, and Barbados, others were first directed toward other federal arrangements by the British colonial office but then eventually sought their own independent enfranchisement. Eric Gairy's Grenada declared independence in 1974, after considering the idea of integrating with Trinidad and Tobago. Then five of the British Commonwealth's "associated states"—Dominica, St. Lucia, St. Vincent and the Grenadines, Antigua and Barbuda, and St. Kitts, Nevis, and Anguilla—sought and won political independence between 1978 and 1983. Anguilla subsequently petitioned to rejoin the British colonial family, and in 1996 Nevis was petitioning to sever its ties with St. Kitts (McElroy and de Albuquerque 1996). Elsewhere, among other European colonial groupings, the Netherlands maintains its widely scattered federation of colonial island territories, and the French *Departements D'Outre Mer* have evolved to become Caribbean extensions of a unified European Union, albeit a francophone extension (Sutton 1995).

The collapse of the federation might have promoted political independence for island territories, but it did not remove the integrationist ideas from the development debate. Heads of government among the Commonwealth Caribbean family of independent nations held annual meetings, if only to keep open the dialogue for greater unity (Caricom 1981). There were several regional interests to foster or to collectively "own": the University of the West Indies was one, the highly successful West Indies cricket team another (Beckles and Stoddart 1995). In December 1965 the heads of government of Antigua, Barbados, and Guyana agreed to form a three-country free-trade agreement, Carifta. Three years later, in 1968, the Caribbean Integration and Free Trade Agreement was expanded to incorporate all ten West Indies Federation members plus Guyana. Carifta admitted Belize in 1974 and the Bahamas in 1983.

In 1973 the formalization of Caricom among the signatories to the Treaty of Chaguaramas as a common market to replace Carifta seemed to herald the strengthening of the integrationist quest. Caricom is based on three principals: (1) a common market based on free trade within the group, a common external tariff, a commitment to the progressive removal of nontariff barriers to trade, harmonized fiscal incentives, and free intraregional movements of capital (notably omitted was a similar commitment to negotiate for the free movement of labor within Caricom); (2) establishment of areas of cooperation and the formation of interministerial committees to collaborate in areas of health, education, science and technology, energy, mining and natural resources management, agricultural development, food, and industry, and cooperation in the development of communications and transportation infrastructure; and (3) the coordination of foreign policies (Thomas 1983). The promises were expansive and the commitments were real, but the performance of Caricom has not been equivalent, either in terms of collective actions nor in terms of cooperative enterprise. The heads of government continue to meet annually, but the political will and community resources have never been sufficient, while the rhetoric and plans are often more ambitious than practical.

WHITHER IN THE 1990s?

The economic crises of the 1980s precipitated a new era of reflection and introspection among national economic planners, Caribbean development specialists, and academic political economists, indeed all of us concerned with the "development" of Caribbean societies. "Diversification" was one rallying cry: spawning policies to promote export-oriented industrialization, expand tourism, and encourage agricultural diversification for niche markets. Nontraditional agricultural exports (NTAE) were held up as the potential niche for Caribbean small farming, but the reality of neoliberal regimes suggest otherwise (Bakan, Cox, and Leys 1993). Producerservices was touted as a new sector where the Caribbean might find a solution (Blackman 1982). "New tourism" was to be promoted enthusiastically (Poon 1993). Caricom still offers itself as an institutional forum and a political vehicle for the coordination of greater regional organization (Maingot 1994). The newest regional forum, the Association of Caribbean States, promises there might be wider Basin representation with Venezuelan and Colombian political interests involved.

External forces and macrostructural imperatives direct and determine each country's policies and practices, scarcely providing the necessary leeway for regional, communal actions, and local practices. Bilateral negotiations through CBI, Caribcan, and the E.U.'s Lomé agreements still dominate (Sutton 1995). Even so, GATT rhetoric insists on sweeping away market protection, and further opening global commerce. Regionally, IMF and World Bank conditionalities reign supreme, leaving little room for the Caribbean Development Bank's multilateral lending programs (Hardy 1995). Integrationist schemes are now being constructed in line with today's neoliberal thinking. The agenda is recast in terms of fiscal and monetary criteria. Political integration remains a mythological ideal, and the open economic systems of the insular Caribbean, now more than ever, are open (Watson 1995).

Serious commentary on the place the Caribbean holds in today's globalizing economy is anything but optimistic (Aponte Garcia and Gautier Mayoral 1995; Watson 1995). With their lens firmly fixed on relations at the national scale, addressing issues of *national* economic space, the *nation*-state, sovereignty, and *nationalism*, such critiques don't focus in on internal affairs nor regional issues, and they definitely do not address microscale issues such as gender relations, family structures, and community-level processes. For example, Watson (1995) sets about studying today's "techno-paradigm shift" at the level of global class relations in the international state system. He convincingly argues that a sea change in the global political economy is dramatically changing the playing field for Caribbean institutions, governments, private capitalist sector(s), international financial institutions and development agencies. He goes on to chronicle the declining significance of the nation-state, the Caribbean's structural dichotomies that limit economic development and enterprise, and the crisis that people and institutions of the region face in the twenty-first century's "seamless global economy." Watson (1995) characterizes this situation as an *end to geography*.

Such a global perspective suggests an end to the geography that was defined by former global-to-national interrelations. It is more likely, however, that the "ending" is merely the subordination of one geography to another geography, and the necessary replacement of this prevailing perspective by others because of the growing complexity of sociospatial relations. Watson hints as much when he posits that the techno-paradigm shift has

> implications for all aspects of human activity, including: the territorial base where humans reproduce the social conditions of their existence and develop material and intellectual culture; the nature, forms and functions of the state; ideology and consciousness, class and gender relations; and international relations in the broadest social sense. (Watson 1995, 76)

What is shifting is the functioning scale of the system, not toward a dominant centralizing tendency that the term *globalization* might suggest, but to a more complex shifting of interaction scales through a spatial hierarchy of "global-to- __?? (global —> national —> regional —> local/communal —> family —> individual) systemic interactions, productions and consumptions of rules and resources, dynamic linkages as well as social actions.

To conclude, Caribbean decision makers need to learn from the mistakes of the past, and neoliberalism appears to be hastening a sea change of global restructuring. But Caribbean people, Caribbeanists, and Caribbean institutions should be examining these new global-to-local relations for ways to forge sustainable paths that *resist* the harsh excesses and dehumanizing consequences of neoliberalism and *challenge* free-market triumphalism rather than acquiesce to its dictates. What is needed are progressive paths that build on yesterday's lessons and spring from the proven strength and continuity of progressive practices, while emphasizing the need to "be careful globally, and act locally."

NOTE

1. The IMF and international financial institutions (banks such as Barclays International, Citicorp, Chase-Manhattan, and Canadian National) are implicated in this indebtedness because they were only too willing to increase debt ceilings, offer new loans to already indebted treasuries, and generally encourage Caribbean finance ministers "to live beyond their means."

SUGGESTIONS FOR FURTHER READING

Richardson, B. C. *The Caribbean in the Wider World, 1492–1992.* Cambridge: Cambridge University Press, 1992. A readable account by a historical geographer of five hundred years in the lives of Caribbean people under a succession of externally directed world economic spheres of influence and power.

Thomas, C. Y. *The Poor and the Powerless: Economic Policy and Change in the Caribbean*. New York: Monthly Review Press, 1988. The most thorough and insightful account of the various models of state-promoted noncapitalist paths toward development of Caribbean countries since World War II.

Watts, D. *The West Indies: Patterns of Development, Culture and Environmental Change Since 1492*. Cambridge: Cambridge University Press, 1987. A comprehensive historical treatment of the environmental changes that accompanied settlement and development of plantation systems, and of the incorporation of Caribbean islands into colonial and postcolonial dependent relationships.

3

Microstates in a Macroworld

Dennis Conway

All too commonly, microstates are dismissed as powerless in today's globalizing (macro) world, solely by allusion to the scale and size of these societies. After all, just about every Caribbean insular territory qualifies, with Cuba as the exception. The South American enclave territories of Guyana, Suriname, and French Guiana might also qualify as de facto microstates if their huge unpopulated interiors are discounted and their settled areas and small resident populations in their Caribbean portions are treated as their "functional" territories (see map 1). It is, however, too naive to equate territorial size, or even resident population size for that matter, with progress, wealth, or even power. In this era, large and small countries of the global economic periphery face problems of resources endowments, dependent relations, external penetration, exploitation, and so forth.

To chart a path that is forward and progressive, this chapter provides a re-evaluation of the positive and negative aspects of smallness, "islandness," and remoteness. The leading question is, Can we identify a set of progressive and possible local responses to move toward a sustainable future for Caribbean island microstates in a neoliberal world?

THE NEGATIVE ASPECTS OF "ISLANDNESS"

The list of negative aspects of smallness and small insularity seems overwhelming. Colonial history left many indelible marks, and the postcolonial experience has not addressed all accumulated deficits, never mind achieving progressive social changes. Political-economic readjustments, ameliorative changes, external forces, and natural hazards have not been accommodating either. These negatives can be summarized as the colonial inheritances, then postcolonial limitations, and, overarchingly, the external influences that have held sway and rendered these microstates relatively powerless, dependent, and vulnerable in the various "eras of development" following President Truman's declaration of such in 1949 (Esteva 1992).

Colonial history has left small Caribbean islands with unbalanced economies. Many continue to rely on a very limited range of agricultural products: primary commodities grown for export under the protection of bilateral arrangements and quota agreements with previous colonial partners. Plantation estate production and adjunct small-farmer production of such staples as bananas, sugar, coffee, pineapples, and citrus fruits have low production efficiency and low or minimal profit margins. For some of these staple products like bananas and sugar, the global price is unprofitable. Government subsidies to these relic, monocrop sectors further weaken the viability of agriculture. International and regional aid to small farmers and attempts to stimulate agricultural diversification, more often than not, have not overcome the sectors' depressed state in postcolonial times. French *Departements D'Outre Mer* are the exception. With their preferential treatment in European markets, Martinique's rum, bananas, and pineapple exports and Guadeloupe's sugar exports are maintaining viability in agricultural production. The recent organization of Geest Industries and organizational changes in the banana trade in the Windward Islands may be a progressive restructuring (see chap. 8). But with the European Union's support of trade preferences under challenge by the current U.S. administration and the WTO, Eastern Caribbean farmers' reliance on their "green gold" may be short-lived.

Colonial history also has left many small Caribbean islands with demographic pressures: high people-land ratios, rural proletarianization, an emerging geriatric problem, and traditions of emigration and circulation as survival and escape strategies from hard times (Conway 1989). Age-selective biases in mass emigrations from several small islands contribute to demographic imbalances in the remaining population. Emigration has depopulated some islands, contributed to gender and youth imbalances, and contributed to the "underdevelopment" or "stagnation" of small island communities (Crane 1971; Lowenthal and Comitas 1962). On the other hand, mass emigration has been a release for the high people-land ratios that the plantation economy bequeathed (Richardson 1992), reducing the pressures for small farm fragmentation, reducing unemployment, even reducing fertility levels, and generally serving as a safety valve in times of crisis, natural disasters, political tension, and social unrest.

Emigration has been castigated for bringing about the dearth of skilled human resources and contributing to a brain drain that has long been posited as a Caribbean malaise (Henry 1990; McKee and Tisdell 1988; Palmer 1984). Arguably of equal significance to emigration is the colonial legacy of societal stratification marked by elitism, ethnic particularism and racism, and imposed social monopolies. Thus, small island societies continue to be conservative, stifling, and lacking the flexibility necessary to foster progressive agency.

Typecasting socially elite groups in the Caribbean in this way may have some substance: bekes of the French West Indies and white Jamaicans come to mind as candidates. Also, attributing similarly regressive social roles and narrow, exclusionary group perspectives to members of enclave emigre communities may be appropriate: Cubans in Puerto Rico and British expatriates claiming their exclusionary position as a country-club elite in any number of the Commonwealth Caribbean territories come to mind as such candidates. Class stratification along racial and socioeconomic divisions, ethnic schisms, and societal monopolies characterizes Caribbean societies today as in the past, despite postcolonial attempts to foster multiculturalism and emerge as less divisive and less stratified plural societies (Smith 1984). Power relations institutionalized during the colonial era are not easily expunged, and the racial and ethnic divisions that were part of the colonial models of authority and dominance are societal legacies with persistence, especially when rearticulated by political rhetoric, class allegiances, and other contemporary forces that see political economic benefits in such societal divisiveness. Simply put, class and ethnic/racial stratification is endemic, with the added complication that a growing middle class now positions itself in between elite and poor strata. The middle class imposes a new set of dictates on society, favoring imported material "wants," pressing their needs for "modern" infrastructures, and competing for land and property shares. Whether the middle strata are reactionary or progressive, divisive or cooperative, remains to be assessed.

In addition to societal divisiveness, colonial plantation legacies bequeath plantation capital's ally and successor, merchant capital (Beckles 1990; Watson 1989, 1994). Merchant capitalists, labeled as the Caribbean's *comprador elite*, have been quite content to prosper by relying on their tried-and-tested, oligarchic control of counterproductive commercial activities. These include import-license monopolistic practices, exclusive cartel control of importing intermediate goods and consumer durables, and recapitalization of commercial enterprises rather than productive entrepreneurial activities and ventures, such as manufacturing and producer services (Ambursley and Cohen 1983; Watson 1995).

Small insular societies in the Caribbean are closed systems in terms of their limited natural resources and capacity to absorb external inputs beyond replacement of existing factors. Indeed, islands have been lauded as ideal laboratories for environmental research precisely because of these closed system characteristics. But as sociopolitical economic systems, all Caribbean nations and territories are open systems. There is external throughput of technology, capital, information, exports, imports, and people, ensuring that island societies are continually receiving, assimilating, interacting with and in part rejecting external impulses. Societies are in constant dynamic transition. Such openness, together with the legacies of an unbalanced agricultural export focus, a conservative *comprador elite*, underutilized human potential and limited natural endowments, produces an external trade dependency that continues to be highly disadvantageous to these small island territories.

An evaluation about a decade ago of the prospects for sustainable development and environmental management of small islands lists a daunting litany of distortions in their political economies:

1. Excessive dependency on foreign aid, with many island countries ranking high on lists of per capita aid transfers.
2. Exports from present-day political dependencies, as well as former colonies, routinely enjoy duty-free or preferential access to "mother country" markets.
3. Negotiations of investment and tax treaties with dominant metropolitan trade partners, which result in beneficial inflows of private capital; however, such negotiated bilateralism has encouraged persistent overvaluation of local currencies to the detriment of their export competitiveness.
4. Historical privileges rooted in colonialism have provided island emigrants with access to metropolitan educational systems and labor markets, resulting in high aspirations but limited domestic opportunities.
5. The above concession-based conditions are vulnerable to reduction or withdrawal, should the sense of metropole responsibility weaken in such "distorted" MIRAGE economies based on Migration, Remittances, Aid, Government, and Education.[1] (Beller 1986)

Small geographical area, fragmented territories, and small population sizes limit Caribbean islands' endowments of natural resources. They similarly impose restrictive limits on domestic production and market sizes and thresholds. Domestic markets are insufficient to support much expansion of local production. Regional trade opportunities are hampered by relatively high transportation costs, low sea transportation service efficiencies and considerable irregularity of service, and a general lack of creditworthiness among their trade partners in Caricom. In the wider region, Cuba and Haiti also suffer from the lack of hard currency, and they have few opportunities to use global financial credit to the advantage of regional commerce.

The smallness of the tax base gives rise to disproportionately high per capita costs of infrastructure, and yet the island societies are pledged to deliver social services and are institutionally structured to support a full-fledged administrative bureaucracy. The democratic models of government adopted by many new Caribbean countries are accompanied by postcolonial institutions that the tax base cannot afford. Shortages of skilled administrative and technical personnel notwithstanding, Caribbean governmental costs remain relatively high per capita, with inadequate performance efficiencies (Baker 1992).

As if small Caribbean islands aren't constrained by social, institutional, and economic limitations to the point of crisis, they may be at their most vulnerable today in terms of their environmental limits and constraints. The assault on these islands' fragile natural resources bases began in earnest when they were "discovered" in 1492 and has since been disastrous for flora, fauna, land, mountain, and marine ecosystems (Watts 1987). There is a very long list of environmental problems: forest clearing, inappropriate land-use practices, soil exhaustion and erosion, coral reef destruction, marine pollution, wildlife destruction and species extinction, introduced species disasters (the mongoose, for example), damaged coastal zone ecosystems, diminished mountain forest ecosystems, wetlands destruction, potable water shortages, and depleted appropriate energy resources. Preservation ethics have been a low priority in the Caribbean until very recently (Conway and Lorah 1995).

Some Caribbean nations are fragmented, consisting of several extremely small dependent island communities that are administered by one government centrally located on the largest island (maps 1–3 show these). The minuscule size of such "island orphans" has led to skepticism over their viability (Lowenthal and Clarke 1980, 1982). There are the Grenadines, some administered by St. Vincent, others by Grenada, and some now privately owned by Europe's "rich and infamous." There are the dependencies of Guadeloupe, Desirade, Marie Galante, Isles des Saintes, St. Barthelemy, and half of Saint Martin shared with the Netherlands Antilles' Sint Maarten. The Bahamas—islands, cays, and reef-shelf islands—are another highly fragmented entity, and the ABC islands of the Netherlands Antilles—Aruba, Bonaire, and Curacao—administered together with the Leeward Antillean islands of Saba, St. Eustatius, and half of Sint Maarten are the farthest-flung collection. Many island clusters have remained intact through political independence, but rarely are inter-island relations free of tension and political conflict, the resource sharing balanced, or the political administration equitable. Perhaps Antigua's neglect of Barbudan interests is an extreme case (Lorah 1995), but it recalls others. Examples include Anguilla's renegotiated colonial status after its people's popular uprising against the Bradshaw regime of St. Kitts and Nevis, and Union island's Rasta revolt seeking separation from St. Vincent and the Grenadines.

The small resident populations of these extremely small island dependencies continue to rely on transfers of revenue and assistance from their major administrative mentors or the former colonial power's coffers. Many experience severe geographical isolation and neglect and must rely on their own meager familial and community resources. Traditions of seafaring among these communities have long meant that those left behind tolerate male absenteeism, ageing, and feminization of their communities. They rely heavily on remittances from absent family members. Some Caribbean microsocieties have been pejoratively labeled "remittance societies" (Richardson 1975; Lowenthal and Clarke 1980). Other relatively recent ethnographic work has personified similar microcommunities in the Caribbean in a more positive light (Crane 1987; Frucht 1968; Olwig 1993).

Though scarcely figuring in a regionwide search for potential progressive paths, these small, isolated, and dispersed communities of Caribbean people, both settled and transient, must be part of the equation. Their lifestyles and life chances should not be neglected in favor of the larger islands. Their vulnerabilities need to be factored into any progressive regional plan oriented toward a sustainable future for Caribbean peoples.

THE POSITIVE ASPECTS OF "ISLANDNESS"

The negative aspects of small island territories seem overwhelming. Can there be any *positive* aspects of smallness and islandness? This author firmly believes that the contemporary experience of Caribbean peoples demonstrates several progressive dimensions that are worthy of our attention and that have potential for positive results (see also Hintjens and Newitt 1992).

Small island societies in the Caribbean have long been under the yoke of external metropoles. Their social stratification is class based, with attendant ethnic and racial ascriptive identities further reinforcing "distancing," "divisiveness," social monopolies, and enclave-elite powerbrokering. Racial polarization and social monopolies characterize the political and social experiences of Guyana, Suriname, and Trinidad and Tobago (Premdas 1986; Ryan 1991; Yelvington 1993). On the other hand, by comparison with Central American societies such as Guatemala, where *indio* and *mestizo* cultural divisions (exacerbated by rural-urban geographical separation) severely prohibit social and cultural cohesion, racial/ethnic divisiveness in the insular Caribbean does not retard the inculcation of a common national identity among Indo- and Afro-Guyanese and Indo- and Afro-Trinidadians. Indeed, national pride and identity is a postcolonial sentiment that Caribbean small island societies have successfully fostered.

Today's generations have moved beyond colonial states of consciousness—sociopsychological constraints and negative identities, including a poor self-image, metropolitan mimicry, Euroclass tensions, prostitution of island-cultural heritages, and feelings of powerlessness and inferiority—demonstrating the fortitude and sustainability of these small societies. The acculturation of new generations of citizens, with their own sovereignty, national pride, sense of national worth, and growing communal commitments to a common purpose, has been easier in some of the Caribbean's small cohesive nations than in other colonial realms, such as Africa. Among the remaining colonial dependencies there are other flexible alternatives to political independence that derive from the island peoples' sense of communal responsibilities and that counter the colonial psychological negativism in larger, geographically divided territories. Virtual self-determination under Commonwealth relations with the colonial power, Britain, has brought Bermuda's people beyond the yoke of colonial despondency, divisiveness, and counterproductive sense of inferiority (Manning 1973). Alternatively, the social cohesion of the French *Departements D'Outre Mer*, Martinique and Guadeloupe, is sorely tested, and the continued social and racial divisiveness that pits metropolitan French identities against island identities, both in the islands and in the metropole (Cabort-Mason 1984; Giraud 1995), can be laid at colonialism's door.

In sum, for many postcolonial societies in the Caribbean, smallness and sociocultural cohesion provide a better context for countering and moving beyond the colonial psychological attitudes of dependency, self-contempt, and feelings of inferiority and powerlessness that Fanon's *Wretched of the Earth* (1967) and *Black Skins, White Masks* (1968) so forcefully demonstrated were the crippling legacies of colonialism. This is not to say that the psychological mentalities imposed by centuries of colonial and neocolonial dependency are completely purged from Caribbean peoples' consciousness. More realistically, progress is observable in the region's Nobel Prize winners, the progress of women in authority, the mushrooming of people's savings movements, and the cultural, musical, and artistic renaissance that is afoot (Bilby 1985; Conway 1983a, 1990; Davis and Simon 1983; Leymarie 1994).

Another characteristic of the Caribbean small island social milieu that lends strength to the people's sense of belonging and national pride is the widely held tradition of emigration and circulation, which is inculcated into the peoples' livelihood option. A geographer earlier observed that for the Miskito of the Far Western Caribbean, migration is a process of "leaving in order to stay" (Nietschmann 1979, 20). They leave while maintaining ties with home and intentions to return, even when not realized. The Miskito seek opportunities in the Caribbean extended social fields in North America, Europe, or other parts of the Caribbean that have become venues along well-worn paths that others have paved. This action embodies a flexible survival strategy for participants, who hold to a Caribbean home as its fulcrum (Conway 1989). Remittances cement ties and meet societal obligations. Returnees influence these island societies, perhaps significantly enough to counter the charges of brain drain that have commonly been laid at the feet of emigration (Gmelch 1987, 1992). Circulators bring pocket transfer-remittances and are target earners during North American mainland sojourns, or they practice petty commercial activity like Jamaican and Dominican higglers, and Trinidadian Rasta suitcase traders and vendors. Portes and Guarnizo (1991) have coined the phrase "Tropical Capitalists" to depict the circulatory behavior of small businessmen and kinfolk who move back and forth between New York City and the Dominican Republic, facilitating the transfer of capital, people, information, and goods in kind. Opinions have changed on the impact of remittances and returnees on Caribbean island societies. Earlier critical and negative sentiments (Brana-Shute and Brana-Shute 1982) have given way to more positive evaluations (Conway 1994; Gmelch 1992).

The wider social fields that extend the Caribbean insular societies beyond their shores is an extended domain for the small community back home. It is a relatively permanent support system with a communal sense of identity and nationalism retained despite absence, even when naturalization and citizenship imperatives in the metropole dictate formal declarations of changes of national allegiance. It was to be expected that Donovan Bailey, the Canadian one-hundred meter gold medalist at the 1996 Atlanta Olympic Games, celebrated that he had "run for Jamaica, my country too." Small islanders, far from being resistant to change, are responsive to changing external environments and circumstances in their lives time and time again caused by external factors and structural forces beyond their control. By developing traditions of migration and circulation as livelihood strategies, they are flexible in their abilities to adapt to changing domestic, regional, and global contexts. Indeed, this mobility allows many to accommodate unforeseen and uncontrolled events via internal readjustments of individual, family, or communal norms and behaviors (Carnegie 1982; Conway 1989, 1994; Richardson 1983, 1992).

What might be the political economic/ecological dimensions that differentiate small island potentials from their larger counterparts in the developing world? Small size or islandness per se may be less a determining factor of advantage or positive aspect than a contributing or accompanying factor. Large countries may or may not have similar positive aspects, but the following additional positive aspects can be attributed to Caribbean small island economies, geographies and ecologies (Jalan 1982; Conway 1990).

Small Caribbean countries, each with its single primate, port city, are well placed to enjoy locational and market efficiencies in the centralized, hierarchical distribution (and supply) of advanced medical, educational, and technological services, while meeting their peoples' needs for such services in more equitable ways. Redundancies perpetuated by regionalism and the geographical dispersion of people requiring such services can be avoided, except in the cases of distant island dependencies. Small countries suffer less from extended lines of transportation and communication; small islands are better endowed than landlocked countries in terms of transportation potential and marketing linkages. The maintenance of transportation and communication networks is facilitated by their limited length and connections. Satellite and optical fiber cable technologies in the communications sectors operate under similar network configurations, thereby reinforcing small islands' advantages, even in today's globalizing era. Also, small countries require smaller per capita spending than larger developing countries on social welfare services, housing, health and educational facilities, and economic infrastructure. Due to the limited nature of fixed capital investments, governments of smaller societies have greater maneuverability to reallocate resources in response to changing needs and priorities.

Small domestic manufacturing and agroprocessing production sectors make it possible for management and labor to enter into progressive dialogues to ensure cooperation and progress toward common national goals of increased productivity, international competitiveness, real wage growth, and security of employment. Even the restructuring imperatives of corporations and business organizations toward "flexible" regimes can be better negotiated in such small industrial communities (Goss and Knudsen 1994). Service provision as a linkage between economic sectors, and as a sector that itself absorbs labor, is ideally suited to small scale operations, where labor-intensive methods substitute for capital-intensive technologies and where needs satisfaction is met by labor intensity in marketing and service functions. Economies of scope, not of scale, can be as easily realized in small scale organizations as in medium-range industrial and service operations. Small Caribbean organizations can be more easily linked to centralized, vertically integrated corporate enterprises as outsource operations, producer services cells, and kit-fabrication specialists and suppliers (Girvan and Marcelle 1990).

Small island nations can undertake development of their most important and abundant factor endowment—human skills. Small island nations can be successful with comprehensive education plans. Education expenditures constitute a major part of the national budget. This is possible because most Caribbean small nations need not invest their scarce resources in building or maintaining large military forces.

Effective fiscal planning can be instituted in small nations through the establishment of a central bank to assert independence in monetary and economic management spheres, to promote development of a national financial system, and to diversify over time via growth of indigenous credit institutions, savings and loans, and commercial banks. As an autonomous authority with responsibility for capital reserves and for maintaining exchange rate stability, the central bank of a microstate can act as an influential adviser to government. It can anticipate changes and suggest policies to the government appropriate to the contemporary fiscal situation of the national account. Since regional economies do not really exist in a small country, the economic impacts of national policies and fiscal decisions can be effectively monitored through central bank accounting of fiscal returns, outputs and inputs, and through the bank's close liaison with government financial ministries and the private sector financial institutions under its jurisdiction. A well-managed central bank can be a progressive instrument for a small nation's monitoring of its economic growth and development, anticipating fiscal squeezes, responding promptly to expansion and contraction needs of the economy, micromanaging the money supply, and providing government with an effective oversight mechanism. This may reduce opportunities for corrupt fiscal practices of government officials and may better inform financial ministries on sound budget practices (Blackman 1982, 1991).

Small Caribbean countries lack many natural resources, but their environmental qualities give them comparative advantages over many larger countries in the hemisphere, and their supply of human resources is abundant and comparatively advantageous too. Tourism has emerged as an important industrial sector for the Caribbean in the post-World War II era, and it is highly elastic in its ability to absorb labor. With appropriate and responsible government oversight, appropriate tourism bundles can be managed and developed to the Caribbean peoples' advantage, despite the industries' checkered record in this regard (Conway 1985; Pattullo 1996a).

To date the environmental, social, and institutional impacts have not been adequately addressed in the initial development stages of many islands' attempts to develop their tourism products, or more correctly, to have their tourism industry *developed for them* (Pattullo 1996b; Lorah 1995). Calls for appropriate "low density styles" of tourism (McElroy and de Albuquerque 1991) are given passing consideration, but are not possible in the mature, high-density "bundles" of mass tourism such as Puerto Rico, the U.S. Virgin Islands, and St. Maarten. Concerns about tourism's externally driven behavior are central to any evaluation of its growth and development potential for Caribbean small islands (McElroy et al. 1987). But small island nations need to seek returns from tourism because of their limited abilities to earn foreign exchange from alternative industries such as agroprocessing, capital goods manufacturing, and commercial fishing (chapter 12 pursues this assessment of tourism and other industries; Ramphall 1995).

Similar risk taking may be appropriate for Caribbean microstates in other service export fields, such as producer services, information technology services, offshore finance, and insurance management (Blackman 1991). However, adequate note needs to be taken of the externally directed forces crucial to these sectors' survival or continued location in the Caribbean. It may well be that little long-term reliance should be placed on these risky enterprises of global capitalism's making. While development options for small islands are limited, the opportunities for successful physical planning may be greater in Caribbean systems than in larger developing nations. This is due to the small scale of the society and the closeness of all involved parties, from local communities, NGOs, and planning officials, to the political center of decision making. All are more responsive to democratic and popular pressures because of the small scale of the society and the interweaving of personal representation with institutional responsibilities. Planning exercises heighten popular participation and strengthen the effectiveness of comanagement and stakeholder, self-management initiatives (see Conway and Lorah 1995). The smallness of social fields leads to continuous popular evaluation of government management. There is the constant pressure of critical commentary in opposition newspapers, on local radio, and by quickly formed protest coalitions, when government actions are deemed ineffective or corrupt and when government high-handedness prompts a rapid national outcry. Participatory political action is relatively common in the history of many Caribbean societies, and trade union marches are to be expected, given their long traditions. And when island children are mobilized, society listens. Authoritarian governments have long held sway, and they still do in a few Caribbean nations. But generally the democratic process is respected and people vote in large proportions. The nations' physical planning processes, though sometimes lacking in sensitivity to local environmental contexts and in flexibility to incorporate local folk and vernacular forms, nevertheless represent comprehensive attempts to undertake appropriate responsibility for the nation's natural resources.

Omitted thus far from this discussion on the pros and cons of the Caribbean's microstates are their strategic weaknesses and geopolitical vulnerability when threatened by international banditry, mercenary adventurism, drug-smuggling, gun-running cartels, and other international criminal activities (Harden 1985; Honychurch 1984; Maingot 1994; Richardson 1992). It may well be that "small is dangerous, and vulnerable" if the power and influence of international criminal activity is not reined in by concerted efforts of the international community (Harden 1985; Ramphal 1983).

However, it is not unreasonable that Caribbean small nations should expect comparable assistance from the global community as that meted out to larger constituencies in the developing South. Indeed, there is a reasonable argument for preferential international assistance and development initiatives for small developing nations. Such assistance might be extremely cost-effective and productive if delivered correctly. Further, small insular societies do require different development scenarios than those designed for large developing economies with their regional disparity problems, national infrastructure difficulties, internal market diseconomies, urban-rural inequalities, and regional ethnic/cultural divisions.

CONCLUDING ON A NOTE OF OPTIMISM

Compared to the problems of many large developing countries in today's globalizing world, smallness and "islandness" may not be such liabilities. Investment per capita ratios might be quite favorable. Success in local, self-help, and stakeholder comanagement projects, microenterprise incubation, and gender- and age-specific initiatives might be more achievable. Of course, the many small Caribbean societies have many problems, including legacies of mismanagement and dependent relations. They are externally dominated and now more than ever "open" societies. But there are also inherited strengths that should not be dismissed. Despite the checkered record of regional associations like Caricom, there are signs that regional cooperation is being actively sought. The islands' political regimes are growing more astute in their international negotiations. Environmental consciousness has been raised to the point that realistic evaluations of island resource bases are being undertaken. Similar assessments are being made of the resident human and social capitals' potentials. We might want to give currency to one of Lloyd Best's (1966) maxims: that management skills and human resource development are the keys to a sustainable future for Caribbean peoples (see also Farrell 1993; Henry 1990). The people's will has never been in doubt. What is needed is the political will, the international community's cooperation and assistance, and the active participation of Caribbean diasporas in the region's plans for the future. Then small can be beautiful and progress can be possible.

NOTE

1. This acronym extends from MIRAB—*Mi*gration, *R*emittances, *A*id, and *Bu*reaucracy—used to characterize Pacific Micronesian states (Bertram 1986). Although people's access to education should be revered as a progressive development achievement, dependent islanders are "educated to emigrate" (Crane

1971). Their educational systems mimic those of their former colonial powers, fueling aspirations for careers not available locally, or so it is concluded.

SUGGESTIONS FOR FURTHER READING

Hintjens, H. M. and M. D. D. Newitt, eds. *The Political Economy of Small Tropical Islands: The Importance of Being Small.* Exeter: Exeter University Press, 1992. The contributors are consultants and scholars, including many acknowledged regional experts and practitioners. This volume of comparative studies takes a positive perspective on the diverse experiences of Pacific and Caribbean tropical islands and their obvious limits, and it stresses their possibilities.

Lockhart, D. G. D. Drakakis-Smith, and J. Schembri. *The Development Process in Small Island States.* London: Routledge, 1993. The contributors are British geographers with interests in the impacts of urbanization, development, and tourism in small country and small island settings, including Caribbean contexts. The unhappy history of many a development project and the current spate of problems these small countries face are themes that recur throughout the contributions.

McElroy, Jerome, and Klaus de Albuquerque. "The Social and Economic Propensity for Political Dependence in the Insular Caribbean." *Social and Economic Studies* 44, nos. 2–3 (1995): 167–93. Why do the sixteen Caribbean territories that have not yet achieved the status of independent nation-states prefer to remain dependencies? This paper summarizes the economic and migratory advantages of the status quo for some contemporary Caribbean colonies.

4

Trade Policies and the Hemispheric Integration Process

Dennis J. Gayle

The trade policies of Caribbean countries are driven by the perceptions and perspectives of elite entrepreneurs, bureaucrats, and politicians. They make policy by evaluating the range of available local resources and market opportunities in relation to the structure of the domestic, regional, and global business environments. In turn, these environments result from continued cycles of interaction between the pivotal ideas and institutions in both public and private sectors. The ideas and institutions define the precise roles of public- and private-sector actors in trade activity.

The pivotal ideas that now define the Caribbean business environment fall under the umbrella of neoliberalism. They include the importance of privatization, deregulation, economic liberalization, foreign direct investment (FDI), sociopolitical stability, reduced tariff and nontariff barriers, and the expansion of nontraditional exports, with a focus on the North American and European markets (these ideas are expounded in chap. 5). The key institutions that encapsulate and articulate such ideas include the World Bank, the International Monetary Fund, and the World Trade Organization. They are reinforced by Caribbean regional development banks, the local offices of international development assistance agencies, embassies representing the region's North Atlantic trading partners, and private sector associations. These neoliberal ideas have been widely implemented at the national and the regional level through Caricom.

This chapter begins by focusing on the fourteen West Indian countries that are members of the Caribbean Common Market (Caricom): Antigua and Barbuda, Barbados, Belize, Dominica, Grenada, Guyana, Haiti, Jamaica, Montserrat, St. Kitts-Nevis, St. Lucia, St. Vincent and the Grenadines, Suriname, Trinidad and Tobago (see map 1).[1] The field of vision later narrows to the Caricom countries of Jamaica and Trinidad and Tobago, which have most aggressively pursued membership in NAFTA, and Barbados, which has concluded that regional interests may best be served by first looking south and west.

I begin by reviewing the NAFTA framework and the discussions to date within Caricom countries as well as between member countries and the Clinton administration. I also review the progress of other relevant hemispheric trade integration processes besides NAFTA. I then examine the post-1982 market opportunities that have resulted from U.S. trade preferences extended to the Caribbean: the Caribbean Basin Initiative and the U.S. Guaranteed Access Program for Caribbean textile exports. The evolving Caribbean business environment is subsequently used as a lens through which to view the responses of Caricom countries to these opportunities and to the possibility of NAFTA accession. I conclude with an assessment of Caricom's hemispheric trade agreement options and prospects.

THE NAFTA FRAMEWORK

The Significance and Perils of NAFTA for Caricom

In November 1993, following an intense debate during which a broad antitrade coalition emerged in the United States, the U.S. Congress voted to ratify the North American Free Trade Agreement (NAFTA). This agreement initiated a process of phasing out tariffs between the United States, Canada, and Mexico over fifteen years, beginning in January 1994, and substantially liberalizing Mexican investment rules. One of the major forces driving U.S. interest in NAFTA was the direct cost to firms of global trade barriers, then estimated at $19 billion per year (*The Miami Herald* 1993, 27 November 1993 sec. A, pp. 1, 7). NAFTA was promoted as the world's largest free-trade zone, comprising some 373 million people with a combined gross domestic product of $6.8 trillion.

If NAFTA lacks the institutional and political attributes of the European Union, such as a legislature and a commitment to foreign as well as macroeconomic policy coordination among members, it nonetheless remains an exercise in deep integration. At least eight aspects of NAFTA are particularly relevant to aspiring Caricom countries. First, the agreement includes reciprocal trade in both goods and services, so that special attention to the potential for sudden Caribbean import surges in any given sector is required, given Caricom's history of protected domestic production, nonreciprocal trade agreements, and lack of serious progress on services trade liberalization.[2]

Second, NAFTA requires prospective members as a precondition to conclude bilateral investment treaties and intellectual property rights agreements with the United States. This means that signatories must extend national treatment to foreign investors from other member countries, apart from specifically excluded sensitive industries, and provide extensive protection to intellectual property rights. It should be noted parenthetically that Caricom countries have yet to collaborate on the revision of related legislation, which has been essentially unchanged since colonial days. Nor have they established a single regional patent office, although some members have instituted national reviews of antitrust legislation and the status of interfirm competition (Stewart 1996, 31–35). That NAFTA's chapter 17 includes detailed commitments regarding copyright, sound recordings, satellite signals, trademarks, patents, computer chips, trade secrets, geographical indications, and extensive enforcement provisions is also worth serious attention on the part of prospective signatories (Sherwood and Primo Braga 1996, 6).

Third, other preconditions for entering NAFTA include unspecified "satisfactory" economic performance, as evidenced by fiscal and monetary stability, low inflation, and market-determined exchange rates, as well as adherence to similarly ill-defined "acceptable" labor and environmental protection standards.

Fourth, companies from all member countries are expected to participate in government procurement projects, an expectation that conflicts with persistent patterns of public sector patronage in the Caribbean (Stone 1980).

Fifth, since the Eastern Caribbean members of Caricom that are also members of the Organization of Eastern Caribbean States tend to be more oriented toward the guaranteed European markets and prices for sugar and bananas afforded by the Lomé Convention than toward the U.S. market (as discussed in chap. 8), intraregional divergences as to the expected net benefits of NAFTA are probable.

Sixth, as a result of the Lomé Convention, Caricom countries would be committed to treat exports from the United States and all European Community countries in an identical manner. This might present a major barrier to the NAFTA accession process, but need not preclude NAFTA parity.

Seventh, the elaboration of committees and working groups under NAFTA would require significant levels of staffing and representation from Caribbean countries. The region has always been hard pressed to provide sufficient numbers of skilled representatives to promote its international interests.

Eighth, the eventual range of hemispheric as well as extrahemispheric membership in NAFTA remains unclear. So does the potential for multilateral negotiations, perhaps primarily involving negotiations among NAFTA, Mercosur, and the Andean Community, as opposed to country-selective extensions of NAFTA. Further, U.S. Department of Commerce officials indicate that they expect future hemispheric trade negotiations to go beyond the requirements of NAFTA regarding product standards, investment protection, and customs procedures, and that the expanding requirements will stress intellectual property and trade in services (*The Economist* 12–18 October 1996, 28).

NAFTA will phase out most tariffs and quotas during the decade to 1 January 2004, with an additional five years allowed for sensitive products. Foreign and domestic investors receive identical treatment, with exceptions and derogation periods varying from seven to fifteen years for automobiles, selected agricultural crops (including sugar and orange juice), government procurement, and financial services. While encouraging economic growth in all three member countries, particularly in Mexico, NAFTA was expected to cause significant net employment losses in vulnerable U.S. sectors, such as low technology, labor-intensive manufacturing, where high tariffs persist, exemplified by apparel, household glassware, and ceramic tiles products. Some analysts projected an increasing U.S. trade deficit with Mexico.

U.S. exports to Mexico grew from a pre-NAFTA level of $27 billion in 1990 to a post-NAFTA level of $49 billion in 1994. In that year, U.S. exports slightly exceeded its imports from Mexico (Weintraub and Gilbreath 1996, 8). Further, the value of U.S. FDI in Mexico rose from $9.4 billion in 1990 to $15.2 billion in 1994. Still, 49 percent of total U.S. FDI continued to be directed to Europe, 17.7 percent to Asia, and only 14.6 percent to Canada and Mexico (Ramirez de la O 1996, 4–5). It was in Mexico that open unemployment increased from 3.4 percent in 1994 to 7.3 percent in 1995, while at the same time real median salaries decreased by more than 50 percent and domestic interest rates soared (Zapata 1996). Further, NAFTA has provided export benefits for only a small number of Mexican companies: 2.2 percent of such enterprises account for 80 percent of the country's non-oil exports. Further, these benefits have remained concentrated in the northern states of Mexico, home to 17 percent of the population, whereas the economies of southern states such as Chiapas and Oaxaca have not expanded (Oppenheimer 1997, 8A).

U.S. Reticence to Expand NAFTA

Despite the fact that U.S. exports have grown with NAFTA, soon after its passage, the U.S. Congress signaled a disinclination to extend NAFTA-style arrangements to Caribbean and Central American countries. Wage levels there are even lower than in Mexico, and U.S. labor unions fear that additional job migration would result.[3] This U.S. disenchantment with NAFTA has continued. For instance, in November 1995, U.S. representative Marcie Kaptur (Democrat-Ohio) introduced the NAFTA Account-ability Act, which called for the certification of gains in U.S. domestic manufacturing, employment, and living standards as a result of the agreement since January 1994, if the United States were not to withdraw. Again, a March 1996 poll conducted among U.S. citizens by the Bank of Boston found that 42 percent of the sample (n = 754) believed that trade agreements result in fewer U.S. jobs, while 48 percent held views less favorable toward free trade than was the case a year earlier; 52 percent supported free trade, but with varying degrees of enthusiasm (Johnson 1996, 4A). During the development of President Clinton's fiscal 1997 budget, which was released at the same time and promptly rejected by Congress, some textile industry representatives argued that the proposed extension of NAFTA parity to Caribbean Basin Initiative products, including textiles, garments, footwear, and petroleum, would cost the U.S. government $2–3 billion over seven years in reduced tariffs collected (Frisby 1996, A20).

President Clinton has pledged since 1993 to seek ways of protecting the twenty-four Caribbean Basin Initiative countries from the loss of U.S. investment and market share to Mexico because of NAFTA. But his declared goal of enhanced regional trade may well remain rhetorical, at least for a while yet. The Summit of the Americas, which was held December 9–10, 1994, and involved all thirty-four elected leaders of the hemisphere, provided a test of President Clinton's willingness to address the goal of enhanced regional trade in a concrete manner. The U.S. negotiating team began by emphasizing noneconomic agenda items, such as effective governance and sustainable development. Under pressure from countries to the south, it eventually accepted a commitment to put a Free Trade Area of the Americas in place by 2005 and to initiate negotiations for Chile's accession to NAFTA. The latter commitment was put aside immediately after the summit. One result was an interim free trade agreement between Canada and Chile, which was explicitly patterned after NAFTA, and was executed on November 18, 1996.[4] During his second term in office, President Clinton will probably renew his interest in hemispheric integration, particularly as the second Summit of the Americas, which is scheduled for early 1998 in Chile, approaches.[5]

Meanwhile, NAFTA has been eroding or eliminating the benefits of CBI trade preferences within sectors such as citrus, cut flowers, electronics, and apparel. Indeed, Mexican apparel now enters the United States at prices that are 8–10 percent below equivalent Caribbean apparel. Mexican apparel exports to the United States continue to surge, expanding at three times the rate of those from the Caribbean Basin. During the first two months of 1996, Mexican apparel exports surpassed those of the insular Caribbean's single largest exporter, the Dominican Republic, amounting to $440 million compared with $207 million (Gayle 1996, 1). The Caribbean Textile and Apparel Institute, located in Kingston, estimates that more than 150 apparel plants were closed across the region, and 123,000 jobs were lost during 1995–96, as a direct result of trade and investment diversion to Mexico (Rohter 1997a). NAFTA also appears likely to benefit Mexico at Caricom's expense in several other product categories, including sugar and perhaps rum, vegetables, citrus, frozen orange juice concentrate, processed fruit juices, fresh fruit, and cut flowers (Gill 1995, 32). Even before the passage of NAFTA, which includes specific dispute settlement mechanisms, an anticipatory shift in extraregional investment, from the Caribbean to Mexico, was observed. Indeed, the value of CBI preferences has also been eroded by the U.S. Andean Trade Preference Act when applied to competing products such as seafood, tropical fruit, spices, rice, and cut flowers.

The global business environment is also threatening for Caricom textile and apparel exports to the United States. It was projected that the 1993 GATT Agreement would reduce the average price of apparel products in the United States by 11.4 percent, or a total of $15.85 billion annually (*The Miami Herald* 19 October 1993, 1C). By phasing out global quotas in the textile sector, GATT radically redistributed, as well as eliminated, jobs in both the Caribbean and South Florida textile sectors.[6] As foreshadowed by the NAFTA debate, detailed implementation arrangements between the United States and the Caribbean across a range of thorny trade issues that are important to the latter, such as agricultural subsidies, textile tariffs/quotas, and market access under the 1993 GATT agreement, have remained elusive.[7] One result, however, was early U.S. and Caribbean consensus on measures to protect the latter's apparel industry from unequal competition with Mexico after NAFTA went into effect. This took the form of parity legislation that was linked to the creation of the World Trade Organization.

The Argument for NAFTA Parity for the Caribbean

The NAFTA parity legislation, the unenacted U.S. Caribbean Basin Trade Security Act, was intended to insure that Caribbean and Mexican exports to the U.S. market enjoyed equal access during a transitional period of ten years. At the same time, it would present the Caribbean with a challenge by progressively raising its rules of origin, which stipulate the share of product value that is local, to NAFTA levels. In return, Caribbean countries would be required to take reciprocal steps to expand market access for U.S. products, strengthen investment guarantees, expand workers' rights, and improve intellectual property protection. At the end of this transitional period, Caribbean countries would be eligible to join the hemispheric Free Trade Area of the Americas.

The argument for such parity legislation is threefold. First, U.S.–Caribbean commercial exchanges have generated nearly 17,000 U.S. jobs a year since the mid-1980s, for a total of over 260,000 such jobs by 1996 (Bernal 1996). Between 1985 and 1995, while Caribbean exports to the U.S. market grew by some 50 percent to $12.5 billion per annum, U.S. exports to the Caribbean market expanded by over 100 percent to more than $15 billion per year (Rohter 1997, 1). This ironic economic interdependence is worth emphasis. For instance, some U.S. labor unions in the apparel industry contend that the CBI has helped to preserve American jobs by systematically reducing joint production costs while establishing a market for U.S. equipment and technology. The second argument in favor of NAFTA parity presents the flip side of this point: Caribbean garment exports rely on U.S. components and labor for up to 70 percent of overall value added. The third such argument is that the Caribbean Basin represents the only world region where U.S. exporters have consistently maintained trade surpluses during the past decade. Some 60 cents of each dollar earned by Caribbean exports to the U.S. market are directed toward purchases of U.S.-made consumer goods, food products, raw materials, and capital equipment (Bernal 1996). The main reasons for Caribbean interest in NAFTA include the perceived need for enlarged hemispheric market access and the encouragement of investment inflows. Yet trade impacts are not always easy to predict. One historical paradox is that preferential or nonreciprocal access to both U.S. and E.U. markets has been accompanied by trade deficits in the former and significantly reduced trade surpluses in the latter (Rampersad 1995).[8]

Hemispheric Trade Integration Beyond NAFTA

In 1991 Argentina, Brazil, Paraguay, and Uruguay formed the Southern Common Market, or Mercosur, under the Treaty of Asunción. Since then, trade within the world's third largest integrated market, after NAFTA and the European Union, has grown by an annual average rate of 3.5 percent, from $10 billion in 1990 to $14.5 billion in 1995. To be sure, internal trade amounted to a scant 1.6 percent of Mercosur's GDP in 1995, compared with 4.5 percent in the NAFTA countries and 14 percent for the European Union. However, on January 1, 1995, Mercosur embarked on the creation of a customs union and in June 1996 concluded a free trade agreement with Chile that was initiated when the latter's hopes for early NAFTA accession were extinguished.

A similar agreement with Bolivia is expected. By December 1995, Mercosur had also agreed to a five-year program for standardizing many trade-related rules and procedures, as well as harmonizing economic policy, while also negotiating a framework for free trade with the E.U. by

2005. In partial consequence, Japanese prime minister Ryutaro Hashimoto expressed interest in initiating a dialogue with Mercosur during a landmark ten-day visit to Mexico, Chile, Brazil, Peru, and Central America in August 1996. Mr. Hashimoto repeatedly pointed out that Japan was Latin America's second-largest trading partner and that 11 percent of all Japanese foreign aid was directed to the region, together with 12.7 percent of all Japanese FDI, valued at $60 billion.

Meanwhile, Brazil initiated a campaign for the creation of a South American Free Trade Area, combining Mercosur and the Andean Pact (IRELA 1995, 28–34). If South American exports to the rest of the world are dominated by primary products, trade liberalization has enlarged the region's internal market for manufactures. By 1996, Mercosur member countries had achieved an income per capita of $5,000, 30 percent above that of Latin America as a whole and attracting external investment valued at approximately $6 billion in both 1994 and 1995 (*The Economist* 12–18 October 1996, 1–6).

On the other hand, an internal World Bank report argues that the fastest growing intra-Mercosur trade items—automobiles, buses, agricultural machinery, and other capital-intensive goods—are not internationally competitive, while common external tariffs exclude imports from more efficient manufacturers (Yeats 1996). Furthermore, Mercosur excludes a range of issues legislated in NAFTA such as trade in services, the treatment of intellectual property, and government procurement.

CARICOM TRADE INITIATIVES

By June 1993, Caricom and Central America's SIECA (Secretariat for Central American Integration) had signed an agreement providing for information exchange and project development, with an eye to expanded regional integration. Later that year, Caricom established a joint trade commission with Cuba to focus on the tourism, biotechnology, pharmacology, and medical equipment sectors. In turn, the Association of Caribbean States was established in July 1994 and formally launched in January 1995. This grouping included a total of thirty-seven states, countries, and territories which planned to complete the membership process, with Mexico, Colombia, and Venezuela providing the center of gravity. By 1994, former Trinidadian prime minister Patrick Manning declared his country's intense interest in NAFTA, observing that the implementation of a Free Trade Area of the Americas would make Caricom obsolete.

In 1996, Trinidad and Tobago, accompanied by Jamaica, mounted a renewed offensive for entry into NAFTA. Trinidad's prime minister, Basdeo Panday, lobbied Mexican president Ernesto Zedillo on behalf of his country's application during a September meeting of the Rio Group in Bolivia. Jamaica's prime minister, P. J. Patterson, commented that although NAFTA included transitional membership exceptions, U.S. negotiators were reluctant to apply these exceptions to the Caribbean.[9] Indeed, the Mexican peso's drastic devaluation in December 1994, as well as the country's economic depression since then, has ironically limited enthusiasm for further hemispheric integration across the U.S. political spectrum, despite Mexico's early repayments on President Clinton's $50 billion line of credit.[10] One U.S. congressional observer commented following the November 1996 elections that the legislative majority that had emerged was neither free trade nor protectionist, but rather nationalist (Gale 1996). Continuing disagreement between congressional Democrats and Republicans as to whether labor and environmental issues should be included or excluded from any negotiating authority granted for the purpose of expanding NAFTA provides a convenient delay for most legislators.

At the March 1996 hemispheric trade summit following the Summit of the Americas, progress toward integration was modest. Participating countries agreed to consider interim steps such as unified customs procedures and investment rules as a prelude to establishing a timetable for talks toward the Free Trade Area of the Americas (FTAA). While the eleven technical working groups established after the summit continue to gather and disseminate significant data, the FTAA process remains overshadowed by serious doubts about the depth of U.S. commitment (Lande 1996). For the United States, the identification of interim steps again proved a convenient obstacle to formal agreements. U.S. posturing was most openly opposed by the Mercosur countries, which have been setting the pace on matters of hemispheric integration.

Prime Minister Owen Arthur of Barbados has argued that instead of focusing on preferential trade arrangements of any kind, and thereby engaging in negotiations to perpetuate trade preferences for their own sake, Caricom ought to focus on enhancing its own international competitiveness. Indeed, the Caribbean region is not prepared to cope with the new realities of its contemporary international economic relations. Prime Minister Arthur has indicated that his government is not anxious to join NAFTA and will concentrate on other hemispheric trade groupings, including Mercosur and the Association of Caribbean States (Arthur 1996; Collins 1996, 4). At the same time, Trinidad and Tobago's announced intention to pursue bilateral free trade and investment agreements with Cuba does not auger well for early NAFTA accession negotiations for that country. Trinidad and Tobago will run up against the U.S. Cuban Liberty and Democratic Solidarity Act of 1996 (better known as Helms-Burton). It creates a federal legal cause of action on behalf of U.S. citizens whose property was confiscated without compensation by Cuba and against those who "traffic" (i.e., invest) in such property.

Despite the serious obstacles between them and NAFTA, Caricom heads of government, at their July 1996 conference in Barbados, agreed to intensify the region's campaign for NAFTA parity immediately after the November presidential and congressional elections in the United States. The plan is to coordinate efforts with Central American members of the Caribbean Basin Initiative, mobilize U.S. groups with Caribbean interests, develop a congressional lobbying campaign by Caricom ambassadors in Washington, D.C., send a Caricom ministerial mission to the U.S. capital, and present a formal request at an unprecedented Caricom-U.S. summit. At the same conference, Caricom decided to pursue a series of bilateral free trade agreements, including both goods and services, with prospective Latin American regional groupings. One such step was taken at the third foreign ministers' conference between Central America's SIECA and Caricom in Costa Rica in November 1996. Caricom and SIECA agreed in principle to sign a free-trade agreement and to establish a Joint Private Sector Commission. On 10 May 1997, while visiting Barbados, President Clinton signed a modest accord with Caricom leaders to improve U.S. drug interdiction capabilities in the region and to provide reduced tariffs for Caribbean textile exporters to the United States. He also indicated support for continued regional banana exports to the E.U., as long as it discontinued its "discrimination" against dollar bananas (i.e., those exported by U.S. firms from mainland Latin American countries).

CARICOM'S TRADE WITH THE UNITED STATES

The Anglophone Caribbean has long benefited from U.S. trade preferences that are based on U.S. national interests and are only incidentally related to the region's economic needs (Gayle 1986, 11–12). It should be recalled that in 1982, when the Reagan administration first proposed the Caribbean Basin Initiative (CBI), at least 87 percent of all existing regional exports to the United States already entered duty-free under the Generalized System of Preferences (GSP), whose time frame was later extended from 1984 until 1993. Whereas the GSP required that 35 percent of all product value be added within a single beneficiary country, the CBI encouraged joint processing within several participating countries and the use of U.S. source materials. To qualify for CBI, articles had to be imported by the United States directly from a beneficiary country and had to include at least 35 percent in processing costs in one or more CBI countries. However, 15 percent of this total might consist of U.S.-made components. The central feature of the CBI was the elimination (over

1984–96) of U.S. customs duties on most imports from Caribbean Basin countries in which they had no particular comparative advantage and therefore from which they would scarcely benefit. The president was authorized to designate noncommunist states as CBI beneficiaries, provided that they had enacted trade and investment legislation that was acceptable to the United States.

Articles ineligible for duty-free treatment under CBI included canned tuna, petroleum and petroleum products, rubber and plastic gloves, leather apparel, handbags, and flat goods (i.e., metal sheets, such as aluminum or steel). Duty-free imports of sugar were strictly limited to current country quotas. Initially, U.S. textile imports remained subject to import quotas assigned to each country and to the MultiFibre Arrangement, which restricts export from developing countries (see IADB 1992, 228–29). In fact, one prime reason for the CBI's failure was the success of Washington, D.C., industry lobbyists in excluding the region's potentially most competitive exports, including sugar, textiles and clothing, shoes, other leather goods, petroleum and petroleum derivatives. Meanwhile, another section of CBI allowed deductions for business expenses incurred in attending conventions held in beneficiary states, provided that a tax treaty with the United States was in effect. In 1984, it was also projected that the Caribbean Basin Initiative would complement the Lomé III Convention, which was concluded during that year, so that in principle, twelve CBI countries could offer interested investors preferential access to both E.U. and U.S. markets.

In 1988, a U.S. Commerce Department survey found that at least 646 U.S. companies had invested more than $1.5 billion in CBI beneficiary states since January 1984, generating over 116,000 jobs across the region. However, the longer term results were predictable. For instance, during 1986–95, the U.S. trade surplus with the Caribbean Basin states steadily accumulated from $297 million to $2.6 billion (Dalley 1996, 25).[11] The only American import growth, amounting to some 10 percent cumulatively, was from nontraditional products, such as seafood, jewelry, handicrafts, and apparel.

In 1995, U.S. exports to the insular Caribbean increased by a record 15 percent, to $8 billion, while U.S. imports from the subregion expanded by one percent to $6.4 billion.[12] The Dominican Republic and Jamaica accounted for 55 percent of all U.S. exports to the Caribbean, with uncut apparel and new and used automobiles constituting the major export components (Jainarain 1996, 37–38). The United States had a trade surplus with every country in the region except Aruba, Trinidad and Tobago, and the Dominican Republic. It is notable that the Caribbean is one of the few world regions with which the United States has consistently maintained such trade surpluses.[13] At the same time, U.S. foreign aid to the Caribbean region has steadily diminished, from some $226 million in 1985 to only $22 million in 1996, consequent upon the demise of the Soviet Union, a diminishing domestic constituency for foreign aid programs, and the decreasing salience of the Caribbean on the U.S. foreign policy agenda. Nevertheless, global security concerns of the U.S. government, such as drug trafficking, environmental degradation, illegal migration, arms proliferation, and problems of public health, multiply within the region (Pastor 1992).

During a visit to Grenada in February 1986, President Reagan announced that CBI countries could negotiate bilateral increases in U.S. import quotas affecting their textile and apparel industries. The Super 807 or 807A program resulted from these negotiations. This program provided that when a U.S. company importing clothes assembled in the Caribbean from fabrics formed and cut in the United States by that same U.S. firm, those clothes were excluded from established country quotas and were subject only to bilaterally agreed limits. As a result, the Caribbean Basin became the most rapidly expanding exporter of clothing to the United States in the world. By 1992, for example, Jamaica's export processing zones yielded $450 million in garment exports, mainly produced by some 28,000 young women who were paid $13–30 per week. Parenthetically, more than a third of the public factory space in these zones was occupied by investors from Hong Kong and South Korea who were seeking to benefit from U.S. trade policy toward the Caribbean (Klak 1994).

In 1993, U.S. apparel imports from the Caribbean Basin as a whole totaled $3.9 billion, which was nearly one-third of all U.S. imports from the region.[14] U.S. imports and exports from Caricom countries in 1994 and 1995 are reported in table 4.1. The final row presents U.S. trade balances with the countries listed in 1994 and 1995 respectively.[15] By 1995, trade in apparel accounted for 25 percent of all U.S. exports to the Caribbean and 60 percent of all U.S. imports from the region, with the Dominican Republic, Jamaica, and Haiti constituting the main trading partners in this sector (Janarain 1996, 39). Caribbean textile and apparel production increased by 21 percent from 1994 levels, amounting to $5.4 billion in U.S. imports.

THE CARIBBEAN BUSINESS ENVIRONMENT

Since the end of the fifteenth century, the Caribbean has produced primary products for export. Today, regional exports such as sugar, bananas, and bauxite have continued to exemplify structural dependence on external markets and preferential arrangements. But in the services and manu-

TABLE 4.1
U.S. Trade with Caricom Countries (In Millions of U.S. Dollars)

Country	1994 U.S. Exports	1995 U.S. Exports	1994 U.S. Imports	1995 U.S. Imports
Anguilla	12.5	14.6	0.3	0.1
Antigua	64.7	97.2	5.6	3.2
Bahamas	685.4	660.5	219.8	170.7
Barbados	161.1	185.7	35.8	38.7
Belize	115.1	100.1	54.2	55.9
Dominica	25.6	26.5	7.3	7.1
Grenada	23.5	26.8	8.0	5.9
Guyana	109.8	141.2	118.7	129.4
Jamaica	1,066.4	1,420.9	789.9	894.7
Montserrat	6.7	4.3	1.0	2.2
St. Kitts-Nevis	45.1	43.6	22.2	23.5
St. Lucia	80.6	81.0	27.8	36.5
St. Vincent	38.2	42.2	5.6	8.0
Suriname	121.8	189.7	46.0	104.8
Trinidad and Tobago	540.8	689.2	1,199.1	1,054.6
Totals	3,097.3	3,723.5	2,544.0	2,535.3
Trade Balances			+553.3 (1994)	+1,188.2 (1995)

Source: Adapted from Wagenheim (1996)

facturing sectors, Caribbean economies have been undergoing significant restructuring since the 1980s. In seeking competitiveness within the evolving global business environment, Caribbean companies have achieved a significant measure of transformation, while the relationship between state and private sector institutions has been redefined by privatization and a degree of deregulation. If the primary product sector has seen little change for several centuries, other Caribbean sectors have repositioned themselves in response to the trends toward globalization and neoliberalism (reviewed in chap. 1).

Seven significant trends can be observed in the Caribbean business environment and among Caribbean firms and investors. First, over time, the services sector has become increasingly important in Caribbean economies, with contributions to domestic product by 1991 that ranged from 81.6 percent in Antigua and Barbuda, to 69.1 percent in Grenada and 53.8 percent in Jamaica (Charles 1993, 18).[16] The most dynamic economic sectors for Caricom countries are tourism (chap. 6), data processing (chap. 7), and clothing (chap. 5), with the latter category benefitting from only selective U.S. trade preferences. Additionally, offshore financial services have become quite important in several countries. Antigua and Barbuda, as well as the Bahamas, have developed special facilities for offshore trust companies. The Bahamas has created a specialty in offshore banking, while Barbados has focused on insurance.

In Trinidad and Tobago, where the declared intention is to become a financial center, there has been a spate of activity involving banks and insurance companies. During 1995, Republic Bank, already the largest bank in Trinidad and Tobago, acquired a majority shareholding in the Bank of Commerce. The country's principal insurance company, Colonial Life, acquired 34 percent of Republic Bank, while owning 21 percent of the Bank of Commerce and 10 percent of the Royal Bank, another major player in the financial sector. Three banks—National Commercial, Cooperative and Workers—merged to establish the First Citizens Bank.

The Barbadian data processing sector includes one of the largest offshore information processing facilities in the world, Caribbean Data Services, with 1,045 employees. Additionally, the Jamaican information sector grew from just two companies in 1982 to forty companies with annual earnings estimated at $30 million by 1992 (*Caribbean Week* 13–26 November, 1993, 48). However, as Beverley Mullings observes in chapter 7 on Jamaica's export information services, the number of such companies fell to twenty-six by 1995, consequent upon the government's withdrawal of fiscal and industrial incentives at the behest of the International Monetary Fund. In addition, the majority of these firms continued to engage in relatively low value-added basic data entry and data-processing services and to pay information sector wages that have remained among the lowest in the world.

Second, within the services sector, tourism has assumed the most important role across the region. It is the only Caribbean Basin industry to have shown steady growth since 1973. In 1990, visitor receipts provided 25 percent of total Caribbean exports, a larger proportion than in any other region of the world (Mather and Todd 1993, 15). Alternatively stated, because of the Caribbean's trade deficits, such revenues from tourism funded more than 41 percent of total regional imports. By 1994, the Caribbean had been the largest regional tourism supplier among the developing countries for a decade, with $12 billion in gross earnings, providing direct employment to 500,000 workers. Between 1970 and 1994, the number of stay-over tourists visiting the Caribbean each year expanded cumulatively by 600 percent, to 13.7 million. Annual cruise ship arrivals increased at an even faster rate, to 2.3 million passengers (Caribbean Tourism Organization 1996, 1).

Within the Caribbean tourist industry today, the overriding issue is how best to improve competitiveness while effectively integrating tourism with national and regional development strategies (such integration is a subject of chap. 6). This dilemma exposes the industry to multiple criticisms on a range of issues, including tourism's foreign exchange leakage (estimates range up to 60 percent), limited links with local economies, environmental degradation, and inadequate local participation in management and ownership (Gayle and Goodrich 1993, 10–11). On the other hand, the fact that favorable factors supporting the growth of Caribbean tourism as an industry do exist is exemplified by the continued profitability and expansion across the region of all-inclusive chains, such as SuperClubs and Sandals.

Third, the contributions of manufacturers to GDP have expanded only modestly since the late 1980s, when they amounted to 15.2 percent in Jamaica, 11.6 percent in Barbados, and 11.2 percent in Trinidad (Trejos and Galles 1987, 74). However, an increasingly dynamic manufacturing sector is emerging. It is led by enterprises within the regionally owned Holding Companies of Neal and Massy and T. Geddes Grant. Key firms include Automotive Components (battery manufacturers, Trinidad), Jamaica Oxygen Acetylene (industrial and medical gases), Caribbean Agro Industries (animal feed, Grenada), and Windsor Manufacturing Company (garments, Guyana). The Eastern Caribbean Group of Companies also exemplifies transregional growth. Flour, animal feed processing, and packaging occurs in St. Vincent, rice production in Guyana, rice processing and packaging in Montserrat, and seafood and poultry production in Antigua.

Fourth, much of the regional manufacturing sector has remained dependent on preferential access to export markets and on external capital. For example, in December 1992, a $20 million joint venture between Sequoia Orange Company of California and the National Commercial bank of Jamaica was established for the development of a ten thousand-acre citrus farm, including packing houses and a juicing plant. This was projected to export 40 million boxes of fruit each year to the United States, Europe, and East Asia and to generate sales of $40 million annually at full production levels. But these expectations were not met, and the venture has since been liquidated.

In another example of dependence on external capital, late in 1993, Ireland's Guinness paid $62 million for a 51 percent interest in Desnoes and Geddes, Jamaica's only brewer. Guinness's intent was to expand the company's bottled drink exports to the U.S. market, especially the flagship product, Red Stripe lager beer. Similarly, in May 1996, Colgate Palmolive purchased Jamaica's Seprod Group of Companies, manufacturers of soaps, detergents, and bleaches, for $224 million. The services sector has also attracted external equity investments, as exemplified by Cable and Wireless' domination of the regional telecommunications sector (discussed in chap. 7), whether as a result of privatization, as in Jamaica, or the persistence of traditional commercial ties, as in Antigua.

Fifth, a trend toward corporate mergers has evolved. For instance, in 1992, the Trinidad-based Neal and Massy Group merged with the Jamaica-based T. Geddes Grant, thus creating the Caribbean's largest and most diversified conglomerate. The expanded Neal and Massy Group included nearly seven thousand employees working at over one hundred companies throughout the region, with an asset base of $266.9 million, with group profits of $44 million during that year (Neal and Massy 1992, 4). The main reasons for this merger were (1) to create a corporate combination that could withstand the Caribbean's traditional earnings fluctuations and (2) to create new synergies.

The then chairperson of T. Geddes Grant, in his letter of recommendation to shareholders, argued that the merger of the two groups would establish the largest and most diversified conglomerate in the Caribbean. During a June 1994 interview, W. Sidney Knox, the chairman and CEO of the Neal and Massy Group, explained the merger using some of the language of globalization and neoliberalism introduced in chapter 1:

> There was need for a broad-based private sector group in the Caribbean, not just overweighted out of Trinidad as Neal and Massy was before the merger, but large in all other areas as well, so that we could make alliances outside of the Caribbean or inside the region with international companies. That need became paramount because the world is changing. The world is globalizing. The world is liberalizing. And the rules being changed are not going to favor the weak, underprepared business entities. (Gayle and Tewarie 1995)

The merger of Neal and Massy with T. Geddes Grant did not survive, mainly due to clashing corporate cultures and senior management styles.[17] In addition, the merger was financed mainly by borrowing, and the resultant interest charges were not outweighed by the profits of the consolidated group.

Sixth, for all Caribbean services and manufacturing companies, just like for all Caribbean governments, the decade to 1996 was characterized by a drive to earn foreign exchange and to stimulate exports beyond the region. Mergers, acquisitions, and corporate restructuring remained part of that trend. For instance, Trinidad's two major state-owned oil companies, Trintopec and Trintoc, merged to become Petrotrin. Cariflex, a private printing company, acquired state-owned Printing and Packaging, while also merging into Cariflex 1995 Limited. Bacardi, the Puerto Rican rum producer, acquired shares in the Trinidad-based Angostura Holdings to forge a mutually beneficial alliance. In Jamaica meanwhile, by early 1996, both large corporations such as the Insurance Company of the West Indies and Jamalco (the Jamaica Aluminum Company), as well as smaller companies in the previously expanding apparel and garments sector, were engaged in extensive downsizing programs (Campbell 1996).

At the same time, efforts to expand regional production and exports of agro-industrial and manufactured products, such as juices, preserves, rums, and flour, as well as furniture, appliances, and even paper continue. By April 1995, some thirty-five companies from across the Caribbean had applied to the Caricom Export Development Project for permission to use the project's "Buy Caribbean" logo on their labels, as evidence of quality. In Grenada and Trinidad and Tobago, some companies were achieving ISO 9000[18] certification and registration by 1994, and the motivation for achieving such registration was intensifying. During the decade to 1996, the Grace Kennedy Exports and Trading Company expanded its export revenue from under $5 million to $15 million as a result of continuous new product development and market expansion to Panama, Mexico, Costa Rica, and Japan. Robert McDonald, managing director of the Jamaica Manufacturers' Association's 1996 champion exporter, reflects his firm's pursuit of higher income export market niches:

> Grace Kennedy Exports and Trading Company is looking for markets which fit a particular profile: markets that have large populations, high per capita disposable income, and low price sensitivity—features which allow one to market at a premium price without great pressure upon one's profit margins. (*Jamaica Weekly Gleaner*, 17–23 May 1996, 13)

The managing director of Grace Kennedy Limited (the holding company of which McDonald's firm is a subsidiary), Douglas Orane, takes the view that Jamaican manufacturers, in order to survive, have to be better than competing companies across the world within the specific niche markets targeted.

Across the region, manufacturing companies complain of an inhospitable domestic environment, the lack of economies of scale, the challenges posed by trade liberalization, and the continuing tendency of governments to view companies as sources of revenue for social welfare initiatives. However, even in the Eastern Caribbean microstates, a small number of companies continue to prosper, as exemplified by Dominica Coconut Products (soaps and detergents), St. Vincent's East Caribbean Group of Companies (grain milling), De La Grenada (liquors, syrups and spices), Dominica's P. W. Bellot (juices), and St. Lucia's Baron Foods (condiments).[19] The common denominators include the entrepreneurial vision to create economies of scope, if not scale, and the creation of high-performance workplaces. A challenge for the Caribbean is how to generate more firms such as these.

Seventh, a much less positive trend is illustrated by the fact that in January-February 1996, nearly one thousand Jamaican workers lost their jobs at companies such as the Insurance Company of the West Indies, Karla Lucea Limited (an 807 garment factory), and the Industrial Commercial Group of Companies. Unemployment mounted to over 20 percent (more than 33 percent among women working in the apparel sector) while price inflation exceeded 2 percent per month and commercial interest base rates averaged 55 percent. In November 1996, Youngone Garment Factory and Manchester Apparel closed, leaving another one thousand employees jobless, partly consequent upon the revaluation of the Jamaican dollar by 12 percent since June. Don Hamilton, a Youngone executive, was reported to have declared that his U.S. customers were unwilling to share the added costs incurred by Jamaican dollar appreciation and planned to move their operations to Mexico (Wagenheim 1997, 15). The government responded to net 1996 textile sector job losses totalling at least forty-five hundred and to reports of declining apparel exports by proposing a program of short-term assistance to investors, intended to reduce operational costs in areas such as rent, security, transportation, and financing.

Similarly, in Antigua and Barbuda, two major insurance companies recently declared bankruptcy, and several large employers, such as Cable and Wireless Limited and Barclays Bank PLC, were in the process of downsizing and laying off hundreds of employees. The government, which constitutes the largest single employer, is also reducing its payroll expenditures. Nevertheless, reengineering or cost-reduction initiatives have been limited by several countervailing forces. These include the strength of Caribbean trade unions, the small size of most firms, negative governmental attitudes toward downsizing, and an interest in avoiding the downsizing experiences seen in the United States.

CONCLUSION

Since 1982, U.S. policy interests have driven a succession of trade preferences for the Caribbean targeting regional exports that are not internationally competitive. As a result, the United States has maintained a consistent and climbing trade surplus with Caricom countries, which have only begun to articulate their distinctive regional interests. Several significant trends characterize the regional business environment. These include (1) the dominance of the services sector, led by tourism, (2) the emergence of an increasingly dynamic but externally dependent manufacturing sector, (3) the salience of corporate mergers, downsizing, and structural adjustment, (4) recession, job insecurity, relatively high unemployment and even higher underemployment, and (5) a drive to expand export production, accompanied by instances of entrepreneurial vision, productivity, and managerial excellence. It is important to stress that any positive trends are largely disarticulated from the U.S. trade preferences available to the region. Yet it is increasingly clear that national efforts across the region to promote an investor-friendly image, particularly to North American and European entrepreneurs, may result in "a race to the bottom" (this argument is developed in chap. 5). Meanwhile, Caricom's trade policy calculus has been dramatically altered by the advent of NAFTA, and by the concept of the Free Trade Area of the Americas. At the global scale, the 1993 Agreement on Textiles and Clothing, which will be implemented through the World Trade Organization, will phase out all textile and clothing quotas by 2003, thus negating the effects of both NAFTA and the Special Access Program for U.S. apparel exports from the Caribbean Basin.

The unmaterialized specter of net employment and export losses from NAFTA in the United States continues to limit Congressional enthusiasm for extending membership to Chile, let alone to the Caribbean Basin and Central America. Consequently, the momentum toward hemispheric free trade remains external to the United States, led by Mercosur, Chile (which recently joined Mercosur), and Canada. Many Caribbean leaders continue to argue that NAFTA is essential for substantially enlarged hemispheric market access and investment inflows. Yet the experience of Mexico to date does not provide reason for unqualified enthusiasm in either respect. Further, several aspects of the NAFTA framework merit much more serious attention from Caricom members than they have yet received. These include (1) the potential for insufficient protection against import surges within small, relatively fragile economies, (2) the need to develop a coherent regional approach to competition and antitrust policy, (3) the need to secure functional definitions of "satisfactory" economic performance and "acceptable" labor and environmental protection standards, (4) the implications of hemispheric access to government procurement projects, and (5) the exact mechanisms that might eventually be put in place for NAFTA expansion.

Meanwhile, several policy fault lines have emerged. Jamaica and Trinidad have applied for accession to NAFTA, on the basis of interim parity arrangements. Trinidad has also announced plans to extend its trade and investment relationship with Cuba, contradicting the recently heightened U.S. economic pressure on the Castro regime. Barbados has rejected the need for NAFTA access, indicating increasing interest in hemispheric trade integration processes beyond NAFTA and looking south to Mercosur and to the emerging Andean Community and the Association of Caribbean States. Indeed, considering Caricom's evolving business environment, a persuasive argument can be made that regional needs for hemispheric market access and the encouragement of investment inflows are not necessarily best met by waiting impatiently in the NAFTA queue, although at least selective parity with Mexico continues to be essential.

NOTES

1. The Bahamas belongs to the Caribbean Community, but not of the Caribbean Common Market. The British Virgin Islands, and the Turks and Caicos Islands, are associate members of Caricom, while Anguilla, the Dominican Republic, the Netherlands Antilles, Puerto Rico, Colombia, and Venezuela are observers. Haiti, Mexico, and Puerto Rico have observer status within several Caricom institutions. Venezuela and the Dominican Republic have applied for full membership.

2. This issue is considered in a June 1994 consultancy report commissioned by the Caricom secretariat.

3. Ford Motor Company provided one model approach to assuaging such fears by encouraging the United Auto Workers to bargain jointly with their Mexican counterparts.

4. Chilean president Eduardo Frei and Canadian prime minister Jean Chretien signed this agreement during the former's three-day state visit to Canada. Although bilateral trade totals only $500 million per year, both leaders believe the accord is a step toward the creation of a Free Trade Area of the Americas.

5. During the 1996 Miami Conference on the Caribbean and Latin America, President Clinton's counselor Mack McLarty commented that during his second term of office the president would expand the special U.S. relationship with Mexico, request congressional approval for fast track authority to negotiate a trade agreement with Chile, and work toward a Free Trade Area of the Americas. How-

ever, Mr. McLarty added that while NAFTA parity was important for the Caribbean, "it may be time to look at changing circumstances" (Bussey 1996, 1C, 8C).

6. By the early 1990s, Florida's annual export proceeds to Caribbean Basin countries amounted to almost $4 billion and over 80,000 jobs (Rosenberg and Hiskey 1993, 14, 24).

7. The current system of U.S. import quotas for textiles and apparel will be phased out by the year 2004. At the same time, most U.S. textile tariffs will be reduced by about 25 percent. OECD negotiators have requested that developing country importers lower their restrictions on industrial country textile exports.

8. This may be explained by differences in trade composition, reciprocal demand elasticities, cross-exchange rate history, as well as the nature of the CBI and Lomé trade agreement themselves.

9. See "Caribbean Report: Trinidad and Tobago Prime Minister Presses for Entry in NAFTA," *The Miami Herald*, 12 September 1996, 18A; and "Jamaica's PM blasts US," *The Jamaica Weekly Gleaner*, 27 September–4 October 4, 1996, 6.

10. The persistence of interest rates some 500 percent higher than those available in the United States has constrained business expansion, while tepid consumer spending has restrained gross domestic product growth. Investors were also discouraged by a 6 percent decline in the value of the peso to a postcrisis low of 8 per U.S. dollar in October 1996.

11. The CBI group includes all Caribbean Community members and signatories to the General Treaty of Central American Economic Integration, together with Anguilla, Aruba, Bermuda, the British Virgin Islands, the Cayman Islands, the Dominican Republic, French Guiana, Guadeloupe, Martinique, the Netherlands Antilles, Suriname, and the Turks and Caicos Islands.

12. The insular Caribbean includes Caricom plus Haiti, the Netherlands Antilles, Aruba, the Cayman Islands, Guadeloupe, Martinique, the British Virgin Islands, the Turks and Caicos Islands, Cuba, and the Dominican Republic (map 1).

13. This occurs while international trade accounts for 25 percent of U.S. GDP, and nearly one-fifth of all goods purchased in the United States are produced abroad.

14. This total was also nearly quadruple U.S. apparel imports from Mexico. However, during 1993, Caribbean Basin apparel exports accounted for only 14 percent of the $28 billion U.S. apparel market (Wagenheim 1996).

15. This table is adapted from Kal Wagenheim, "U.S. Trade with the Caribbean Basin, January–December 1994, 1995," *Caribbean Update*, 12, no. 4 (May 1996): 23. "F.a.s" means "free alongside ship," while "c.i.f." includes cost, insurance, and freight charges.

16. As Charles (1993) points out, however, problems of measurement persist. For instance, government is typically linked with "other services," while the retail and wholesale sectors are often combined with hotel and restaurant activities so that it is not always easy to make valid comparisons among countries.

17. There were deliberate cross-appointments of managers from both groups, and two executives from the T. Geddes Grant Group were appointed to the board of the new parent company. However, the Neal and Massy management style was

fast-paced, informal and pragmatic, underpinned by formal strategic planning. By comparison, the T. Geddes Grant management style reflected a stronger sense of hierarchy, status, and fragmented leadership.

18. ISO 9000 is an increasingly accepted certification of quality, provided by the Geneva-based Industrial Standards Organization.

19. Mark Lee, "OECS Manufacturers Struggle for Survival," *Caribbean Week*, 25 May–7 June 1996, 39–40. The OECS countries consist of Antigua and Barbuda, Dominica, Grenada, Montserrat, St. Kitts and Nevis, St. Lucia, and St. Vincent and the Grenadines (see map 2).

SUGGESTIONS FOR FURTHER READING

Bryan, Anthony T., ed. *The Caribbean: New Dynamics in Trade and Political Economy*. New Brunswick, N.J.: Transaction Books, 1995. A study produced by the University of Miami's North-South Center. The contributors tend to accept the need for trade liberalization within the Caribbean, some more enthusiastically than others. Rather than debate the implications of market liberalization, the chapters consider issues such as the viability of free trade arrangements with North America, the erosion of preferential treatment, and the requisites of Caribbean competitiveness in a global economy.

Jainarain, Charles I. *Annual Report on Trade 1995–1996: U.S., Florida, Latin America, and the Caribbean*. Miami, Fla.: Summit of the Americas Center, 1996. A unique compilation of trade statistics and commentary focused on the areas mentioned in the subtitle. Jainarain is the former director of research at the Beacon Council in Miami, and current executive director of the Summit of the Americas Center at Florida International University. This discussion is practitioner-oriented, not an academic analysis.

Stone, Carl. *Democracy and Clientelism in Jamaica*. New Brunswick, N.J.: Transaction Books, 1980. A seminal study of interest group politics and patronage in Jamaica that explains why policy is often flawed in both formulation and execution. This work has been frequently cited by subsequent scholars.

5

How States Sell Their Countries and Their People

Thomas Klak and Garth Myers

> "We are not in anybody's backyard, and we are definitely not for sale."
> —Maurice Bishop, in 1979, one month after taking power in Grenada's New Jewel Movement revolution (Conway 1983b, 3)

How ironic his words were! The Reagan administration was not amused by such defiance, however, and soon after taking office in January 1981 began work toward toppling Bishop's regime. At an OAS meeting in Washington in 1981, Reagan made an assessment and a warning that everyone knew was directed at Grenada:

> In the Caribbean we above all seek to protect those values and principles that shape the proud heritage of this hemisphere. Some, however, have turned from their American neighbors and their heritage. Let them return to the traditions and common values of this hemisphere and we all will welcome them. The choice is theirs. (Hersh 1991)[1]

Then the United States chose to distance itself diplomatically from the tiny island and conducted a mock invasion exercise in the Caribbean clearly aimed at Grenada. When Bishop traveled to the U.S. capital in 1983 to assuage concerns about Grenada's international relations and development priorities, he got the cold shoulder. Upon his return home from cajoling Washington, the radical fringe of the New Jewel Movement arrested him and murdered him amid the ensuing chaos and struggle for power. In the words of the U.S. ambassador to the Eastern Caribbean at that time, Sally Shelton Colby, that murder and power struggle provided the United States with "an enormous piece of luck" that it could use to justify the invasion it had long been planning (Hersh 1991). A predictable sequence of events followed: an election of the U.S.-chosen presidential candidate, an inflow of modest U.S. aid (including funds to complete the airstrip Reagan insisted Bishop was building for Soviet warplanes), and a pro-U.S. policy. Although these events have perhaps left it less sanguine than many of its neighbors about neoliberal development policy (Wiley 1997), the Grenada government now joins the chorus by selling its country and people to foreign investors in nontraditional export sectors.

But those are the details of Grenada's turbulent recent history (see also chap. 2; Ambursley 1983b; Conway 1983b, c; Clark 1987; McAfee 1990). This chapter is less concerned with the particularities of Caribbean countries that have led to their present situation and more concerned with the remarkable elements of sameness in their current development policies. Bishop's "not for sale" challenge in fact followed a similar claim by Jamaica's Michael Manley. The U.S. government also sought to destabilize Manley, who eventually was forced to conform to the neoliberal order (see chap. 2). Indeed, over the last two decades, states throughout the global periphery have rather abruptly converged upon neoliberalism. The associated promotion of foreign investment and nontraditional exports has expanded apace.

Yet only recently, interpretations of the workings of global economy based on dependency theory were still popular with Grenadian and many other Caribbean and Third World scholars, state planners, and even the person on the street who had benefited little from foreign investment and trade (Kay 1989). For countries of the global periphery, dependency theory sees foreign investment and international trade as problems rather than solutions. States therefore promoted import substitution industrialization (ISI) to counteract the negative effects of historical trade dependency. Given this abrupt policy about-face toward neoliberalism and nontraditional exports, we ask three questions in this chapter. First, how do states make the case to investors that their countries are now neoliberal converts? Second, how do they attempt to differentiate their countries from the myriad of others pursuing similar policies? And third, to what extent do those portrayals correspond with the countries' ground-level reality?

We pursue these questions by focusing on four Caribbean countries that are broadly representative of regional diversity—Barbados, St. Lucia, Jamaica, and Haiti. They represent the breadth of the Caribbean region in terms of level of development (see tables 2, 5.1; note that the income figures in the two tables result from different measures). The four countries are also fairly representative of the Third World as a whole: they have limited strategic importance in global geopolitics and have economies that at the outset of their industrial experiences could be categorized

TABLE 5.1
Selected Development Indicators for the Case Studies

Country	Adjusted Real GDP/cap	Rank on the Human Development Index
Barbados	$5,850	25th out of 174 countries
St. Lucia	$3,795	76th
Jamaica	$3,180	86th
Haiti	$1,050	145th

Source: UN (1996, 135–37)

as underdeveloped. Despite their diversity and some differences in sectoral emphasis, each promotes itself as an industrial export platform. Their neoliberal policy pursuits offer a spectrum of regional experiences, as well as insights into the neoliberal trend across the global periphery. Our main focus is on the investment promotional materials that governments compile and disseminate to prospective investors, obtained from the responsible public agencies. While we focus in this chapter on four Caribbean countries, the analysis is situated with respect to a broader research project aimed at decoding and critiquing neoliberal development efforts across the global periphery (Klak and Myers 1997; Myers and Klak 1998).

This chapter reviews the themes represented in the guidebooks and compares them to what the countries and the manufacturing sectors are like behind the advertising facade. In particular, we are interested in the promotional themes and underlying reality associated with export processing zones (EPZs). These are labor intensive manufacturing centers that involve the import of raw materials and the export of factory products (Gereffi and Korzeniewicz 1994; Klak 1995a). Usually, export processing occurs in state-designated free zones that are created to streamline importing and exporting and to sidestep national laws that privilege some domestic social groups over foreign industrial exporters. In some cases, such as Barbados, the state has not designated free zones proper, but nonetheless offers a package of infrastructure and incentives to encourage foreign investment for export manufacturing which parallels that found in countries with official EPZs (Schoepfle and Perez-Lopez 1989). In all countries, some government incentives and subsidies extend to manufacturers located outside designated free zones, so it is important to expand the analysis beyond simply those sites, as we do here.

Over ninety countries worldwide now offer export processing zones. This global homogenization of development policy emerged from a confluence of three exogenously controlled factors (Mody and Wheeler 1987; Klak and Rulli 1993): massive foreign exchange shortfalls in less developed countries, the search by international investors for cost-saving components in manufacturing, and the spread of neoliberal ideas that encourage open economies, foreign investment, and nontraditional exports (Williamson 1990, 1993). Falling output from and demand for traditional primary product exports and foreign debt caused the crises that inspired EPZ development. These led states into structural adjustment agreements and their component industrial export policies. EPZs primarily attract manufacturers seeking bargain-priced and compliant labor as a cost-saving component of global commodity chains. They are often prepared to relocate if provoked by social instability or by exogenous changes in trade policies or production methods (Gereffi and Korzeniewicz 1994; Klak 1995a). This degree of exogenous control over export processing suggests that Caribbean countries have only limited latitude for capturing benefits (Kaplinsky 1995).

EPZ politics are understudied, and EPZs are frequently judged by simple enumeration of their impacts on jobs and exports (e.g., Schoepfle and Perez-Lopez 1989; World Bank 1992; Tirado de Alonso 1992). EPZs are far more consequential to Third World development than that. A comparative analysis of EPZs offers many insights about the direction of and prospects for Third World development. EPZs are emblematic of the broader neoliberal agenda, inasmuch as both emphasize open economies, foreign investment, nontraditional exports, privatization, and a withdrawal of the state to the role of "market facilitator" (Williamson 1990; Krueger 1993). EPZs are also crucial testing grounds for the intersection of neoliberalism and the agendas of domestic social groups. In this chapter, to encompass the wider significance of EPZs as manifestations, symbols, and harbingers of neoliberal development policy, we employ the acronym EPNDP (Export Processing within Neoliberal Development Policy).

FOREIGN INVESTMENT PROMOTION IN ITS BROADER POLITICAL-ECONOMIC CONTEXT

Since most policy makers and planners in the Third World have embraced the neoliberal approach to development, it falls to them to convince the foreign investors upon which neoliberalism so heavily relies that countries long wary of their intentions are now firmly procapitalist. But a chorus of governments of the global periphery has emerged seeking to lure in the same investors. Thus it becomes necessary for countries to craft eloquent and elaborate story lines in an effort to appear distinctive and worthy of receiving fastidious international capital. In essence, states need to aggressively advertise, promote, and sell their countries and people.

These investment promotional materials are only one part of a multifaceted venture by investment-hungry governments to sell their countries as neoliberal sites. Besides the guidebooks, governments devote much money and effort toward advertising themselves at trade shows, opening and operating investment promotion offices in the countries of desired investors, and placing materials in single-page ads or even entire supplementary advertisement sections in business magazines and trade journals. Several Third World countries operate Web sites advertising their free zones. While space does not permit an extensive analysis of all of these forms of advertising, it is important to note that the materials analyzed here contribute to a multidimensional effort to lure investors.

Advertisements for neoliberal development policies attempt to lure export manufacturers as well as investors emphasizing other economic sectors. Investment in tourism, nontraditional agriculture, and offshore bank accounts are often sought as well. Still, even with these inclusions, the investment promotion materials do not tell the whole story about Caribbean development. They communicate few details about such crucial elements of local political economy as the built environment (outside of the industrial export sector), social welfare programs, and informal or non-commodified activities. The guidebooks are nonetheless crucial statements of how a Caribbean government wishes to present the country to the outside world. They are representative of the new proinvestment and outward-oriented messages that governments are conveying domestically. The guidebooks can therefore be read as guides to the hopeful positioning on the neoliberal bandwagon by governments in the global periphery.

ANALYSIS OF INVESTMENT PROMOTION

This section describes the text language, photographs, and maps in the investment guidebooks for the four countries under study. At the most general level, the guidebooks present a deep irony: guidebooks that are ostensibly providing descriptions of countries as sites for investment pay little attention to the actual context of the countries. To the contrary, much of the writing in the guidebooks adheres to a standard textbook outline of features known to be attractive to foreign industrialists: political stability, proinvestor policies, infrastructure, cheap and productive labor, incentives, and preferential market access (Chandra 1992; Dicken 1992). In general, context is highlighted only to the extent that it adds charm or additional opportunities for profit to the generic, proinvestor features.

Research on investment promotion on a broader array of peripheral countries has demonstrated that the advertising package which accompanies EPNDP typically combines three themes: neoliberal and contextual depiction (pledges of subsidies, an open economy, and cheap and unorganized labor; tropical paradise and friendly natives), science fiction (dreams of high technology, telecommunications, informatics, and sophisticated exports), and strategic omission (exclusion of strife, resistance, hardship, and societal degradation) (Klak and Myers 1997). The pro forma "geography-less" renditions in the guidebooks suggest that the neoliberal prescription has little tolerance for spatial and contextual differentiation. This is sensible inasmuch as the global economy has been characterized as moving toward conditions of "hypermobile capital and frictionless space" (Watts 1994, 373).

These neoliberal development policies prompt a new type of geographical investigation in the form of discourse analysis (as discussed in chap. 1). Whereas the discipline of geography has traditionally sought to interpret physical and human landscapes and contexts, the neoliberal era is now encouraging a new line of analysis of "mediascapes." These are the newly constituted images of countries that states put up for sale in the international marketplace (Appadurai 1990; Sachs 1992). Countries of the South create and advertise mediascapes to designate themselves as operational members of the newly emerging neoliberal world. Rather than providing contextual descriptions, the investment promotional materials tell hyperbolic stories about the countries they promote (Roe 1991). In this way export promotion and investment agencies help "produce, transmit and stabilize development 'truths' " (Watts 1993, 263–64; Escobar 1988), which if repeated endlessly, the state planners hope will actually become true. The guidebooks' narratives and images create "strips of reality" (Appadurai 1990, 9) that embody North Atlantic notions of development and the usefulness of Third World places as investment platforms.

The Basic Advertisement Package: Investment Incentives, the Ideal Location, and Stability

Fiscal incentives like tax holidays, tariff exemptions, and low wages form the core of the promotional message in all four of our cases. The availability of financial incentives is the guidebooks' most frequently mentioned theme (table 5.2), closely followed by the obviously important theme of industrial infrastructure. Other common themes are discussed

TABLE 5.2
Frequency of Themes in Investment Guidebooks by State

Theme	Barbados	Haiti	Jamaica	St. Lucia
1. Incentives	4+	4+	4+	4+
2. Infrastructure	4+	1	4+	4+
3. Labor quality	3	2	3	4+
4. Peace and stability	3	2	2	3
5. Ideal location	2	1	4+	2
6. Open economy	3	2	2	2
7. Tropical paradise	1	2	2	3
8. Profitability	4+	0	1	2
9. Environmentalism	0	1	0	0
10. Social welfare	0	1	0	0

Source: Authors' survey of investment guidebooks
Note: Numbers in the table indicate how often a theme is mentioned in each country's guidebooks (4 + means four or more).

later because they represent different categories of advertisement. The incentive theme is reinforced by pledges and commitments to economic liberalization, free trade, deregulation, and private sector development. We categorize these under the heading "open economy," the sixth most frequent theme in the guidebooks (table 5.2). The investment guidebooks for all countries except Haiti make grandiose claims about being the ideal competitive location for profitable investments. "Profitability" is the eighth most common theme (table 5.2). Haiti's recent history disallows the credibility of such a claim. (Recent controversies over conditions in garment factories in Haiti are discussed in chap. 12.)

The typical set of EPZ investment incentives, provided by all four Caribbean governments, includes

- Provision of factory space and industrial infrastructure
- Personal assistance with establishing operations and residency, as well as with identifying markets
- A "one-stop" streamlined permit acquisition process
- No or low tariffs and taxes for a multiyear period or even in perpetuity
- Duty-free and unrestricted import of production inputs into the zones
- Unrestricted foreign ownership and exchange
- No export duties
- Unlimited capital and profit repatriation
- Nationality-blind treatment of investors for loans and services
- Worker training programs

- Various explicit or effective operational subsidies
- Access to the markets of emerging regional free trade blocs
- Guarantees against nationalization

All of the guidebooks offer these thirteen incentives in one form or another. The precise levels and duration of subsidies in each category show some variation among the cases. Besides the explicit benefits listed in the guidebooks, informal benefits extend the incentives to include commitments that officials at the highest levels of government will respond promptly and decisively to their concerns (Klak 1996). Peripheral governments are willing to provide these incentives because, in neoliberal thinking, foreign investment is the basis for economic growth and national prosperity. However, given freedom from taxation, allowances for repatriation of profits, low wages, and limited development of backward and forward linkages to the local economy, the connections between foreign investments and local benefits are at best tenuous and contingent on effective policies. These concerns are elaborated below.

Besides a host of incentives, exporting from less developed countries also qualifies investors to take advantage of various trade agreements, such as the Lomé Convention, the Caribbean Basin Initiative and its Super 807 supplement, the Multifibre Arrangement, and the General System of Preferences, thereby gaining preferential access to the world's largest markets (chap. 4 discusses these trade policies). Foreign investors are invited to fill the special market-access quotas that are allotted to Third World countries, but which they themselves cannot meet. Note the imbalance between core and periphery in the current arrangement. Peripheral countries are offered special access to markets in wealthy countries, but these quotas are largely filled by firms from the wealthy countries (Klak 1996).

To complement the economic components of their advertisements described thus far, each government highlights its relative position proximal to potential investors and markets. This strategy of claiming to be the "ideal location" is the fifth most frequent theme in the guidebooks (table 5.2). The guidebooks demonstrate that by viewing itself as the center of the world and by using creative cartography and embellishment, virtually any place on earth can portray itself as absolutely central and accessible (Klak and Myers 1997).

Some guidebooks also employ a tactic of grouping the country for analytical purposes with the East Asian NICs. Barbados, for instance, notes that it is "slightly smaller than Singapore." Jamaica describes itself as having market access "unequaled by its Far East counterparts." St. Lucia draws conspicuous attention to the presence on the island of manufacturers from "Korea, China and Hong Kong" and quotes of endorsements from them at several junctures. For countries seeking investment, references to East Asia are salesmanship by inference for geographical position, potential market access, political stability, openness to investment, and the cutting edge of the twenty-first century global economy (Henke and Boxill 1998).

Unfortunately, none of the four countries can claim a track record that approaches the NICs' record for economic growth and a relatively equitable distribution of benefits, although Barbados comes closest (see chap. 2; World Bank 1993, 1995). This is primarily because state capacity (Brautigam 1996) is weakly developed in the Caribbean. That is, states have difficulty enforcing their own rules for revenue generation and implementing their development agendas in a cost-effective way (Klak 1996). Few Caribbean states effectively execute proactive, astute, and "agile" policies (World Bank 1993a; Marshall 1996). Such policies would invest in infrastructure, increase worker productivity, facilitate backward linkages and otherwise foster comparative advantages, creating the basis for endogenous benefits from EPZ policy in a cost-effective manner. These can be expensive public investments, whose value can only be determined by net positive impacts on the EPZ sector. The unreality of comparisons with East Asia makes for dramatic disjuncture between the imagined development base and the actual one.

At first glance these exaggerations and embellishments may seem unremarkable. Television commercials and other advertisements constantly inundate us with false and hyperbolic claims, thus blurring the distinction between rhetoric and reality, truth and fiction. Media manipulation is almost accepted as normal. But in this case, governments are selling their countries and people as private-sector marketing departments and celebrity spokespersons sell consumer commodities. Governments are marching in unison to the neoliberal beat, giving testimony to the power and reach of the neoliberal turn. It is worth recalling that only two decades ago it wasn't this way. Third World countries have dramatically reversed the direction of their development policy and their attitude toward foreign investors and international trade.

All guidebooks promise investors an efficient welcome mat, security from nationalization threats, and a future free of social upheaval. Barbados assures potential investors that "all political parties [are] middle of the road." St. Lucia calls itself "stable and customer-friendly," a characterization that conveniently misplaces the island's growing political polarization, which is creating a divisive "climate of fear" that is of deep concern to its citizens (Lee 1996). Jamaica's conflictual postindependence politics (see note 1 and Eyre 1986) are drowned out by guidebook reminders of "the land of Reggae Music, Red Stripe Beer, Tia Maria, Blue Mountain Coffee, and Rum." This notion of "peace and stability" is the fourth most common theme in the guidebooks (table 5.2). It combines aspects of neoliberalism with the strategic omission of contextual information—the past matters only inasmuch as it tastes great and is less filling. Unless it is alluring, the past is ignored or recast in a peaceful light in the promotional materials.

Perceived political stability drives investment decisions more than actual political circumstances. As a Mexican reporter recently observed, "an adverse editorial in the *New York Times* or *Washington Post* can do more damage to a Latin American government than a thousand large scale demonstrations" (Rubio 1995, 4). Development planning promoters must perform a juggling act with respect to political stability. The difficulty for state planners comes when they attempt to attribute the perceived stability on which foreign investors insist to societies that are highly unequal, include large numbers of people for whom a middle-class lifestyle is inaccessible, and are served by electoral processes and other outlets through which the people's discontent can be aired.

The "Profits in Paradise" Theme

The warm climate that Caribbean governments advertise refers to both their natural environments and their newly acquired attitudes toward foreign investors. On the one hand, the guidebooks describe the attractiveness and benefits of a tropical locale; this is the seventh most frequently occurring theme (table 5.2). On the other hand, it would not be logical to address industrialization in four insular, tropical countries without recognizing that tourism is itself a vital (if not the principal) source of foreign exchange (as chap. 6 discusses). The guidebooks play on this environmental double entendre, for example, "St. Lucia: The Perfect Climate for Investment Opportunities."

Regarding tourism's economic role in the Caribbean, former Jamaican prime minister Michael Manley (1996, ix) states that "the governments and leaders of the Caribbean have finally and almost unanimously come to the view that tourism is anything from 'an important' to 'the most important', to 'the only' means of economic survival for their states." Like foreign investment for nontraditional export production, tourism too is widely viewed as the region's "engine of growth" (Manley 1996, x). For many developing countries, tourism has been linked directly to the free-zone industrial model. Most guidebooks make this linkage by their emphasis on seeking high-end, wealthy tourists (de Kadt 1979). According to the model, many of these tourists will be businesspersons who will note investment opportunities during their vacations. Thus tourism will feed the EPZ plan.

This EPZ-tourism theme is abundantly clear in the photographs chosen to illustrate investment materials. They typically include unspoiled beaches that are empty except for perhaps a European or white American couple, lushly forested mountain vistas, and various other recreational settings. Often, though not always, the tropical paradise is depicted as devoid of local people who might tarnish the promotional image of serenity, peace and solitude in a vacation getaway. Materials from Barbados, an Afro-Caribbean society with one of the world's highest population densities, illustrate this tendency most obviously.

The awkward combination of tourism themes with industrial ones—where foreign investment is advertised as an escape to unspoiled locales and as an engine for economic growth and profits—is captured by this testimonial from a foreign investor in St. Lucia's guidebook: "When you first get here, you're convinced you've discovered a gem, and you want to keep it a secret. But you realize international business is good for you and St. Lucia. So, you're happy to spread the word." The hegemonic position that business interests are universal interests, as chapter 1 discussed, is central to the neoliberal discourse.

Another aspect of selling the Caribbean for export manufacturing is portraying the workforce as being of high quality. Labor quality is in fact the guidebooks' third most common theme (table 5.2). But this is not an easy sell, since the guidebooks simultaneously portray the islands as blissfully laid back, and the Caribbean people are widely stereotyped as "slothful" (Richardson 1992; Crick 1989). Another complication occurs when the investment guides boast of the low wages that are paid to Caribbean workers. Even as they advertise tropical labor as an investor's bargain, guidebook writers also stress that low wages buy an energetic and increasingly productive workforce. Barbados, for example, claims its information-service workers equal their U.S. counterparts for productivity, but at only one-third the wage and turnover rates. Given that these industries include a range as broad as typesetting, software development, and litigation support services, such a claim would be virtually impossible to establish.

The other countries try to strike a balance in their guidebook rhetoric between productivity and good-heartedness. St. Lucia claims only "75–85 percent" the productivity of U.S. workers across all industries, but its proportionately lower wages make it an even better deal than Barbados. St. Lucian workers are baldly said to be "as warm and friendly as the landscape and possess remarkable dexterity and manipulative skills for assembly work and manufacturing." Jamaicans, too, are said to have an "easy going lifestyle" in one sentence of the guidebook and to be "the friendliest, most industrious people you'll find anywhere" in the very next line. Taken together, these labor messages show how investment promoters attempt to create an investor's paradise: a blissful and laid-back tropical setting with easygoing workers who are willing to work for little.

They are, nevertheless, highly productive and industrious. Welcome to the extraordinary world of neoliberal mediascaping!

The "Science Fiction" Theme

Illusions of scientific grandeur punctuate much of the photographic and textual information in the guidebooks. Many photos straightforwardly display either free-zone buildings and grounds or transport facilities. But a large share of photographs are specifically targeted to wooing investors associated with "high-technology" industries: computers, electronics, information processing, and telecommunications. Some thirty-six of the ninety-five guidebook pages with photographs have high-technology imagery as their focal point. Computers and computer-training facilities, as well as other high-technology equipment related to industries such as medical equipment engineering or pharmaceutical production, figure prominently in all guidebooks with photos.

Only Haiti, hurriedly compiling and distributing its photocopied promotional materials in the chaotic, postcoup context of 1995, offers no photographs. Although now Haiti is scrambling to try to reconstruct its EPZ sector, it was early by regional standards in developing EPZs under Jean-Claude Duvalier. The homogenizing effect of neoliberalism is suggested by the way that first Aristide and now Preval are attempting to rejuvenate a Duvalier policy as EPNDP (Dupuy 1997).

At one level the guidebook messages concerning telecommunications belie the simultaneous claim that the country is the most centrally located place on earth. All guidebooks with photos and drawings display satellite dishes, presumably to assure investors that the peripheral country is networked into the global telecommunications systems (fig. 5.1). Images are complemented with text descriptions (e.g., St. Lucia's) claiming that it possesses "a telecommunications network that is as sophisticated as any found in major metropolitan areas." One Asian investor is quoted as saying that telephone access is as good to South Korea as it is inside that country (a cost comparison is not included; fig. 5.2). The message to investors is that they can profitably separate off and relocate labor-intensive portions of global commodity chain production processes to remote locations (Gereffi and Korzeniewicz 1994). There they can pay bargain-level wages but still be highly accessible to decision-making centers and markets thanks to advanced telecommunications.

Although presented as factual, the guidebooks convey less of the existing reality of EPZs than of a fictional (and improbable) technological future to which they aspire, often based on patterns laid down by the East Asian NICs. As Dicken (1992, 181) recounts, "In 1986, following the unexpected recession of 1985, the Singapore government announced . . .

Figure 5.1. Depiction in a Jamaican investment promotion guidebook captioned "The JDI Digital Network."

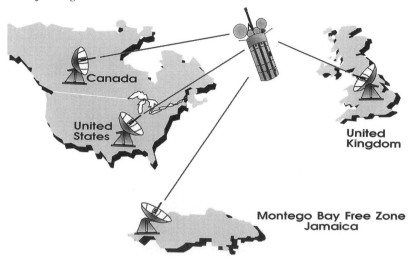

Source: Jamaica Digiport International, Ltd. (JDI), *The Jamaican Advantage: An Economic Alternative* (n.d.).

measures to move away from being merely a labour-intensive assembly site to a high-technology, knowledge-based economy." Barbados has moved in that direction. With wage costs of around $2 per hour which have priced it out of the labor market for garments and most other assembly operations, Barbados by the mid-1990s seems to follow Singapore's earlier reorientation by emphasizing financial and information services (table 5.3). But Barbados's reorientation seems more of a reaction to the exodus of low-wage seeking firms than a proactive policy building on past success with lower-order exports. It is worth reviewing Barbados's historical record with export-oriented industries to illustrate why many analysts are judging EPNDP as essentially a "race to the bottom" (Marshall 1996, 447).

By Caribbean standards, Barbados earlier exhibited precocious EPZ-style development and employment benefits. From the late 1960s until 1980, Barbados's industrial exports grew by 28 percent per annum. By the early 1980s, Barbados was by far the largest per capita industrial exporter in the Caribbean, with electronics and garments contributing the most. During a decade and a half of industrial export expansion, wage rates grew to around $2 per hour. This was because the Barbadian state regularly increased the wage index so that it nearly kept up with consumer price inflation while maintaining the local currency's exchange rate

Figure 5.2. Depiction in a St. Lucian investment promotion guidebook.

Growing...

Augmenting a system of paved roads, a major new highway program under construction will further improve transportation throughout the island.

Water is abundant and is distributed through a system of reservoirs and filtration plants, all of which conform to strict international standards. Another water treatment plant, storage reservoir and pumping station are now under construction, thus increasing the island's ability to distribute water efficiently.

A modern electrical system provides reliable electric service at 240 volts, 50 cycles.

"It is absolutely amazing to my colleagues in Korea that they can reach me as fast by phone in St. Lucia as in Korea."

Sang Won Cho
KOCIA MILLS

Source: St. Lucia National Development Corporation, *St. Lucia: Investment Opportunity . . . Here and Now* (n.d.). (Note that Kocia Mills has since left the islands with thousands of dollars of unpaid bills and payroll.)

and purchasing power against the U.S. dollar. Both of these proworker policies were unusual for the Caribbean (Thomas 1988, 272–75). Since 1983, however, Barbados's industrial exports have plummeted, declining to only one-third their previous high in just three years (they were about $1,100 per capita in 1983 and only about $300 per capita in 1987; Klak and Rulli 1993, 125). By far the largest contributor to this collapse was the computer-industry giant INTEL, which phased out its production facilities in the mid-1980s and relocated them to the Dominican Republic,

TABLE 5.3
Economic Sectors Emphasized in the Texts of the Investment Guides

Economic Sector	Barbados	Haiti	Jamaica	St. Lucia
1. Primary production	0	40	0	15
2a. Basic manufacturing	24.3	40	36.4	25
2b. Scientific or high-technology manufacturing	44.6	0	27.3	20
3a. Transport and shipping	0	0	18.2	10
3b. Financial services	28.4	0	18.2	10
3c. Tourism	2.7	20	0	20
Total	100	100	100	100

Source: Authors' survey of investment guidebooks
Note: Numbers are percentages of the country total, rounded to nearest tenth.

where wages are far lower. The $2.16 per hour paid to Barbados's semi-skilled workers in export industries as of 1988 was uncompetitive with the many other Caribbean sites where workers take home far less than $1 per hour (Deere et al. 1990, 149). The growing number of U.S. tariff advantages since the early 1980s for U.S. industries to produce in virtually any Caribbean country except Cuba has removed Barbados's earlier more market-based attractiveness to U.S. firms. As a growing number of EPZs across the Caribbean region compete for the same investors, policies that allow for rising working-class wages and purchasing power, as in Barbados, make the country unattractive to foreign industrialists.

Unfortunately for the governments of Barbados and many Third World countries aspiring to EPNDP, to the associated employment opportunities, and even to emulating the East Asian miracle, rhetoric alone will not yield a cutting-edge position in global trade. Few aspirants have been able to approximate the East Asian NICs' policy dexterity in response to changes in the world economy. As Conway notes in chapter 2, however, other aspects of the national development policies of the Barbadian state have been sound, and are even worth emulating in other Caribbean countries. That said, the constraints Barbados is under with respect to attracting foreign investment in manufacturing for export affect the entire region, and are difficult for even the better managed governments to overcome.

The Guidebooks' Neglected Themes: Politics, Agriculture, Environment, Social Welfare

The images that the guidebooks omit are as significant as the ones they include. Their absence directs potential investors' attention away from what we consider crucial contextual features of the countries. The guidebooks suggest that part of the promotion of stability and a pro-investment climate involves avoiding politically related photographs and discussion. The reality of regime turnover or divisive politics need not dampen the image of long-term political stability. Only one political figure, St. Lucia's former prime minister John Compton, appears in any guidebook. Little of substance concerning local cultural or social achievements appears in the guidebooks—yet another calculated political silence. St. Lucia's materials proudly refer to its two Nobel Prize recipients (Arthur Lewis in economics and Derek Walcott in literature), and Jamaica's promotional materials refer to its legacy of "acclaimed political leaders, sportsmen, scientists, entertainers, [and] artists." But neither country's guidebooks refer to these facets again or with any specificity. Neither Derek Walcott's poem "The Swamp" nor Bob Marley's tune "Buffalo Soldier" is likely to tap investor confidence. "No news is good news" when it comes to creating an investor-friendly political mediascape.

Although monocrop plantation agriculture historically has been the economic base of all four countries, agriculture is nearly absent from the guidebooks—only one photograph shows agricultural activity. Those few agricultural processes discussed in the texts are primarily associated with neoliberalism's nontraditional exports, such as hydroponic gardening and cut-flower "factories in the field." Primary product industries receive substantial mention only by Haiti (table 5.3), which had a bleak economic profile in 1995 when the advertisement was distributed. The other guidebooks generally underemphasize actually existing traditional and low-technology economic activities while exaggerating the extent to which the country has already attracted high technology firms. The guidebooks promote basic manufacturing (e.g., garments, electronics assembly), but references to it (as a share of themes mentioned, see table 5.3) are far below its actual share of EPZ activity in all four countries. Tourism is similarly underrepresented relative to its major economic significance to these countries. In contrast, scientific, high-technology manufacturing, information processing, and financial services, which are rare within the sample group, are the sectors most frequently emphasized in Barbados and Jamaica. In St. Lucia they are the second most frequently emphasized sector (table 5.3). Countries that are economically farther ahead (Barbados in particular, and even St. Lucia and Jamaica compared to Haiti) realize that to continue playing and benefiting from the EPZ game, they must position themselves as ripe for investment associated with the information age, however unrealistic these aspirations may be.

The guidebooks are also largely silent in regard to issues such as environmental protection, social justice, human welfare, and poverty reduction. Evidently these themes are not deemed appropriate to the neoliberal model of EPZ promotion (table 5.2). The promoters know (as international advisers can inform them) that investors are wary of environmentalist agendas (Vanderbush and Klak 1996). Investors seldom locate in a country in order to reduce poverty there. Hence, with a few exceptions, the guidebooks minimize references to the country's environmental laws and say little about investors' other social responsibilities. To the contrary, the guidebooks explicitly attempt to sell their countries on the basis of remarkably low cost of labor and/or lack of trade union power. The guidebooks' omission of social responsibility is ironic in that the governments are sold on the EPNDP model as a means of reducing poverty and expanding opportunities, and they sell it as such to their constituents in political campaigns or the local media. But that sales pitch speaks to audiences other than fastidious international investors. Rather than social concerns, investors want to read about incentive packages and other giveaways that will make their investments superprofitable, often at the expense of local people. The absence of environmental and social welfare themes in the materials promoting investment is a distressing sign of the long-term instability and unsustainability of the neoliberal approach to development (as discussed in chap. 1).

It should be noted that only Haiti's guidebook mentions social welfare and the need for environmental protection. In the post-Duvalier era of reconstruction, perhaps Haitian investment promoters believe that these issues, whose historical neglect is nothing short of appalling (Wilentz 1989; Dupuy 1997), will finally get some attention. Compared to Duvalierism, neoliberalism looks promising. Thus the poorest Caribbean state demonstrates that the homogenization revealed by critical analysis of the guidebooks is by no means total. For the most part, the guidebooks signal that the country preparing them is a signatory to the neoliberal world order. They demonstrate considerable similarity regarding discursive tactics, messages, and promises to capital. Yet distinctions remain. Haiti's guidebook stands out the most (see tables 5.2, 5.3), and not simply because of its grammatical errors or lack of glossy photos. Barbados boasts of its literate, "self-assured and cultivated people," St. Lucia lists its Nobel Prize winners, and Jamaica jams in a note of reggae. The most that Haiti's guidebook can offer is "sanguineness" (which is more than Grenadians can muster at present; Wiley 1997) about the future amid a clearly desperate plea for any kind of investment, anywhere in the country. A note of pessimism almost inevitably seeps in, where the other guidebooks have, as the Barbados case shows sometimes quite visibly, whitewashed their past and present.

BEHIND THE MEDIASCAPES IN ST. LUCIA AND JAMAICA

We turn now to a brief review of the actual record of EPNDP in two of the four cases in order to compare and contrast them in greater detail with the mediascapes reviewed thus far. In the spirit of self-reflection and self-critical analysis described in chapter 1, these vignettes are offered as alternative conceptualizations of their EPNDP efforts to the mediascapes. The invitations to international capital in the guidebooks must ultimately deliver the ground level reality to which they refer. This reality is inevitably more multifarious than the guidebooks suggest. Investors discover on site that local history and struggle preclude an unproblematic absorption and implementation of the neoliberal project.

The realities of Jamaica and St. Lucia, as far as reaping benefits from industrial export policy is concerned, are far more complicated than the mediascapers claim. Relative to other developing countries, these two cases are in the "middle of the pack" in development indicators, where Barbados lies far above and Haiti well below most of the globe. By Caribbean regional standards, St. Lucia and Jamaica have achieved moderate levels of human and economic development, and so their experiences and obstacles parallel those of many other countries.

St. Lucia

St. Lucia is an Eastern Caribbean microstate. Such small countries have been characterized as unstable and "economically crippled" (Harden 1985; Cole 1996, 9). Discussion of the impending phaseout of the E.U. Lomé market guarantees for bananas prophesies economic doom for the Eastern Caribbean (Wiley 1996). St. Lucia's macroeconomic profile offers little additional promise: bananas contribute half of export revenues, it increasingly relies on tourism, and it has followed EPNDP convention by emphasizing foreign investment in garment factories. Compared to neighboring Jamaica, St. Lucia is disadvantaged in terms of economic size, industrial base and infrastructure, regional influence, and proximity to U.S. markets (McKee and Tisdell 1990). On the political front, St. Lucia's two major parties are more ideologically similar than Jamaica's, but their recent public quarrels and partisan newspapers suggest a descent into polarized factionalism.

While smallness, economic fragility, and political factionalism pose challenges to development, St. Lucia and other microstates can undoubtedly reap local benefits from EPNDP. St. Lucia has some positive features that are unusual in the global periphery. It has attracted and maintained a cohort of electronics exporters that Jamaica has long and arduously, but unsuccessfully, sought. As a share of free-zone employment, St. Lucia is less dependent than Jamaica, Barbados, and Haiti on garments (Willmore 1993). A considerable portion of its EPZ activity is not relatively uncompetitive Fordist mass production (Sayer and Walker 1992). Instead, it exhibits competitive qualities such as employee engagement and development through flexible job rotations and quality circles (Goss and Conway 1992; Goss and Knudsen 1994). Its EPZ wage rate of around $1 per hour exceeds the rates of most of Central America and the Caribbean, including Jamaica and Haiti (Klak and Myers 1997). St. Lucians occupy most EPZ management positions (Willmore 1993). Its state policies have encouraged considerably more backward linkages than those of Jamaica (Willmore 1993, 1994).

Despite these positive features, however, foreign capital flight from St. Lucia's garment sector has recently exposed a vulnerability attributable to state policy's overemphasis on foreign investors and low-skill assembly operations (St. Lucia National Development Corporation 1995). With the great majority of foreign garment producers closing down operations over the last few years, St. Lucians have been left bitter from the experience. One St. Lucian commentator captures the sentiments of many locals:

> The failure of the garment projects in the various industrial zones . . . is a direct consequence of the intense global competition in that area of trade. After all the hype about job creation, transfer of skills, and so on, our people and institutions ended up getting the shaft, as unscrupulous investors fled, even with the hard-earned money of workers, and in some cases the savings of depositors. (Vitalis 1996, 2)

Thus St. Lucia's EPZ sector has both positive and negative features. In the literature comparing countries for EPZ development, St. Lucia is enigmatic. Willmore (1995) groups it with South Korea and Mauritius, and contrasts them with Jamaica and the Dominican Republic to illustrate how sound policies promoting local benefits pay off. Kaplinsky (1995) counters that the critical variable is not policy but market access: U.S. quotas and tariffs restrict exports from the Caribbean; Asia and Africa have more options. This regional distinction has considerable validity (Deere et al. 1990; Safa 1995), and suggests the relative power of exogenous forces over endogenous policies to determining EPNDP results.

A regionally based interpretation, however, leaves St. Lucia's local benefits compared to other Caribbean islands, Jamaica for example, to be explained. We believe that the positive aspects of St. Lucia's industrial export sector are facilitated by elements of cooperative pluralism (Schmitter 1974), and by relatively effective state policies (Brautigam 1996). Similar to the situation found to varying degrees in other Eastern Caribbean microstates, St. Lucia has a relatively high level of equity, traditional reciprocity, social peace, community consciousness, and political stability and transparency (this idea is discussed in chaps. 2–3; World Bank 1993b). St. Lucia is not plagued with the racial and ethnic divisions found elsewhere; fewer than a few thousand citizens are not of African descent. The St. Lucian state's policy transparency and accessibility are attractive to both domestic and foreign investors, and they are features in critically short supply in much of the global periphery, including Haiti (Hey and Klak 1997). Besides fostering backward linkages, state policy has also contributed to EPNDP through St. Lucia's educational attainment (which is below that of Barbados, similar to that of Jamaica, and greatly exceeding that of Haiti; UN 1996). Educational equity extends to women, as they account for more than half of students and 61 percent of faculty at the university level (Seager 1997, 86–87). These elements of national inclusiveness and state policy encourage the use of the cooperative flexibility in industrial production that is competitive in the post-Fordist era (Goss and Knudsen 1994; Sayer and Walker 1992). Electronics may be more suitable to flexibility and more tolerant of St. Lucia's higher wages than garments, thus explaining St. Lucia's recent decline in the latter.

Jamaica

Since the 1980s relations among the state, capital, and labor in Jamaica have been characterized by distrust, tension, and the pursuit of narrow self-interest, making it more factionalized than Barbados and St. Lucia (Klak 1995a). At the same time, Jamaica displays significant pluralist elements, including a societal commitment to two-party, Westminster-style electoral politics, consensus on civilian rule, well-organized interest groups with access to the state, prominent trade unions representing about a fifth of workers, open political debate in the press, and a free flow of information and views (Stone 1980). However, these elements of societal cohesion are threatened by the growing poverty, desperation, and disenfranchisement precipitated by the country's economic crisis and structural adjustment. The state is committed to the neoliberal development model as evidenced by removal of ISI protections and barriers to international capital flow, social service reduction, state shrinkage, and policy unity between the two parties (Culpepper 1991; Klak 1995a, 1996). While its cuts to social welfare spending under the rubric of structural adjustment have been called "savage" (Anderson and Witter 1992), the state has been less aggressive about promoting nontraditional exports. Local benefits from EPNDP have been only modest. Taken together, Jamaica's general features of economic crisis, restructuring, poverty, and tentative state leadership make it representative of many peripheral countries pursuing EPNDP (Nelson 1990). Three aspects of Jamaica's experience with EPZs are worth highlighting because they suggest that it serves as a test case for the obstacles to neoliberal industrial export development in the global periphery.

First, *state policies have not adequately supported the sector.* For a brief moment in the mid-1980s, Jamaica was declared a neoliberal development model for the Caribbean (McAfee 1994). Under Reagan-ally Edward Seaga as prime minister, there began a concerted effort toward free zone development and promotion. But Jamaica's EPNDP, as in the Caribbean generally, seems in practice more of a reaction to a crisis of foreign exchange and debt than a well-orchestrated economic reorientation (Levitt 1991; Klak 1995a). This seems attributable to a combination of state weakness with regard to development policy, factionalism on the part of workers and local investors that undermines EPNDP, and pluralist elements that pull the state in many directions besides those leading it effectively to execute strategically crafted policies that could generate competitive advantage and local benefits (Porter 1990; Evans 1995; Marshall 1996).

Second, *despite early promise, the results of nontraditional export promotion thus far are modest.* Although Jamaica's EPZ sector builds on certain ingredients, including several policy components that are favorable to the accrual of local benefits, few have materialized. Favorable ingredients include the island's geographical and electronically based accessibility and familiarity to the United States, including a high-speed telecommunications "digiport" created through public-private partnership (figs. 5.2, 5.3), adequate industrial infrastructure, relatively sound educational and training systems, and large numbers of underemployed workers. Yet foreign investment and exports have grown only haltingly, and certainly not at a vibrant pace that would open possibilities for expanding local benefits. Sectoral diversification has advanced little beyond garments (Klak 1996); employment has expanded only modestly beyond physically exhausting entry-level positions; attempts by EPZ workers to organize have been suppressed (Kelly 1989); factionalism is rampant (as evidenced by deep suspicion of other classes and a widespread aversion to factory work); culture clash further inhibits cooperative relations, especially between Afro-Caribbean workers and U.S. and Asian plant managers; policy effectively discriminates against local investors, contributing to their scarcity compared to foreigners (as discussed in chap. 7; also Mullings 1996); backward linkages are practically nil (Willmore 1994); and net foreign exchange is hampered by the large public subsidies to EPZ firms (Klak 1996). The garment sector is now on a precipitous decline with over 4,500 jobs (or more than 10 percent of total) lost to plant relocations in 1996 alone, according to the Caribbean Textile and Garment Institute (Rohter 1997a).

Third, *Jamaica's neoliberalism and pluralist elements stand at a crossroads.* Both are deeply entrenched, but most of society is increasingly dissatisfied with their results. Political openness creates volatility when combined with growing inequalities, deteriorating living conditions for many, high un- and underemployment, crime,[2] discontent, and a sense of futility (Anderson and Witter 1992; de Albuquerque 1995; Chevigny 1996). A result is growing factionalism, which in turn creates a perception of instability that runs counter to the guidebook messages and repels the foreign investors and tourists on which Jamaica's development policies depend (Klak 1994). Jamaica is a test case for what happens to EPNDP and Westminster politics when they are deeply entrenched, but are judged unsatisfactory because they have delivered inadequate rewards.

CONCLUSION

A collapse in traditional export markets and an overexposure to foreign indebtedness brought economic decline and swelling poverty to the Caribbean in the 1980s. Caribbean governments responded to these events with some prodding from the IMF, the World Bank, and Western governments, with a rapid economic opening and incentives to attract foreign capital to produce for export. They aimed to emulate East Asia's industrialization trajectory. Indeed, there has been a remarkably rapid global unification of policy around a neoliberal development model (as chap. 1 recounts).

But the myriad of subsidies and enticements that governments of the Caribbean hold out to fastidious investors as their version of EPNDP have become virtually ubiquitous. Countries therefore cancel out each other's attractiveness. Perhaps Caribbean planners consider the generous incentives as short-term public investments for longer-term national development gains. In practice they function more like mandatory antes for entry into a high stakes poker game against a sea of international competitors, most of which are ill equipped and can scarcely afford to play. Pressures are great to pile the incentives ever higher, still with no guarantee of payoffs. In many EPNDP cases, poor countries have given away the bank before the investors even show up in port. One result is that the foreign debt of the great majority of Caribbean governments is now worse than ever, whether it is measured in U.S. dollars or as a share of per capita GDP or exports (see table 2).

The investment guidebooks examined in this chapter proclaim that the countries are unequivocal converts to neoliberalism. This is a message crafted for both external investor and internal mass audiences. Through the guidebooks, states try to paper over actual existing local conditions, reactions, and resistance, but it takes more than words to make true domestic converts, and neoliberalism has been unable to deliver adequate material goods in the Caribbean. The people's reactions include unproductive behaviors on the job and destabilizing behaviors society-wide, thereby serving to thwart the states' agenda of neoliberal transformation. States too, reflecting their institutionalization under past political agendas, prove to be more neoliberal in print than in practice. EPZs and their promotional policies are quintessential representations of the current experiments with neoliberal development planning, but our evaluation of them suggests that these experiments are flawed. Their obvious contradictions and instability make EPZ policies dangerous. They contribute to creating and entrenching a new and qualitatively different set of economic conditions in their host countries. These countries are exposed to greater trade dependency and international vulnerability after a long and troubled history of such arrangements. EPZ policies thereby contribute to propelling countries down a flawed development policy path while constricting options for alternative and more stable and sustainable approaches. The promotion of export manufacturing demands a high price from Third World governments and workers in exchange for fleeting and inadequate levels of foreign investment.

NOTES

1. For an explanation that draws on cultural mythology to account for why U.S. leaders have portrayed the hemisphere in such terms, see Kenworthy (1995).

2. Jamaica's annual murder rate of 70/100,000 ranks second in Latin America and the Caribbean, behind Colombia's 89.5 and far ahead of Brazil's 19.7 (*Latinamerica Press* 1997).

SUGGESTIONS FOR FURTHER READING

Agnew, J., and S. Corbridge. *Mastering Space: Hegemony, Territory and International Political Economy.* New York: Routledge, 1995. This work examines the importance of geography to the current period of globalization. It incorporates the political theory of Antonio Gramsci into its analysis.

Colclough, C., and J. Manor, eds. *States or Markets? Neoliberalism and the Development Policy Debate.* Oxford: Clarendon, 1991. This edited volume collects the works of numerous (mostly British) scholars of development studies. Its analysis of theoretical matters is highly accessible.

Watts, M. "Development I: Power, Knowledge, Discursive Practice." *Progress in Human Geography* 17 (1993): 257–72.

———. "Development II: The Privatization of Everything?" *Progress in Human Geography* 18 (1994): 371–84. Parts 1–2 of a trilogy of pieces by Watts. Taken together, they provide an array of references for development studies research. Any term paper should start with this trilogy to understand the debates and create a bibliography.

III

CARIBBEAN DEVELOPMENT POLICIES IN A NEOLIBERAL ERA: CASE STUDIES

The next four chapters zero in on specific economic sectors and on revealing case studies of development policy. In chapter 6 Janet Henshall Momsen focuses on the rural areas of Barbados, St. Lucia, Montserrat, Jamaica, and Cuba, and on tourism and agriculture. The chapter evaluates the extent to which tourism and local agriculture complement each other, as would be preferred in an integrated development strategy. Tourism has become the largest sector of many Caribbean economies. Policy makers emphasize the potentially positive effects of tourism on agriculture, especially in terms of new market outlets. Tourist demand for varied and high-quality food has for decades been seen as a stimulus to domestic agriculture. This, it is said, should increase and diversify agricultural production. The evidence, however, suggests that until recently tourism has often been detrimental to agriculture, because of competition for land and labor resources, inflated land and food prices, increased imports, and demonstration effects on the consumption and migration patterns of the local population. This chapter explains these predominantly negative effects. It also explains why in a growing number of Caribbean countries tourism and agriculture are developing the complementarity that the model suggests. These new trends are in part explained by a maturing of tourism's relationship with domestic and regional suppliers, as well as by growing tourist interest in creole cuisine. The trends hold the promise of future expansion of backward linkages from tourism into the local economy and of efforts at filling export market niches for high value food products.

In chapter 7 Beverley Mullings assesses the development potential and problems of a distinctive nontraditional export industry—information processing services. The development prospect of this sector entails incor-

111

porating local labor and nurturing local firms to take advantage of expanding opportunities in the global data processing industry that earns $1 trillion yearly, of which information processing services is a component. Drawing on a detailed analysis of the rise and fall of information services in Jamaica, Mullings explains why this industry, which has real potential (however narrow) for growth in employment, wages, managerial expertise, and backward linkages into the local economy, has stagnated in terms of all these criteria. She identifies the problem in terms of inadequate state support for local firms; continued policy steering and dampening by traditional, nondynamic private elite; investment fear on the part of foreigners; and an extremely narrow role allotted to Jamaican firms and workers by U.S. outsourcing firms. Rather than propelling Jamaica to a heightened position in the international division of labor in the global economy as the neoliberal model predicts, the information services sector has slumped and entrenched the gender, class, and international inequalities that have characterized this peripheral capitalist country over the long term.

In chapter 8 James Wiley focuses on the Eastern Caribbean island of Dominica, reviewing its traditional export troubles, neoliberal export diversification strategy, and prospects for the future. Historically Dominica has been reliant on a single agricultural export. The most recent of these is bananas, sold to Europe under favorable terms for Dominican farmers. The European Union, with prodding from the WTO and the U.S. government, which wants U.S. multinationals to sell more bananas in Europe, is now phasing out those preferential terms and its guaranteed market. In response, Dominica is going to the other policy extreme by promoting a wide range of nontraditional products that it hopes will find new markets and bring new sources of foreign-exchange earnings. Wiley documents how difficult it is for Caribbean countries to move from export sectors that are based on a few goods to ones that are experimenting with an array of vegetables, fruits, seafood, flowers, tourism, and assembly operations. The review of Dominica's diversification efforts reveals the tremendously vibrant public- and private-sector activity in microstates often perceived externally as backward, passive, and undynamic.

Wiley explores an essential question of whether Dominica's "scattershot" approach to generating foreign-exchange earnings will identify some product niches with considerable promise or whether Dominica is replacing monocrop and single market dependence with a new form of vulnerability. In other words, is Dominica trying to do many things at once while not doing any of them well? In many ways this tiny island illustrates the difficulties the world's many micro states face while under pressure to adjust quickly and effectively to new global political-economic realities.

In chapter 9 Paul Susman shifts attention to Cuba, its post-Soviet economic crisis, and how policy makers have borrowed heavily from neoliberalism while trying to retain elements of state socialism. Cuba's state socialist system is usually analyzed as a unique case, largely distinct from problems affecting its Caribbean neighbors and global capitalism (Klak 1994). In light of the tendency to view Cuba in isolation, Susman's analysis is refreshing and revealing. He employs a comparative approach and in so doing draws parallels between Cuba's crisis dimensions and policy responses, as well as those across the Caribbean and worldwide, even in rich capitalist countries. Cuba's "special period" of post-Soviet adjustment coincides with what can be called the special period for the capitalist model of development throughout the Caribbean and elsewhere. Decades of efforts to fit into the global capitalist economy have led Cuba's neighbors to high structural unemployment, economic stagnation, policy dependency, and reliance on outmigration as a safety valve.

With these cautions firmly in mind, but faced with the daunting task of reconstituting virtually all of Cuba's trade ties, policy makers have incrementally opened the country for foreign investment, and have expanded and then limited domestic self-employment entrepreneurial activity. Domestic policies now include farmers' markets' selling surplus directly to consumers, parallel market activity in many consumer goods, legalized use of the U.S. dollar, and the beginnings of a conversion of the entire currency to a dollar equivalent. Production policies include encouraging foreign investment by allowing (at least partial) foreign ownership of enterprises in Cuba, promoting tourism, reorienting state investment to enhance product development for global markets, and reconfiguring large state farms into autonomous and productive cooperatives. For Cuba, the basic question is whether state socialism can survive and stand alone in a capitalist world to which it increasingly must open for trade, capital, and political relations. Given the experience of many Caribbean capitalist experiments past and present, in which there are vast gaps in living standards and opportunities between the wealthy and privileged few and the impoverished and subjugated majority, Cuban efforts to preserve equity and access merit high priority during its neoliberal transition and insertion into the global economy.

6

Caribbean Tourism and Agriculture: New Linkages in the Global Era?

Janet Henshall Momsen

The globalization and democratization of tourism began in the 1960s. A newly affluent middle class endowed with ever increasing amounts of disposable income and leisure time started to take advantage of relatively cheaper air fares, and propelled tourism to its current status as the world's largest industry. Between 1960 and 1996 world international tourist arrivals per annum grew from 69 million to 593 million. The latter figure was a 4.6 percent increase over 1995. Earnings from tourism, excluding airfares, grew by 7.6 percent to $423 billion, both figures being the highest on record (*Economist* 1997, 115). At the beginning of the 1990s tourism employed 112 million people worldwide, 6.5 percent of the total global workforce (CTO 1992).

Stay-over tourist arrivals in the Caribbean have grown even faster than the global rate, increasing from 4.2 million in 1970 to 14 million in 1994, while cruise passenger arrivals rose from 1.2 million in 1970 to 9.8 million in 1994 (CTO 1981, 1994). The proportion of the world's visitors going to the Caribbean increased from 2.6 percent in 1976 to over 4 percent in 1996 (CTO 1992, 1995; *Economist* 1997). For many Caribbean countries tourism is the strongest and fastest growing sector of the economy and the insular Caribbean as a whole ranked ninth in the world in terms of tourist receipts in 1990, according to the International Monetary Fund. By 1994 the Caribbean Tourism Organization estimated that its thirty-four member states grossed $12 billion from tourism and in 1995 predicted that the region's tourist industry would grow by 6.3 percent annually over the next sixteen years, twice the expected rate for the world as a whole (Pattullo 1996).

Tourism's contribution to gross domestic product in a territory fluctuates with visitor expenditure and reflects changing opportunities in other economic sectors. Over the last decade, growth has been fastest in the French and Dutch West Indies and in Cuba, which doubled its tourist arrivals between 1991 and 1996 (CTO 1992; *Caribbean Insight* 1997). On the whole, the smaller islands are most tourism dependent, with visitor expenditure averaging more than half of GDP between 1985 and 1994 in Anguilla, Antigua and Barbuda, St. Lucia, the Turks and Caicos, and the U.S. Virgin Islands, and more than one quarter in Aruba, Barbados, the Bahamas, Bermuda, Cayman Islands, Grenada, Montserrat, St. Kitts-Nevis, and St. Vincent and the Grenadines (CTO 1994). Even the more diversified economies of the Greater Antilles, especially the Dominican Republic and Jamaica, had years in which tourism was a substantial contributor to GDP at 19.2 percent in 1988 for the Dominican Republic and 37.2 percent in 1991 for Jamaica (CTO 1992).

The Caribbean as a whole ranked fifth in the world in terms of tourist stay-over and cruise arrivals in 1994 (*Economist Intelligence Unit* 1996). The Caribbean islands have generally high *tourism density* ratios (the number of tourists per square kilometer on any one day) and *tourism penetration* ratios (the number of tourists per thousand local inhabitants at any one time; see table 6.1). Tourism penetration ratios are highest in the smallest islands of Aruba, Anguilla, and the Cayman Islands. Tourism density ratios show similar patterns, being highest in the small, densely populated islands of Bermuda, Aruba, and the British Virgin Islands (table 6.1). Although most islands have exhibited increases in both ratios since 1982, some of the countries with long established substantial tourist industries, such as the Bahamas, Bermuda, and the U.S. Virgin Islands, have falling penetration ratios indicating a perception that optimum visitor levels in relation to the local population have been exceeded.

After many years of intraisland competition for visitors, the Caribbean now has a regional tourism research organization, the Caribbean Tourism Organization based in Barbados, and some joint advertising. Efforts are also being made to differentiate between the attractions of individual islands with some emphasizing ecotourism (Dominica), health tourism (St. Lucia), all-inclusive resorts (Jamaica and St. Lucia), or history (Nevis and Barbados), while Cuba offers some of the cheapest package holidays. This new regional approach to Caribbean tourism marketing, which encourages differences while recognizing the need for cooperation, is a reaction to the region's situation of unequal power relations of wealth, race, and class that are manifested at several geographical scales. This can be seen (1) at the world economy level between core nation hotel and travel companies and peripheral host nation's tourist boards; (2) at the Caribbean regional level between small, resource-poor, tourism dependent islands and larger, wealthier Caribbean countries with more diversified economies; and (3) at the local level between largely poor, black rural hosts and

TABLE 6.1
Caribbean Tourism Penetration and Density Ratios

Country	Penetration Ratio 1982[1]	Penetration Ratio 1991	Density Ratio 1982[2]	Density Ratio 1994
Anguilla	17	115	1	12
Antigua & Barbuda	34	61	6	15
Aruba	60	156	21	57
Bahamas	94	92	1	2
Barbados	30	46	18	31
Bermuda	136*	110	141*	133
Bonaire	39	80	1	4
British Virgin Islands	212	320**	16	31
Cayman Islands	77	120	5	18
Curacao	14	27	4	11
Dominica	6	14	1	2
Dominican Republic	3	7***	n.a.	1#
Grenada	8##	19	2##	6
Guadeloupe	12	14***	3	5
Jamaica	6	10	1	3
Martinique	8	9	3	4
Puerto Rico	5	6***	2	3
St. Kitts & Nevis	20	44	3	9
St. Lucia	17##	26***	4##	9
St. Vincent & Grenadines	8	14	2	3
U.S. Virgin Islands	73*	54*	24*	19

Sources: Caribbean Tourism Organization; *Caribbean Tourism Statistical Report,* 1991 and 1995. Barbados: CTO.
*1985; **1990; ***1989; #1992; ##1983
[1]Tourism density ratio: The average daily number of tourists per square kilometer
[2]Tourism penetration ratio: The average daily number of tourists per thousand local inhabitants

rich, white urban guests. Such inequalities have encouraged a focus in studies of Caribbean tourism on the social and economic costs and benefits of tourism and its impact on local cultures (Bryden 1973; Pattullo 1996). Unusually, in this chapter, I focus on backward and forward linkages between tourism and other sectors of the economy, particularly the relationship with the former dominant sector in the region's economy—agriculture.

TOURISM-AGRICULTURE RELATIONSHIPS

Developing countries have embraced the growth of tourism as a welcome source of foreign exchange, investment, employment, and economic growth. For the small islands of the Caribbean with few resources except sun, sand, and sea, tourism has been seen as the sine qua non of development (as discussed in chap. 5). The projected economic benefits of tourism, however, have proved illusory. Government planners and foreign consultants have argued for over three decades that tourism will stimulate other sectors of the Caribbean economy, notably agriculture (Sergent 1967; Brown 1974; Gomes 1993). Their rationale is based on the belief that the tourism-driven demand for more varied and higher quality food will stimulate farmers to both expand and diversify agricultural production. Unfortunately, there is little evidence to suggest that the international tourism industry has been successful in developing backward linkages to local agriculture sufficient to stimulate growth in the agrarian sector.

Numerous scholarly studies have noted the failure of these predicted linkages to form (Momsen 1972, 1973; Belisle 1983; Latimer 1985; Telfer and Wall 1996). There are many constraints inhibiting the development of these linkages. Belisle (1983, 505) suggested that these include "physical, behavioral, economic, technological and marketing obstacles." Lack of marketing, transport, and storage facilities may also hinder food distribution from producer to consumer. Certain environmental characteristics of the Caribbean—small, crowded islands with little physical variation that are vulnerable to climatic extremes of drought and high winds—contribute to the difficulties in forging such linkages (Latimer 1985). Others, including Bryden (1973), Belisle (1983), and Britton (1991), argue that the organizational structure of the international tourism industry, in which foreign-owned hotel chains have strong links to overseas food suppliers, itself acts as a barrier to developing links with domestic suppliers. A recent theoretical study of the effect in the Bahamas of replacing a quarter of food imports with food supplied by local farmers suggested that no definite conclusions regarding net positive or negative effects could be drawn. Although there would be an improvement in the tourist multiplier and in agricultural employment, there would also be increased import of agricultural inputs and some job losses in trade sectors (Taylor, Morison and Fleming 1991). Some have even suggested that rather than stimulating local agricultural development, tourism actually demands a higher level of food imports, which increases the burden on scarce foreign exchange reserves. Indeed, Pérez (1973–74, 480) concludes that "in converting former agricultural monoculture economies to travel monoculture, tourism renews and reinforces the historical process of underdevelopment." Bryden (1974) also suggests that, at least in the smaller islands of the region, there may in fact be a perverse relationship between agriculture and tourism, leading to what he calls "immiserating conflict."

Much of the failure can be traced to historical factors and unequal power relations between producer and consumer. The region has always been trade dependent as captured in the old adage that "the Caribbean produces what it does not consume and consumes what it does not produce" (Deere et al. 1990, 4). As long as export-oriented agricultural production was profitable, few farmers were interested in producing for a small local market with limited purchasing power. Consequently, production of foodstuffs for the domestic market was left to women working as small farmers in most Caribbean countries (Henshall 1984). Women farmers receive little attention from extension agents and so food production utilizes traditional methods often with low productivity. National governments are generally unaware of this gender bias. Structural adjustment in the 1980s with its concomitant currency devaluation translated into higher consumer costs and greater impoverishment. Many women, often single mothers, were forced back to subsistence production to feed their families, but at the same time higher prices of imported goods increased opportunities for petty commodity production and small-scale producers serving domestic markets (Klak 1995). It was already evident in the 1970s that small-scale commercial vegetable and poultry farmers producing for the tourist market were predominantly men (Momsen 1972, 1974). As prices for export crops fell in the 1980s, large-scale, mostly male farmers with greater resources and better access to credit and government advice began to take advantage of the growing tourist demand for fresh food.

However, linkages between agriculture and tourism are not restricted to production. Tourism can influence agriculture in five interrelated ways. First, it can offer alternative employment opportunities and therefore raise the reserve price of agricultural labor and encourage migration from farming to tourist areas (Brown 1974). Second, competition for land between recreation and agriculture may raise land values and so remove some agricultural land from food production. Third, tourist activities may modify land use and land values around resort areas. Fourth, tourist demand for high-value and quality food may provide incentives for farmers to increase and diversify production or increase food imports. Fifth, tourism may create aesthetic uses for rural land, encouraging preservation of some rural environments and creating associated recreation-based jobs in rural areas.

In the most extreme cases, tourism is reported to actually displace agriculture by competing for land and human resources. In Antigua the agricultural sector had virtually disappeared by 1992, having declined as the tourist industry grew. Bryden (1973, 47) claimed that this was due to direct competition for land between tourism and agriculture, while O'Loughlin (1968, 147) observed that "tourism has tended to make the sugar industry even less economic by forcing up wage rates." More recently the collapse of Antigua's agriculture has been blamed on environmental degradation, not competition from tourism (Lorah 1995). Weaver (1988) in his "plantation model" of tourism development suggests that in general the demise of agriculture lies in planters' transferring investment funds by planters to take advantage of higher returns in this sector. It has also been suggested that tourism, through its demonstration effect, increases consumption of imported foods by local people (Bryden 1973, 1974; Belisle 1983b; Momsen 1986). These dangers should not be exaggerated, however, as hotels are usually built in dry coastal areas unsuitable for agriculture (Momsen 1973). Greater variety in the local diet reflects a general rise in living standards that may be a result of tourism-based prosperity, but is not necessarily a copycat relationship. In many cases tourism and agriculture may be seasonally complementary in terms of labor demands. By reducing un- and underemployment it raises local incomes (Momsen 1986).

The majority of the economic benefits from conventional Caribbean tourism actually accrue to transnational corporations and foreign entrepreneurs. The proportion of the tourist dollar that stays in the tourist's Caribbean destination, the *tourist multiplier*, is lower than in most comparable tourist regions. This is because hotels depend on imported furnishings, equipment and food, and the range of locally produced souvenirs is limited (Bryden 1973). Efforts to maximize the economic benefits from tourism have focused on tourist numbers, expenditure, and length of stay. However, backward linkages to agriculture can also help by increasing consumption of local produce by tourists and so improving the tourist multiplier effect (Telfer and Wall 1996).

Gomes (1993, 157) calculated that food and beverages served in Caribbean hotels, including the costs of delivering the meals and drinks to visitors, accounted for over half (56.7 percent) of the total revenue per room.

On the basis of these calculations he estimated that $1,680.57 million was spent on food and beverages by Caribbean tourists in 1990 (Gomes 1993, 160). Earlier calculations suggest that Gomes understates domestic benefits from Caribbean tourism. Gooding (1971, 94) pointed out that although almost two-thirds of food consumed by tourists was imported into Barbados in 1968, if import duties and taxes, local transport, and mark-up to local distributors and wholesalers are included, an impressive 52 percent of the money spent on tourist food stayed on the island. Further, in the last three decades more food consumed by tourists in Barbados has been locally grown (Alleyne 1974; Momsen 1990) than predicted by Gooding. Clearly, local production of food can make an important contribution to the balance of payments in a tourist-dependent economy such as those of many of the smaller islands of the Caribbean. In addition, better linkages between tourism and agriculture not only represent an important mechanism for the stimulation of local farming but may also help to spread the benefits, by converting rural people into economic stakeholders and beneficiaries of the tourism industry. In this way such linkages improve the sustainability of both agriculture and tourism.

This chapter examines tourism-agriculture linkages in relation to changes in state policies, the maturity of the tourism industry, and the type of tourism. These aspects are illustrated by case studies based on fieldwork over several decades in Barbados, St. Lucia, Montserrat, Dominica, Jamaica, and Cuba. Despite the popular belief among development planners that agriculture is one of the sectors with greatest potential for linkages, it has been noted as recently as 1996 (Telfer and Wall 1996) that very few studies examine the precise nature of the linkages between tourism and agriculture in the Caribbean and other lesser developed regions (Belisle 1983; Bowen, Cox and Fox 1991). The questions concerning tourism-agriculture relationships addressed in this chapter are central to an assessment of the neoliberal transition in the Caribbean. Can local food production be revived by tourist-created demand and contribute to the economic diversification and multipliers sought after in the neoliberal era? Or will local food production be destroyed in the competition for land and labor resources and by imported foodstuffs, so that tourism is essentially another Caribbean economic enclave with minimal capacity for foreign exchange earnings?

Economic Policies and Tourism-Agriculture Linkages

The economies of Caribbean islands are being transformed from a production to a consumption base, as are many rural economies around the world (Marsden and Arce 1995). For three hundred years the islands have produced tropical crops such as sugar, bananas, and cotton for the metropolitan powers. But now they have become recipients of visitors from the North determined to consume the local resources of sun, sand, and sea and increasingly unspoiled tropical rural scenery and ecology. Thus the Caribbean rural economy is in the process of being transformed from a food regime based on settler colonialism largely dependent on foodstuffs (Buttel and Goodman 1989) to one in which transnational and regional food networks are reconfigured by the globalization of tourism (Goodman and Watts 1994). Many tourists want the same fast foods they eat at home, as seen in the spread of take-out pizza, hamburger, and chicken outlets throughout the region. Fish-and-chip shops have become popular in areas with increasing numbers of British tourists. However, a growing proportion of Caribbean tourists, especially those attracted by ecotourism and heritage tourism, represent the new consumerism, which demands healthy natural food produced by a sustainable agriculture that does not damage the environment. Friedmann (1993, 35) links such agriculture to the politics of relocalization and posits that a "new agriculture would emphasize proximity and seasonality: a food delivery system rooted in local economies." This trend should promote linkages between tourism and agriculture in the Caribbean.

In the 1960s the small resource-poor Caribbean islands saw tourism as a type of development through import substitution industrialization (ISI). They promoted this nascent industry with low start-up taxes and by allowing tax-free import of furnishings and equipment. Gradually, hotels that in the 1960s imported most of their food were forced to use local products as governments introduced quotas on food imports. In this way St. Lucian chicken producers, who could not compete with imports on the basis of cost because of the need to import feed, were guaranteed a market (Momsen 1986). Brown (1974) notes that from 1964 Jamaican hotels faced increasing restrictions on imports, and so they substituted locally grown fruits and vegetables for imported fresh and canned produce. Today the Cuban government imposes import restrictions on food imports for tourism, but as discussed below, foreign-owned hotels have the power to negotiate to import a greater share of their food requirements.

The structural adjustment programs of the 1980s forced most countries of the Caribbean to abandon import substitution. The introduction of neoliberal policies encouraged a focus on exports, especially of nontraditional goods. Tourism is now seen as a special case of a nontraditional export (Brohman 1996b). With the loss of protected markets for the traditional plantation staples, nontraditional agricultural exports expanded and many farmers have also found tourist markets.

The stringent structural adjustment programs imposed on several islands by the International Monetary Fund in the 1980s encouraged tourism as one of the few viable economic alternatives (see chap. 5). By the

1990s tourism was being promoted even more vigorously as the Caribbean became increasingly politically marginalized by the end of the Cold War and excluded from its traditional markets by free-market trading blocs such as NAFTA and the European Union (as discussed in chaps. 4, 8). The effect is clear, as the CTO pointed out in 1995: "Trading blocks such as the NAFTA and the European Community have made it increasingly difficult for traditional Caribbean manufacturing and agricultural industries to remain competitive, giving tourism an even higher priority throughout the region" (CTO 1995a). Thus the E.U. in the third protocol (1986–90) of the Lomé convention noted "the real importance of the tourism industry" for the Caribbean after barely mentioning it in the two previous five-year protocols. The West Indian Commission, set up to consider the Caribbean's future in the post-Cold War world, also recognized the "strategic position that tourism has come to occupy in the region" (West Indian Commission 1992, 106).

THE GROWTH OF CARIBBEAN TOURISM

Many Caribbean countries have only recently turned to tourism. Cuba and the Bahamas, being closest to the United States, were the first. Although time series data are not always strictly comparable, it appears that the total number of tourists in the Caribbean rose from 45,100 in 1919 to 131,400 in 1929. It reached 430,000 in 1938, when 37 percent of visitors went to Cuba (mainly Havana) and 13 percent to Nassau (Anglo-American Caribbean Commission 1945). However, the main growth of tourism is a post-Second World War phenomenon, with the region receiving 1.5 million visitors in 1959 and 2.5 million by 1965. Puerto Rico, where government encouragement of tourism began in 1948 (Barasorda 1963), replaced Cuba as the leading tourist destination after Cuba's 1959 revolution. As long distance air travel became accessible to a wider group of people, Caribbean tourism grew by 10 percent per year in the late sixties and early seventies, reaching a total of 7.3 million in 1973. The first oil shock of 1974 halted this rapid expansion, although renewed growth in the late seventies brought a new peak of 11 million visitors in 1980.

This impressive growth should not obscure that the industry continues to be vulnerable to (1) global problems such as economic recession and the Gulf War, (2) economic problems in the nations sending tourists such as growing unemployment or negative adjustments of the exchange rate, and (3) political and environmental problems in the host nations, such as political instability in Haiti and Grenada, hurricane damage in the Virgin Islands, and volcanic eruptions in Montserrat. Such problems led to the first decline in world tourist numbers in 1982 with a further decline in

1991 (CTO 1992). Individual islands exhibit considerable fluctuations, reflecting tourist perceptions of local problems. Yet tourism has now spread to even the smallest islands. In 1994 Cuba received more than twice the number of tourists it did in 1958 and the region as a whole had 14 million stay-over and 9.8 million cruise-ship passenger visitors (CTO 1995). Falling long-haul airfares and the decline in the U.S. dollar exchange rate against European currencies has led to an increasing proportion of European visitors, who now outnumber Americans in most of the Lesser Antilles.

The Caribbean depends on tourism more than any other developing world region, according to the Caribbean Tourism Organization (Pattullo 1996, 12). In 1993 the *Economist* magazine noted that for the Caribbean "tourism is the only sector of regional GDP that has consistently increased its share of total income during the 1980s. In some places tourism accounts for up to 70 per cent of national income directly and indirectly" (*Economist* Intelligence Unit 1993). Tourism revenues offset more than 41 percent of the Caribbean's total import bill, and six countries (Antigua, Bahamas, Barbados, Grenada, St. Kitts-Nevis, and the Dominican Republic) earned more from tourism than from all other exports combined (IMF 1993). Thus for the Caribbean tourism has become a last resort of major economic importance.

BACKWARD LINKAGES

The region must reduce the leakage of tourism-derived earnings from the region, in order to maximize its financial return from tourism. The Tripartite Report of 1966 stressed that "though tourism can be the prime generator of economic development, growth cannot be based on expanding tourism alone. Tourism must be supplemented by a major effort in the direction of import substitution, particularly of food items. . . . The agricultural sector must grow in order to provide increased exports and import substitutes" (Sergent 1967, ix, xi).

Agricultural responses to tourist demand were very limited because export agriculture was flourishing and individual islands thus could not guarantee reliable supply, year-round availability, and consistently high levels of freshness and unblemished appearance, which the hospitality industry demanded (Momsen 1972, 1973; Belisle 1983a, b). The proportion of locally produced food consumed by visitors varies with the ownership and size of the accommodation establishments, the type of tourist, the ability of local producers to respond to tourist demand, and the government's attitude toward fostering the sectoral linkage. It also varies with the maturity of the industry. Sometimes failure to expand linkages may be caused by conflict between the interests of local producers and those of the traditional wholesale and retail trades whose livelihoods depend on imports. The issue is further complicated where government obtains a significant proportion of revenues from taxes and duties levied on imported products (CTRC 1986).

Government control is particularly important in Cuba. There is a single official state food wholesaler from whom hotels must procure food with payment in dollars. This state supplier buys from producers in pesos at low prices set by the state, so there is little incentive for quality and quantity improvement. Cuban hotels must buy all their inputs through official channels, but foreign-owned and foreign-managed hotels can negotiate a contract that allows for use of imported items for which they are often granted a tax break (Everleny 1995). Many foreign hotel chains import 40–60 percent of their food depending on the season, mainly from Canada, Mexico, Chile and Spain. One of the Cuban producers, Cultivos Varios, has divided a state farm into 204 fincas and pays individual producers half the profits. It allows them to make decisions on the daily division of labor as well as on the distribution and use of profits. It also provides them with land for crop production for their own consumption and for sale. This new system resulted in a doubling of production between 1994 and 1995 (Cultivos Varios 1995).

The quality of Cuban-produced food, as measured by size, appearance, and taste, is often poor and about a quarter of it is returned by hotels as unsuitable for tourist consumption. A lack of imported pesticides and chemical fertilizers makes it difficult to control damage from pests and disease, although Cuban farmers have made great strides in use of organic pest control and fertilizer (Rosset and Benjamin 1996). Poor handling and inadequate storage facilities also result in damage to fresh produce. The imposition of a two-tier system of import controls clearly discriminates against Cuban-owned hotels, which is reflected in an occupancy level half that of hotels that are foreign owned or managed (Everleny 1995). Cuban tourism has nonetheless grown rapidly, with tourist arrivals passing the million mark for the first time in 1996, an increase of 35 percent over 1995 (Caribbean Insight 1997). That growth and the two-tier food supply system provide a window of opportunity for unofficial and illegal entrepreneurship, and some small producers were seen selling to Cuban hotels during fieldwork in 1995. The Cuban situation shows that even under the most stringent conditions of internally and externally imposed import substitution, quality is the key to production for the tourist market.

TIME SERIES ANALYSIS OF TOURISM-AGRICULTURE LINKAGES

For five islands—Jamaica, Barbados, St. Lucia, Montserrat, and Dominica—data are available for comparisons of tourism/agriculture linkages over time. These islands have very different types of tourism (CTO 1995). Jamaica has the largest tourist industry, with two-thirds of visitors coming from the United States. Two-thirds of its hotel rooms are concentrated in the major resort areas of Ocho Rios and Montego Bay (CTO 1992). Barbados has both mass package-holiday tourism and traditional élite tourism. Well-known show business personalities, as well as other wealthy people, maintain holiday homes there. Tourist accommodation is predominantly in self-catering apartment-hotels, which represented two-thirds of tourist beds in 1995, or hotels, which have an additional 21.9 percent of the beds (Barbados Statistical Service 1996). The single largest group of tourists are European (38 percent in 1995), coming primarily from Britain, Germany, and Scandinavia. St. Lucia, which attracts only about half the annual number of tourists who visit Barbados, has a similar proportion of European tourists (40 percent in 1992) who come mainly from Britain, Germany, and Italy. In 1992 61 percent of tourists stayed in hotels, many of which are inclusive resorts (St. Lucia, n.d.). Dominica received 52,000 tourists in 1993, only about one-third of the number visiting St. Lucia. Of these tourists, 36 percent came from France or the French West Indies, reflecting the influence of Dominica's location between Martinique and Guadeloupe. These French visitors spend more than other visitors on meals outside their hotels, and they visit the island for its tranquility, natural history, and the Carib territory (chap. 8 focuses on Dominica; CTO 1994a). Montserrat received some 21,000 tourists in 1993, but 38 percent came from North America and 44 percent from other Caribbean countries, and 79 percent of tourist accommodation was in apartments or villas (CTO 1994b).

The type of hotel and tourist affect the pattern of local food consumption. For example, Montserrat has a very small population and, like Dominica, many long-stay visitors. Fifteen percent stay more than three weeks, compared to 9.5 percent in Barbados and 11.2 percent in St. Lucia. Tourist food consumption in Montserrat can influence local food production to a greater extent than on larger islands. Although tourist food consumption is generally a small proportion of a country's total consumption, it is concentrated on certain high value products such as steak and lobster, and it is seasonally and spatially specific.

Lundgren (1971) identified five stages in the development of tourism's linkages with local food producers. In stage 1, hotels are being established and they have little effect on local food producers. In stage 2, links with local farmers are formed, and by stage 3 wholesaling and bulk purchasing are in operation. In stage 4 there is a rise in hotel demand, transportation networks improve, and goods are obtained from a wider area. In stage 5 agglomeration economies come into play. Expanded resort facilities drive out nearby farmers, long-distance supply lines become consolidated and regional agricultural specialization develops. This model may be interrupted by exogenous factors such as drought or windstorms or government regulations. The stages may be accelerated by changes in the tourist market, as evidenced by the expansion of European holiday makers, many of whom may be more prepared than North Americans for culinary adventures.

In 1968 Jamaican hotels imported 69.4 percent of their food. Floyd (1974, 429) remarked that "the hoped for stimulus for Jamaican peasants and livestock farmers to produce high quality foodstuff has, as yet, failed to materialise." Between 1965 and 1972 the import content of food and beverages consumed by tourists in Jamaica varied from 66.3 percent to 79.3 percent (Brown 1974, 137). Yet by the early 1980s the proportion of imported food had decreased. Belisle (1984b) reported that although the amount of local foods consumed by Jamaican hotel visitors varied from 20 percent to 95 percent of the total, the mean import level, weighted by size of hotel, was 45.8 percent. Fieldwork by Rickard and Carmichael in 1993 revealed that Jamaican hotels had increased their use of local suppliers. Further, a complex supplier network had developed with small contractors collecting food products from inland, more distant, farmers (Rickard and Carmichael 1995), with supplies from Caricom producers becoming important. These changes appear to provide empirical support for Lundgren's staged model, indicating that Jamaica may have reached the final stage of the model.

In Barbados, Gooding (1971) surveyed three hotels, a guesthouse, a supermarket, and several wholesalers, and estimated that in 1968 only one-third of tourist food by value and half by weight was produced locally. This did not differ markedly from the local/import ratio of the general Barbadian diet at the time. In 1990 a survey of twelve hotels and twelve apartment hotels in Barbados, constituting about 40 percent of all such accommodation on the island and one-forth of all tourist lodgings, found that over 90 percent of the beef and lamb consumed by tourists was imported while most of the other meat and fish was produced locally, as was milk, eggs, vegetables, fruit, and soft drinks (Momsen 1990). Two-thirds of the alcoholic drinks by value were imported. This appears to indicate a big improvement in local supplies, although the two most expensive items, alcohol and beef, were still mostly imported. According to Gooding the constraints limiting increased consumption of local products were first of all price, followed by quality and availability. By 1990 the ranking had changed and expanded, with lack of variety, marketing inefficiencies, guest preference, and price, in that order, being listed by hotels surveyed.

In St. Lucia in 1971 I found that 70 percent by value of the food consumed by tourists was imported, but that the small locally owned hotels imported only about one-third of their food supplies (Momsen 1972).

These hotels usually belonged to the local élite who used their estate land to grow food for their hotel guests. At that time the foreign-owned hotels were quite new and had not developed local market networks, and therefore tended to use wholesalers in Florida and Puerto Rico for most of their supplies. By 1983 a survey of only the largest hotels in St. Lucia found that the proportion of imported food had fallen to 45 percent by weight and 58 percent by value with only about one-third of vegetables, fruit, and seafood imported (CTRC 1984). The main items imported were beef and dairy products.

In Montserrat in 1973 the proportion of imported food varied from 63 percent for the largest hotels to only 20 percent for the small, locally owned guesthouses visited mainly by people from elsewhere in the region. At this time 81 percent of the hotel rooms were locally owned, and the proprietors, like some in St. Lucia, generally depended on their own plantations for fresh produce. In 1992 all the hotels and guesthouses surveyed in Dominica were locally owned, and many grew their own vegetables and fruit. Most tried to buy locally produced goods, but "price is more important than loyalty to the region" (Sharkey 1994). Shortages of certain commodities were blamed on attempts by government to protect local producers by banning imports and on shipping problems. A recent survey in Barbados (Momsen 1990), which included apartments and hotels, estimated that 48 percent of operating costs were for food and beverages while in Dominica the equivalent statistic was 35 percent (Sharkey 1994). Both of these figures exclude staffing costs for preparing and serving food. The difference in the figures for Barbados and Dominica probably reflects the higher level of locally owned and smaller hotels in Dominica and the island's greater agricultural productivity.

Although it was estimated for the British Virgin Islands that one hundred hotel rooms could support only two market gardeners working full time for the tourist industry (Elkan and Morley 1971), field surveys found that approximately thirty farmers provided produce directly for the occupants of St. Lucia's 747 hotel rooms in 1971 (Momsen 1972), while eighteen farmers in Montserrat grew produce for the 120 hotel rooms on that island (Momsen 1973). However, none of these farmers was entirely dependent on the hotel sector, as demand fluctuated with hotel occupancy rates. Farmers tended to respond primarily to the local demand for fruit, vegetables, eggs, and poultry, which was growing in response to the tourist demonstration effect, a long-term secular trend in tastes, and to rising personal incomes.

In both St. Lucia and Montserrat maturity in the tourism industry has brought increased linkages with agriculture. Agriculture ministries on both islands carefully monitor demand and supply of local produce. In Montserrat by the mid-1980s, the government had instituted programmed production, import restrictions, and intensive field monitoring of the 136 carefully selected primary farms. The National Plan aimed for eventual local self-sufficiency in vegetables and some fruits, and also in beef, pork, and lamb (Bass 1984). St. Lucia had a modern, well-equipped meat processing facility and began producing jams and snack foods for hotels in the early 1980s. In 1984 St. Lucia had only 152 vegetable farmers compared to the 195 recorded in 1971, but their production was carefully monitored and weekly information on prices and availability of produce was widely disseminated. For the first time in many years St. Lucia registered a positive balance of trade in food products in 1984, largely because of the main export crop of bananas.

In the 1990s, with the banana trade with Europe under threat, St. Lucia is further intensifying the linkages between tourism and domestic agriculture. In 1994 the St. Lucia Hotel Association and the Ministry of Agriculture jointly launched an "adopt a farmer" pilot program with the two largest all-inclusive resorts on the islands, Sandals and Club St. Lucia. Farmers were to interact directly with hotels and provide goods selected from a list of required items. They could then borrow against this agreement (Pattullo 1996). Nevis, which had its first large resort hotel open recently, has taken similar steps. A task force of the Ministry of Agriculture regulates production and imports, and it acts as a negotiating agent between the farmers and the hotel. The task force offers farmers a guaranteed market and in return demands produce of high quality (Pattullo 1996).

Overall, the last two decades have seen an increase in the use of national and regional produce following the broad outlines of the Lundgren model. Both Barbados and Jamaica have attained a food-supply network similar to that described in the final stage of the model. Since the early 1980s there have been pressures to reduce government intervention. Yet a realization that backward linkages from tourism to local agriculture would only occur if both demand and supply were stimulated and marketing was improved has forced governments to become more proactive in this field (OAS 1984). Neoliberal policies have forced Caribbean governments to move beyond simple import substitution to global competition where quality of output is vital. Today, with the expansion and maturity of the Caricom trade in agricultural products and the rapid growth of tourist demand, regional and local specialization has developed. Tariffs that restrict imports from non-Caricom countries have encouraged intraregional trade in foodstuffs. Barbados now imports much of its shellfish from other Caricom members and its fruit from St. Lucia. Dominica and Montserrat grow fruit and vegetables for other islands, especially Antigua. At the same time, fresh-food production has been taken up by large-scale farmers who produce for both the local tourist market and the export market in local food crops among West Indians living overseas. Caribbean growers have also moved into nontraditional agricultural products such as tropical flowers and plants for metropolitan markets as well as for the large tourist hotels.

Tourism itself has developed a commodification of place (Britton 1991) that can be appropriated to develop a saleable commodity. Thus hotels and restaurants can develop menus based on local fresh foods presented as regional specialties. In an interview with a hotel manager in Dominica in 1992 we were proudly told, "Our restaurant has an islandwide reputation for top-of-the-line authentic food." When asked if tourists were interested in eating local foods all Dominican hotel and guesthouse owners said yes. One noted that Americans preferred a "less-embellished meal." All restaurants in Dominica offered creole cuisine (Sharkey 1994).

Vacation-based acquaintance with such authentic local dishes and food products can generate a market for food and beverage souvenirs. Production of such souvenirs has been a major growth industry for many Caribbean agroindustries. Souvenir foodstuffs are usually sold in small amounts in expensive and eye-catching packaging so that the unit price is much higher than on the local market. Typical souvenir food items in the Caribbean are rum, brown sugar, coffee, jams, jellies, spices, hot sauce, and tropical fruit juices. These satisfy the well-traveled tourists' search for authenticity (Urry 1990) and enable Caribbean producers to sell high value-added products without export shipment costs. In turn, if the link between place and product is successful, then markets in the visitors' home countries may expand. This is already occurring for specialty rums such as Barbados's Mount Gay and coffees such as Jamaica's Blue Mountain.

GENDER IMPACTS

The gender impacts of changes in the tourism and agriculture sectors are multifaceted rather than unidirectional (Momsen 1994). Studies in the early 1970s found that small farmers producing for hotels were more likely to be male than female (Momsen 1972, 1973). Yet the people selling fresh fruit and locally processed food products to tourists on the beach were mostly women (Momsen 1994). Where nontraditional agro-industries have developed, most notably in the Dominican Republic, young women provide most of the workforce, picking, grading, processing, and packing items such as fruit, flowers, vegetables, and spices (Raynolds 1994).

The tourist industry employs men and women in generally equal numbers, although hotels often employ more women than men. It is often young women who leave the farm to work as maids in hotels, salespersons in tourist stores, or prostitutes. Young men work as waiters, run water sports, and do beach trading in jewelry and drugs with prostitution as a sideline (Momsen 1994). Older men combine part-time farming with work as hotel gardeners and handymen or taxi drivers. Women with children often farm while also doing some beach trading and sometimes babysit tourists' children. Thus tourism offers opportunities that attract young people away from farming and thereby accelerate the decline in young entrants into agriculture in much of the Caribbean. Although pay is often low, tourism is seen as a more glamorous occupation with easier working conditions than agriculture.

CONCLUSION

After years of failure to develop backward linkages to agriculture, tourism is integrating more and more with local producers. Such tourism-agriculture linkages are a product of the maturing of the Caribbean tourism industry, a side effect of the globalization of food consumption habits (discussed further below; Goodman and Watts 1994), and a reaction to the new barriers imposed on traditional Caribbean agricultural exports by NAFTA and the E.U., which have forced farmers to become innovative in their search for alternative crops. Simultaneously, Caribbean farmers are seeking increased value added for their products and developing agricultural businesses such as the manufacture of jams, pickles, fruit juices, and perfumes and the packaging of spices and ground coffee. These enterprises are often small and depend on exploiting traditional local specialties such as St. Lucian coffee, Jamaican spices, and Dominica fruit juice. They sell predominantly within Caricom, but also exploit the tourist market through hotel consumption and direct sales of souvenirs to tourists. In most of the Caribbean the scale of production is increasing and firms are moving towards meeting regional markets rather than limiting themselves to national ones. Larger-scale producers are generally better at providing hotels with more consistent quality and regular supplies of produce. In Cuba, however, the inefficiencies of state farm production are enabling small-scale entrepreneurs who can offer better-quality produce to benefit from the rapidly growing tourist demand. Many small producers throughout the region are choosing to farm without expensive imported chemical inputs because they can no longer afford them. They then sell their output at premium prices that exploit the wealthy tourist's desire for organically grown produce.

This growth in tourist consumption of local foods is partly attributable to the globalization of diet, which leads to greater homogenization of world tastes and greater familiarity with international cuisine. The growth of international hotel and restaurant chains has made the hospitality industry one of the most global. Workers are trained centrally in order to maintain the quality of the particular chain. Then they move from country to country as they are promoted within the firm. The impact of such corporate practices is very noticeable in the Caribbean with the rapid replacement of expatriate chefs and managers by internationally trained West Indians. Several studies have shown that locally managed hotels with indigenous chefs are more likely to utilize local foodstuffs (Momsen 1972, 1974).

At least one day a week, many hotels offer a menu of national dishes that use local produce but are cooked according to more sophisticated tastes. However, Butler's (1980) model of the tourist cycle is relevant here, as large-scale mass tourism is most resistant to dietary experimentation. Pattullo (1996, 41) notes that in Barbados "farmers complain that the hotels tell them that their guests only have a fish-and-chip palate." Thus the trend away from beach-based mass tourism to niche tourism such as ecotourism in Dominica (Sharkey and Momsen 1995) and health tourism in St. Lucia (Goodrich 1993) is helping to improve linkages between tourism and local agriculture, especially with the expansion of organic farming (Sharkey 1994).

Today, the food being served to tourists throughout the Caribbean is more varied and is proudly advertised as coming from local sources, indicating a successful turnaround in marketing strategies. Creole cuisine is sought out by more and more visitors, and souvenir food and beverage items are increasingly popular. However, the producers benefiting from this improvement in the linkages between agriculture and tourism are likely to be male farmers with large acreages rather than the traditional small-scale woman subsistence farmer. The companies developing souvenirs often belong to expatriate entrepreneurs. Despite the unequal distribution of benefits, backward linkages from tourism are expanding. After thirty years of halfhearted attempts to develop economic linkages between tourism and agriculture, the closure of their traditional markets for plantation crops has finally forced Caribbean governments and farmers to take the global market visiting their shores seriously and to capitalize on it.

SUGGESTIONS FOR FURTHER READING

Goodrich, Jonathan N., and Dennis J. Gayle. *Tourism Marketing and Management in the Caribbean*. London: Routledge, 1993. Largely written from the perspective of the hospitality industry, this book is the first comprehensive analysis of its kind to be published. Its many short chapters describe specific new developments in Caribbean tourism. The eighteen contributors are all outstanding practitioners, tourism directors, or scholars. As often occurs with compendiums, the contributions vary in quality.

Momsen, Janet H. "Tourism, Gender and Development in the Caribbean." In *Tourism: A Gender Analysis*, edited by Derek Hall and Vivian Kinnaird, 106–20. Chichester: Wiley, 1994. A look at the gendered impact of tourism in the Caribbean with most of the evidence drawn from fieldwork in Barbados.

Pattullo, Polly. *Last Resorts*. London: Latin America Bureau/Cassell, 1996. A thorough, up-to-date study that is interestingly written by a knowledgeable journalist and a Caribbean tourism operator.

7

Jamaica's Information Processing Services: Neoliberal Niche or Structural Limitation?

Beverley Mullings

In 1986, as part of its program of structural adjustment, the Jamaican government pledged its commitment to the development of a new service industry based on the export of information-processing services. These services involve the collection, transmission, storage, processing and display of information, using communications technology such as computers and telecommunications equipment. This industry therefore encompasses a broad range of activities from keying in information for magazine subscriptions or health-insurance claims to providing computer-aided design (CAD) services for engineering operations and the development and conversion of software for a wide range of applications. Studies conducted by the Jamaican government in 1986 envisaged that an industry based on the export of information services would be of significant benefit to the island's development because it would provide foreign exchange earnings, employment, and technology transfers. Now, ten years later, the export information processing industry in Jamaica remains relatively small, specializing in the provision of low value-added services and relying on sweated female labor. In 1995, for example, of the twenty-nine firms involved in the provision of information processing services in Jamaica, 59 percent were engaged in the provision of basic data-entry and data-processing services, with a much smaller percentage of the industry providing other higher value-added services such as geographic information systems (GIS) (7 percent), telemarketing (7 percent) and software development (17 percent) (table 7.1). This chapter examines the factors that have limited the growth of the information processing service indus-

135

TABLE 7.1
Regional Distribution of Information Processing Companies in Jamaica by Type of Service, 1995

Type of information processing	Kingston	Montego Bay	Other	Total	%
Data entry	11	4	2	17	59
Telemarketing	0	2	0	2	7
GIS	1	1	0	2	7
Software and consultancy	5	0	0	5	17
Subtotal	17	7	2	26	90
Sales, training, & marketing	2	0	1	3	10
Total	19	7	3	29	100
Percentage	66	24	10		

Source: JAMPRO and JDI, March 1995

try, with an aim of identifying the role played by (1) sociocultural and economic structures and (2) human agency at both the local and the global level. In doing so, this chapter argues that neoliberal export-oriented industrialization strategies have been pursued without due regard for the local, cultural, and structural realities of the Jamaican economy and society. It concludes that without an industrial strategy that is sensitive to the political and sociocultural structures that influence economic change, Jamaica will continue to pursue programs of industrial development that neither contribute to reducing existing inequalities nor encourage sustainable forms of industrial development.

STRUCTURAL ADJUSTMENT AND INDUSTRIAL RESTRUCTURING

The policies of neoliberal macroeconomic stabilization and adjustment that have characterized World Bank and IMF lending since the 1980s represent the single most important influence on the shape and character of recent industrial policy in Jamaica. Policies of adjustment in Jamaica for the most part have focused on macroeconomic policies such as abolishing or liberalizing foreign exchange and import controls in order to remove barriers to free trade and devaluing currency to make locally produced goods and services more globally competitive. The longer-term restructuring of industry has constituted an equally important, interrelated objective. Guided by its neoliberal underpinnings, industrial policy under structural adjustment has focused largely on stimulating economic growth through promoting sectors that promise to be lucrative sources of foreign exchange earnings.

Export-Oriented Industrialization

A major component of this export-oriented strategy has been the creation of new industrial spaces designed to attract foreign direct investment. As discussed in chapter 5, efforts to diversify exports have generally focused on attracting new assembly operations in free trade areas known as export processing zones (EPZs). EPZs in Jamaica have been attractive to foreign investors because they provide locational facilities as well as generous fiscal and labor incentives. Incentives range from direct concessions such as 100 percent tax holidays on profits in perpetuity and duty-free imports of capital, consumer goods, and raw materials to more indirect ones, such as the public provision of factory sites, utilities, infrastructure, arrears subsidies, and interest rates.[1] The only requirement on investors in these enclave areas is to conduct all transactions in U.S. dollars and to sell all finished goods and services outside of the Jamaican market.

The importance of EPZs to Jamaica's export-oriented industrial strategy cannot be overstated. Between 1981 and 1995, gross exports from the free zones increased from $14 to $317 million (PIOJ 1987, 1996). This resulted in actual foreign exchange earnings of $65 million and employment for 15,373 persons[2] in 1995 (Willmore 1994; PIOJ 1996; Raymond 1992). A number of new export industries have gravitated to the EPZs. The most prominent of these include garment assembly and manufacture, nontraditional agricultural products,[3] and information processing services. Of these three industries, garment manufacture has provided the highest foreign exchange earnings. In comparison to garment manufacture, information processing has been a far less lucrative free-zone activity. Despite the fact that exports grew tenfold, rising from $1.5 million to $17 million between 1986 and 1991 (JAMPRO 1993), this sector's contribution to exports constituted just over a tenth of the value of exports from the garment sector.

While the state's emphasis on neoliberal export-led growth strategies has been largely influenced by the loan conditionalities imposed by international lending agencies, its willingness to implement those strategies can also be seen as indicative of the state's response to the structure of competition that has developed within the global economy over the past fifty years (Thomas 1988). Innovations in technology have increased the volume and pace of international flows of goods and services and has led to the increased internationalization of production. Domestic markets no longer account for the majority of the sales of manufactured goods, since the markets for most major industrial products are now international, facilitated largely by the activities of foreign direct investors primarily from multinational corporations (MNCs). Such "globalizing" tendencies as were discussed in chapter 1, however, are also occurring in an environment of growing regionalism. The consolidation of supranational trading and economic blocs, for example, is indicative of narrowed trade opportunities facing countries that are not incorporated (Hirst and Thompson 1992). While trading blocs like the European Union and NAFTA are not new, they have increased in number, territorial scope, and function, conferring competitive advantages on member states in areas such as information technology, telecommunications, and biotechnology.

While the policy-based strategies of international lending agencies, as well as the general trend toward more diversified trade in global markets, represent some of the most powerful influences on current Jamaican industrial policy, they are not the only ones. Also of importance has been the relationship between particular political regimes in Jamaica and various local interest groups, the struggles among various interest groups themselves, and the impact of these struggles on the actual implementation and outcome of policy. As the study of the export information processing service industry demonstrates, the combination of these global economic trends and local social relations has produced a complex set of uncoordinated and often contradictory practices that have limited this industry's prospects for sustainable development.

Export Information Processing Services

Despite its relatively marginal contribution to foreign exchange earnings in Jamaica, there are potential benefits to be derived from the export of information processing services. In 1995 the value of the global information processing industry was estimated to be over $1,000 billion, with the United States accounting for approximately 40 percent of revenue. Within North America alone, there were over 27,000 sites with data-entry operations that employed over 10 million people in 1995 (fig. 7.1). While much of the industry is still composed of in-house sites within sales or distribution departments, technological advances have allowed several segments of the market to open up, allowing firms to outsource to regions or countries that offer lower-cost services. As a result, service bureaus in 1995 represented about 60 percent of the volume of information process-ing services with over seven hundred data-entry bureaus serving the United States alone.

In recognition of the potential employment and earnings to be derived from the global information processing market, the Jamaican government decided to create an enabling environment for the development of such an industry. In its development plan for 1990–95 the Jamaican government outlined its commitment to the development of this industry. It stated that

> the export of information services is seen as an area for immediate action by Government. In the last 5 years the industry has grown from 2 to 29 compa-nies, 25 of which are Jamaican owned and operated and located outside the free zones. The United States possesses a large and growing market for these services, with revenue from data processing totaling some $27.1 billion in 1989, an increase of 13 percent over 1988. (PIOJ 1990, 84)

In the five-year development plan the state's belief in the developmental potential of export information services was clear. They suggested that, in keeping with the growing contribution of services to gross domestic product worldwide, export information services in Jamaica could rapidly

Figure 7.1. The global value of information processing services, 1995.

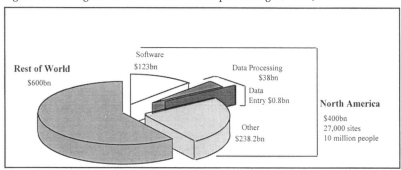

Source: Adapted from Schware and Hume (1996).

increase foreign exchange earnings and savings. This industry was also attractive because it had the potential to provide employment for semi-skilled women, a group that experienced high levels of unemployment. Particularly for women under twenty-five years of age, where unemployment levels were almost twice that of their male counterparts (PIOJ 1995), the expansion of this sector was seen as desirable. Other potential advantages to be gained from the development of information services for export included the environmentally friendly nature of an industry that relied on telecommunications infrastructure for transmission and the relatively low start-up costs associated with setting up individual firms.

The Rise of Export Information Processing Services

In order to encourage the growth of this industry the state introduced two types of incentives—one infrastructural and the other fiscal. High speed data transmission technology was considered essential to the industry's success because it would allow foreign investors and their clients to outsource jobs to Jamaica and receive the processed data instantaneously through direct computer links. In so doing, potential clients could maintain control over paper-based data, which would not need to be transported physically to Jamaica to be processed. The government therefore sought to facilitate high speed data transmission through the construction of a teleport. This plan came to fruition in 1989 when the Jamaica Digiport International (JDI) was constructed in a free zone area in Montego Bay (see map 3). The digiport was built by a consortium composed of the privatized telecommunications company Telecommunications of Jamaica (TOJ), its parent company (Cable and Wireless) and AT&T. It offers services such as international long distance (ILD), advanced 800 services, switched 56 services, and dedicated private lines for data transmission of speeds ranging from 56kbps to 1.5mbps at volume discounted rates (these are explained in table 7.3 below).

The JDI was situated in the Montego Bay free zone in order to attract investors who would provide foreign exchange to the government through their rental of free-zone factory space, infrastructure, and related activities carried out in the free zone, as well as local employment. In exchange, investors were given access to the fiscal incentives made available to free-zone investors.

Fiscal incentives were also provided to investors who were located outside the free zone through the Export Industry Encouragement Act (EIEA) and the Industrial Incentives Act. Under these two pieces of legislation investors were able to benefit from tax holidays, as well as customs and excise duty remissions for periods of between three and ten years. In addition to the direct incentives provided to companies setting up infor-

mation processing firms, the state also provided indirect support by establishing a training program for prospective data-entry operators under
the Human Employment and Resource Training (HEART) scheme. The
ability to access these incentives, however, was short-lived. In response to
an IMF loan facility negotiation[4] the incentives offered under the EIEA
were withdrawn in 1989 (JAMPRO 1993; Pearson 1993, 291). In 1995 a
moratorium was placed on further assistance under the Industrial Incentives Act.

The Rise of a Local Export Sector

The response of the private sector to the incentives provided by government in the early 1980s was extremely encouraging. Between 1983 and
1990 the number of firms exporting information processing services from
Jamaica increased from two to thirty-seven (table 7.2). The successful
expansion of the sector, however, was largely due to the growth of locally
owned companies, the majority of which were located outside the JDI.
The industry was unusual in this regard because it attracted a new breed
of Jamaican entrepreneur, the black, middle-class professional, who normally would not have come to own the means of production (Pearson

TABLE 7.2
Spatial Distribution of Information Processing Service Companies in Jamaica,
1985–1995

Year	Inside EPZ	Outside EPZ	Total
1985	0	2	2
1986	0	3	3
1987	1	8	9
1988	2	n/a	n/a
1989	4	25	29
1990	8	29	37
1991	7	n/a	n/a
1992	8	20	28
1993	9	20	29
1994	11	19	30
1995	7	19	26

Sources: Jampro's list of companies providing information processing services (various
years), exporters of information group (1989), PIOJ (1990), data supplied by the Jamaica
Digiport International

1993; interviews with Jamaican owners of data entry firms 1994). Given the dominance and control held by minority ethnic elites[5] in the traditional manufacturing and services industries, and the extension of this power to the political arena (Gordon 1991; Reid 1977; Stone 1980, 1991), the growth of the information processing industry represented a small but significant change in the class and racial structure of Jamaican industry.

While the local private sector responded enthusiastically to incentives offered by the state, their foreign counterparts did not. The lack of commensurate growth in the number of foreign direct investors to the JDI led to a curious situation: the majority of the industry (located outside of the free zone area) had access neither to high-speed data transmission technology nor to the more generous incentives of the JDI. The punitive effect of the differential incentive structure on investors with local currency was highlighted in 1989 when a group representing local information processing firms, the Exporters of Information Processing Services (EXIS), criticized the government for failing to provide the local industry with support even though it was clear that they had contributed significantly to the development of the sector, employing approximately 2,000 persons and contributing $10 million per year to the local economy (Exporters of Information Group 1989). The complaints of the largely locally owned segment of the industry went largely unheard as the government continued to support the JDI's efforts to attract investors with foreign currency to the free zone. New investment outside the digiport dwindled to a trickle when the moratorium on incentives to investors located outside the free zone area was implemented (Mullings 1995).

The structure of the industry that was created very early on has not significantly changed. Most industry is still located outside the digiport without access to the incentives currently offered to their foreign competitors. While local firms now have access to the high speed technology provided by TOJ, the cost of these services is considerably higher than those offered by the JDI. In 1995, for example, a three-minute international call made by a firm outside the digiport would cost between two and five times more than if made within the JDI. Similarly, a company using a 56kbps data tarnsmission line in its operations would pay double the amount in monthly charges that a similar firm in the digiport would (table 7.3). The impact of the duality created in the industry can be seen in the subsequent growth of the industry. Between 1990 and 1995, the number of companies located outside the digiport fell steadily from twenty-nine to nineteen, while those in the digiport peaked at eleven companies in 1994 and then fell to seven in 1995 (table 7.2). While part of this decline can be explained by the search of these largely foreign owned firms for more advantageous locational opportunities (four companies, for example, relocated to North America[6] in order to take advantage of

TABLE 7.3
A Comparison of Selected International Telecommunication Services Provided by TOJ and JDI in Jamaica, 1995

Type of Service	TOJ	JDI	% difference
IDD[1] Toll Rates (Based on 3-min. call)	3.23-3.82	0.57-1.68	230-570
Switched 56-Half Channel[2]			
Installation charge	1,500.00	1,995.00	-33
Monthly fee	200.00	100.00	200
(Rate/minute)	0.75-1.25	0.43-0.80	160-170
Leased Channels[3]			
T-1 half channel/month	21,980.0	18,000.0	120
T-1 full channel/month	49,500.0	n/a	n/a
Installation charge	5,000.00	n/a	n/a
56 kpbs/month	2,800.00	1,812.00	150
Installation charge	1,500.00	n/a	n/a

Source: Data provided by TOJ (Telecommunications of Jamaica) and JDI (Jamaica Digiport International)
[1]International Direct Dialing
[2]A private digital transmission line capable of transmitting data at a rate of 56 kilobits per second
[3]A private digital transmission line capable of transmitting data at a rate of 1.544 megabits per second

its cheaper telecommunications and operational costs), the inability to make workers conform to the requirements of this Taylorist industry was also a push factor.

Factors Behind the Fall of the Information Processing Industry

Shortsightedness on the part of the state, particularly its response to the changing global economic environment and the pressures from its international lenders, limited the growth of the industry. In responding to the policy-based adjustment programs of the IMF and World Bank, the Jamaican government instituted policies that satisfied their demand for a reduced role from the state in industrial development. These policies, however, were particularly injurious to the development of an indigenous, export-oriented private sector because they focused exclusively on short-term foreign exchange earnings rather than longer-term local industrial development. Thus the unequal access to low-cost, high-speed data transmission services between investors with foreign currency and those without, as well as the early removal of fiscal incentives to investors outside the free zone, created a dual industry that stunted the long-term growth of the industry. While the state created the duality that currently characterizes the industry, there were other factors behind its limited success. Technological advances, insufficient resources for finance and marketing, unstable firm-supplier relationships, and reliance on unsustainable forms of work organization have also contributed to the decline of this sector. Superimposed on an already biased enabling environment, other local and global structural constraints have further constrained the sustained development of export information processing services.

Technological Advances

Very early on in the industry's history, Jamaica established itelf as a data-entry locale, competing with countries like the Philippines, Mexico, and China on the basis of a supply low-cost labor. Data entry was identified as a profitable service to export because there already existed a pool of English-speaking workers with typing skills who could be trained quickly for computers. Jamaica's geographical proximity to the United States allowed firms to send paper-based documents to Jamaica by courier, have them converted to computer readable formats, and returned on disk by air freight or courier in as little as twenty-four hours. While data entry represented a segment of the industry where Jamaica had a comparative advantage, it was also the lowest-value-added, rapidly disappearing part. Data entry has become an obsolete service as technological advances such as optical character recognition (OCR), bar code systems (BCS), and on-line transaction processing (OLTP) have reduced the need for many paper-based data conversion jobs. In addition, high-speed data transmission capabilities have eroded much of the geographical advantage that arose from Jamaica's ability to promise a quick turnaround of processed data. As technology minimized the competitive advantages conferred by proximity to North America, the main export market, Jamaica acquired new international competitors from the Philippines, Bangladesh, and China. By the 1990s the international competitive environment had changed significantly to one where quality of service was becoming as important as cost to importers of this service. The benefits therefore of an efficient labor force and the ability to provide information processing services for which there was a high value added became even more important than the ability to provide a cheap service.

Inadequate Financial and Marketing Resources

Local firms were also hampered by the general lack of financial resources to improve and market their services. Early entrants from the local segment of the industry, for example, experienced significant difficulties in gaining access to venture capital from the local financial institutions. While the state provided some financial concessions under the Export Industries Encouragement Act and the Industrial Incentives Act,[7] their early discontinuation triggered a shakeout in the industry as firms that were still in the learning process found themselves with full fiscal responsibilities. The learning curve for the new entrants was particularly steep because few had estimated the costs involved in finding markets for their services (Mullings 1995). Most were insufficiently prepared for the large financial commitment that was required for them to adequately compete with local and international data processing firms for contracts. Although the government provided some amount of marketing support, few of the entrants to the industry employed rigorous marketing programs. In addition, the withdrawal of government support to the local industry had a negative effect on the local financial sector which began to view the local industry as a high-risk sector (Exporters of Information Group 1989). The local banking sector was reluctant to provide financial support to the industry, and this was identified by many local companies as a major reason for their slow expansion. As a local manager and owner of a data entry firm in Kingston described it,

> because it is a new high tech area that few people understand they [the financial institutions] are not favorably disposed to this type of business. So they therefore very grudgingly give you some support, and you will find out in business that if you get inadequate support it is sometimes worse than getting no support at all. Because if you get no support, you're supposed to close the doors and go out of business. If you get inadequate support it gives

you a shot in the arm and you continue, but because it is inadequate, it is not enough to pull you out of the hole so what you put in also gets spent and gets wasted. (Interview data 1994)

Without financial support, many of the local companies could afford neither to modernize their computer hardware and software nor to take advantage of more efficient modes of data transmission. The inability to finance technological improvements not only worsened the situation but it also created a vicious cycle. Many firms were unable to secure contracts because their operations were less efficient and obsolete; without contracts, few were able to secure the financing needed to modernize their operations. In interviews other managers alluded to the fact that unless the traditional owners of capital in Jamaica found the information processing industry to be a lucrative endeavor from which they themselves could profit, the local segment was unlikely to receive financial support in the future. One manager, for example, felt that unless the telecommunications company TOJ, currently chaired by Mr. Mayer Matalon,[8] became an exporter of information services, the local segment of the industry would never be able to benefit from the cheaper telecommunication services.

Unstable Firm-Supplier Relationships

The relationship between firms entering the industry and their markets has been equally problematic. Unlike Barbados, where the information processing industry is dominated by three large firms that are the back offices of major U.S. corporations,[9] firms in the Jamaican industry have been of two main types: local firms seeking U.S. markets for their services and U.S. service bureaus in search of lower-cost labor. The subcontractual relationship, while promoted by many as an innovative, flexible approach to the production process (Scott and Storper 1990; Teague 1990; Thompson et al. 1991), has provided few benefits to subcontractors. Both local and foreign-owned subcontracting firms must constantly find markets to sell their services to in order to remain profitable. The inability to secure dedicated markets was a factor that contributed to the failure of many of the early entrants and created an industry characterized by an unstable organization of work. The prevalence of subcontracting in Jamaican information-processing firms has had a significant impact on the stability of the industry as a whole, since it would appear that the overwhelming rationale for this type of firm-supplier relationship has been to minimize perceived risks and responsibilities.[10]

The instability of the subcontractual relationship is demonstrated in the difficulties experienced by firms in maintaining a constant flow of contracts. Most data-entry firms in Jamaica receive jobs from companies seeking to contract out specific data conversion jobs. Few local companies manage to secure a sufficient number of long-term contracts to maintain a constant flow of work. As one manager stated, "Short-term contracts mean that if you are doing a project for three months you will have to staff up to deal with that. At the end of three months if you do not have another contract starting exactly behind that one, then you're back down to a valley situation" (Mullings 1995).

Different constraints face the segment of the industry located in the free zone, where the majority of firms are the back offices of U.S. service bureaus. Most of these firms have located in Jamaica in order to take advantage of the island's lower labor costs and the incentives offered by the free zone. Unlike the local segment of the industry, the free zone segment has been constrained by the relatively high turnover rate of companies. Between 1987 and 1995 twenty firms entered the free zone and eleven left it. The firms that left the industry remained in operation for an average of three years. For particular subsectors of the industry the turnover rate was even higher. Between 1988 and 1995, for example, six telemarketing companies started business on the island but remained in operation only two years. Companies that left the JDI cited a number of reasons for their decisions to close their operations. In the case of one telemarketing and one data-processing company, the high cost of the telecommunication service made their operations unprofitable. In the case of another data-processing firm, the manager was dissatisfied with the quality and productivity of recruited labor and subsequently relocated to the United States. While the dominance of the higher-paying tourist industry in Montego Bay partly explained difficulties that were experienced in recruiting suitable workers, the very low rates of pay and poor working conditions were also contributing factors.

Unsustainable Work Processes

Much of the instability of employment in the industry can be attributed to the relationship between exporting firms in Jamaica and their importers overseas. Because the majority of the firms in the Jamaican industry subcontract their services, few have direct control over output levels and therefore respond to changes in demand by varying the size of their workforce. This type of worker flexibility has been particularly damaging because the industry has not been able to secure a stable labor force. Firms are continuously recruiting, training, and laying off workers. Firms therefore find themselves in a vicious cycle where the inability to reap the benefits of a stable, mature workforce limits the extent to which firms are able to expand or deliver a stable, consistently high-quality service. The impact of this form of labor flexibility is doubly damaging, however, because the industry is increasingly perceived by potential employees as a form of employment to be avoided.

The organization of labor in the Jamaican data processing firms can best be described as *flexibly Taylorist* because it combines elements of labor flexibility with rigid controls over the work process itself. Despite the perceived white-collar status of information processing, the organization of the work process is quite similar to blue-collar factory production. In fact, the organization of data processing work in Jamaica is similar to that described by Soares (1991, 156), who describes data-processing centers in Brazil as factories in which the raw materials are the data-entry documents that roll along the assembly line.

In terms of labor flexibility, data-entry services in Jamaica display many of the features described by Atkinson and Gregory (1985) in their model of the flexible firm. Atkinson and Gregory identify four main types of flexibility: numerical flexibility, functional flexibility, distancing (particularly through subcontracting), and pay flexibility. Numerical and pay flexibility (the ability of employers to vary the amount and value of labor used at short notice) and distancing (the ability of employees to be spatially removed from markets through a range of subcontractual arrangements) are the most prevalent features of the Jamaican information processing industry.

Like the Atkinson and Gregory model, most data-entry firms in Jamaica maintain a very small group of core workers, largely supervisors, some keying staff and staff involved in data quality control. These employees are full-time workers and they are assured a basic wage or salary even when there are no jobs to be done. In most information processing firms, data-entry operators form the bulk of the peripheral workforce. These workers occupy a very unstable position in the industry because although most are described as full-time employees, they function as part-time workers in terms of the conditions under which they are employed. Most data-entry operators, for example, are paid at rates that are closely tied to the availability of work. During the periods when a firm has no contracted work, such workers are either laid off until there is a need for their services or are kept on at a subsistence wage until more work comes in. In 1995 subsistence rates of J$100 (U.S. $2.85) per day were quoted by workers.

Not surprisingly, issues of both pay and conditions represent the most dissatisfying aspects of the industry in the workers' eyes. Jamaican data-entry operators are among the lowest paid information workers in the Caribbean and the world. In 1994 it was estimated that the average data-entry operator earned U.S. $0.80–1.00 per hour. While higher than the hourly wage commanded by workers in the garment manufacturing industry (estimated at $0.88 per hour in 1995 [JAMPRO 1995]), this rate is much lower than that earned by secretaries, who presumably would have similar skills. Low wages are a significant source of discontent for workers in the industry, but the incentives and punishments built into the calculation of wages are an even greater problem.

Most companies pay a basic wage with a variety of performance-related bonuses. Among data-entry firms, the basic wage quoted in interviews was $400–550 per week for a forty-hour work week (U.S. $13–18 at January 1994 exchange rates). This is slightly above the existing minimum wage of $400 (U.S. $12) for a forty-hour work week. Above this basic wage, the average data-entry keyer's take-home wage is directly related to the number of accurate keystrokes input per week. The wage rates offered for work completed above the basic wages varies, however, according to the type of job that a firm has been contracted to do. Simple jobs such as credit cards are the cheapest ($150 or U.S. $4.40 per 1,000 records), while more complex jobs such as handwritten legal documents are more expensive. Workers are paid according to the complexity and subsequent cost of a particular job. In interviews, managers stated that the average worker engaged in an average job would earn $1,200–2,000 per week (equivalent to U.S. $40–67 per forty-hour week at January 1994 exchange rates).

The ability to electronically monitor individual accuracy and speed also allows managers to reward or punish workers through the wage process. Workers who are able to accurately key at the speeds set for particular jobs are often rewarded with higher rates of pay. Those who are unable to meet daily or weekly targets are likely to be paid at basic rates of pay or may even have deductions taken from their wages for mistakes made. The penalties for mistakes may be high. One company that paid its workers on a per-record basis, for example, penalized for mistakes by deducting amounts equivalent to the value of one record if more than two mistakes were detected per hundred records keyed. The impact of this form of wage compensation on the instability of employment in the industry is tremendous because no worker is able to predetermine what the monetary value of her work will be.

Poor Management-Worker Relationships

The poor image of the export information processing industry in the eyes of its workers goes beyond issues of instability of employment. In interviews with workers in the industry it became clear that the relationship between workers and management as well as the structure of the work process itself was as problematic as the instability of employment and low levels of remuneration. Not surprisingly, the high level of control over the work process combined with the rigidity of the division of labor produce a tense relationship between workers and managers. It is at the level of management-worker relations that the Jamaican export information industry demonstrates a hybrid version of flexible Taylorism. This method of organizing work harks back to the colonial experience with its embedded class and racial relations (Charles 1992; Klak 1995; Sunshine 1988). The sharp class divisions that have historically characterized Jamaican society have created an especially top-down and rancorous relationship between managers and workers (Manley 1975; Stone 1986, 1991). In the export information industry, not only did workers feel that they were viewed by management as easily replaceable components of the work process, but many argued that they were treated as less than equal human beings. This feeling was expressed by one woman who stated:

> You only see their names on the door . . . you don't see the manager for three months or four months or more. [When you do] you don't even get "hello, how are you" or "good morning." They just pass and look at us, the dogs! They cannot say hi or good morning . . . because they are better than you . . . they don't rap with you. Listen, you are not in their class! (Interview data 1995).

The sustainability of top-down management styles based on scientific management methods is currently being questioned (Cole and Mogab 1995; Cowell and Boxill 1995; Soares 1991). But the structure of the markets in which most data processing firms compete encourages firms to adopt strictly monitored work processes that minimize scope for creativity. The product of the current organization of work, in both local and foreign-owned segments, is a demoralized labor force whose main concerns revolve around trying to leave the industry rather than trying to achieve occupational mobility within it. In nearly every interview, managers expressed dissatisfaction with the overall educational level of data-entry staff and their dedication to the job. Many felt that new entrants to the industry lacked skills in comprehension and mathematics, which severely limited productivity. In focus group interviews, however, workers explained that the current organization and instability of work, the low levels of pay, and the absence of any prospects for occupational mobility all resulted in low levels of motivation. As one worker explained:

> Certain people . . . if they're getting low pay and they're comfortable they will not leave. But if you're getting no salary, you're pressured by management and you're treated like shit . . . there is no form of motivation, nothing! (Interview data 1995)

The high levels of staff turnover, low productivity, and motivation among workers are indicative of employee demoralization. Few workers view the industry as a place to start a career, and many enter the industry with the principal hope of gaining computer skills that will make them more attractive to prospective employees in the banking and insurance sectors.

Not surprisingly, labor turnover in the industry is very high, with workers averaging two or three years within any one firm (Mullings 1995). Most workers remain in the industry between four and six months before moving into clerical and secretarial positions in private sector companies. The high levels of turnover have been damaging to the industry, as few firms have been able to reap the benefits of an experienced workforce. For example, firms reported in 1994 average annual turnover rates of 50 percent (survey data 1994), with one company reporting that the number of workers who had left within the year was equivalent to three times his present level of staff (120 persons). These reported turnover rates are much higher than those found in the survey of data processing firms in North America in 1992, where turnover rates of only 8 percent were reported (The Association for Work Process Improvement 1993). High turnover and low motivation damage the industry, and prospective investors are beginning to view Jamaica as an unsuitable place to outsource processing jobs. Unlike Barbados, where average wages are higher[11] and where the image is one of an efficient service, the Jamaican industry is increasingly being viewed as one that is cheap but not efficient.

Toward a Sustainable Export Information Processing Service Industry: Exploring the Options

Under the aegis of neoliberal structural adjustment, Jamaica has embarked on policies that have been short-term, uncoordinated, and subject to the demands of local and global hegemonic groups. These policies have limited the expansion of the export information services sector and have encouraged forms of work organization that are deeply exploitative of labor. As an industrial strategy, neoliberal export-oriented industrialization appears to entrench rather than eliminate existing inequalities, since the market at all times favors capital flows to sectors that promise the highest rates of profit. As the export information processing industry demonstrates, the inequalities between men and women, rich and poor, elites and nonelites, and local and foreign investors have all been heightened under this industrialization strategy. The entrenchment of existing inequalities under neoliberal, export-oriented industrialization is demonstrated in the high proportion of women who work in the strictly monitored data-entry firms for extremely low rates of pay. While the fact that these women are employed is positive, given the high level of female unemployment in Jamaica, the low pay and the instability force women to depend on their families and other social networks for survival. Given that these flexibly Taylorist industries represent the main forms of formal sector employment currently open to semiskilled women, it is likely that the gender inequalities that currently exist will intensify as fewer alternatives for employment become available.

The tendency to entrench existing inequalities, which appears to be a feature of neoliberal export-oriented industrialization, can also be seen in the strategies used by large international corporations to ensure their own profitability. While export-oriented industrialization in Jamaica has focused on attracting foreign direct investment, this strategy has not been successful. Few foreign corporations have been keen to take the responsibilities and risks associated with offshore investment. Most have sought instead to minimize both by contracting out routine jobs. Building an export sector based on subcontracted information services, however, is fraught with instability, particularly for countries like Jamaica that specialize in the export of the least value-added services. Jamaica's reliance on subcontracted data entry, in this regard, represents an entrenchment of its position in the international division of labor because the services that it exports are low in value but high in terms of the number of alternative suppliers.

Jamaica's pursuit of a neoliberal, export-oriented industrialization strategy has been neither stable nor sustainable. The social relations that affect the industry's progress—exogenous policy pressure from international institutions such as the IMF and the United States, clientelist relations between elites, and worker resistance to the industry's demand for high levels of efficiency at low wage levels—are not mutually supportive. For the information-processing industry to develop in ways that can be sustained in the long term, the state must become more active, transparent, and democratic in its formulation and execution of industrial policy. Unless Jamaica can begin to invest in the human and physical resources required for entry into higher value-added market niches, it will continue to be the global outpost for cheap exploitable labor, and the vicious cycle of poverty, inequality and exploitation will only deepen in its intensity. Investing in human and physical infrastructure, however, is a costly endeavor with long-term rewards. Given the state's inability and the local private sector's reluctance to finance such expenditures, alternative ways of investing in social infrastructure must be sought. One potential solution may lie in the formation of regional alliances, particularly with other countries in the Caribbean Basin (see chap. 4). By developing and sharing resources for the training and education of workers in the industry, common standards of excellence, pay, and working conditions could be set. This would go a long way toward stabilizing wages in the region and facilitating the development of higher value-added services. Many of the islands in the Eastern Caribbean are now beginning to offer informatics services. Their presence is a competitive threat for those islands already involved in this export sector. In an environment where regional re-sources for the development of social infrastructure were shared, the entry of other Caribbean neighbors could signal the first step toward a more enduring and sustainable industry.

NOTES

1. In 1992 the lease rate for a standard factory building was $4.25 per square foot per annum, with a minimum requirement of 10,000 square feet.

2. A survey of garment factories in Kingston in the late 1980s found that 88.9 percent of the workforce was female (Willmore 1994). Given the high level of unemployment among women under twenty-five (in 1993, 31 percent), the free zones provide an important source of employment.

3. These refer to winter vegetables, horticulture, and ethnic food crops and fruit.

4. The World Bank and the IMF dissuade governments from picking strategic sectors to subsidize investment, arguing that it would distract governments from their preferred role as providers of infrastructure, and would lure capital away from labor-intensive "less strategic sectors" to high-wage, capital-intensive sectors.

5. Reid (1977) argues that economic power in Jamaica is held by twenty-one families joined by a range of mutually supporting interest groups.

6. Including Mexico.

7. These concessions included tax holidays and customs and excise duty remissions for three to ten years.

8. A powerful local elite that Reid (1977) describes as one of the five richest families in Jamaica.

9. Pantin (1995) notes the dominance of these large employers in the Barbadian informatics industry. Of the fourteen firms exporting these services in Barbados in 1995, three provided 72 percent of total employment. One, American Airlines, operates a back office that provides ticket processing services and employs just over 1,000 workers (or almost 50 percent of the jobs; Freeman 1993).

10. Klak (1994) argues that media images of crime and violence in Jamaica have been damaging to the economy because they have increased investor perceptions of the level of risk. The concept of risk, however, goes beyond perceptions of crime. Subcontracting has also become the preferred investment strategy of multinational investors because it allows companies to achieve assured quality of product or service without direct participation or control over the work process.

11. The average hourly wage in Barbados in 1994 was U.S. $2.44 compared to U.S. $0.90 in Jamaica (Schware and Hume 1994).

SUGGESTIONS FOR FURTHER READING

Freeman, C. "Designing Women: Corporate Discipline and Barbados's Off-Shore Pink-Collar Sector." *Cultural Anthropology* 8 (1993): 169–86. Describes the role of female workers in foreign-owned offshore data entry companies in Barbados through a case study of one such firm (1989–91). The clerical work in these information-based businesses resembles earlier assembly-line work in manufacturing plants because of its low pay, low skill, and repetitive nature. These workers constitute a newly gendered, proletarianized class.

Schoonmaker, S. "Regulation Theory and the Politics of Global Restructuring." *Current Perspectives in Social Theory* 15 (1995): 213–44. Provides a strategic-theoretical approach to regulation theory, and shows that political debates over world trade are regulatory attempts to create political conditions for capital accumulation by states. States, in turn, both manipulate regulatory measures and attempt to alter the principles that govern present institutions. The trade of information shows how conflicts between states and capital, and between industrialized and industrializing countries, structure an international market for trade in services.

Dunn, H. "Caribbean Telecommunication Policy: Fashioned by Debt, Dependency, and Underdevelopment." *Media, Culture and Society* 17 (1995): 201–22. Factors contributing to the current monopoly of telecommunications networks and operating companies by Cable and Wireless, a British transnational, are reviewed. Ongoing British imperialism in the current policy and network structure of telecommunications in the Caribbean results from reliance on foreign capital, technology, and managerial expertise. Discusses the implications for delivery of basic telephone services and for regional development.

8

Dominica's Economic Diversification: Microstates in a Neoliberal Era?

James Wiley

While contemporary trends in the global economy challenge virtually all countries, few encounter trials as severe as in small island states traditionally reliant on one or two foreign exchange-earning primary-sector commodities. Many Caribbean nations today confront this problem. Advances in technologies largely developed elsewhere have enhanced the mobility of capital, altered production systems, and allowed for more flexible sourcing of inputs that threaten to destabilize the already dependent economies of the region. Watson (1994a) describes these processes as a techno-paradigm shift that undermines the ability of the traditional nation-state system to manage national economies. Market liberalization is a requisite for globalization and defines neoliberalism, supported by the United States, the World Bank, and the IMF, as its underlying ideology (Watson 1994b). The ensuing shift deemphasizes "extensive resource-driven technologies" in favor of innovative technologies, implying changes in social processes in the affected countries.

This chapter focuses on the efforts of Dominica, a small Eastern Caribbean state whose exports are dominated by bananas, to adapt to the new realities of international trade. In Dominica, the more general problem of adjusting to economic globalization is exacerbated by two potentially devastating events: a recent change in the European Union's banana import policy and the imminent demise of the Lomé Convention, which now affords Dominica preferential market access to the E.U. The latter, anticipated in 2002, stems from the Uruguay round of General Agreement on Tariffs and Trade (GATT) negotiations that led to the creation of the World Trade Organization (WTO). The WTO has a charge to eliminate special arrangements that interfere with free trade and enforcement powers, outcomes championed by the United States. These two developments offer strong stimuli for Dominica to pursue a path of economic diversification, but this ironically occurs at a time when its small size proves more disadvantageous than ever in achieving economies of scale that permit greater efficiency and price competitiveness. Thus, Dominica exemplifies the tightrope walk described by Conway (chap. 3) faced by the many Caribbean microstates in a macro world economy.

Small size is not the only variable of importance to the contemporary situations of countries like Dominica. Rather, size interacts with other variables, including a tradition of highly specialized economies, declining terms of trade for primary sector goods, metropole-oriented transport linkages, a shortage of citizens trained in skills necessary to compete in the emerging international division of labor, and a legacy of marginalization dating from the colonial period, to name just a few on the negative side. Smallness, though, offers several possible advantages as well, including higher levels of social cohesion, more effective planning (since planners are closer to the objects of their efforts), and a greater potential for psychological decolonization (see chap. 3; Conway 1991).

The degree of smallness also matters. Hong Kong and Singapore have small territories but populations of several million, while Dominica tallied fewer than 75,000 in its 1991 census, a number that doesn't grow because of the vast emigration (described in chap. 10). This creates a important difference with regard to internal market size. The two city-states also have beneficial physical situations allowing them to play an entrepôt role. Benedict (1967) noted this interaction between location and small size, comparing highly accessible Luxembourg to the remote Seychelles. Dominica and its neighbors lack such advantages and spawn few enterprises based on location, reducing the number of development options available to them. A narrow resource base and small domestic markets can lead to greater economic specialization and dependence on international trade. Together with relative remoteness, this can also yield less diversity in trading partners, something more characteristic of island countries in the Caribbean, the Pacific, or the Indian Ocean than of small European states. Distance also increases export and import costs (Conway 1991).

Public sector finances are also affected by small size (Conway 1991). Very small populations pay a higher per capita price for such basic services as health care, education, and transportation, since the costs of the necessary infrastructure can be amortized over relatively few people (Benedict 1967). This ultimately limits creation of the conditions within which development can proceed. It also renders unwise (or perhaps even inapplicable) neoliberal prescriptions for public sector downsizing such as those that have characterized IMF interventions in many countries (Harris 1996).

The situation encountered by Dominica raises several questions that may appropriately be considered within the broader context of restructuring in the Caribbean Basin. *What role* is there in the future world economy for microstates, particularly island countries, that are unable to generate economies of scale and, therefore, be price competitive for virtually any product? A more suitable question may be, *Is there in fact a role* for such countries in the emerging world economy? A subsequent question, assuming an affirmative response, would be, *What policy initiatives* are needed to address these challenges? Finally, will such initiatives yield *independent* development or will they represent a new version of *dependent* development? The case study presented here attempts to shed light on these issues in a way that suggests applicability beyond Dominica's specific circumstances to those of several of its neighbors.

This chapter, based on interviews, document reviews, primary and secondary sources, and personal observations, considers the challenges confronting Dominican diversification within the greater context of globalization and neoliberalism, and the specific context of the assets and limitations of its small size (chaps. 1, 3 set the context). It begins with a brief explanation of the trade issues conspiring to produce the current crisis. Second, it concisely profiles the country's banana industry to illustrate the difficulty inherent in reorienting its economy away from this dominant export. Third, it assesses the special difficulties intrinsic to the introduction of new products, including market development and infrastructure. Next, government responses to the impending crisis are reviewed, along with several internal and exogenous factors that will affect the outcomes of its efforts to prepare for a postbanana future. By way of conclusion, the chapter evaluates Dominica's prospects in an era of neoliberalism by attempting to answer the questions raised above, at least in a preliminary manner. In the final analysis, its very small size dictates a creative development strategy that does not attempt to compete based on price. The obstacles it encounters and whatever successes it may achieve will prove to be of significant interest to other microstates.

CHANGING THE RULES OF TRADE: BANANAS, THE EUROPEAN UNION, AND THE WTO

Richardson (1992) has described the Caribbean as a region subjected to influence from outside forces, each time generating a response that, in the long run, has helped shape the distinct character of the area and its people. This established pattern continues through the 1990s as once again, decisions and events elsewhere are affecting the basin, challenging Caribbean creativity. Today, the two important sources of change are the E.U. and the newly created WTO.

The complexity of banana geopolitics is indicated by the fact that, among the thousands of products imported by E.U. members, bananas were the last for which an accord was reached within the Single European Market (SEM). Created by the Maestricht Treaty (1991), the SEM mandates that member states develop common policies for all goods imported from nonmembers. SEM rules replaced previous single-country trading arrangements. The significance of this stems from the fact that the banana is the most important, by volume traded, of the world's fresh fruit and vegetable (FFV) commodities, and the E.U. comprises its largest market.

The new banana importation scheme, Council Regulation 404/93, was signed in February 1993 and went into effect on 1 July 1993. The extra time required to negotiate the accord reflected the debate it generated. Much of the controversy can be attributed to the fact that previous banana import policies differed with regard to sources, prices, and tariffs, yielding a highly segmented banana market. As the nature of this segmentation would shape the new regime and, ultimately, affect Dominica's banana exports, a very brief description is appropriate here.

The sources of bananas consumed by E.U. residents fall into three major categories. First, four members, Spain, France, Greece, and Portugal, produce the fruit themselves, though at high labor costs. This internal production is not subject to tariffs. E.U. banana-producing zones are categorized as marginalized regions and qualify for annual agricultural subsidy programs offered to such areas by the European Commission. Council Regulation 404/93 protects banana production in these areas from lower-wage competitors elsewhere by making them eligible for the subsidies.

The second source category involves twelve African-Caribbean-Pacific (ACP) countries linked to former colonial powers in the European Union through the Lomé Convention. This group, including Dominica, is covered by a special banana protocol within Lomé IV, the current accord, and receives preferential access to E.U. markets. Britain is among the E.U. members importing from ACP growers, though at high prices reflecting relatively inefficient production methods among the twelve. Dominica's protected annual market allocation is 71,000 metric tons, which exceeds production levels for the 1990s.

"Third country" producers constitute the final source of E.U. bananas. These are mostly Latin American countries whose industry is dominated by Chiquita, Dole, and Del Monte, large multinational corporations (MNCs) from the United States. Their bananas are more efficiently produced on huge plantations with low labor costs and would, in an unregulated market, likely displace E.U. and ACP bananas. Council Regulation 404/93 established a two million-ton tariff quota for such imports (Article 18), but this quantity falls short of the 1992 total of 2.4 million metric tons of "third country" bananas imported by the E.U., 99 percent of them from Latin America.

Council Regulation 404/93's impacts are far reaching. A detailed description of the pre-1993 E.U. banana market, the new import regime, and its impacts appears in Wiley (1996). Of central interest to this chapter is what it all means for Dominica. At first glance, the new policy seems to protect the island's growers from greater competition by precluding the unrestricted market conditions that the SEM ostensibly intends to create. While this is the case, it also contributed to price convergence within the E.U. banana market, leading to price rises in formerly unrestricted markets but bringing about price declines in previously restricted market countries, including Britain. It is the price decrease in Britain that currently affects Dominica, yielding lower payments for the country's primary export commodity. In addition, the policy itself is under attack by the U.S. government, which, representing the interests of its MNCs, filed a complaint before the WTO. A favorable decision could destabilize the Caribbean banana industry even more rapidly than the second change of importance, which follows.

While the new E.U. banana regime generates short-term problems for Dominica, longer-term impacts on the country's banana industry will be generated by the WTO and its greater penetration into trade matters involving the agricultural sector. This will bring about the demise of the Lomé Convention with the expiration of the fourth round in 2000 and no renewal currently foreseen. Though Lomé is neocolonial in nature, maintaining dependency relationships between E.U. members and their former colonies, the convention is crucial to many ACP states, particularly smaller ones. It shields them from directly competing in world markets. The products covered by Lomé are mostly primary sector commodities. Many are tropical goods, not affecting European production. This was even true of bananas due to the segmented nature of the pre-1993 E.U. market. Through Lomé's STABEX program, the E.U. attempts to reduce the price fluctuations that characterize primary sector goods so that the ACP states can rely on more stable income from their major exports from year to year (Gonzáles 1995). This constitutes a form of aid within an otherwise trade-oriented plan but conveys a recognition of the structural problems inherent in North-South relations within the world economy.

Dominica will be seriously affected by the end of Lomé. Without it or a similar accord, the country loses its preferential access to British consumers and will be forced to compete in that and other markets. That is not something it is currently prepared to do, as a review of the structure of its major industry indicates.

DOMINICAN GOTHIC: THE FAMILY BANANA FARM

Had Grant Wood ever attempted to paint a Dominican equivalent of his famous *American Gothic*, he would surely have selected one of the country's many banana farmers as his subject, for it is the family farm that lies at the heart of the island's economy, just as it does in neighboring St. Lucia and St. Vincent. An understanding of the structure of banana cultivation is essential for an appreciation of the problems that lie ahead for Dominica.

The banana is the latest in a line of crops that have dominated Dominica's landscape since the arrival of Europeans more than three centuries ago. According to Honychurch (1995), coffee was the principal crop of the early colonial planters. It was followed in turn by cocoa, vanilla beans, oranges, grapefruit, and limes, ranking Dominica as the world's leading exporter of the latter during the 1930s. Each of these stages was characterized by a high level of specialization; thus, contemporary banana dependency is merely a new rendition of an old theme that has seen one dominant crop replaced by another when market conditions for the former decline (Robinson 1995). This time, though, the country faces a very different global economy as it prepares once again to search for substitutes for its principal foreign exchange earner.

The rise of banana cultivation in Dominica in the early 1950s occurred as a result of British colonial policy. To quell growing unrest in its colonies in the region, Britain sought new economic activities to replace enterprises then in decline. Jamaica, the principal supplier of bananas for Britain, could not meet growing postwar demand, leaving an unfulfilled market share. Geest Ltd., a British company with Dutch origins, was invited to establish a banana industry in the Eastern Caribbean, including Dominica. The company already had a distribution network in place in Britain, and this was utilized to market bananas. Unlike the U.S. banana multinationals operating in Latin America, Geest did not enter directly into the production phase of the industry; thus large, infrastructure-laden, foreign-owned plantations have never characterized Dominican banana cultivation. With market quotas and tariff-free access guaranteed, Geest established a monopoly over the Windward Islands' banana industry, serving as sole transporter and marketer of the fruit shipped from Dominica, St. Lucia, St. Vincent, and Grenada (Thomson 1987), until it sold its banana operation at the end of 1995 (as discussed below). The Geest ship visited those islands weekly, loading produce for shipment to

Southampton in Britain. Significantly, each island alone is incapable of generating sufficient volume to merit its own weekly call, a fact severely reducing Dominica's leverage in negotiating prices and market access for its goods.

Scale, therefore, is important to consider when profiling Dominica's banana industry. The island's precipitous terrain—its difficult topography caused Trouillot (1988) to label it a "patchwork of enclaves"—works against the development of large plantations. Much of the cultivation occurs on inclines, often rather steep slopes. While plantations did exist during the colonial period, their size was modest by world standards. Most were broken into small holdings during the 1970s and 1980s, yielding an array of family farms worked by yeoman farmers. While the number of such units decreased in recent years, the Dominica Banana Marketing Corporation (DBMC), a parastatal agency that markets the country's bananas, counted 5,779 in 1993 (DBMC 1994). Overall, banana farmers represent 20 percent of the labor force, so their fortunes substantially affect the nation's socioeconomic well-being.

The majority of Dominica's farms range in size from 1.5 to 5 acres. Most families grow other crops in addition to bananas on their land, including food crops (Robinson 1995). Small size and steep slopes conspire to produce yields that are lower than those of large Central American plantations endowed with level terrain and good soils. Farms are undercapitalized and agricultural credit is a frequent problem, exacerbated in recent years by the financial difficulties of the DBMC (DBMC 1994). Bananas, though, continue to be a labor-intensive crop and offer the advantage of year-round production. With the Geest system still in place (without Geest itself), farmers harvest each week, trucking their produce to port on Thursdays to meet the arriving banana ship. This ritual is followed by the weekly issuance of a paycheck, an event uncommon in other agricultural sectors. This increases the difficulty of luring farmers away from bananas toward other crops, a process essential to any diversification effort.

In late 1995, Geest's Caribbean banana operations were purchased by a consortium composed of Fyffes, Ltd., an Irish MNC that operates in the United Kingdom (UK), and the Windward Island Banana Development Corporation (WIBDECO), an umbrella organization that includes the banana marketing boards for Dominica, St. Lucia, St. Vincent, and Grenada. WIBDECO holds 50 percent of the shares in the joint venture and is jointly owned by the governments of the four countries (Durand 1996). The very recent nature of the purchase and the interruptions to banana production and trade caused by the three devastating storms of autumn 1995 render a current evaluation of this move impossible. However, the necessity for its success is indisputable, as failure would be cataclysmic for all four states. It figures prominently in Dominica's diversification plans, which anticipate piggybacking other goods on the banana boats headed to Britain (Harris 1996).

Despite the limitations of its banana-driven economy, Dominica has experienced considerable progress since the 1960s, a process chronicled in detail by Honychurch (1995). Physical infrastructure has improved dramatically, though many needs remain, as discussed below. Dominica was once one of Britain's poorer colonies. But its 1995 per capita GNP of U.S. $2,450 now approaches many of its regional neighbors, while its infant mortality rate has fallen below ten, making it one of the Caribbean's best (see table 2). Begging is rare. Malnutrition problems that plagued the country in the past are virtually unknown today (A. Martin 1995), and the basic appearance of the populace indicates that health standards are considerably higher than in most other developing countries. Great strides have been made in preventive health through the opening of a network of seven district clinics, placing services within ten miles for 100 percent of the population. Subclinics staffed by nurses reduce this distance to just three miles (E. Williams 1995). This has contributed to the near eradication of many tropical diseases and a life expectancy at birth of seventy-seven years, highest in the region (PRB 1995). In some years, maternal mortality is zero (W. Fevrier 1995).

Education has also advanced, particularly at the secondary level. Dominicans describe their educational program, based on the British examination system, as "rigorous" and speak of it with great pride. According to data compiled in 1991, nearly 90 percent of those five years of age or older were attending or had completed primary school, while nearly 25 percent of those fifteen or older were attending or had completed secondary school (CSO 1995a). Basic schooling is critically important to the functioning of the country's banana farmers who, after all, are independent businesspersons. Higher education remains beyond the reach of the vast majority of Dominicans, though the island is home to a teachers' training college, a community college, and a distant-learning center of the University of the West Indies. Housing is the major deficiency in the country's social infrastructure. Many houses, particularly in rural areas, lack indoor plumbing, and are built by their occupants.

THE CHALLENGE: PREPARING FOR THE EXPIRATION OF LOMÉ

Once again, Dominica faces the need to reorient its economy and replace its dominant export crop. In this round, it must do so as an independent country within a global economic context that threatens to increasingly marginalize small states. Unlike the island's previous transitions, though, early indications from the government suggest little desire to merely replicate the pattern of substituting a new dominant export crop for bananas. Instead, the stimuli noted above have led the government to adopt diversification as its economic goal. Ironically, this unfolding effort occurs at a time when economies of scale have become more important than ever for countries competing in the global market place. While diversification is an attempt to reduce the vulnerability inherent in specialized economies, expansion into a wider range of goods works against the achievement of such scale economies.

Even without the pressures imposed by economic globalization, diversification is and will continue to be a difficult, often painful process fraught with challenges. It is more complicated than simply deciding what to grow or produce. The array of issues involved in the production and trade of bananas above indicates the wide range of matters that must be considered *for each product* that might be included in a diversification mix. Numerous questions must be raised—and answered—for each product. Does the country have appropriate factor endowments to cultivate/produce the good? What inputs are needed? Where can these be obtained (locally or through importation)? What infrastructure needs to be developed for the new industry? What labor is necessary and what training programs must be implemented to provide that labor with the requisite expertise? How will the new products be transported to markets? Where will those markets be and how can access to them be obtained? Who will provide competition within this industry?

Such a short list is obviously incomplete, but it should convey the complexity inherent in any diversification effort. To it, though, should be added a series of questions, such as those of Thrupp (1995), confronted by most Latin American and Caribbean countries currently promoting nontraditional agricultural exports (NTAEs). Among these: Is the activity environmentally sustainable? Who are the real beneficiaries of the program? How will relations among various levels of the social structure be affected? How much will markets depend on ever shifting dietary preferences? Does the activity promote the penetration of multinational capital? The track record with NTAEs already accumulated by many developing countries provides cause to consider such issues very seriously before proceeding.

In Dominica's case, a series of internal and exogenous factors add to the challenges reflected in the questions raised above. The former include a limited natural resource base. Good volcanic soils and a benign climate offer great potential to cultivate a wide variety of agricultural goods, but these advantages are partially offset by the difficult terrain that renders large-scale operations impossible in most of the country. It lacks exploitable mineral wealth, suggesting that its industrial potential is limited to agricultural processing or the assembly of finished goods from imported inputs or parts manufactured elsewhere. The latter category involves additional costs, thereby lowering any eventual earnings from the activity.

Infrastructure is often a grave problem for Dominica. The country has a system of feeder roads that sufficiently link most agricultural areas to the port facilities at Woodbridge Bay (the primary commercial port facility, three miles north of Roseau, the capital) and Portsmouth (the second largest city; see map 2). But Dominica lacks an airport able to accommodate jet planes. The two modest airports at Canefield (on the Caribbean coast, just north of Roseau) and Melville Hall (northeastern Dominica) handle only small planes, reducing the efficiency of air cargo use and necessitating an additional transshipment point elsewhere in the region (often Antigua; see map 2). The lack of direct flights from Europe and North America also affects the development of tourism and information processing (discussed further below). With a population of 75,000, insufficient public sector revenues render construction of a jetport impossible without external funding. The airport situation remains a severe constraint on the country's diversification efforts.[1]

A reorientation of much of Dominica's labor force is essential to the diversification program. According to DBMC reports, the country currently is exerting a substantial effort to upgrade the skills of its banana farmers in order to enhance the quality and quantity of their output. Similar training will be necessary for all other crops and animal products included in the anticipated export mix. Each will involve such functions as site preparation, seedling propagation, efficient care during the growth period, proper harvesting methods, packing, and postharvest handling. Under such programs, farmers incur great risks and are offered few guarantees of success. The critical stage of market development that is so essential to their ultimate prosperity occurs *after* the farmer has already switched to the alternative crop. Dominica has the advantages of a well-educated, English-speaking labor force, which is beneficial to tourism and information-related industries. One benefit of the country's otherwise disadvantageous small size is that diversification does not need to yield a large number of new jobs for Dominica to realize its employment-generation goals. It can, therefore, pursue modest projects, knowing that each will have a positive impact on the small labor force.

Exogenous factors also add to the difficulty of achieving a diversified economy. Among these are the aforementioned market development process, enhanced competition from new sources, the need for assistance on infrastructural matters, and the inability to affect commodity prices. Based on information obtained in several interviews, market development appears to be an imprecise science, particularly when operating from such a small base. The country is unable to afford its own trade missions and must rely on efforts promoted by international organizations. It often participates in Caricom, Caribbean Tourism Organization (CTO), or Organization of Eastern Caribbean States (OECS) programs. While opening channels that would be difficult to create alone, such group marketing obscures the country's identity, an already grave problem due to name confusion with the Dominican Republic. The National Development Corporation is currently debating whether Dominica is well served by its participation in such ventures, aware, however, that the price of attempting to go it alone is high (Edwards 1995).

Trade fairs constitute another market development thrust. The Dominica Export Import Agency (DEXIA), a parastatal organization responsible for trade facilitation, frequently represents the country and its private sector interests at established trade fairs in such potential market countries as the United States, France, Germany, and Britain (Clarendon 1995). Through such efforts, the country is able to tap into an established process without bearing the costs inherent in creating its own trade mission. These fairs also present a risk. Such a small country can becomes "lost in the shuffle," particularly when its participation occurs under the aegis of one of the larger groups (e.g., OECS or CTO).

DEXIA also monitors market prices and researches competitors for most of Dominica's goods except for bananas, which remain the DBMC's responsibility. New competitors for several of Dominica's potential products have entered the marketplace, which represents a daunting prospect for the country's diversification program. The recent reentry into world markets of South Africa, whose great agricultural potential and production profile place it in direct competition with several Caribbean states, is causing particular concern, an irony given Dominica's strong support of the antiapartheid struggle. Brazil, with its large plantations, equatorial climate, and dire need for export earnings to service its foreign debt, represents another challenge to Dominican diversification, especially in the area of citrus fruits. The issue of scale strongly suggests that small island states will be unable to compete with any large country that seriously pursues production for export of a given good.

Another external factor that will govern Dominica's eventual success in diversifying is its ability to obtain funding for necessary infrastructure projects. The larger airport is, perhaps, the most critical. A plan to build an airport capable of receiving jet planes already exists, and the U.S. Army Corps of Engineers is committed to preparing the site once a donor has been found to fund the actual construction. Dominica looks to the E.U. for this funding but, as yet, no commitment has been forthcoming. An alternate plan would involve private foreign capital and a link between the airport project and the construction of a two-hundred-room hotel (Fadelle 1996). Other forms of shipping must be considered as well. For each, several elements including storage, transportation, and packing facilities must be in place for the program to function. The Diversification Implementation Unit (DIU) of the Ministry of Finance and Development handles many of the negotiations behind these efforts, focusing on the mechanics of the program. It was successful in obtaining Japanese government funds to build a fisheries pier in Roseau, dedicated in 1995, that will allow the country to develop its fishing potential in conjunction with the two-hundred-mile territorial limit permitted under the UNCLOS (Harris 1995). This Japanese aid carries a price (although government officials do not publicly acknowledge it): Dominican support of Japan's pro-whaling position in opposition to the International Whaling Commission's ban on commercial whaling. This places the country at odds with its customary support of proenvironment positions in other fora and, some suggest, with its stated goal of becoming an important ecotourism destination (A. Martin 1995).

One additional factor influencing the success of Dominica's diversification efforts is its inability to affect world prices for virtually any good it may choose to produce. Even with a dominant crop like bananas, its exports represent less than one percent of the world total and have no impact on market prices when those are based on supply and demand factors. Thus the country continues to be on the receiving end of prices determined elsewhere. This increases the risks to individual producers who shift to new activities, and it mirrors the dependent development cycle reflected in the country's earlier economic transitions.

THE RESPONSE: DOMINICA'S DIVERSIFICATION PROGRAM

Despite such daunting challenges, Dominica is moving ahead with its diversification program. It has no choice but to do so, although it has some latitude as to how it may proceed. In mid-1995 and early 1996, when this chapter was researched, efforts in three major categories of the economy—agriculture, tourism, and industry—were already in progress. Each of these areas is briefly reviewed below.

Agriculture

Agriculture is the sector receiving the highest priority, since it will be most negatively affected by current trends in the world political economy. Disruptions in the agricultural sector will spill over into other sectors if its problems are not addressed, since 30.8 percent of the active labor force is employed in the primary sector, mostly in agriculture, including 40.2 percent of all males (CSO 1994). To assist with planning in agriculture, the government in 1995 was conducting the Dominica Agricultural Census[2] in consultation with the Food and Agriculture Organization (FAO). The previous census had been realized during the 1960s when the country was still a colony; the plan is to regularly update the 1995 census so it may serve as a base line for further planning.

Several efforts were already in progress, not waiting for census results or the outcomes of E.U. banana or WTO negotiations. These reflect both a wide array of initiatives and a high degree of institutionalization, with participation at the national, regional, and extraregional levels. The Ministry of Agriculture's *Crop Development Plans, 1993–95* (CDPs) outlines the initial development paths to be followed with a variety of crops that fall into the NTAE category for Dominica. Subsequent plans will be developed as necessary for each crop. Included in the plans are anthuriums (both local pinks and hybrid varieties of these flowers), tree crops such as avocado, mango, cocoa, and orange, passion fruit, hot peppers, plantains, root crops such as tannia and yams, and ginger. Each CDP presents a strategy that includes target acreage, training programs for farmers, and anticipated markets. Attention is paid to the technical support services needed for each crop and training needed in such areas as postharvest handling, in recognition of its impact on the quality of the eventual export. Several CDPs are notable for their modest scales, such as goals of 550 acres for avocadoes and 850 acres for mangoes, while another (ginger) even identifies *hucksters*[3] as a potentially significant outlet. The implementing agencies are also identified; for most crops this includes various branches of the Ministry of Agriculture (MoA) itself, though, frequently, aid programs (USAID and the Republic of China [Taiwan]) or organizations such as the Caribbean Agricultural Research and Development Institute (CARDI)[4] or the aforementioned DEXIA are involved. USAID provided a U.S. $1.5 million grant administered by the MoA and aimed at assisting with crop development and establishing a central livestock farm to serve as a stock supply source for community-based livestock centers. The grant also paid for improvements to feeder roads (now completed), and for the construction of a hot-water plant to combat anthracnose diseases in mangoes. It came rather free of conditions except to stipulate that chemicals not be used for any of the crops involved (Grell 1995).

Other diversification crops are included in the MoA's New Opportunity Crop Development Programme. Among these are melon, pumpkin, breadfruit, and bay leaf (MoA 1992). A third group is not directly targeted by the above government programs, but will receive MoA support when initiated by private sector concerns. They include ornamental plants, aloe vera (considered an industrial crop), the Irish potato, and various vegetables. Still other efforts are evident in travels around the island. A French agricultural cooperation project focuses on pig production to decrease the need to import pork; vegetable and fruit production to boost intraregional exports; tropical flowers such as pink and red ginger, heliconia, bird of paradise, and anthuriums; and a marine management program for the Soufriere Bay area (at the southwestern tip of the island; Ehret 1995). Dominica's location between and historical linkages with Martinique and Guadeloupe underlie French interests in the island. An aquaculture project to raise prawns and tilapia, a rapid-growing fish of African origins, was originally funded by USAID. It was taken over by the Taiwanese during the mid-1980s and now continues on a small scale—just three farmers—under the MoA (Magloire 1995). The ministry also manages seven plant propagation stations in various locations around the island to provide stock for many of the crops mentioned above, as well as for carambola, sweet peppers, pineapple, sweet potatoes, and dasheen.

Additionally, recent global trends toward the institutionalization of tropical agriculture are evident in Dominica. The FAO (UN), DEXIA (Dominica), and CARDI (Caricom) have already been mentioned. The OECS is involved through its agricultural diversification coordination unit (ADCU), which provides technical support to the MoA and training programs for farmers. The ADCU also attempts to avoid duplication of diversification efforts for export crops among OECS member states, though it is limited to an advisory function (Satney 1995). The OAS is represented by the Interamerican Institute for Cooperation in Agriculture, which indirectly abets the diversification process through its involvement in plant/animal protection and quarantine, tropical fruit development, support for farmers' organizations, and technology generation and transfer (U. Martin 1995). In a larger country, such efforts could proceed independently of one another, resulting in much duplication and wasted resources. Dominica's scale prevents this from occurring; the staff of these organizations work in close proximity and meet regularly. An outside observer is struck by the rather high degree of cooperation, consistency, and singularity of purpose, not often found elsewhere. It offers an example of smallness being an asset.

The impressive variety of initiatives must contend with several of the obstacles noted above. Flowers, for example, are dependent on efficient transportation, as freshness is of ultimate importance. The lack of direct flights adds to the time between cutting and delivery to market and to the transport cost. The flowers generated by the French-sponsored project spend up to one week in transit on their route from Dominica to Antigua, then on to Heathrow (London) and Paris. The Dominica-Antigua leg of the journey adds $0.50/kilogram to the $1.00/kilogram cost of transport from Antigua to Europe (Ehret 1995). Such extra costs do not bode well for competitiveness in the country's new endeavors. The price of imported inputs must also be considered. While French breeding pigs are brought in at no charge to Dominica, the MoA's anthurium project imports plant stock from the Netherlands at approximately $4.00 *per plant*, with the expectation that each hybrid will produce seven flowers per year for up to five years. The high value of each plant mandates further expenditures on special plant sheds. They house raised flower beds built of bamboo with soil covered by coconut husks (Magloire 1995). Such endeavors are risky, especially considering the flower's three-week postharvest shelf life, assuming proper handling.

The special challenge of market development generally noted above particularly applies to agriculture. The difficulty is exacerbated by the wide variety of crops currently included in the diversification program. Dominica is pursuing regional and extraregional markets for various products. The drier, touristic islands to its north offer potential opportunities to sell a range of agricultural goods for consumption by residents and guests alike. Similarly, the cruise industry currently thriving in the region utilizes the kinds of fresh produce that Dominica can cultivate. Both of these markets are now being targeted. Outside the Caribbean, the problem of connecting with possible buyers increases, as noted above. A recurring fruit fly problem and USDA rules keep the U.S. market off limits for many Dominican FFV exports (OECS/ADCU 1994a), but northwestern Europe and Canada are two areas whose climatic complementarity suggests the plausibility of greater future primary sector trade. The issue of connecting with specific buyers in those places, though, remains a difficult one to resolve, given the limitations of the trade fair system already described.

Tourism

Given Dominica's environmental endowments, exquisite beauty, and climate, it is logical that tourism follows agriculture on the country's diversification priority list. Until now, the island has avoided its neighbors' path in pursuing the resort-oriented mass tourism market. Instead, it has used its reputation as the "Nature Island" to attract ecotourists and specialty tourists, including scuba divers, for whom the island is well-suited. The result is a distinct profile for its tourism industry relative to most others in the Caribbean region that, given the country's need to diversify, presents both challenges and opportunities.

This distinct tourism profile is reflected in the scale, hotel ownership, source regions, inputs sourcing, and tourist activities. The scale of the industry has remained small, despite recent increases in visitor numbers. Excluding passengers on cruise ships, only 65,331 people visited the island in 1994, modest in light of the numbers registered by several other

Caribbean destinations (CSO 1995) but significant when related to total population (see chap. 6, especially table 6.1, for comparisons). The small number mirrors the accommodations available, just 757 rooms in 1994, including hotels, guest houses, apartments, and cottages (CSO 1995). Despite this, the high rate (95 percent) of local hotel ownership (Edwards 1995) differs from Caribbean norms and minimizes the problem of leaking tourism earnings that characterizes the industry in many developing countries. While much of the region depends on the North American market, Dominica receives visitors from diverse regions. Omitting Dominican nationals returning home for visits, Europe contributed 24.9 percent of the foreign visitors in 1994, while North America provided just 20.5 percent. More than half (52.9 percent) came from other Caribbean states, with Martinique and Guadeloupe responsible for nearly 30 percent of the total (CSO 1995). Latin America and Japan are still largely untapped markets, while the United States represents another potential growth area.

This diversity of sources of tourists renders the country less vulnerable to the impacts of economic slumps in individual First World nation-states. The local accommodations ownership pattern extends to the sourcing of inputs for the tourism industry, particularly food. The country's diverse agricultural potential allows the hotel and restaurant sector to obtain most of its needs without importing, setting the country apart from neighbors that continue to import the majority of their food for their resort tourism sectors (discussed in chap. 6). This extends tourism's multiplier effect in Dominica, where it is estimated to be greater than one, compared to less than one for most of the region (H. James 1996). Finally, with regard to activities, the island lacks the broad, sandy beaches common to resort tourism elsewhere in the region. Thus, the touristic experience there tends to emphasize active pursuits such as hiking, diving, and birding.

As Dominica confronts the need to diversify, its tourism industry finds itself at a crossroads. It must grow in a way that contributes to the goals of the diversification effort (discussed below). Such growth, though, threatens to generate tensions within the industry itself, challenging the ecotourism base that has been its mainstay thus far. This has already been manifested in the growth of the cruise-ship sector. Arrivals in that sector increased from 4,924 in 1990 to more than 122,000 in 1994 (CSO 1995), with further growth anticipated to follow the June 1995 opening of Roseau's new pier. Large ships such as the *Carnivale* and *Festivale* now include the island on their itineraries. Each call disgorges more than a thousand passengers who spend an average of just $29 per person, though generating a boom for Dominica's taxi drivers and craftspersons. Many feel that this form of tourism is incompatible with ecotourism, as the day-tripping cruise passengers descend on many of the same sites visited by the longer-term ecotourists, undermining the ambiance of the nature experience for the latter group. There are considerable sentiments for channeling cruise-ship visitors to a limited number of the more accessible attractions, including the Emerald Pool (centrally located in the interior, but easily accessible from Roseau) and Trafalgar Falls (in southwestern Dominica, a few miles inland from Roseau). The idea is to upgrade the capacity of those sites to handle large numbers, leaving the rest of the island to those preferring more indepth encounters with nature. The accommodations sector of the industry also feels that its needs, primarily infrastructural, have been neglected in favor of pier development for cruise ships, although it should be recognized that many visitors from the French islands who overnight on Dominica also arrive by boat. Again, the airport issue remains of paramount importance to the accommodations sector as access to the island continues to be difficult.

The government clearly favors further cultivation of the country's ecotourism and specialty tourism potential. No interest in trying to compete in the resort tourism sector was expressed by officials in either the Ministry of Tourism, Ports, and Employment or the Division of Tourism of the National Development Corporation (NDC). Rather, there was a strong desire to diversify Dominica's product *within* the ecotourism area. This could involve including the island on the itineraries of First World nature-travel companies and the development of educationally oriented programs sponsored by universities. The former is another example of both opportunities and obstacles. A review of brochures issued by such companies indicates a dearth of Caribbean programs, evidently reflecting the perceptions of ecotourists that the region has little to offer. Fadelle (1996) reports little progress in promoting joint itineraries with other islands, and he attributes this to a lack of interest among local hotel owners who are unwilling to share their profits with the agents who would necessarily be involved in such cooperative ventures. The latter could include both study-travel programs and longer-term research visits hosted by institutions like the Springfield Environmental Protection, Research, and Education Center managed by the Dominica Conservation Association (A. Martin 1995).

As with agriculture, market development for tourism remains a major challenge. Promotion of mass tourism is often easier, since much of it occurs within multinational corporations that link airlines, hotel chains, and major tour packaging companies under one umbrella. Sales of packaged programs result from the distribution of colorful brochures to thousands of travel retailers in communities throughout North America, Europe, and elsewhere, with 800 numbers offering easy access to reservation systems. Locally owned Dominican hotels and the small regional airlines that service the island are financially unable to join these computerized networks, whose countless operatives—local travel agents—are often unable to distinguish the country from the larger Dominican Republic. Adding to the challenge is the profile of their target population, which is dispersed, very independent, and difficult to reach. Dominica does participate in regional programs such as the Caribbean Tourism Organization but as one of thirty-two members once again encounters the problem of a submerged identity (Edwards 1995).

Manufacturing

The third arena of diversification efforts—industry and informatics—has received less attention than agriculture and tourism, but NDC officials indicate that this is now changing (Fadelle 1996; Gregoire 1996). The diminutive internal market looms as a deterrent to progress in manufacturing, and most production oriented toward local consumers needs an external market to make the effort viable. This has proven difficult to achieve despite some positive recent developments. Agricultural processing represents the logical target area within manufacturing, but results have been mixed. The local banana industry failed to generate adequate demand for one of its most important inputs—the fifteen kilo cartons used to pack bananas. The plant closed and the boxes are once again imported. Coconut production and processing were targeted expansion industries following Hurricane David's devastation of existing crops in 1979. A concerted effort to encourage many farmers to begin cultivating coconuts faltered in light of the mixed success of the plant and the decline in prices for copra, the dried coconut meat used in making coconut oil. In 1995, the plant was purchased by Colgate-Palmolive to manufacture soaps, lotions, and creams (see table 2), and the NDC is optimistic about future expansion.

Bello Products, Inc., represents the island's exceptional success story, boosting the credibility of an export-led industrialization model. Founded in 1939 and locally owned, it focuses on highly specialized products like hot pepper sauce, gourmet coffee, bay rum lotion, fruit juice concentrates, and tropical fruit jellies that are produced primarily for foreign consumers but are also sold locally (Fagin 1996). Bello purchases a variety of domestically grown crops for use in its products; its success or failure in developing foreign markets therefore affects diversification efforts in agriculture as well as in manufacturing. DEXIA often represents the company's products at trade fairs abroad. Despite its success, Bello faces transport challenges that await other potential Dominican industries. Its owner, Vantil Fagin, recounted a March 1996 situation in which he tried to ship an order to Guadeloupe, the island directly north of Dominica. There were no direct options available, and the most viable alternative was to arrange shipping via Miami, Florida. He characterized shipping among the islands as "dreadful," and his tale exemplifies the hub-and-spoke system that has characterized Caribbean shipping patterns since the colonial period.

Kubuli Brewery and Beverages, Ltd. opened in late 1995 and appears poised to mirror Bello's achievements. German-owned with local shareholders, Kubuli uses Dominica's fine water to brew its beer for domestic consumption and, by March 1996, had succeeded in cornering a major share of the market. It plans to diversify into water bottling, eventually manufacturing its own plastic bottles. Other small-scale manufactures include garments such as school and work uniforms, T-shirts (although shirts marketed to tourists are still imported), plastic bags and shoes, rum, plastic molding, and furniture. In addition, there is a water bottling plant that already produces for export within Caricom (Gregoire 1996).

The interagency cooperation noted above occurs in the manufacturing sector through NDC, USAID, ADCU, and MoA participation in a program to develop a Caribbean label for marketing processed foods. This multi-island concept is intended to promote a "healthy island" image that (it is hoped) will become sufficiently recognizable abroad to engender consumer brand loyalty. This venture also extends backward into the primary sector through NDC/ADCU/DBMC efforts to wean farmers away from bananas and into other crops (Fadelle 1996).

In 1995, information processing became a consideration in the diversification effort (H. James 1995). An OECS study funded by the World Bank investigated the potential for development of a telecommunications services and operations industry within the Eastern Caribbean, including Dominica. Preliminary results indicate both potential and obstacles. High literacy rates, computer skill levels, and labor force availability were all noted favorably in the as yet unpublished study (OECS 1995). Problem areas included wage rates that are higher than those in other developing regions and the high price of international dialogue communications. In Dominica's case, the latter is due to the monopoly enjoyed by Cable and Wireless Ltd., which reaps huge profits despite the high per capita costs of infrastructure development on the island. A follow-up study at the level of OECS is attempting to link countries with companies; subsequent implementation of the program, should it proceed, will occur at the national level. Some foreign investors have begun to express interest in Dominica, and the government proposed draft framework legislation for the industry in early 1996 (Fadelle 1996). NDC and Ministry of Finance personnel are well aware of the footloose nature of the industry described by Mullings (chap. 7), but its employment potential still makes it desirable as a diversification component. According to Heather James (1995), one sizeable company can create two thousand jobs offshore. At Dominica's scale, obtaining just a share of such a program would yield a relatively great benefit to the nation's employment situation and also a vulnerability, since the employment source would be in the hands of a few international investors.

AN EXPORT NICHE MARKET STRATEGY

Dominica is leaving few stones unturned in preparing for a post-Lomé world. At a time when many debt-ridden developing states are seeking quick fixes to their fiscal crises via the NTAE route, Dominica is forging a diversification effort notable for its breadth and its attempts to maintain traditional egalitarian values.

The key to success for the emerging programs described above is the *niche market* strategy, a term used by several officials during interviews (see also chap. 1). It provides the glue that binds together many seemingly disparate elements. The niche market approach is oriented toward overcoming the disadvantages of the country's small size by focusing on production of specialty goods for which a factor other than price is the primary purchase consideration. This alleviates the need to achieve the economies of scale that Dominica can never realistically expect to attain and accentuates those items for which the island's endowments are well suited.

There are three basic ways, not mutually exclusive, in which this tactic can be (and is being) implemented. First, upscale and specific ethnic markets in developed states are being identified for unique items whose high quality offsets price in the decision to purchase. For Dominica, gourmet coffee, cut flowers, hot pepper sauce, and nature tourism all fit into this category.

Second, other niche markets can be identified where there are gaps in competitor countries' annual crop cycles that render the other producer(s) unable to fulfill the demand for tropical agricultural goods in northern markets. Such gaps may be just one month long for different products, but when that month coincides with Dominica's ability to harvest, a niche can be exploited. Thus it hopes to supply Europe with citrus crops during Israel's export gap each October and to sell avocadoes to Hispanic groups in the United States between California's growing seasons each November through March (OECS/ADCU 1994b). A similar result can be achieved within the region by supplying nearby islands and cruise ships during brief periods when the customary provider is "down."

The third category of niche involves establishing relationships with individual retail firms, rather than entire countries, in larger nation-states such as the United Kingdom, Germany, or Canada. Through this process,

Dominica could supply a variety of goods to one wholesaler that already has a distribution network through one or more chains of retail grocers. Conceptually, the niche-market concept is sensible. It reduces the negative impact of small size and lack of price competitiveness on the nation's economy. As a strategy, it corresponds nicely to the island's scale. It recognizes that Dominica does not need to find large niches in world markets. Small ones are sufficient to help the country achieve its job creation needs. Implementation, though, will be difficult because the challenges identified above are magnified in complexity when constraints for so many goods must be resolved simultaneously.

SUMMARY AND CONCLUSIONS

The scattershot nature of Dominica's diversification effort seems to increase the country's difficulties; it adds to the long list of problems needing solutions. When questioned about this, DIU director Carey Harris said it is intentional, as the country cannot afford to miss any potential opportunity. He anticipates achieving stability with some goods while others, particularly those bound for extra-regional markets, may never be secure income producers. The wide range of items included in the program, once established, will serve to reduce the vulnerability now inherent in a situation where one product dominates the country's economy and export profile.

The goals of this program, as articulated by Harris (1995), go beyond specific production targets to include (in order) preserving democracy, increasing the standard of living of Dominica's farmers, and generating foreign exchange. The first goal clearly draws on the second while preventing the third from dominating policy as it does in many countries. In essence, these goals convey a recognition of the negative impacts that economic collapse would have on the stability of the country's democratic system. Other, compatible, goals defined by the NDC's Sheridan Gregoire (1996) include employment generation, environmental protection, technology transfer, and skill development. This philosophy guides Dominica's diversification program in a direction that emphasizes the well-being of its people and the sustainability of production, even if that means reduced short-term earnings.

While it wishes to attract foreign investment capital and assistance, it seems unwilling to engage in the massive giveaways described by Klak and Myers (chap. 5). In this Dominica seems to differ from other nation-states in the region, from many Latin American countries pursuing NTAEs as described by Thrupp (1995), and from the will of some international agencies. Dominica attaches greater priority to *socioeconomic* development to maintain social stability and protect the country's environment. This commitment is exemplified by the fact that the country does not allow any major forest exploitation (A. James 1995). Its forests serve as the watershed for its high-quality drinking water, one of its keys to positive health indicators and an exportable commodity in its own right, as noted above. While the market and private sector are valued, the country prefers a more flexible approach to diversification than that usually mandated by external actors, even when this may yield slower growth at the macroeconomic level.

In its diversification program, Dominica may reduce the vulnerability that has always characterized its highly specialized economy, but it is never likely to achieve stability. The niche market approach will require continual effort if it is to be sustainable. Its flexibility will be tested regularly by consumer tastes that change frequently, especially those tastes emanating from upscale markets. New varieties of products will need to be developed, each necessitating adjustments on the part of farmers or other producers with the attendant risks involved in those processes. New competition is certain to arise, adding to the challenges already at hand.

Dominica can never realistically expect to achieve a truly independent form of development in the global era. The island's scale and its inability to affect global trade dictate its dependent status. Its diversification strategy, however, represents a break with past patterns and may ultimately come to represent a new, more benign form of economic dependency than the colonial or neocolonial versions that preceded it. While it may seem strange to describe any form of dependency as "benign," the newly emerging form offers more options than were available during those earlier eras. Unlike the current banana crisis, no single crop will dictate the island's fate. Dominica's new development path will still render it economically dependent on rulings made elsewhere, but the current situation seems to allow greater latitude for local decision-making than in previous periods. This should enable Dominica to draw more heavily on the creativity of its people, which is its great strength and in the Caribbean tradition. The people will devise the variety of solutions needed if diversification is to succeed there.

Is there a place for countries such as Dominica in the future world economy? Dominica is struggling to ensure that it has a spot in the emerging global trade milieu. It has already demonstrated a strong grasp of the dilemma that it faces, a matter threatening the country's very existence, and has begun to take inventive steps to confront its problems while simultaneously providing a measure of prosperity for its people. Its program announces to the world that Dominica prefers trade to aid, in keeping with current preferences of the world's economic powers. Many obstacles remain and new ones will certainly arise, but by intelligently reconciling the scale of its aspirations to the reality of its situation, i.e., by "thinking small" and emphasizing a wide range of modest targets, Dominica is positioning itself to ensure its survival in the neoliberal era.

NOTES

1. The need for external assistance to construct a jetport capable of stimulating other economic sectors is reminiscent of 1980s Grenada. There, the Cuban/Soviet presence, in part to build a runway for jumbo jets, led to the U.S. invasion, ironically supported by Dominica's prime minister, Eugenia Charles.

2. Census results were unavailable when this research was conducted, but the effort focused on farmer profiles, crop profiles, and land use information.

3. Hucksters are independent small-scale traders who purchase goods directly from the producers and carry them via local ships, often ferries, to neighboring islands. Trouillot (1988) describes them as an "alternative export circuit," noting their importance to northern Dominica, for which Guadeloupe comprises a market. Hucksterism persists in much of the Eastern Caribbean particularly for agriculture. An informal activity, it remains beyond most forms of data collection so its full importance is unknown.

4. CARDI is a nongovernmental organization funded by Caricom and its English-speaking member states, providing technical assistance and agricultural policy recommendations.

SUGGESTIONS FOR FURTHER READING

Honychurch, Lennox. *The Dominica Story: A History of the Island*. London: Macmillan Caribbean Publishers, 1995. The volume is the primary historical work on Dominica. Honychurch chronicles the island's social, economic, and political history against the geographical backdrop of its unique physical environment.

Thomson, Robert. *Green Gold: Bananas and Dependency in the Eastern Caribbean*. London: Latin American Bureau, 1987. The "green gold" of the title refers to the color of bananas prior to their shipment to northern markets. Thomson chronicles the development of the banana industry in the Eastern Caribbean states of Dominica, St. Lucia, St. Vincent, and Grenada, illustrating how the industry maintained the economic dependency of those countries into the postcolonial period.

Thrupp, Lori Ann, with Gilles Bergeron and William Waters. *Bittersweet Harvests for Global Supermarkets: Sustainability and Equity in Latin America's Agroexport Boom*. Washington, D.C.: The World Resources Institute, 1995. This volume takes a critical look at the current rush into nontraditional agricultural exports in Latin America and the Caribbean. Many problems are highlighted, drawing on detailed empirical evidence from several Latin American countries. The study calls into question the basic assumption of widespread benefits from export agriculture's diversification for the host countries and their people.

9

Cuban Socialism in Crisis: A Neoliberal Solution?[1]

Paul Susman

This chapter examines the Cuban government's response to the economic crisis associated with the decline and collapse of the Soviet Union along with the loss of the favorable CMEA socialist bloc trade relationship. Cuba's efforts to become more competitive globally while maintaining its socialist achievements and direction have resulted in tension. Cuba's search for a more flexible approach to developing a "socialist-oriented economy" emerges while the prevailing worldview is that Marxian socialism is dead. This chapter explores possible substitutes for socialism. These lie along a relatively narrow spectrum from neoliberalism to capitalist social democracy.

Should Cuba pursue a neoliberal path? Cuban options are constrained by virtually hegemonic global capitalism in which neoliberals see free markets as the path to economic prosperity and political freedom. Neoliberals do not allow the state to intervene in the market for the purpose of providing social welfare, fearing market-distorting behavior. Drawing on a liberal model of the state and the economy, neoliberals treat the market as the natural embodiment of the modern social contract. The entire world is being pressed into this neoliberal mold (as discussed in chap. 1).

During the post-1989 crisis in Cuba, called the "special period in time of peace," government agencies and nongovernmental organizations have proposed a variety of reforms. The key economic reforms resemble the neoliberal programs adopted in other countries. As the Economic Commission for Latin America summarized the neoliberal reforms (ECLAC 1996a):

> Although different in many respects, all the reform processes have pursued the goals of macroeconomic stabilization and international competitiveness

179

through fiscal discipline, trade liberalization and financial deregulation, the freer functioning of market mechanisms, greater reliance on private investment and new incentives and regulatory frameworks.

Cuba's neoliberal policies include efforts to (1) rationalize production and downsize the labor force; (2) encourage self-employment and small private enterprises; (3) legalize dollars and stabilize the peso; (4) shift toward privatization in agriculture; (5) establish new farmers' markets; and (6) encourage foreign investment. Many of these have been implemented unevenly, and with potentially profound effects on Cuba's efforts to build a socialist society. These policies stem from Cuba's search for a path out of the crisis. They constitute part of a shift "from a planned economy to a more flexible, socialist-oriented economy," according to Cuban minister Rodriguez (Caivana 1994, 3).

Changes in the internal political climate also affect Cuba's efforts to survive this special period. Cuba's economic crisis is associated with an initial governmental willingness to expand participation in civil society. For example, since 1989 Cuba's nongovernmental organizations (NGOs) experienced explosive growth, reaching about 2,200 by 1994 (Gunn 1995, 1–2). Most of these are actually government-funded organizations designed to attract foreign capital. However, other NGOs emerged that took advantage of new openings for religious and cultural groups, and they felt increasingly empowered to operate in the public space. Cuban leaders fear that advocates of greater democracy want the latitude to discuss the development of capitalist property relations. Thus these new groups were the objects of tightened government control, as members of dissident groups. In February 1996 the government denied permission for a large conference, but only after waiting until arrangements had been made by the Concilio Cubano, representing "130 human rights, dissident, and unofficial professional groups." The conference was intended to be "a plural, democratic and constructive encounter" (Rohter 1996). On the other hand, Castro has clearly extended an olive branch to the Catholic Church in arranging the first papal visit to revolutionary Cuba in January 1998.

Incessant U.S. efforts to increase pressure on Cuba and subvert the revolution provide the Cuban government a continuing rationale for limiting civil liberties. Citing comments by the head of the U.S. State Department Cuba Bureau, the Cuban government claims that some small dissident groups are politically and financially backed by the United States and should be treated as such (*Prensa Latina* 1996). There is of course a long record of U.S. financing of opposition groups. Economic hardships, difficulties in meeting basic needs, and new pressures from the Helms-Burton bill have Cuban leaders responding strongly to perceived threats. In its 23 March 1996 report, the Communist Party Politburo discusses the U.S. two-track policy against Cuba. The first track is represented by the "blockade, seeking economic asphyxiation." The second track is based on subversion. Thus, any indication that the United States is behind nongovernmental organizations in Cuba is seen as a threat. Using a second-track rationale, the Cuban leadership dismissed the head of the research institute, Center for the Study of the Americas, whose promarket reform and prodemocracy positions became too strident for the adaptive, responsive approach to policy that has always prevailed in Cuba and, by implication, too much of a challenge to Castro's decision-making style (Politburo Report 1996). The government also declared flatly that there are no NGOs in Cuba; civil society expresses itself in other ways than through NGOs.

Are the Cuban regime's economic and political responses sufficient to carry Cuba out of the crisis and enable it to survive with its socialist goals intact? Pastor and Zimbalist's (1995, 8) recent interim assessment of the Cuban transition represents a prevailing scholarly opinion: "There is now an acceptance of significant elements of capitalism, with political and economic consequences that remain unclear."

This chapter argues, to the contrary, that the consequences of capitalism are all too clear and that the Castro regime is walking a tightrope, seeking to benefit from the introduction of some capitalist practices while simultaneously trying to contain the onslaught of global capitalism from without and profit-seeking behavior within. Understanding Cuba's efforts to retain sovereignty and what the regime considers its key accomplishments requires attention, then, to internal economic and political tensions and to external pressures and experiences. Cuba's "special period" coincides with what may be called the "special period of the capitalist model of development" throughout the Caribbean and elsewhere.

THE GLOBAL CONTEXT OF CUBA'S SPECIAL PERIOD

Cuba's crisis is not isolated. Crisis tendencies are evident in all regions of the global capitalist world as well as in the transition economies of the former Soviet bloc countries. Typical outcomes for people around the world include, for example, falling real wages, growing temporary (versus permanent) work, along with increased job insecurity and declining access to social services. Social polarization and income polarization go hand in hand. The scale of dislocation and income loss, as well as the heightened consciousness and reality of vulnerability, exceeds anything seen since the Great Depression.

One crisis indicator, slow economic growth, is evident in the advanced capitalist countries. For instance, in France, Germany, Italy, and the United Kingdom, growth in 1993–96 has been below the 2.8 percent of the 1980s. From 1979 to 1994, unemployment, another crisis indicator, increased in the G7 countries from 13 to 24 million, or in other words from 4.8 to 7.4 percent of the labor force. Unemployment would be even higher if the figures included another 4 million who stopped looking for work and an estimated 15 million part-time workers who would prefer to work full time (ILO 1996, 10). New jobs tend to be in the service sector (accounting for 98 percent of employment growth in Canada and the United States from 1984 to 1995, for example) and much tends to be in the form of temporary jobs (Shorrock 1996, A6). The globalization of production (even the threat of moving overseas; see chap. 1) tends to weaken the bargaining power of any individual country's labor force. Cuts in government social expenditures exacerbate the impacts for middle- and low-income people. It is no surprise that income polarization is growing, especially in societies that have adopted the most aggressive neoliberal free-market policies and rhetoric. Examples include the United States, Canada, and France, as well as the transition economies of Eastern Europe and Russia, where aggressive neoliberal programs have opened great holes in the social safety nets.

Social problems are met in neoliberal rhetoric by calls for new rounds of market reforms around the world. The reforms typically entail measures intended to enhance conditions for capital, stabilize currencies to ensure returns on investment, and encourage market formation. Neoliberal programs seek to overcome imbalances between government expenditures and revenues, and between money income and commodity availability. This serves as a rationalization for reductions in social expenditures, deregulation of capital, and redistribution of social income from labor to capital, evident throughout the capitalist world. Such cuts not only limit access to food, education, health care, public transportation, and other social services, but are associated with declining real incomes for significant portions of the population and other real effects, such as the rise in many countries of industrial accidents, illnesses, and deaths (GNN 1996). Many states need to pay interest on public debt which often leads to new consumer taxes. The neoliberal argument also extends the economic reforms to the political arena in its claim that less government equals more freedom.

Do neoliberal reforms offer Cuba a desirable path? A brief examination of outcomes of neoliberal reforms around the world suggests that (1) the capitalist market model offers no panacea, (2) a transition from socialism to capitalism is anything but smooth, and (3) if the context of capitalist crisis is global, the very notion of abandoning a socialist vision to pursue capitalist development does not offer a solution to social, economic, and political crises. Latin America and the Caribbean provide ample evidence of the impacts of neoliberal reforms.

Crisis in Latin America and the Caribbean

Faced with high real interest rates, skyrocketing debt levels, falling export prices, and a sharp curtailment of new loans, Latin American and Caribbean governments adopted similar neoliberal programs in a desperate effort to attract new capital inflows.

Yet, even as they adopt these reforms, in contrast to the free market rhetoric of neoliberalism, they are faced with foreign aid packages that are often tied to specific market interventions that favor financial capital, especially in its portfolio form, and disadvantage investments in production. U.S.-backed debt relief in Latin America, for example, has been linked to debt *securitization*, or converting bank debt into bonds. In the 1990s, portfolio capital investments were at a level about twelve times higher than in 1983–89. They leave the economy vulnerable to decisions by portfolio managers to shift capital elsewhere in response to global opportunities and relative risk (Henwood 1966, 14). This, of course, compromises a country's ability to pursue a long-term development plan based on available capital. In contrast, Cuba's neoliberal type reforms are not predicated on the promise of foreign aid, as discussed below.

A new round of market reforms in Latin America is a desperate effort to achieve growth and restore the confidence of foreign investors.

> This realism is being imposed across borders by the international investors on whom Latin America depends for financing. Argentina, for example, can't afford to alienate investors, because it's spending more than it collects in tax revenues, which remain depressed by a weak economy. This year, it's expected to top nearly $9 billion from international markets. . . . This commitment to reform reflects not only pressure from bond market vigilantes, but also a lack of alternatives. (Friedland 1996, A15)

In Latin America the neoliberal fiscal stabilization goal of cutting inflation seems to be succeeding in the 1990s. The Inter-American Development Bank attributes "most of the decline to a fall in noninterest spending," or over a decade of slashing social expenditures as a share of GDP (IADB 1995, 11). Despite the negative consequences for poor people, slashing social expenditures is at the center of a neoliberal program.

Latin America's economic growth is concentrated in the largest countries and its benefits reside in the largest companies (Altimir 1996). Nearly half of all capital inflows to Latin America and the Caribbean went to Mexico (1991–94), and most of the rest went to Argentina, Brazil, and Chile. Even as these four countries experienced a sixfold leap in the constant dollar value of the equity market (stocks), reflecting large capital inflows, their current accounts deficits grew to $45 billion, suggesting a fiscal destabilizing process. Fiscal tightening in Latin America and the Caribbean meant squeezing wage earners. The share of wages in GDP declined significantly over the last twenty years.

After more than a decade of pursuing a neoliberal agenda, the predominant regional outcome is high debt and high unemployment, growing income polarization, and low growth rates. Latin America and the Caribbean, viewed as a region (excluding Cuba) have been unable to achieve the 6 percent growth rate the World Bank and IMF believe will lead to increased employment, reduced poverty, and reduced social polarization. Government subsidies for social welfare programs are cut to help keep down fiscal deficits. Despite following the neoliberal formula, "In 1995 only nine (countries) saw their per capita GDP overtake 1980 levels" and of these only two countries, Colombia and Uruguay, achieved levels of inequality lower than those prior to the crisis (and, in the first case, only temporarily) (ECLAC 1996b). Aside from Chile, cited as marginally reducing inequality in the early 1990s, "In the other economies current levels of inequality are significantly higher than before the crisis."

Given outcomes throughout the capitalist world of increased inequality, rising unemployment, and persistent vulnerability to global market conditions, it is no wonder that Cuba has not leaped to embrace the full gamut of neoliberal reforms. Yet despite such consequences, Cuba's need for capital inflows and more favorable terms of trade places it under intense pressure to become globally competitive in market terms.

Russia and Eastern Europe: Lessons for Cuba on a Market Transition

The contradictions in a transition to a capitalist market system should not be underestimated. The 1990–95 decline in GDP by over 40 percent in Russia and Eastern Europe suggests the scope of the problems (East Database 1996). Since 1989 Cuba has been able to witness the impacts of such a transition around the world, and is therefore wary about following neoliberal programs as seen in Russia and elsewhere.

Changes in Russia are illustrative. Even the U.S. State Department concedes that "as it moves from a centrally planned economy to a free market system, the Russian economy has undergone considerable stress." That GDP plummeted by over 50 percent from 1990 to 1995 begins to describe some of this "stress" (U.S. State Department 1995). Maintaining social services, infrastructure, and basic provisions has been impossible in Russia. Since the push for privatization of state assets with the economic reforms begun in 1992, the private sector has grown to account for at least half of that shrinking GDP and the workforce. As in advanced capitalist countries, in Russia there is also a fundamental restructuring of the labor market toward more insecure wage labor positions (which were 73 percent of job openings in 1995), and away from salaried positions (Zalesova 1996). Only IMF funds (intended for other uses) have allowed the government to meet some government payroll obligations and prevent popular political repudiation of the regime and total economic collapse. Given these changes in the economy, it is no surprise that "the gap between rich and poor appears to have widened; about 20 percent of the population lives below the official poverty level" (U.S. State Department 1995).

The Russian transition to a market system has also brought declining health indicators, including shorter life expectancy and a resurgence of preventable diseases because of falling immunization coverage. An assessment of the reforms by the U.S. State Department identifies underfunding of health programs in the context of broad social and economic changes in Russia along with residual problems in a health care system from the Soviet era. Environmental health issues also contribute to public health problems. Serious crime problems have emerged since 1989. So terrible are the impacts for so many people that even Boris Yeltsin, a reform stalwart, had to campaign on a more moderate reform platform in the June 1996 election.

CUBA: BRIDLED NEOLIBERALISM?

The collapse of the Soviet Union and the Eastern bloc meant a drastic loss of aid and trade for Cuba even as U.S. pressure intensified through the passage of the Torricelli and Helms-Burton bills. The magnitude of the shock to the Cuban economy is reflected in a 75 percent drop in its imports (1989–94). In the face of capital shortages and severe hardships, the Cuban government has proclaimed a need to mobilize for survival and called this era the "special period in time of peace."

Programs and policies of the special period aim to more efficiently utilize domestic resources and labor, substitute domestically produced alternatives for scarce production inputs and consumer goods (including medicines), and create a business climate attractive to foreign capital. What makes the Cuban response to crisis conditions so interesting is that it appears to accept many capitalist economic practices, but with restrictions aimed at maintaining its commitment to socialism. Understanding the motivation for such a mobilization necessitates a review of Cuba's dependence on Eastern Europe and the former Soviet Union, the island's internal economic weaknesses, and domestic calls for both economic and political changes.

Cuba's Capital Shortage after the Collapse of the Eastern Bloc

Cuba's capital shortage followed the loss of Soviet bloc trade and aid. Soviet grants and loans were crucial to Cuba's economy. For example, Mesa-Lago (1993a) estimates that from 1960 to 1990, total Soviet aid to Cuba amounted to about 65 billion pesos, of which about 25.7 billion were loans. Without this aid, economic crisis would have hit Cuba much earlier. About two-thirds of Cuba's total trade deficit with the Soviets accumulated in the 1980s, with about half in the last four years of the decade. By the mid-1980s, Soviet aid and favorable trade arrangements for Cuba may have accounted for more than 22 percent of Cuba's national income. Part of this aid took the form of favorable terms of trade for Cuban sugar. But after smaller-than-expected harvests, Cuba had difficulty in meeting its sugar export commitments to the Soviet Union. In the 1986–90 period, Cuba had to spend $398 million in precious hard currency, or about 20 percent of its total hard currency export earnings, to buy sugar on the world market to fulfill its export obligations (Mesa-Lago 1993b).

Even though Cuba's terms of trade with the Soviets deteriorated by about 36 percent between 1986 and 1990, Mesa Lago calculates a net gain of about $10.1 billion for Cuba compared to what world market prices would have brought. But declining terms of trade in the late 1980s and domestic inefficiencies led Cuba to announce its "rectification" campaign aimed at economic rationalization and political mobilization.

Facing its own crisis, the Soviets continued to reduce aid to Cuba. For example, in 1991, the Soviets paid $0.25 per pound of Cuban sugar, 60 percent less than what they paid in 1990, although still two times the world price. By 1992, Soviet subsidies to Cuba were eliminated with sugar and oil prices set at world market levels, thus exacerbating Cuba's trade deficit and capital shortage. Despite "free trade" rhetoric in the United States and elsewhere, only 10–15 percent of world sugar is traded at market prices. Ending the Soviet price subsidy therefore placed Cuba among a small minority of "free market" sugar producers. As it only received $.09 to $.10 per pound, Cuba's revenues dropped sharply (Blasier 1993, 148). The island also relied heavily on oil imports from the Soviets for energy and for reexport to bring in hard currency. By 1990, oil reexports ended. The Cubans' favorable exchange ratio of a ton of sugar for 4.6 tons of oil rapidly disappeared so that by 1992, one ton of sugar brought in just slightly more than one ton of oil (Mesa-Lago 1993a). Cuban debt spiraled upward with the end of concessionary arrangements. Debt to the USSR jumped from about $24.5 billion in November 1989 to $27.6 billion a year later, and to $28 billion by September of 1992 (Mesa-Lago 1993a; as table 2 notes, most recent figures estimate Russian debt to be $20 billion).

In addition, Cuba was heavily dependent on the Eastern bloc through-out the 1980s for oil, food, and other essential raw materials. About 84 percent of its trade was with the CMEA socialist bloc countries. Cuba experienced an immediate hard-currency crisis when the CMEA ended all special concessions to Cuba in 1992. The Eastern bloc collapse forced Cuba to cut its imports from $8 billion in 1989 to $2 billion in 1994 as its export earnings collapsed and Soviet guarantees of Cuba's trade deficits were withdrawn. An indicator of the devastating impact of the loss of Soviet bloc aid and trade is the change in Cuba's GDP which grew at an average annual rate of 4.3 percent from 1959 to 1989. In the subsequent four years (1990–93) it declined by almost 35 percent.

Following the devastating loss in Eastern bloc trade, Cuba had to find new trading partners. It began to vigorously pursue Latin American and Caribbean links, signing partial agreements with the Latin American Integration Association, participating in the Association of Caribbean States, and forming closer ties to Caricom. By the end of 1996, Cuba had trade relationships with 108 countries, although the top ten countries account for two-thirds of it: Canada, Spain, Mexico, China, France, Russia, Venezuela, Netherlands Antilles, Italy, and the Netherlands. Trade with the western hemisphere, including Canada (10 percent of Cuba's trade alone), Latin America, and the Caribbean, accounts for 40 percent of its trade, while 32 percent is with the E.U. countries (Lee 1996a).

A high level of import dependence continues the hard-currency hemorrhage. Imports account for over half the food consumed in Cuba, including all soybeans and wheat, and about 98 percent of oils and fats, 99 percent of butter, 90 percent of beans, and about half of the rice (Alvarez 1994). Even as Cuba found new export outlets leading to an export growth of 10 percent in 1995, it still had to contend with an import dependence that was reflected in a 30 percent growth in imports linked to efforts to fuel the economy (in many instances, quite literally) (Cubaweb 1996).

The same growth pattern continued in the first six months of 1996, with exports jumping 32 percent and imports 54 percent, compared to the first half of 1995 (Cuban Ministry of Economy and Planning 1996). But economic growth continues to center around traditional primary products, such as sugar production (accounting for about half the export earnings), nickel, fisheries, and tobacco, and on tourism. Continued reliance on sugar means that small harvests contribute to Cuba's economic woes. To increase its harvest and earnings, Cuba has borrowed money from foreign sources to purchase fertilizers and herbicides. In a not atypical situation when hard data are difficult to find, one hears different values of new debt incurred for the harvest. One claim is that $135 million was borrowed from ten foreign banks and corporations on terms including a

25 percent profit share from sugar sales beyond a stipulated norm (La Riva 1996). Another estimate is that the government borrowed $300 million in high-cost, short-term credits and that the additional revenues from any increased harvest just covered the loans (Rice 1995, 3D). In any event, national debt remains a central concern and broad economic indicators are dramatically down despite recent growth (see table 2). The upturn since 1994 reflects Cuba's efforts to restructure its economy and trade relationships and to attract new foreign investment (discussed below).

Shortages and Responses

Notable achievements of the revolution are in jeopardy as a severe capital shortage, combined with intensified U.S. embargo limits and the purchase of industrial inputs, hampers the ability of the regime to maintain expected levels of services. Translated into everyday impacts on the population, the special period has meant a dramatic decline in the standard of living. Food shortages appeared and Cuba's famous health care system faced medicine and supply shortages (Benjamin 1994, 2). Reduced weight in children is one outcome, and a slight and temporary increase in infant mortality is another. By December 1996, however, the rate had declined to a record low of 7.9 per 1,000 live births from 9.4 in 1995 (Osa 1997; another estimate put the IMR at 9.0 for 1996 [table 2]). Another outcome, brought on by nutritional and vitamin deficiencies and lack of medicines (blocked by U.S. embargo), contributed to an epidemic of optic and peripheral neuropathy, which affected more than 50,000 people between 1991 and 1993. In addition, a UNICEF report raises concerns over Cuba's water supply since, in mid-1996, the principal chlorine production plant functioned at only 50 percent capacity due to shortages in spare parts. Difficulties in providing safe drinking water constitute the "worst threat to children's health" (Granma International 1997). Educational programs suffer as well. A paper shortage has meant fewer books, including school texts.

Housing construction and maintenance have been cut severely and petroleum-based transportation and production are not always maintained. Housing shortages continue to plague urban people disproportionately. Self-help housing in rural areas, in which people utilize available materials, is less feasible in the city. Unable to pay for materials and renovation, new construction in Havana slowed almost to a complete halt in the early 1990s. During the construction activity leading up to the 1991 Pan-American Games, the workers went on strike when the government announced that the new buildings would become part of the tourist infrastructure. The government then agreed to use some for housing, a continuing need throughout the revolutionary period. Havana neighborhoods that were already in need of repair and renovation when the "special period" hit continue to deteriorate.

Havana has experienced some of the worst impacts, especially food shortages. Transportation patterns had to be altered, and fuel shortages led to a reduction from 30,000 to about 7,000 vehicle trips per day. To replace petroleum-based vehicles, Cuba imported (from China) or manufactured two million bicycles. In the countryside, farmers resorted to oxen and horse-drawn carts to replace trucks (Castro 1996).

Not only has agricultural production suffered the loss of fuel, fertilizers, and other chemical inputs during the special period, but transport to the city has been cut as well. The revolution's gains in nutrition and equality of access to essentials were suddenly altered as rural people were better able to access locally grown food. Feeding the urban population has proved to be a logistical problem as well as a source of political discontent.

Special period policies may promote contradictory environmental outcomes because the driving force is survival rather than a particular long-term vision. Fuel, fertilizer, and money shortages motivate experiments in organic agriculture that have international experts excited by the possibilities of a sustainable system. At the same time, and at the other end of the environmental-technological spectrum, the government announced a joint project with Russia to raise additional funds to resume construction of the Juragua nuclear power plant near Cienfuegos (map 3). This time the goal is to attract a third party investor who would "earn back a $300 million investment in seven years" (New York Times News Service 1996).

Special-Period Policies

During the special period the government has promoted policies to enhance Cuba's international economic position at the same time it has explored new ways to use domestic resources to overcome shortages in food, medicine, and raw materials. Some of the export-oriented efforts include continued development of biotechnology and pharmaceutical industries. On the domestic side, there are experiments in organic agriculture and efforts to find old and new medicinal uses of locally grown plants. These are driven by petrochemical and capital shortages. These efforts on the international and domestic levels are the subject of considerable public-relations hype, although they play a minor economic role. Central to the special period are efforts to reshape the Cuban economy to more effectively utilize its scarce resources while making itself attractive to foreign capital. Central to the latter are programs similar to the neoliberal approach taken elsewhere in the Caribbean.

On 26 July 1993, Cuba's national holiday, President Castro announced a series of policies addressing issues of excess currency, commodity shortages, and increasing numbers of unemployed. Included were legalization of the dollar, private-sector employment (self-employment) in over a hundred categories, dollar bank accounts, and agrarian markets. The state would also seek to attract foreign investment in joint ventures. Each of the reforms may be interpreted as shifting, albeit under pressure, to more capitalist forms of societal organization.

The sacrifices, hardships, and "rehabilitation of the domestic economy," as the Cuban government describes it, seem to be paying off in economic performance. Cuba's GDP grew by 0.7 percent in 1994, 2.5 percent in 1995, and reportedly 7.8 percent in 1996 (J. Rodriguez 1997). This is above the 3.5 percent average for Latin America and the Caribbean in recent years. The region's growth is attributable, in part, to a $10 billion jump in direct foreign investment from 1995 to 1996 to a total of $30.8 billion. Cuba has also been recently able to attract foreign capital (reviewed below).

To what extent does Cuba's embrace of market principles open the door to capitalism? To what extent are the Cuban market reforms following a neoliberal model? It is often difficult to discern differences between what a capitalist and a socialist might advocate under crisis conditions. Paying close attention to what Fidel Castro says may provide some insight into the direction of the Cuban revolution. In a 30 April 1996 speech Castro celebrated

> what the people have learned and how the idea of economic efficiency . . . has taken hold. Controls, savings, efficiency, loss reduction, increased earnings, profitability, the fight for enterprise profitability, the tremendous battle to save a factory, to keep it from closing because of its economic and social importance, all this can now be observed.

Only the last item on his list would not appear in a capitalist neoliberal rendition. Priorities in socialist Cuba differ from the ones in capitalist countries. For example, new labor policies announced at the 17th Congress of the Central Organization of Cuban Trade Unions in April 1996 followed nearly a year of discussions involving virtually all workers in Cuba. The dialogue generated 70,000 proposals from local organizations that in turn shaped the focus of the congress (Campbell 1997). Thus, while layoffs and labor restructuring in capitalist countries are often sudden and surprise announcements for workers, in Cuba many of the policies are firmly in the realm of a highly politicized population.

On the other hand, Cuba's overall economic efforts follow the basic outline of the rest of the region's neoliberal reform program. For example, the Ministry of Economy and Planning discussion in 1996 of the continuing transformation of the economy could have occurred in almost any capitalist country:

In the first few months, these transformations have focused on rehabilitating domestic finances, downsizing production and service capacities, restructuring labor, and reorganizing self-employment. In addition, progress has been made in restructuring the banking sector while the process of economic opening to the outside world has continued.

Some of these specifics are discussed below as examples of Cuba's form of neoliberal reform.

"Rationalizing" the Cuban Workforce

Because of price controls, guaranteed incomes, and a shortage of commodities, inflationary tendencies have been present continuously since 1959. During the special period inflationary pressures have soared with the combination of greater commodity shortages, increasing numbers of unemployed receiving wage compensation without producing new wealth, and continued price controls on essential items. Guarantees of employment have been problematic throughout the revolutionary period. From early on, worker absenteeism and low productivity plagued Cuba's state enterprises. Without socialist-bloc aid, and faced with shortages of fuel, production inputs, and capital, wasteful and inefficient production could no longer be absorbed. In addition, the government has tried to move people back into agricultural labor to substitute for machines idled by parts and fuel shortages. Efforts at labor shifting have been coupled with reduced quotas for professional higher education. Given over thirty years of promoting formal education and relieving the population of labor drudgery, this new emphasis on manual labor has understandably faced resistance.

To make plants more efficient, state subsidies to individual enterprises have been reduced, forcing greater accountability for resource use. With plants operating at only 30 percent of capacity in 1995, it is no wonder that Cuba downsized the labor force in state enterprises (La Riva 1996). A 4 May 1995 Cuban newspaper headline proclaimed, "Employment-Cuba: Full Employment Is a Thing of the Past." By then, rationalization measures had led to the elimination of about 140,000 jobs (Acosta 1995). An additional 11,000 cuts in government ministries and civil service positions were planned for 1995/96. The real unemployment rate is hard to discern. The Cuban government places it at 8 percent (1995–96), while a Cuban NGO claims 40 percent of the labor force unemployed (including one-third of the male and two-thirds of the female labor force), as of 1993 (ANEIC 1994).

A smaller workforce and more careful resource use led to a productivity increase of 8.5 percent in 1996. Part of the new economic program, the Direct Incentive Program, ties wages to productivity. The number of workers included in the Direct Incentive System jumped from 17 percent of state enterprises and cooperatives in 1995 to about 23 percent (830,000) in 1996 (Rodriguez 1996). As a result, while productivity grew by 8.5 percent, average salaries jumped 6.8 percent (from 190 to 203 pesos/month).

By 1996, total subsidies to state enterprises fell to a quarter of the 1993 level (and were kept under 1400 billion pesos, or about 200 billion less than budgeted). Resource efficiency and employment rationalization seem to be paying off. In 1996, for the first time in a decade, net earnings of state enterprises exceeded subsidies by 756 million pesos (M. Rodriguez 1997).

One of the hallmarks of Cuban socialism, its social safety net, has been tattered during the special period, as the conditions of work illustrate. The government provides unemployed workers with alternate job offers. Surplus workers, or those transferred permanently or temporarily to jobs of similar technical demands, may receive the same salary as in the previous job. Available workers, or those for whom new jobs are unavailable, are entitled to 60 percent of their pay, although some claim much lower figures. When jobs are offered but declined, unemployment compensation is limited to one month. In 1994 the government budgeted $97.2 million to cover these social security payments, and it allocated $154 million in 1995, thus cutting into the savings from rationalization substantially. Even with such allocations the social safety net has been weakened. A study by the Association of Independent Cuban Economists reports that 88.9 percent of respondents (of 117 nuclear families surveyed) claim that their sources of income, including social security payments, are inadequate to meet the cost of living and they must engage in other activities to make up the shortfall (ANEIC 1995). As the regime introduced charges for previously free services, it soon recognized that some people, especially retired people and unemployed single mothers, were not receiving basic necessities. In response, by the end of 1996, the government proposed to exempt payments for services and in-kind assistance to households with demonstrated need (Lee 1996b). This has yet to be implemented nationally.

While rationalizing employment in the state sector, another policy legalized self-employment. Special period rationalization measures and unemployment pressures led many people to seek income in a variety of small-scale, mostly service activities. Officially about 200,000 people, or about 5 percent of the workforce, and perhaps that many again unofficially, now engage in self-employment (Ministry of Economy and Planning 1996). According to the Communist Party Politburo (23 March 1996):

It is evident that the figure is much higher, since there are thousands more who engage in self-employment of some kind or another without the necessary authorization. Self-employment will necessarily grow in the near future, since the inevitable struggle for economic efficiency demands the rationalization of the excess labor force.

The government wants to encourage up to another 500,000 people to become self-employed (Acosta 1995).

The Dollarization of Cuba: Illegal and Legal Forms

Black market and informal market growth accompanied increasing unemployment, galloping inflation, and growing commodity shortages. Driven by an explosion in illegal activity that threatened the social fabric and by an uncontrolled de facto devaluation of the peso, the government in July 1993 made it legal to possess dollars and announced the intention to gradually make pesos convertible with other currencies. At the same time, the state established an official parallel market with special stores in which Cubans could buy imported goods for dollars. As the peso free fall continued, it reached new lows relative to the U.S. dollar, with a black market exchange rate of 150:1 in April 1994. Those with dollars were able to attain significantly better living conditions than those without, and this growing inequality fueled the rise of large parallel and black markets (Rice 1995, 3D). Special period shortages have led to many other forms of illegal activity. Eckstein describes a large part of it as "producers and distributors" who "siphoned off goods for private profiteering." Black-market trade became pervasive and may have grown "from $2 billion in 1989 to $14.5 billion by mid-1993—exceeding the value of official retail trade" (Eckstein 1994, 124).

The regime saw increased currency valuation and stability as essential to establishing foreign-investor confidence and attracting new investment. High inflation, low exports, and high imports increased the budget deficit, which Castro reported as reaching 34 percent of GDP in 1993 (Castro 1996). Thus one dimension of the economic policy was to reduce significantly the number of pesos in circulation, improving the peso/dollar exchange rate, and thus helping to reduce the budget deficit. In early 1994 there were about CP$12 billion in circulation, but by June 1996, CP$2.8 billion had been cut. The Ministry of Economy and Planning cites the improving value of the peso against the dollar in the informal market, dropping from an average CP$32.1/U.S.$1 in 1995 to CP$19.2/U.S.$1 in 1996. Between the currency policy and efforts to increase exports, by 1994 the budget deficit dropped to 7.4 percent of GDP, and to less than an estimated 6 percent by 1995 (*Business Week* 1995). More recent figures from the Cuban Ministry of the Economy and Planning show the budget deficit at only 3.6 percent in 1995 and 2.4 percent in 1996 (Rodriguez 1997).

Legalizing dollars and establishing parallel markets has allowed the government to regain some control over the value of the peso while offering the population improved access to commodities and some protection against dollar-driven local currency devaluation. Yet the shortages of the special period continue and so does the advantage of access to dollars. One fear is that stark income distinctions may give rise to a new class system. Analco (1995, 23) observes that

> there is an evident transfer in the country of the homes, autos, jewels, works of art and other wealth that some families possess into the hands of people who have access to dollars, who could now be considered the new rich, among whom one does not find, paradoxically, many government leaders and members of the top staff of the Cuban military. Among the "new rich," one can find, incredibly, waiters and cooks' assistants and maids and taxi drivers, porters, etc. There are also executives of corporations, Cuban representatives of foreign firms and others who by their activities are linked to the dollar sphere. These people have displaced with their level of income scientists, doctors, top academics, lawyers, engineers and other professionals, as well as teachers who by government disposition and sphere of work have no access to the much desired dollars.

Inequality continues to grow along with Cuba's "dual economy" in which some workers are in the dollar sphere and others receive wages in pesos. To address some of the inequality and raise revenue, new graduated income taxes on both hard currency and peso incomes were enacted.

The Partial Privatization of Agriculture

In 1993, as one response to special period food shortages, the government began replacing most state farms and sugar plantations with basic units of cooperative production (UBPCs), a new form of workers' cooperatives. Coop members own the equipment and means of production, although the land remains state property. Thus UBPCs represent not only privatization, but the profit motive as the organizing principle. It was hoped that the possibility of profits would provide production incentives, and agricultural output did indeed respond. It grew 17.3 percent between 1995 and 1996. Because UBPCs have the right to hire and fire workers, new possibilities arise for the UBPC management to act in a capitalist class capacity relative to nonmember employees. However, the number of nonmember employees remains small. By the end of 1993, about 87 percent of the land held in state sugar plantations had been converted to cooperatives. UBPCs were extended to other agricultural sectors as well and by the end of 1994 occupied 40.6 percent of Cuba's agricultural land, leaving state enterprises cultivating just 29.8 percent of the land

(Deere 1995, 14). Thus the public sector contains state enterprises while UBPCs are a new mixed private/public sector. The private sector consists of existing cooperatives, in which farmers combine their privately held resources, and individual farmers.

Farmer's Markets

Until the special period farmer's markets, surpluses from both public and private sources had been sold to the state for a premium. For a short period in the early 1980s individual farmers were allowed to sell their surpluses directly to the public in "peasant farmer's markets." Although these enterprises immediately relieved urban food shortages, Castro ended them in 1986, fearing the emergence of a new class of farmer millionaires. However, after food shortages in the 1990s generated an uncontrolled black market with soaring prices, the government in October 1994 once again permitted farmer's markets (Pastor and Zimbalist 1995, 10).

Unlike the earlier farmer's markets, all producers outside the sugar cane sector, not just individual farmers, can sell surpluses in the new markets. The government still rations essential foods to ensure universal access, although availability remains a problem, especially in Havana. In a successful effort to counter the black market and bring down prices, the government's Gaviota state enterprises dumped large quantities of pork on the new farmer's markets. Overall, the return to farmer's markets seems to be making food available at lower prices, even as the state enterprise role in farmer's markets declines. One indication of this success is that, as of June 1996, sales in the farmer's markets were 27 percent higher and prices 35 percent lower than one year previous (Ministry of Economy and Planning 1996). In addition, the state introduced a tax on the value of projected gross sales to bring in revenue, control profiteering, and encourage, by means of lower tax rates in Havana, a greater supply of foodstuffs to the capital. Farmer's markets operating with pesos, not dollars, also provide a means of absorbing excess currency. Because the peso now has exchange value in farmer's markets, it is increasing in value compared to the dollar.

The success of the farmer's markets is accompanied by the emergence of a new group of vendors serving as intermediaries between growers and consumers. While vendors are still small in number, the Politburo is especially concerned about both privilege and people's extraordinary responsiveness to market opportunities. Given the extreme economic hardships, contradictions with socialist consciousness once again arise, as do questions of whether it can be achieved and/or sustained.

Foreign Investment

Cuba's domestic efforts to rein in inflation, establish peso convertibility, and achieve higher levels of productivity are designed to improve economic performance and attract foreign capital. In 1996 foreign investment accounted for 3 percent of Cuba's GDP and employed 5 percent of the labor force (*Prensa Latina* 1996). From 1989 to 1995, foreigners invested $2 billion in tourism, mining, transportation, and other industries (Navarro 1995). Significant investors in telecommunications come from Mexico, in tourism from Spain, with about 2,300 hotel rooms in the Sol Melia, Guitart, and Riu hotel chains, and from Canada, with Sherritt Nickel. At least 300 companies from 43 countries have invested in Cuba.

These investments are contributing to Cuba's GDP growth. For example, tourism earnings were up nearly 50 percent in 1996 compared to a year earlier, the hotel sector accounting for the largest growth of investment at 107 percent. In 1996, an additional $300 million was invested in the tourist industry alone. Foreign tourists increased from 250,000 in 1985 to over 1,000,000 by the end of 1996. Another recipient of foreign investment, nickel production, grew 31 percent in 1996.

Cuba has aggressively pursued foreign capital through trade missions and fairs, and by altering the legal arrangements for foreign participation and investment. But Cuba still faces foreign investment constraints. As it seeks greater global integration and greater regional integration with Latin America and the Caribbean as its natural trading partners, Cuba has to respond to external pressures. Politically, members of the E.U., responding to U.S. pressure, are pushing for democratic reform as a basis for doing business. Even if business opportunities arise, Cuba has still to create a commercial infrastructure capable of operating in an unprotected competitive setting. In addition, Cuba needs to develop personnel who are skilled and knowledgeable in international finance, commerce, and exchange. It already has established and continues to develop qualities attractive to foreign capital, including, according to Regueiro (1994, 10–11), a stable political/social order, a safe business climate and protected investment, growing relations in Latin America, a highly qualified labor force, existing idle productive capacity, and strong scientific potential in such sectors as pharmaceuticals, biotechnology, and computerized medical equipment. Indeed, *Radio Havana* (10 April 1995) cited a study ranking Cuba among the thirty lowest-risk countries for foreign investment.

While a standard neoliberal program calls for opening the entire economy to foreign investment, Cuba has focused on attracting foreign investment to the export sector, not production for the internal market (Regueiro 1995, 7). Thus, attracting foreign capital is one side of Cuba's policy, while the other side is trying to shelter the internal economy from global capitalism and trying to maintain an extensive (socialist) safety net. Yet pressures on the fragile socialist economy are intense. One indication of how rapidly conditions are changing in Cuba (and for Cuba on the world scene) is that in less than one year, from September 1995 to May

1996, Cuba enacted two new laws aimed at attracting foreign capital. The first (discussed in the next section) establishes new, more liberal ownership possibilities, tax-free profit repatriation, and labor arrangements for foreign capital. The second institutionalizes export-processing zones. Further, in response to intensified U.S. pressure on foreign investors in Cuba through the Helms-Burton bill, the new law permits foreign plant operators to sell 25 percent of their goods inside Cuba, thus eroding previous domestic safeguards. Four initial free zones are being built, three in Havana, and one in Cienfuegos, described for public relations purposes in the international edition of the Cuban newspaper *Granma* as "about 300 kilometers southeast of Havana and near the Colón duty-free zone at the Panama Canal" (Rodriguez 1996; see maps 1 and 3 and the parallels to neoliberal free zone promotion in capitalist countries described in chap. 5).

By the end of 1996, Cubans had drafted rules to regulate a new private-insurance sector for businesses. In a departure from popular reliance on a state-provided social welfare system, there is now discussion of legislation to cover individual insurance policies for accident, life, and property and to regulate special private funds for education and retirement. Clearly, the special period has brought a significant shift in thinking about the role of the state. As Dr. Ramon Martinez Carrera, president of the boards of directors of insurance companies in Cuba, put it:

> We have moved forward from that ideal situation, in which only the state worried about these matters and the rest of us considered ourselves consumers, to a much more balanced and complementary situation where, without the state completely pulling out of the picture, we can begin to make a contribution and take certain precautions. (Rodriguez 1996)

The New Foreign Investment Law

In September 1995 a new foreign investment law (Law no. 77) expanded opportunities for investors beyond the limits of the previous 1982 Decree-Law no. 50. It offers foreign investors the options of majority control in mixed enterprises, total foreign ownership and control, and assurances against expropriation, including an indemnity of the investment at its commercial value. The law still protects public health, education, and the industries run by the armed forces from foreign investment, although in these excepted sectors some foreign investment may occur with government approval. For example, the armed forces sector in Cuba now operates an "entrepreneurial system" that may be open to foreign investment. In a strong (desperate?) bid for foreign investment, the law permits

> free transfer abroad, in freely convertible currency, of the foreign investor's profits or dividends received from the joint enterprise as well as the amounts

due him in case of termination, sale or cession of his part, or the liquidation, in any form, of the joint enterprise. The transfer of these funds to his country or to any other country will be tax-free. (Fernandez 1996)

In return for these investment concessions, foreign firms pay a tax of 30 percent on net profits. The tax increases to a maximum of 50 percent for natural-resource industries. In addition, the employer must pay 11 percent taxes for utilizing the Cuban workforce and must also contribute 14 percent to the social security fund. Enterprises with any foreign investment must maintain a Cuban bank account, thereby providing the government with a hard currency float.

The Labor Regime under the Foreign Investment Law

Especially interesting is the form of "labor regime" established by Law no. 77 (continuing the practice established under Decree-Law no. 50). A Cuban government employment agency mediates the labor market. Included in the agency's tasks are hiring and worker dismissal and replacement. Workers are paid in Cuban currency by the state employment agency, but the agency is paid in hard currency by the foreign investor. The drive for hard currency in Cuba may overwhelm concern for working conditions, and it already diminishes possibilities for worker participation in decision making. The Cuban government's role raises the specter of a new class system, with the state acting as coinvesting capitalist or as capitalist intermediary between foreign capital and workers. In either case, exploitation is a concern. One U.S. journalist claims that Cuban geologists receive less than $10 per month while foreign companies pay the government $2,700 (*Wall Street Journal*, 5 August 1996, A18).

Socialist equality and justice are irrelevant to foreign capital (see chap. 5). A willingness to operate in Cuba stems from potential profits in production for international as well as Cuban markets. Profitability, as the minimum condition for investment, motivates government policy. Given Cuba's crisis conditions, a direct relationship between the state and foreign capital may be essential to the regime's survival.

While trying to encourage foreign investment, Cuba is quite concerned about the negative impacts of foreign capital. The demonstration effect of wealthy tourists, growing prostitution tied to the tourism industry, imbalances created by the positive employment conditions in joint ventures with capitalist enterprises, and what is perceived as the inevitability of corruption associated with capitalist business practice are all concerns and fears for the continuing revolution. As a Politburo report (1996) comments, "foreign capitalists establishing joint ventures in Cuba are also leaving their mark on our workers' consciousness." Efforts to attract foreign capital involve both institutional accommodations and a cultural reorientation by the state and population. Once pressure for cultural change is introduced, openness to a fuller market and political participation may follow.

THE MARKET AS A DOUBLE-EDGED SWORD

The Central Committee of the Cuban Communist Party sees achieving production efficiency as central to surviving the crisis of the special period. At the same time, the Politburo advocates "accelerating, improving, and prioritizing political and ideological work" and maintaining the fundamental socialist goals of equality (Politburo Report 1996): "The market is part of the solution, but above all the national economic plan is the key. Without a plan, without the preeminence of the state that guarantees it, there is no socialism, nor can there be." Both "market" and "plan" are at the heart of the strategy. Can these be reconciled? This is not a new question (Nove 1983). Is it possible for Cuba to forge a new system in which the strengths of market coordination are combined with social justice, equality, and the fundamental goals associated with a Marxian vision? Should Cuba abandon the Marxian emphasis on class struggle? Is it possible for Cubans to extend market relations without re-creating a capitalist class system? Can the social-equity objectives of the revolution survive a market-linked revival of capitalist consciousness?

The various special period policies raise questions about the distinction between market reforms that may promote Cuban socialist objectives and those reforms that may undermine it. These questions are not answered here, but they constitute the backdrop for reconsidering markets as central to Cuba's economic dilemmas.

Capitalist Markets and Their Threats to Cuban Socialism

Capitalism and capitalist market relations are associated with a particular organization of society. Under capitalism, market exchange becomes the central means of obtaining necessities and participating in society. People must go to the "market" for the goods and services they need and become "commodities" themselves when they sell their labor power to earn money. Inherently unequal class positions emerge tied to relative command over society's resources. But on the labor market, as in other markets, power is highly unequal between the buyers and sellers of wage labor. Thus the turn to the market as central to the solution of economic crisis in socialist countries would seem to contribute to the further breakdown of social order. In Cuba, for example, the new UBPC agricultural cooperatives' ability to hire and fire workers (although still in practice on a small scale) significantly alters social relations among people. Such workers, without access to sufficient property or means of production, are forced onto the labor market, where their ability to produce a surplus value beyond the wage redefines the essence of social relations in society.

The implications of extending market relations in Cuba are therefore profound. Inherent inequalities associated with power in market transactions threaten Cuba's social equality. Socialism in Cuba has meant the pursuit of equality for people and regions, at least rhetorically, in as full a sense as modern society discusses. Thus, inequalities based on class, race, gender, and geography have been targeted by the revolution since 1959. Geographical inequalities were addressed by redefining provincial boundaries and emphasizing provincial growth poles, beginning in 1975. The underlying objective was to minimize urban/rural and interprovincial disparities (Eckstein 1994).

Equality in Cuban socialism includes both the political and economic spheres. In the economic sphere, both production and consumption activities should, at least in theory, be equally dispersed and accessible, and, ultimately, defined by democratic process. To the extent that planning overcame income, production, and access inequalities brought about by market mechanisms, the spatial distribution of economic activity was altered. The Cuban experience is one of having overcome a society and landscape that was highly polarized in 1959. Over the course of the revolution, Cuba has achieved one of world's most equal societies (Susman 1987). From total urban primacy and vast urban/rural disparities in 1959, Cuban society has closed the gap. Able to emphasize its social goals, in part because of the cushion of Soviet aid, Cuba until recently downplayed the importance of spatially efficient and often lower-cost clustering of economic activities. Exchange, mediated by need rather than the market, means that prices do not define social roles. Efforts to achieve socialist goals included using central planning instead of the market to coordinate economic activity. Central planning's ability to avoid assigning market-determined prices to many goods helped Cuba escape from the spatially, economically, and socially polarizing tendencies of capitalist societies, including those that prevailed before the revolution. It is only in the context of the present market reforms and the relentless search for economizing possibilities that social and spatial polarization threaten to reemerge.

Capitalist markets are "fixed sites where the play of supply and demand form prices and thus allocate individual incomes and class positions in society." Thus, capitalist markets constitute a social relation with a de facto class composition, and markets become "the sites where life chances were distributed (and ruined) through price fluctuations" (Altvater 1993, 57). Beyond their economic function, markets tend to spatially bias access and outcomes, including sites of future investment. Markets also tend to have gender, race, and age biases. Reintroducing market relations brings the danger that inequalities and biases that were substantially diminished under Cuban socialism will quickly reappear; women and blacks may suffer. Reversals in conditions and in consciousness could happen quite quickly, for capitalism is a force to be reckoned with. For a society envisioning expanded market relations, the historical record is extensive. Given the relatively short time since the revolution to reorient society toward socialism, a return to a market ideology that abandons socialism would seem altogether too easy. The Soviet turn from planning to the market occurred, as Altvater (1993, 17) put it, "with quite staggering ease." For Cuba he comments that "this leads one to suppose that even after forty years, little had been deposited in the system by way of a social, or socialist, alternative substance."

E. P. Thompson's (1963, 90) classic study of the emergence of capitalism in England is also instructive. He documents capitalism's alteration of ideology and culture. Within just a few generations of capitalist relations in the countryside, long-standing claims to the land by the mass of the population disappeared. Instead, acculturated to capitalist production, the population dropped its active opposition to capitalism and instead focused narrowly on "working day struggles." The coming of the market quickly eroded rights to land. In England, Marx tells us (1976, 878), "a mass of 'free' and unattached proletarians was hurled onto the labor market by the dissolution of the bands of feudal retainers." For the Cubans now being hurled onto the labor market or seeking profits in UBPCs or in self-employment, market exchange begins to define the importance of people in society. Tendencies for class distinctions to reappear come not only from employment in foreign-financed joint ventures but also from many kinds of market relations.

To the extent that the Cuban government restricts markets by limiting the scope of self-employment, regulating farmer's markets, and restricting the prerogatives of foreign capital, the ravages of capitalist expansion may be contained. Even with containment, however, income inequalities and unequal use of money tend to promote values antithetical to the revolution. The power of money promotes dissolution of community (Harvey 1985). Those competing in capitalist markets seek their advantage at the expense of others. As Marx (1976, 381) long ago observed, "Under free competition, the immanent laws of capitalist production confront the individual capitalist as a coercive force external to him." Within a country pursuing market-based relief to crisis, such tendencies must be examined carefully.

The Option of Market Socialism

If unfettered market capitalism fails to maintain basic social-equity goals, what about a form of "market socialism"? This question resurfaced in the post-1989 era in many forums, and it became a central discussion point for people in and outside Cuba seeking a survival strategy. But throughout this Cuban search for a survival strategy is an underlying reference to Marx's analysis and critique of capitalism and his vision of emancipation, social justice, and equality.

This is at the heart of the Cuban dilemma, for a capitalist class system is antithetical to socialism, and unregulated capitalism is incapable of promoting (1) a high degree of equity/social justice and (2) efficient utilization of all social resources, including labor power. In addition, increasing attention is going to capitalism's incapability of adequately responding to (3) issues of sustainable economic activity, especially in environmental terms. These goals, or at least the first two, have constituted the socialist agenda for over a century. Since the collapse of the Soviet bloc, and in the face of both external and internal pressures on Cuba, many see significant market reforms as the only option. Socialists, identifying weaknesses in central planning, often advocate "market socialism," while capitalists call for neoliberalism—opening the economy to unbridled market forces.

Market socialists offer political and economic arguments to support their position. As a political argument, market socialism offers to establish social justice, equity, and democracy as primary values. Drawing legitimacy from both liberal claims for civil liberties and socialist equity, market socialism claims to combine the best of a history of civil liberties associated with some capitalist societies with the magic of the market, while leaving behind the inequality and injustice so closely tied to capitalism. But what is the basis for property relations, and what is its distinction from capitalism? Can a market socialist system in a small, open economy suffering an extreme capital shortage survive? Is efficient use of resources in a capitalist market system of relative resource abundance compatible with a socialist definition of efficiency in a context of relative scarcity?

Is Central Planning the Problem?

The main example of nonmarket socialism, the former Soviet Union, proved a powerful influence on Cuba, which copied elements of Soviet planning and organization and maintained adherence to the system even after the Soviets abandoned it. But the Soviet bloc socialist alternatives to capitalism were not self-sustaining, did not adequately protect civil liberties, and suffered declining support among the people. Perhaps these failings were due to the unfortunate Stalinist legacy, delegitimizing socialist claims to democracy while failing to continuously improve standards of living. Without strong popular support, often dependent on the extent of popular participation in decision making, revolutionary goals are difficult to achieve. In addition, there are many obstacles to constructing a socialist society in the midst of a global capitalist system. Having a vision of social justice and efficient resource use is not the same as having a blueprint complete with economic organizational principles to attain those goals.

Soviet central planning did not meet either economic or political democracy goals. Soviet "democratic" centralism and planning remained in practice a top-down hierarchical structure with sharp limitations on popular input. In both the former Soviet Union and Cuba, inefficiencies, inappropriate pricing strategies, and errors led to uneven access to production and consumption.

Advocates of market socialism believe that central planning is theoretically and empirically incapable of ensuring efficient resource use. One problem arises from the centrally planned economy's guarantee of full employment and income without respect to performance. Thus many state enterprises operate on a "soft budget," ignoring both real resource costs and real losses that may arise in production. Central planning contributes to inefficiencies in which monetary costs exceed gains. Gross inefficiencies and waste in the former Soviet Union and Eastern European economies were abundant. Despite these problems, during the seven-year period up to 1988, the former Soviet Union achieved GDP annual growth rates averaging 3.5 percent, and the rest of Eastern Europe achieved rates of 3 percent (Griffin and Khan 1995, 162). This exceeded the below 3 percent growth rate for the OECD market economies. Without the much celebrated inefficiency of central planning, who knows how high the growth rate would have been? Once capitalist market reforms began in the Eastern bloc countries, their growth rates all plummeted, and by 1990 they were negative. While the centrally planned economies of the Soviet bloc were not a model of efficient management, it may be that the failures stem not from central planning per se, but from the lack of democratic participation in decision making. The Soviet bloc may be more of an argument for promoting strong popular involvement than an argument against central planning. This is especially worth considering in light of the respectable standard of living achieved under central planning and its precipitous decline since.

Thus there is no clear empirical guide for determining whether or not state intervention is efficient or what limits of such intervention should be. Different outcomes may follow if the decision to intervene is based on a democratic process to determine economic priorities or by a hierarchical imposition of a central plan. Market socialists emphasize economic performance and democratic politics. But the viewpoint of most market socialists is the transition from capitalism to socialism. In contrast, the question before Cuba is how to maintain socialism while embarking on a market-based economy.

Cuban Interest in the Chinese Path

Should Cuba emulate the Chinese experience? Some point to China as a successful example of a transition from centrally planned socialism to a new system that includes economic liberalization. Before market reforms, centrally planned China's growth rate already was substantial, at 5.8 percent from 1968 to 1978. Following reforms, the GDP has grown even more rapidly (Griffin and Khan 1995, 163). But China, unlike Cuba, was not operating in a crisis situation, and the Chinese context is quite different. The Chinese fourteenth party congress in October 1992 confirmed the goal of creating a "socialist market economy." Can socialism be maintained in China by relying on foreign investment, advantaging urban industrialization, and accepting massive unemployment? Growing inequality, especially urban/rural disparities along with increasing unemployment, is serious enough to warrant a reconsideration of Chinese economic policy. Social instability may follow along with higher unemployment (beyond the estimated 100 million unemployed in the rural sector and millions in the urban sector) and social polarization. The Chinese nondemocratic political system is able to respond and adjust to changing circumstances without organized opposition. Griffin and Kahn see this as central to China's reforms (1995, 195):

> One must be careful not to push historical parallels too far, but the Chinese experience does suggest that maintaining firm political control during a period of systemic change in the economy has enormous advantages. This point is especially true if the style of reform is experimental, flexible and incremental—as it was in China—so that the reformmongers receive a steady flow of information that enables them to monitor progress during the transition.

The Cubans confront an inflation problem stemming from shortages; the Chinese are dealing with inflation linked to investment rates that exceed economic growth, and with problems in distribution, rising food prices due to government purchases, and industrial inefficiencies. Whereas the Cubans are searching the world over for investment, the Chinese have been inundated. For example, from 1979 to 1994, China received $84.54 billion in foreign direct investment, but most of it, 72.4 percent ($61.19 billion), arrived in 1992–94. Most sectors in China are open to foreign companies competing against state enterprises, a situation not yet envisioned in Cuba. However far the market reforms in China have gone, the government still intervenes in markets both directly and indirectly, often distorting market signals to achieve political aims. Thus, the market governs, but at the government's pleasure.

The Chinese effort to achieve macroeconomic stability by controlling inflation, allocating resources to the most profitable sectors, and ensuring the value of the currency is similar in many ways to the Cuban effort. Austerity programs all take on the same general appearance, at least to those finding more austere cupboards, even though the economic conditions leading to the programs may be very different.

For Cuba, the lessons of China may be much more in terms of the political process than in borrowing Chinese policy. Tad Szulc (1996), describing the China model as appealing to Castro, says:

> China has come up with the perfect solution for the survival of a "socialist revolutionary" society: Create a market economy, with large-scale foreign investment, while brutally forbidding political freedom. Mr. Castro has often said he wants to avoid the mistakes of Mikhail Gorbachev, who he thinks brought about the collapse of the Soviet Union by permitting both economic reform and political liberalization.

Thus, from the socialist side, the Chinese have embarked on market reforms with at least a fifteen-year record of greater inequality, greater social and economic polarization, and higher unemployment, all within the context of a politically repressive regime. But even the Chinese government has been unable to stop the extension of market forces into realms previously reserved entirely to the political sphere. In Shanghai, for example, a stagnant real-estate market in the East Shanghai development zone led the municipal government to entice people to buy high-cost apartments by offering residency permits with the privileges of Shanghai citizenship.

> In doing so, the city has thrown open its once jealously guarded gates, and turned the residence card, a powerful tool of Communist political control, into a commodity. Nearly 20 years of market-oriented reforms have weakened most elements of the Communist Party's web of control. State affiliated work units, once all powerful arbiters of everything from workers' housing to political status, have steadily lost authority as the private sector expands. (Kahn 1996, A9)

With remarkable prescience, Marx and Engels (1980, 39), speaking of the force of capitalism, declare that

> the cheap prices of its commodities are the heavy artillery with which it batters down all Chinese walls . . . and compels all nations, on pain of extinction, to adopt the bourgeois mode of production; it compels them to introduce what it calls civilisation into their midst, i.e., to become bourgeois themselves. In one word, it creates a world after its own image.

Cuban Central Planning and Pressures for More Market Reforms

Central planning continues to prevail in Cuba, even with its market reforms, although the old central planning body (JUCEPLAN) has been replaced by a new group more responsive to the flexible demands of the times. While new trade and investment agreements are announced every month, the crisis of the special period continues. Able to negotiate deals with foreign companies, decide on production incentives, and proceed with its plans, the government's ultimate decision-making authority remains intact.

But pressure to alleviate the hardships of the special period and calls for more open society-wide dialogue continue. Interest in greater market reform is growing as different segments of the population favor market reforms for various reasons. The promarket population includes some of those displaced from work during the special period who see little or no opportunity to improve their well-being without entrepreneurial activity. These include those displaced from jobs due to rationalization, including geographic consolidation. Some of the promarket reform people are spurred on by the clear benefits to those able to operate in the dollar economy. Service sector jobs, especially those catering to tourists, offer access to dollars. Also among those in the dollar economy are people receiving remittances of hard currencies from abroad, which disproportionately go to lighter-skinned Cubans, reflecting the composition of families who left Cuba previously. Urban and rural access to necessities and to markets also differs, as discussed earlier. Thus a closer analysis would reveal growing class, race and spatial divisions within society. Promarket positions are associated with such factors as location, gender, skin color, and, of course, a desire for a better life.

Another promarket reform position, shared by people outside Cuba with other motivations, is the belief that free markets are synonymous with democracy. Although most Cuban socialists would disagree, there is a strong, unquestioned assumption about this unity in many quarters. Supported by the major global political, economic, and cultural institutions, a flourishing democracy is seen as essential to a healthy economy, and this is linked to the "freedom" to participate in the market. In addition, Cubans who support socialism but reject the remnants of Soviet-style planning and constraints on civil liberties join in advocating market reforms. For example, Juan Antonio Blanco, the founder of an NGO named after a priest, the Felix Varela Center, believes it essential to explore alternative paths to socialism given the realities of the post-Soviet world and the desire for greater democracy (Blanco 1994).

CONCLUSION

The Soviet Union is gone, socialist regimes have collapsed in Eastern Europe, and China's market reforms, implemented by a repressive state, have produced the familiar outcomes of greater inequality, unemployment, and dislocation. Only Cuba holds out, but for how long? This epoch would have us believe that socialism is dead; neoliberal solutions to the world's dilemmas prevail. It is no wonder that this epoch gave us Fukuyama's *The End of History* (1992) in which the historical conditions that led to socialist ideology are whisked away, class differences are eliminated as an analytical category, and harmony supposedly prevails. Political democracy becomes the universal goal and economic conflict ceases as a category. Confusing political outcomes with economic policies, agents of global capital, such as the IMF and World Bank, advocate neoliberal economic reforms as the road to (economic) openness and, by implication, political democracy.

Cuba's special period coincides with the "special period of the capitalist model of development." Capitalism's strong crisis tendencies are evident the world over. The way out of the crisis, according to the dominant voices of the capitalist world, is to pursue neoliberalism. Cuba observes similar outcomes to such neoliberal reforms, whether in the advanced capitalist countries, Latin America, the Caribbean, or the former Eastern bloc. These include greater inequalities across the population and space, uneven development, and the limitations on some people's abilities to achieve decent standards of living. Yet, in the face of its harshest crisis, and without alternative sources of capital and credit, Cuba has pursued a course of macroeconomic stabilization and of seeking greater international competitiveness through neoliberal reforms.

But according to the government and the Communist Party, Cuba's reforms are intended to protect and perpetuate the revolution's goals, not to abandon them. Along with market reforms are strong efforts to save the health system. Openings to foreign production and commodities are accompanied by state initiatives to stimulate domestic food production and to develop sustainable agricultural practices that require fewer artificial inputs.

The question of whether there is such a thing as limited capitalism remains the great mystery of the special period. In other words, can the government just use profits to motivate farm cooperative production? Is it possible that the labor relations inherent in profit-seeking enterprises, whether farms or foreign corporations, may escape the conflicts of class relations? Will private-property rights over the means of production held by foreign companies disadvantage local producers?

For Cuba to pursue a fully capitalist model of development under great duress would be to abandon the gains of the revolution in precisely those arenas of equality and justice and the beginnings, perhaps, of a transformation of consciousness away from the capitalist market model. Indeed, Cuba has moved toward the neoliberal model of macroeconomic reforms, modifying property institutions, and allowing the profit motive to guide a growing share of its citizens. Statistical indicators suggest that these reforms have improved economic conditions. Cuba is also experimenting with new, nonstate, political institutions and a more open policy toward individual religious beliefs. Throughout the crisis and transformation, the state remains the central political and economic actor, able to curtail these openings and reforms and to set the agenda for striving for a more just society. But in the face of new domestic profit incentives, market relations, and the growing presence of foreign capital, will the Cuban people maintain the will and the consciousness to strive for a more just society?

NOTE

1. I would like to acknowledge the many helpful comments made by Tom Klak, John Peeler, and Linden Lewis on previous drafts of this paper.

SUGGESTIONS FOR FURTHER READING

Eckstein, Susan. *Back from the Future: Cuba under Castro*. Princeton: Princeton University Press, 1994. This book presents a careful analysis of domestic and global influences on Cuban policy decisions and shifts and makes clear that Castro does not simply rule in a totalitarian state. Contradictory interests within the government and society result in policies reinforcing one interest or another, even if often producing nonoptimal economic outcomes.

Rosset, Peter, and Medea Benjamin, eds. *The Greening of the Revolution: Cuba's Experiment with Organic Agriculture*. San Francisco: Global Exchange, 1996.

———. "Cuba's Nationwide Conversion to Organic Agriculture." *Capitalism, Nature, Society* 5, no. 3 (September 1994): 79–97. Faced with cash, fuel, and chemical shortages, Cuba has launched an experiment in organic agriculture that may become a model. Its transformation of agricultural inputs is attracting worldwide attention.

Smith, Lois M., and Alfred Padula. *Sex and Revolution: Women in Socialist Cuba*. New York: Oxford University Press, 1996. This is a thorough and provocative study of women's issues including, for example, women's rights and social conditions, problems of sex discrimination, and employment opportunities.

IV

CONTEMPORARY CARIBBEAN ADAPTATION THROUGH MIGRATION

In recent decades people's motivations for migrating have been studied in terms of "push" and "pull" factors. Push factors propel people to leave, while pull factors lure people to new places. Today both push and pull factors offer powerful incentives for Caribbean emmigration, and arguably they are stronger now than ever. The incentive to migrate (especially to the United States) is enhanced on both ends by economic, media, and policy trends emanating primarily from the United States. The next two chapters emphasize ways in which people from the Caribbean, more than any other region, continue to use international migration, circulation, and remittances as a survival strategy. Chapter 10 presents a broad overview of the main characteristics of Caribbean migrants and related social and economic features, while chapter 11 focuses in on Trinidadians who emigrated to the United States before returning home.

More specifically, in chapter 10 Aaron Segal reviews the main types of contemporary migration, their economic dimensions, and their differences among Caribbean states. Emigration is unpacked to distinguish the contributions of short-term visitors, return migrants, swallow migrants who recycle regularly, brain drains, urbanization, refugees and asylum seekers, and other migratory movements. Chapter 10 also scrutinizes the nature of Caribbean diaspora communities in Canada, France, the United Kingdom, the United States, and the Netherlands with emphasis on second and subsequent generations born abroad and their contacts with Caribbean societies. The analysis of migration is complemented by a discussion of key related demographic trends in the region such as fertility, net emigration, and age distribution. The chapter concludes with a discussion of the past, present, and future effects of emigration on Caribbean sending countries and on overseas receiving countries. Caribbean migration is projected to continue at a high level due to economic differentials and opportunities, social networks of friends and families, geographic proximity and low commercial air fares, and widespread and deep expectations of higher standards of living that cannot be achieved at home.

In chapter 11 Roger-Mark De Souza explores crucial economic and cultural linkages between the North Atlantic and Caribbean regions through migration flows. While Caribbean societies are connected to the North Atlantic region in many ways, migration-related connections are among the most central. One of the most remarkable and well-established migration patterns involves emigration and return of West Indians, wherein return is commonly realized through circulatory mobility patterns, temporary labor schemes, or permanent return. De Souza's rich and revealing data for Trinidadian migrants who return home illustrate such controversial and misunderstood hemispheric issues as remittances, brain drain, upward mobility, the generation of sources of capital, North Atlantic racism, and other comparisons and contrasts between the Caribbean and North Atlantic experiences. Through an examination of local images and motivations for return migration to Trinidad, chapter 11 explores this longstanding response by Caribbean people. Local messages and images of return reinforce the collective perception that return is beneficial and a status-conferring path to upward mobility. Return migration is a key response by citizens to perceived shortcomings in the development policy prescriptions of their governments. It helps explain why these policies often don't keep Caribbean peoples on their island homelands and gives insight into why and under what conditions they return.

10

The Political Economy of Contemporary Migration

Aaron Segal

The international political economy imposes severe constraints on densely populated and heavily trade-dependent Caribbean countries. They have little control individually or even collectively over such matters as access to external markets, terms of foreign investments and technology transfers, and legal emigration. Historical commercial preferences for sugar, bananas, and other agricultural exports to North America and Western Europe have been seriously eroded for Caribbean countries. Economic and political strategies now revolve around pursuing market niches such as tourism, offshore banking, and migrant labor schemes, where there is some kind of comparative advantage in a ferociously competitive global economy. The movement of people, often on a preferential basis on the part of receiving countries, has long been an important niche strategy, although it is not often considered in concert with national development policies.

The Caribbean has experienced greater impacts, both in absolute and relative terms, of migration than perhaps any region on the planet (Duany 1994). Throughout most of the Caribbean's colonial history (and after the Indians were decimated) chronic labor shortages, high infant mortality, and low fertility were addressed by bringing in people to work. In the modern era available work has never caught up with labor in intentionally overpopulated societies (Richardson 1992).

Between 1500 and 1900, approximately 4 million slaves were imported from West Africa, followed after emancipation by 200,000 indentured male laborers from India, 125,000 from China, and smaller numbers from Dutch Indonesia. The abolition of slavery prompted the importation of indentured laborers to Guyana, Trinidad, Cuba, and other countries on a lesser scale between 1840 and 1920 (Richardson 1992). Many served out their contracts and returned home. Others brought wives and stayed on, often leaving plantation work to open their own farms or shops. Between 1880 and 1920 there was a Caribbean-wide immigration of modest numbers of Syrians and Lebanese, mostly Christians bearing Ottoman Empire passports. Unlike Chinese, Indian, and Javanese migrants, these "turcos" (as they were known) often intermarried with locals, especially Catholics.

Interisland migration began with the abolition of slavery, especially from Barbados and several smaller islands such as Grenada. The emancipation of British colonial slaves in 1832 prompted some exslaves to move to Guyana and Trinidad in pursuit of land and life as peasant farmers rather than estate workers (Marshall 1981). Interisland migration began on a major scale during the first failed French attempt to dig the Panama Canal and the second successful American effort from 1900 to 1920 (Richardson 1989). Several hundred thousand construction workers were recruited throughout the West Indies, especially Barbados and Jamaica. Although most returned, a significant West Indian population stayed in the Panama Canal Zone. Some second-generation Panamanians emigrated north along the Caribbean coasts of Panama and Nicaragua. Ironically, an eighteenth-century migration from the Caribbean island of St. Vincent to the Belizean and Honduran coast consisted of indigenous people fleeing British conquest and enslavement (Gonzalez 1969).

The abolition of slavery resulted in a massive labor exodus and a desperate need for replacements. Hundreds of thousands of Haitians were recruited between 1880 and 1930 to work on Cuban sugar estates, and then most of them were deported during the 1930s depression (Lundahl 1982). Smaller movements saw Puerto Rican sugar-estate workers migrating to Hawaii, and Haitians to the Dominican Republic. In 1937 the Dominican government ordered the massacre of Haitian migrants. Movements mostly occur from small, impoverished islands to better-off neighbors, consisting typically of unskilled, mostly young, men willing to move in response to labor-market pulls, the prospects of cash earnings, and inexpensive passages.

Since World War II an estimated 5 million Caribbean people have emigrated to France, the Netherlands, the United Kingdom (until it closed its doors in 1963), Canada, and the United States (Segal 1993). Patchwork national policies in receiving countries have controlled these movements, including the nearly one million Cubans and Haitians who entered the United States as political refugees. The pull factors have been higher earnings, kinship networks that assist with adjustment, and geographic proximity with low air fares. The push factors have included stagnant local economies, massive unemployment and underemployment, the decline of agricultural exports and wage labor, the failures of industrialization efforts to generate jobs, and the high personal expectations, especially kindled by information from relatives and friends abroad.

Emigration levels are determined by arbitrary receiving-country rules with negligible Caribbean inputs. Puerto Ricans and U.S. Virgin Islanders have unrestricted access to the United States as citizens. Similar rules apply for French Antilleans to France and Netherlands Antilleans to the Netherlands. Everyone else in the region must take their chances with strict Canadian and U.S. immigration quotas and eligibility criteria. The rules can change as in 1994 when Cubans and Haitians were removed from automatic asylum/political refugee status.

Yet the conflict remains between moving jobs to people and moving people to jobs. Most Caribbean governments are trying to do both. For example, Dominican Republic emigrants congregate in the low-paying garment trades in New York City while even lower paid Dominicans work in the textiles sector or the country's export processing zones. Highly mobile foreign capital looks for inexpensive, semiskilled workers in both places although not the same firms. The Caribbean is locked into an international political economy with two options: (1) to encourage citizens to emigrate and send back remittances and (2) to stay home and work in low-paying tourism and export processing.

DEFINITIONS OF THE CARIBBEAN REGION

There is no consensus on the geographic definition of the Caribbean. Definitions differ over fundamentals, criteria, and the concept of region (Segal 1984). In this book the Caribbean is defined as constituted by the archipelago stretching 2,000 miles from the Bahamas to the two-island nation of Trinidad and Tobago. It adds four mainland territories that historically, culturally, and geographically share more with the islands of the Caribbean Sea than with their mainland neighbors (see map 1 and table 1). These include Belize, Guyana, French Guyana, and Suriname. Belize has a mixed West Indian, Maya Indian, and Central American population and maintains a historical orientation towards the West Indies (also known as the Commonwealth Caribbean). Yet Belize is also in many respects a Central American country. As of a few years ago, Spanish replaced English as the most common native tongue.

The people of Guyana are principally Indo-Guyanese, Afro-Guyanese, or Amerindian. Although its educational, legal, economic, and political contacts with the West Indies have been fragile since independence in 1966, Guyana is still closer to the West Indies and the rest of the Caribbean than to South America. It has few ties with Amazonian Brazil and has maintained a long-standing border dispute with Venezuela.

French Guyana is a sparsely populated overseas territory of France with nominal connections with neighboring Brazil and Suriname. Its closest cultural and political ties are with Guadaloupe and Martinique.

Suriname, like Belize, Guyana, and French Guyana, is on the Caribbean periphery, isolated by demography, geography, and an aluminum-based economy that depends on European markets. The population includes people of Javanese, Creole, Hindustani, Maroon, and other origins. Dutch is an official language, providing loose ties with the Netherlands Antilles. During the 1980s a radical Surinamese military regime cultivated political and economic ties with Cuba, but these were not lasting.

The pan-Caribbean emigration flow continues, with Guyanese emigrants in New York City, Belizeans in New Orleans, and French Guyanese in France. A quarter of the population of Suriname emigrated to the Netherlands at independence, when Dutch citizenship was offered (Richardson 1989; Segal 1993).

In 1997 the Caribbean includes about 38 million people living in sixteen independent and ten nonindependent states, varying from colonies like the islands of Anguilla or the Turks and Caicos to the partly autonomous Puerto Rico and the six Netherlands Antilles islands (table 1; PRB 1996). Linguistically, Spanish dialects are spoken in Cuba, the Dominican Republic, and Puerto Rico, constituting two-thirds of all Caribbean peoples. English, in several West Indian dialects, is spoken to one degree or another in all thirteen West Indian countries by about 6 million people. French, the official language of the French overseas departments and territories, is spoken by about 1.5 million people. A French-based Creole with its own spelling is the lingua franca of Haiti, the French possessions, and the once French colonies of Dominica and St. Lucia. It is used by an estimated 5 million speakers, mostly Haitians. The resurgence of linguistic nationalisms has also been felt in the Netherlands Antilles, where there are about 200,000 speakers of a Spanish-derived Creole called Papamiento. Sranan-Tnang, a mixture of African and English words, is a unique lingua franca for the more than 300,000 multilingual Surinamese.

Attempts to reduce the inherent fragmentation of the Caribbean have taken several directions. The West Indies is a group of thirteen English-speaking independent states that are linked by the trade encouraged by Caricom (see chap. 4), the multicampus University of the West Indies, a regional secretariat based in Guyana, and several other regional institutions. Dominated by Jamaica, Trinidad and Tobago, and Barbados, the West Indies has not realized its potential since the breakup of the 1958–62 West Indian Federation, but it has not been a clear failure (West Indies Commission 1992). Although it conducts a decennial census, the West Indies is neither a geographic nor a demographic entity. It constitutes less than 20 percent of the total regional population, and its migration experience is only part of a bigger picture.

A final internal subcategory is the nonindependent Caribbean, an array of small and large islands with a total population approaching six million in 1997: Puerto Rico, the U.S. Virgin Islands, the Netherlands Antilles, the French Antilles, and French Guyana. These islands possess extraterritorial citizenship that guarantees freedom of movement to and from the metropole. While reliable public opinion or other data are lacking, the available evidence suggests that one reason for rejecting independence is the desire to retain freedom of migration (McElroy and de Albuquerque 1996). However, residents of Anguilla, the Turks and Caicos Islands, and other British possessions such as Bermuda or the Caymans do not exercise freedom of movement.

DEMOGRAPHIC TRENDS

The Caribbean has used mass emigration to facilitate a rapid demographic transition to low fertility and low mortality (United Nations 1989). Except for Haiti, whose demographic data and experience differ from the rest of the region, the demographic transition has been achieved in two decades or less, among the fastest rates in the world. Although controversy continues over the role of migration in this transformation, the process is clear. Beginning in 1945 and continuing to the present, mass emigration has reduced significantly the number of women of childbearing age, has reduced their fertility in receiving countries, has raised the age of marriage or first child among Caribbean emigrants, and has resulted in large numbers of children being born overseas. Except for Cubans and Haitians, who represent perhaps 15 percent of the five-million Caribbean diaspora, this emigration is classified by the U.S. government as voluntary. Moreover, this emigration has been largely gender balanced unlike the movement of male mine workers to South Africa or unskilled Algerian men to France and Belgium.

Further education at home, the availability of contraceptives and family planning, and modest economic growth in 1970–90 combined with the emigration of young women to accelerate the demographic transition (Segal 1991). A crude estimate on a pan-Caribbean basis, rather than individual islands, is that net emigration contributed to about 20 percent of the rapid decline in birth rate.

Over several decades net emigration comprising 5–10 percent of the total population of each Caribbean society has combined with the youth of emigrants (usually 15–40 years old) to both displace births overseas and to lower fertility. It has also lowered the fiscal burden on educational, health, and other facilities. However, the exodus of a better-educated and perhaps better-motivated segment of the population has resulted in a brain drain. Remittances on the order of several hundred million dollars a year (mostly to Jamaica, Barbados, Haiti, and Puerto Rico) have largely gone to household consumption, not investments (World Bank 1995). Slowly growing Caribbean economies have been unable to generate the kinds of employment that might have reduced emigration. However, household studies indicate remittances are used for small-scale investments (Conway 1992). Thus emigration has been neither a panacea nor a stopgap: its primary beneficial effect has been to speed up the demographic transition.

The cultural impacts of mass emigration have been the subject of extensive speculation and are alleged to include inappropriate imported consumption and cultural values, diffusion of unrealistic expectations, and many other undesirable results (Deere et al. 1990). What is often overlooked is that emigrants have taken advantage of opportunities abroad that were unavailable at home (Palmer 1990).

Emigration may also have contributed slightly to very impressive health gains in much of the Caribbean. Reductions in birth rates and total population sizes have made it possible to spread health expenditures more equitably and to serve even smaller populations more efficiently, since health expenditures are a low priority for all Caribbean governments except Cuba. World Bank data show that life expectancy in years in 1993 was 76 for Barbados, 76 for Cuba, 76 for Martinique, 75 for Guadaloupe, 75 for Puerto Rico, 74 for Belize, 74 for Jamaica, 73 for Netherlands Antilles, 72 for Trinidad and Tobago, 71 for Suriname, 70 for the Dominican Republic, 66 for Guyana, and 57 for Haiti. These compare with 80 for Japan, 78 for Switzerland, 78 for the Netherlands, 77 for France, 76 for the United Kingdom, and 76 for the United States (World Bank 1995). The control of tropical diseases, a health services infrastructure, and modest standards of living enable much of the Caribbean to nearly match developed countries in life expectancy.

Similar World Bank data for infant mortality per 1,000 live births indicate impressive gains in spite of slow-growth economies. For example, infant mortality in the Dominican Republic dropped from 88 per 1,000 live births in 1970 to 40 in 1993; from 43 to 14 in Jamaica; from 44 in 1970 in Trinidad and Tobago to 18 in 1993; and in Puerto Rico from 28 in 1970 to 11 in 1993 (World Bank 1995). Cuban infant mortality declines are even more impressive, although their decline has slowed as a result of post-1988 economic woes (see chap. 9). In contrast, Haiti has not improved high infant mortality rates in over twenty-five years (see table 2 for the most recent IMR figures).

Data on birth and contraception rates also suggest important gains in health in spite of slow economic growth. Crude birth rates (measured per 1,000 population, 1980–93) fell from 41 to 26 in the Dominican Republic, from 34 to 21 in Jamaica, from 28 to 21 in Trinidad and Tobago, and from 25 to 18 in Puerto Rico (World Bank 1995). Comparable data on emigrant birth rates from these countries are not available, but one would expect to see even sharper declines. Similarly, we have little data on contraceptive use by diaspora women. Figures for the Dominican Republic indicate that 56 percent of married women of childbearing age used contraception in 1988–93, and 55 percent in Jamaica.

These transformations of infant mortality, life expectancy, crude birth rates, and contraception use suggest that much of the Caribbean is close to stable population size, given another decade or two of net emigration. Again, the major exception is Haiti, where the annual population growth rate is estimated at close to 3 percent and the demographic transition has barely begun. The World Bank projects the total fertility rate for the Dominican Republic at 3.0 in 1993 and 2.7 in 2000; at 2.3 for Jamaica in 1993 and 2.1 in 2000; at 2.4 for Trinidad and Tobago in 1993 and 2.2 in the year 2000; and 2.2 for 1993 and 2.1 for the year 2000 for Puerto Rico (the population is stable at 2.1 children per woman; World Bank 1995). The latest total fertility estimates for Haiti are 4.7 in 1991 and 4.2 in the year 2000 (World Bank 1992). Cuba is not a member of the World Bank, but its national estimates for total fertility are in the range of Puerto Rico's.

Essentially, most of the Caribbean, except Haiti and a few smaller islands like Grenada and Dominica where fertility is still dropping, have achieved a demographic transition, a life expectancy that is close to rates in rich countries, and a nearly stable population. This has been done with slow or even negative economic growth rates (Cuba, Trinidad and Tobago), thus questioning the correlation between health and per capita income (World Bank 1993). Net emigration was only a secondary factor in these gains. Its most important demonstration effect may have been on women who stayed at home and postponed marriage, used contraception, and pursued further education.

MIGRATION DATA

The Caribbean and its diaspora compare favorably with most world regions in terms of demographic and migration data. National census data are available and reliable for all countries except Haiti, which has never had a 100 percent national census and depends on irregular 5 percent urban samples. Data for the West Indies census are collected on a subregional basis with delays in publication. Migration data are much more problematical at the Caribbean level due to difficulties in distinguishing emigrants, temporary visitors, return migrants, tourists, and other visitors. The reciprocal flow of visitors makes Puerto Rican, Dominican, Jamaican, and other national data less than fully reliable. Immigration data for receiving countries omit illegals and often confuse tourists, legal immigrants, migrant workers, and other categories (Duany 1994).

In spite of these difficulties, data on migration can be pulled out of receiving-country censuses, ethnographic studies, surveys of minority racial and ethnic groups, and naturalization, legal resident, school enrollment, and other data sets. While there are several studies of individual diaspora communities, there is an absence of comparative research, very little work on second and later generations born abroad, minimal research on return migration, and only one pioneering study of migrant recycling (swallows) (Hernandez and Scheff 1994). Thus we have a reasonable picture of the massive 1945–90 Caribbean exodus, but only a superficial understanding of the comparative and evolving nature of the diaspora, or of ongoing contacts with home countries (see chap. 11).

URBANIZATION

Urbanization continues at a fast pace throughout most of the Caribbean, in societies that are already highly urbanized. Causes include the decline of export and domestic agriculture, the concentration of government and other services in a single, primate city, and the failure to provide adequate incentives for the growth of secondary and tertiary cities. A consequence of the rapid urbanization under conditions of low economic growth is the proliferation of slums, formal and informal urban unemployment, soaring crime rates, and rising social and class tensions (Cross 1965; Potter and Conway 1997).

The urban population as a percentage of the total population rose from 40 percent in the Dominican Republic in 1970 to 63 percent in 1993. From 1980 to 1993 the annual urban growth rate was 3.9 percent. The capital city of Santo Domingo had 51 percent of the total urban population in 1991, nearly four times the size of Santiago, the second city. Jamaica's urban population grew from 42 percent of the total in 1970 to 53 percent in 1990; an annual growth rate (1980–93) of 1.9 percent. Kingston by 1990 accounted for 53 percent of the total urban population, dwarfing all other Jamaican cities and facing problems with employment and housing. Trinidad and Tobago has become one of the Caribbean's most urbanized countries. The urban population as a percentage of the total population rose from 63 percent in 1970 to 71 percent in 1993, a 1980–93 annual increase of 2.2 percent. However, Port of Spain accounted for only 12 percent of the total urban population, with San Fernando being one of the few secondary cities in the region to rival the capital.

Puerto Rico has experienced galloping urbanization, growing from 58 percent of the total population in 1970 to 73 percent in 1993, a 3.0 percent annual increase. San Juan, an unrivaled primate city, held 53 percent of the total urban population in 1990, more than all the other cities and towns combined (World Bank 1995).

Cuba and Haiti represent the polar contrasts in regard to Caribbean urbanization. Cuba has used strict limits on urban residential construction, work permits and restrictions on job and residence changes, and other policies to keep the population of Havana and its suburbs at about two million. The overall urban population of Cuba has been severely restricted, and no city has been allowed to rival Havana. Since 1959 the Cuban government has made many rural social-service investments, including the creation of eighty-three new rural towns (see Eckstein 1994, chap. 6). Haiti has placed no restraints on urbanization and has concentrated most services and commerce in its capital, Port-au-Prince, a swollen city with a totally inadequate infrastructure and harrowing municipal problems. Between 1970 and 1991 the urban population of Haiti increased from 20 percent of the total to 29 percent, an annual average growth rate for 1980–91 of 3.8 percent, with Port-au-Prince holding 56 percent of the total urban population, nearly ten times the size of its nearest rival, Cap Haitien. The growth occurred while the Haitian economy was regressing. Most secondary cities and towns declined in population, and there was a massive voluntary and refugee exodus (Segal and Weinstein 1992).

How has emigration affected urbanization? The second city for most Caribbean countries has become New York, Miami, Toronto, Amsterdam, Paris, or London, the destinations of 80 percent of all Caribbean emigrants (Levine 1987; Patterson 1987, 1994). Emigration has probably slowed the rate of urbanization while raising expectations that promote a move to the capital city. Earlier generations of emigrants went directly overseas from rural areas, but more recent migrants are coming out of the urban sprawls.

Rapid urbanization is also associated with environmental problems such as air pollution, toxic waste disposal, sewage, and polluted water supplies. Only Bermuda has banned private vehicles. Puerto Rico, Trinidad, Barbados, and other Caribbean countries are trying to reconcile finite island space with nearly unlimited imports of passenger vehicles. There is little investment in improved public transportation (Cuba has imported hundreds of thousands of bicycles from China), and roads compete with other uses for public space. Short-range electric-powered vehicles or other modes of transport that could save on fuel imports and pollution emissions are largely ignored.

RACIAL/ETHNIC DEMOGRAPHICS

Although North American concepts of racial classification are generally rejected, there is no Caribbean consensus as to how to count people racially. Most governments have simply decided to forgo such classifications. However, there is a widespread perception that there has been a disproportionate emigration of well-educated whites and a lesser if also disproportionate emigration of mulattos, or brown persons from urban, educated backgrounds. Thus Cuban-Americans in the United States are considered to be 95 percent white, while Cuban society itself is perhaps 40 percent black and brown (Masud-Piloto 1988). Guesses are proffered that there has been disproportionate emigration of white and brown Haitians, brown West Indians, and East Indians from Guyana and Trinidad. Dominican emigration to the United States and Puerto Rico is considered, on the basis of scanty evidence, to be largely brown and white with few blacks (Dunning 1996).

Emigration is changing the racial and social mix of each Caribbean society, but the consequences are poorly researched and understood. For one, it has loosened the hold of tiny white minorities on plantation agriculture and other enterprises, especially in the West Indies. Secondly, it has resulted in the exodus of Chinese communities from Cuba and to a lesser extent Jamaica, Trinidad, and Guyana. Thirdly, it has produced a steady outflow of small businessmen of Lebanese and Syrian origins from Haiti, Cuba, and other countries, and of frustrated East Indian businessmen and professionals from Guyana and Trinidad. On the home front, emigration has facilitated social mobility by Afro-Caribbeans as well as black and brown intermarriage in several countries.

INTERISLAND MIGRATION

Currently there are two distinct patterns of interisland migration. The first is the historical movement of mostly young, adult males to seek formal- and informal-sector work anywhere from Haiti to the Dominican Republic, the Bahamas, the French Antilles, and as far as French Guyana (map 1; Segal and Weinstein 1992). In spite of appalling working conditions and meager earnings, Haitians, often landless, move legally and illegally in search of work in nearby countries, especially the Bahamas. So do poor, mostly rural Dominicans, risking the hazardous passage to Puerto Rico where they stay or seek to move on to New York City. Citizens of Grenada and other Windward Islanders (Dominica southward) continue to migrate for work to Trinidad and Tobago, as do Leeward Islanders (Guadeloupe northward) to the larger economies and job opportunities of the U.S. Virgin Islands (see map 2). Most of these movements have persisted for several decades.

The new pattern of interisland movement consists of migrant workers, often with their families, moving to nonindependent islands that are experiencing tourism, construction, and land booms (see industries in table 2). Destinations include both Dutch and French sides of St. Martin, Anguilla, the Caymans, the Turks and Caicos, and other islands with native populations of 50,000 or less (CSA 1996). There is a real possibility that foreign-born people with their children will outnumber locals, especially as some locals migrate. The burden on education, health, and other services has already become an issue. Although the absolute numbers involved in these movements is less than 100,000 at present, it is not clear whether these are temporary migrant workers and/or prospective permanent residents. Migrants include Dominicans, Haitians, and residents of many small islands. Receiving countries may well resort to restricting work permits and naturalization to avoid locals being outnumbered by immigrants.

ILLEGAL EMIGRATION

Geography, distance, costs, risks, aggressive interceptions at sea, and legal avenues for entry severely limit illegal Caribbean emigration overseas. Since 1991 a few Haitians sailing in fragile vessels have managed to avoid interception by the U.S. Coast Guard and arrive in South Florida. An unknown but probably modest number of Dominicans have braved the perils of the Mona Straits to enter Puerto Rico illegally. Since 1994 Cubans attempting to enter the United States illegally by sea are being returned, although Cuba has not been allowed to fill its annual quota of 20,000 legal emigrants. Illegal emigration from the Caribbean to Canada or to Western Europe is on a minimal scale.

Most illegal entries occur when tourists overstay, particularly in the United States and Canada. Although the number of tourist visas issued per country annually is known to the INS, how those visas are used is poorly documented. Persons with relatives and friends can readily fly to New York, Miami, or Toronto on a tourist visa and then melt into the local Caribbean diaspora community where niche employment and false papers are available. There have been no further Canadian or U.S. amnesties for illegals since 1986, but the chances of being apprehended while resident in North America are slim. The use of overstays based on tourist visas has been documented for people of the Commonwealth Caribbean, Haiti, Dominican Republic, and others.

LEGAL EMIGRATION

Legal emigration from the Caribbean is subject to multiple variables and a few imponderables. Cubans and Haitians are no longer eligible for asylum and refugee status except on a case-by-case basis. However, Puerto Ricans and U.S. Virgin Islanders enjoy freedom of movement as U.S. citizens, as do French Antilleans and Guyanese in France, and Netherlands Antilleans in the Netherlands as citizens of the kingdom. All other Caribbean sending countries depend on receiving country laws, quotas, admissions criteria, and asylum conditions. These are subject to political change and are fraught with uncertainty. Moreover, the United Kingdom is virtually closed for West Indians, including family reunification. Meanwhile Canada and the United States are considering legislative changes that would reduce global immigration quotas, limit the extent of family reunification, revise quotas for professional workers, make immigrant sponsors responsible for certain public costs incurred by immigrants, and other measures.

When freedom of migration is allowed in and out of a North Atlantic country, migration correlates closely with perceived economic opportunities in a countercyclical manner. Thus, when the rate of growth of the Puerto Rican, French Antillean, or Netherlands Antillean economies exceeds that of the metropole there tends to be net cyclical return flows (INSED 1990). The reverse net flow occurs when metropole economies are outpacing those of the islands. What is remarkable about these reciprocal flows is that they are countercyclical in spite of per capita incomes being three times or more higher overseas. The data suggest that in the absence of serious economic deterioration holders of non-Caribbean citizenships exhibit a strong preference for remaining in the Caribbean.

Earlier rates of naturalization in Canada and the United States correlate positively with future legal emigration. West Indians, Haitians, Cubans, Surinamese, and other Caribbean peoples have relatively high rates of acquiring legal resident and naturalization status. This makes it easier for them, even if family reunification quotas are cut back, to legally sponsor close relatives. Several Caribbean governments have responded by legally granting dual citizenship, although no data are available on the takers or the legal implications.

It is projected that Canada and the United States, under distinct sections of immigration laws, will continue to allow 200,000–250,000 Caribbean emigrants to enter annually, with 200,000 entering the United States. West Indians with advanced education are particularly well placed to take advantage of Canadian and U.S. rules regarding the entry of professional workers. U.S. quotas of 20,000 per year for most countries enable Caribbean sending societies to reunite many immediate families. However, all bets are off should there be a drastic change of regime in Cuba, where pent-up demands to emigrate are abetted by close relatives living in the United States (Perez 1994).

Projections for continued legal emigration are subject to many variables and unpredictable changes, whether a new Caribbean refugee crisis or a persistent anti-immigration mood in the United States. On a small scale the diaspora is engendering niche economic enclaves for the import of specialized products from the homeland, such as tropical fruits and cassettes of island music. Dominicans, Haitians, West Indians, Puerto Ricans, and others have engaged in small-scale retail and wholesale trade with their home countries, as well as service-sector travel agencies, banks, and other enterprises. Even though the purchasing power of the five-million-member diaspora is probably slightly greater than that of the 38 million residents of the Caribbean, it has barely been mobilized for trade or investment. The exceptions are the large-scale return home visits for Carnival, Christmas, and other occasions (Olwig 1993). The World Bank estimates remittances to the Dominican Republic at $25 million in 1970 and $362 million in 1993; $3 million in 1970 for Trinidad and Tobago and $6 million in 1993; $29 million for Jamaica in 1970 and $139 million in 1992; and $13 million for Haiti in 1970 and $47 million in 1990 (World Bank 1992, 1995). These are probably underestimates, since remittances flow through many channels that are difficult to document. However, the modest scale of these figures and the tendency for remittances to be spent on immediate consumption suggest that the diaspora is not investing in home-country bonds, mutual funds, or retirement housing on a significant scale, or in other employment generators.

Legal emigration allows some of those whose educational achievements and aspirations surpass local resources and opportunities to leave. It does not allow the urban poor, the discontented, the unemployed, or the underemployed to leave. It is only a brain drain in the sense that Caribbean societies have invested scarce resources in the education of those who leave. Trying to count their potential contribution if they had stayed or returned is not possible (see chap. 4 for a discussion of roles they could play).

The worst effects of legal emigration are on the poorest of Caribbean societies. Haiti has experienced a massive outflow of doctors, nurses, engineers, and all other categories of scarce professionals (Segal and Weinstein 1992). Remittances do not come close to compensating. Smaller islands such as St. Kitts, Nevis, Monserrat, and Dominica have become "remittance" societies with large numbers of children and elderly dependent on transfers from abroad (Rubenstein 1983; Stinner and de Albuquerque 1982). Even the dollarized sector of the Cuban economy functions through remittances sent from Miami. The Caribbean is becoming a region of haves and have-nots based on access to remittances from relatives and friends in the diaspora. Yet legal emigration contributes to tourism (when emigres temporarily return), to some technology transfer, to the realization of educational goals, to keeping expectations alive for some, and in a minor way to generating trade and external savings for otherwise stagnant economies (see the Trinidadian example of these in chap. 11).

SWALLOWS MIGRATION (RECYCLING)

Swallows, or recyclers, are persons who regularly over a sustained period of time divide their residence and/or employment between two or more countries. The term first came into vogue to refer to pre-World War I Italian laborers who regularly migrated to and from Argentina as harvest workers. They were known as swallows after the famous nesting habits of these migratory birds. The first reference to swallows in the Caribbean is to Trinidadian musicians of the 1930s who regularly visited New York City to make recordings, given the absence of recording studios in Trinidad until the 1970s (Manuel 1995).

In principle, there are no legal impediments to recycling for legal residents and citizens of Puerto Rico, the U.S. Virgin Islands, the French Antilles, and the Netherlands Antilles, as well as all members of the Caribbean diaspora who have legal residence or citizenship overseas. As naturalization accelerates in Canada and the United States among members of the Caribbean diaspora, and as the numbers of offspring born overseas grow, the potential number of swallows may be close to 8 million. Absolute numbers will continue to grow through citizenship by birth and by naturalization, and with continued flows of legal emigrants. The granting of dual citizenship by many Caribbean governments also facilitates recycling by improving chances for employment at home.

SECOND AND SUBSEQUENT GENERATIONS

The second generation (the first generation born abroad) and later generations of immigrants have received little research attention among the Caribbean diaspora. There are frequent references to the second generation in ethnographic studies, but little systematic research (Henry 1994; Chaney and Sutton 1987). There are even fewer comparative studies of Haitians in Montreal, New York City, and Miami, or West Indians in London, Toronto, and New York City. National census and other data are often not easy to disaggregate by generations nor is it easy to locate rapidly dispersing second generations.

However, by the year 2000, second and later generations will outnumber many first generation diaspora in spite of continuing emigration, intermarriage, and declining fertility. This has already happened among West Indians in the United Kingdom, where emigration was cut off in the

1960s, and among Haitians in the Bahamas, where there have been large-scale deportations (Marshall 1980; Nanton 1995). It is already happening among West Indians in Canada and the United States, and Puerto Ricans in the continental United States (Henry 1994; Palmer 1995; Pessar and Grasmuck 1991).

The emergence of second and later generations merits further research on several grounds. One has to do with assimilation, multiculturalism, and other components of personal, ethnic, racial, and national identities. A second topic consists of relations with homelands, emergence of pan-Caribbean identities as in the North American-staged Caribbean carnivals (Kasinitz 1992), the nature and incidence of intermarriage, and, of course, social, educational, and economic mobility. The scattered evidence suggests that Caribbean second generations, starting from very different backgrounds and levels, are achieving impressive social and professional mobility, primarily, like second generations from other regions, by investing in education (Palmer 1995; Henry 1994; Boswell and Curtis 1984; Fitzpatrick 1987).

FUTURE CARIBBEAN MIGRATION

The research agenda for the next decade of Caribbean migration studies needs to be a mix of the old and the new. There needs to be further tracking of legal migration and its effects on sending and receiving countries, much better ways of studying illegal migration through tourist over-stays, new research on interisland migration to new growth poles such as St. Martin, and new work on changing racial and ethnic compositions due to migration and on swallows. Modern research on Caribbean migration began with studies of the Puerto Rican exodus to New York City in the late 1940s and has continued over five decades to cover an extraordinary diversity of topics and groups. Its next logical direction is to compare and contrast the experiences of second and later generations in all five receiving countries with significant Caribbean first- and second-generation populations. Like swallows research, this involves research teams from several countries and some method of longitudinal analysis.

Legal and illegal emigration from the Caribbean will continue unless the United States imposes and implements drastic controls. At the same time innovative forms of emigration such as recycling are likely to become more important and visible. Migration will continue to be neither a safety valve nor an entirely negative or positive factor in sending countries. It will be a mostly positive factor for receiving countries, adding to their music, arts, and human resources the talents of several million productive persons and their offspring.

SUGGESTIONS FOR FURTHER READING

Palmer, Ransford. *Pilgrims from the Sun: West Indian Migration to America*. New York: Twayne, 1995. The best single work on the experience of Caribbean peoples in the United States.

Pessar, Patricia, ed. *Caribbean Circuits: New Directions in the Study of Caribbean Migration*. New York: Center for Migration Studies, 1997. A comprehensive and timely study of both the migrants and the conceptualizations used to understand their movements, livelihoods, and cultural patterns.

Segal, Aaron. *An Atlas of International Migration*. Oxford: Bower, 1993. This book is the only existing comprehensive cartographic documentation of the major and minor human migration flows among countries, past and present. It is a basic reference book with data and maps for those interested in any specific aspects of migration or regions.

11

The Spell of the Cascadura: West Indian Return Migration

Roger-Mark De Souza

> Those who eat the cascadura will, the native legend says,
> Wheresoever they may wander, end in Trinidad their days.
>
> (MacMillan 1977)

In Trinidad and Tobago, legend has it that those who eat a fish called the cascadura will return to the islands no matter where they wander. Such images, coupled with aspirations of material well-being and upward mobility, fix and reinforce a collective perception throughout the West Indian (W.I.) islands that return migration is beneficial and confers status.[1] This chapter shows how this perception is paramount to understanding W.I. return migration. It perpetuates emigration and return as a valid local response to overcoming the limitations imposed by small-island life, it helps explain why government policy prescriptions often fail to keep West Indians on their island homelands, and it gives insight into why and under what conditions expatriates return.

Current approaches in migration analysis conceptualize return in various ways. "Return" is understood as the reentry of a citizen who left with the intention of spending at least a year abroad, and upon returning intended to spend at least a year in the homeland. This corresponds to the United Nations' recognition of "one year" as a duration of significance for defining a migrant and coincides with recent research suggesting that most of those who stay beyond the time allocated on their visas, "overstayers," leave the host country within one year (Conway 1994). This kind of international movement is scarcely documented, however, in large part because of data inadequacies. In response, returnee samples are usually obtained through networking techniques such as the snowball sampling one used for the sample analyzed in this chapter.

The life stories of the one hundred Trinidadian returnees examined here reveal that return occurs across the categories of gender, age, ethnic origin, and social status. There were more female returnees than male (60 percent versus 40 percent). Fifty-four percent of the total sample were 30 years and under, 41 percent from 31 to 55, and 5 percent above 55. Additionally, the five major ethnic groups were represented in the sample (African [49 percent], East Indian [18 percent], *Callaloo*/Mixed [16 percent], white [11 percent], and Chinese [6 percent]). It is difficult to draw conclusions about ethnicity and return, as no statistics exist on the ethnicity of those who emigrate in the first place. The majority of the returnees were professionals (54 percent), with the remainder being skilled and unskilled workers, students, retirees, and unemployed (see table 11.4).

How applicable is the Trinidadian example of return to its neighboring W.I. islands? With a view to effects on mobility, Trinidad and Tobago (T&T) exhibits two key differences from its neighbors, and also some similarities. First, regarding differences, its ethnically diverse population carries implications for emigration. The roots of ethnic divisiveness in T&T lie in a history marked by labor schemes that established rank according to race. Even though today those divisions are less obvious, certain sectors of the population continue to believe that some ethnic groups seek economic gains at the expense of others. Recent research indicates that the income disparity between Africans and East Indians, on the one hand, and Syrians/Lebanese, Chinese, whites and Callaloos, on the other, has decreased but has not disappeared (Yelvington 1993). This preoccupation with race has escalated into acts of violence in times of crisis. During a black power uprising in the 1970s, some Chinese were assailed while others, fearing unmerited persecution, sought refuge in North America (Millett 1993). A similar attitude was evident during the attempted coup d'état in 1990 when businesses run by Syrians were singled out for attack. When it was suggested that these businessmen had brought these assaults on themselves, some threatened to leave Trinidad. In fact, some Indo-Trinidadians have used unsubstantiated racial-persecution claims to gain refugee status to enter Canada. These kinds of tensions may not be evident in other W.I. islands and may impinge on Trinidadians' decision to return.

The second important difference is the relative prosperity Trinidadians enjoy, especially from the 1970s oil boom (table 2). Hikes in oil prices brought a fivefold increase in fiscal earnings from petroleum between 1972 and 1982. As a result, unemployment was reduced to less than 10 percent of the economically active population, and imports, primarily of luxury items, increased elevenfold (Instituto del Tercer Mundo 1990). This petrodollar bonanza enabled the government to initiate ambitious plans to modernize T&T. Under the direction of the prime minister, Dr. Eric Williams, the oil industry was nationalized and OPEC pricing policies were established. At the same time, investment by transnational corporations was encouraged. This economic prosperity opened professional doors for skilled expatriate Trinidadians who were looking for an avenue for return.

Despite these differences, however, the underlying forces driving mobility decision making in T&T—a strong migration ethos, difficulties of expatriate life, substantial enclave network formation, and creative mobility-based strategies of coping with adversity—are quintessential W.I. characteristics that inform all international W.I. movement (as reviewed in chap. 10).

WEST INDIANS AND THEIR ISLAND HOMELANDS: PEOPLE ON THE MOVE

West Indians have always been on the move. Historically, as players in plantation economy dynamics, inhabitants of these islands always moved in and out of the region. As a result, people who live on these islands today have always looked outward, in part because they inhabit geographically limited spaces and in part because their ancestral and ethnic links have come from other lands. As Segal explains in chapter 10, beyond this historical legacy lies a combination of demographic, geopolitical, and cultural realities facilitating and perpetuating the migration culture of the West Indies at present.

Continued population growth combines with already high population densities, limited employment opportunities, and increasing urbanization to force West Indians to seek external avenues of escape. Migration presents a logical solution given existing transnational ties, such as historical and cultural links to former colonial motherlands, enclave networks with W.I. communities abroad, and the proximity to and desirability of life in North America. The validity and the acceptance of the migration solution are affirmed in both official and popular ways. W.I. governments, either actively or through their inaction, encourage their peoples to migrate, thereby sanctioning migration as a national escape valve (Carlson 1994; Maingot 1994). At the same time, the sheer numbers of emigrants, coupled with cultural images and anecdotal evidence of West Indians overcoming homeland limitations through migration, fuel and confirm migration as an individual survival strategy. Indeed, migration has become a cultural icon that defines the typical W.I. experience.

West Indians take advantage of these opportunities. Table 11.1 shows the high level of legal immigration to the United States and Canada, revealing a near doubling of Caribbean immigrants since the 1960s (Carlson 1994). U.S. residency application records from 1969 to 1989 show that,

TABLE 11.1
Legal Immigration into North America from Selected Caribbean Territories,
1980s

Country	United States	Canada	% of Total Nationality
St. Kitts & Nevis	10, 587	521	26.4
Antigua & Barbuda	12,555	706	17.0
Grenada	10,483	1,991	13.3
Guyana	92,393	--	11.5
Jamaica	207,762	34,046	10.0
Barbados	18,404	3,059	8.9
St. Vincent & the Grenadines	7,340	1,741	8.1
Anguilla	683	8	5.0
Trinidad & Tobago	37,947	12,911	4.2
Dominican Rep.	226, 853	2,063	3.3
Bahamas	6,477	422	2.9
Haiti	126,379	22,316	2.4
Cuba	163,696	1,292	1.6

Source: Kurlansky (1992)

on average, 5,871 Trinidadians per year successfully completed the application procedure (Conway 1994). Such figures, together with documented and undocumented illegal immigration, unsubstantiated refugee claims, and creative mobility strategies, appear to lend credence to the belief that West Indians are anxious to leave their homeland (Chaney 1987; Conway 1994; Maingot 1994).

Governments of the West Indies have welcomed these escape valves because until the 1970s, long-term emigration was primarily undertaken by unskilled individuals. From the mid-1970s onward, however, highly educated professionals such as nurses, doctors, teachers, and scientists have been at the vanguard of this emigration stream. From 1962 to 1968, for example, T&T lost 143 doctors and dentists, 170 engineers, 629 nurses, 784 teachers, and 909 other professionals, mostly in the productive 20–34 age group. It was calculated that in the 1970s the West Indies as a whole was losing some 14,000 skilled personnel per year (Maingot 1994). Additionally, nonreturn ratios of 30–50 percent and higher have been reported for W.I. educators, officials, and students residing abroad (Daniel 1983). This skilled emigrant departure is troubling for two reasons. First, it affects development plans through a loss of investment monies, expertise, and talent that could help implement a shift toward service and high-technology economies. Second, it suggests that members of this talent pool are not content in their native land and that additional factors, beyond the state's inability to provide adequate opportunities for them, are not strong enough to keep them on their island homelands. As Carl Stone has remarked, "These migrants are not unemployed; they do not dislike their countries, they are frustrated by the lack of opportunities. They know, like all past generations did, that migration is the widely accepted avenue for dealing with those frustrations" (Maingot 1994, 197). In this sense state policy is contradictory. On the one hand, the state is happy to have some of its people leave; on the other, it is unable to retain those whose skills it needs for the new nontraditional export economy, some of whom hold the possibility of generating local employment opportunities to give even more citizens a reason to stay (chap. 4 makes a related point about the Caribbean's human resource mobilization problems).

SOME ANALYTICAL LENSES ON WEST INDIAN RETURN MIGRATION

Return migration is somewhat of a conundrum in W.I. demographic analysis. Informally recognized because it is anecdotally and culturally prevalent, it remains poorly documented and, as a result, difficult to analyze. This is not surprising. Prior to the 1960s, migration literature in general only made fleeting references to return migration. King (1986) suggests that this was largely due to the difficulty in obtaining satisfactory data and was furthered by the conception of migration as a one-way process, perhaps supported by little recorded return movement at the time. This analytical gap regarding return migration is remarkable, given that Caribbean people had made widespread use of it for centuries (as discussed further below).

By the 1960s four studies of Caribbean return migration were completed. Davidson (1969), Patterson (1968), and Philpott (1968) dealt with the return of West Indians from Britain, while Alvarez (1967) examined Puerto Rican return migration from the United States. The worldwide recession in the 1970s and 1980s encouraged further analysis of W.I. return movement as North Atlantic host societies no longer held out the promises they once did (Conway and Glesne 1986; Nutter 1986; Thomas-

Hope 1985). Even though the subject has gained more recognition today, many published works mention it only tangentially, focusing instead on other aspects of the migration question such as decision making, integration abroad, and the consequences of emigration for the home country (James and Harris 1993; Kasinitz 1992; Palmer 1990; Thomas-Hope 1992; Western 1992).

Researchers who have examined W.I. return movement conceptualize four return patterns. These patterns are useful conceptual tools that capture the extent, pervasiveness, and commonalities of return in W.I. societies.

The first, a *mobile livelihood system* (Conway 1992; Rubenstein 1982), envisions return as part of a circular or seasonal movement wherein the major concern is economic survival. This approach is demonstrated by patterns habitually referred to as "circulation," "cyclical migration," "circular migration," "commuting," "temporary recurrent migration," and "transient migration." They frequently include migrants exhibiting temporary labor mobility patterns such as international vendors, contract workers, itinerant labor migrants, and international business commuters (Thomas-Hope 1985). These migrants traditionally stay abroad for periods of six months and less, but this varies according to contractual agreements or commitments back home. Because of these short sojourns abroad, not many migrants in this category are captured in the sample analyzed in this chapter.

A second conceptualization, a *double passage* (Gmelch 1992; Thomas-Hope 1985), captures longer-term return by stressing that return migration is the long term reentry of a national after an extended period abroad. It also indicates that return migration is not really a question of economic necessity, but more an issue of individual will. These long-term migrants have been divided into settlers, students, and long-term circulators (Thomas-Hope 1985). Their time abroad tends to be longer than six months and could extend to several years, depending on individual circumstances. Most of the migrants in the sample fell into this category.

A third conceptualization, *return visitation*, considers repetitive visits of West Indians living abroad in the form of "metropolitan" tourist and business visiting flows (Conway 1994). Figures for this flow between T&T and North America and Britain indicate that over 78 percent of all visitors in 1990 were either business visitors or visitors destined for private accommodation with kin, friends, or relatives (Conway 1994). These short-term visits of nationals living abroad are important because they are a reflection of the diaspora's attachments to the homeland.

Fourth, *swallow lifestyle movement*, captures those West Indians who consciously move back and forth as a lifestyle (see also chap. 10). Such strategies have been facilitated by liberal citizenship laws (Kasinitz 1992).

Thirty-nine percent of the sample hold legal status for T&T only, while the remaining 61 percent possess citizenship or residency status for T&T and another country. Of the latter, 51 percent enjoy dual status with Canada, 21 percent with the United States, 18 percent with the United Kingdom, and the remaining 10 percent with various countries. A 1988 amendment to *The Citizenship of the Republic of Trinidad and Tobago Act* gives legal sanction to dual citizenship. It permits migrants to secure citizenship in the host country and then return to T&T without fear of losing citizenship privileges in either country. All W.I. citizens now maintain full citizenship rights even if they become citizens of another country, and in some cases such rights are extended to their foreign-born children and grandchildren.

THE PREVALENCE OF WEST INDIAN RETURN: THE CASE OF TRINIDAD AND TOBAGO

Historical, anecdotal, and statistical evidence suggests that as long as there have been streams of out-migration in the West Indies, countervailing streams of return have existed (Thomas-Hope 1985). In Trinidad, for example, from the eighteenth century onward, the leading plantocracies of the French Creoles and later British Creoles would send their children to Europe to be educated and then have them return to assume key leadership positions on the island. In the nineteenth century, Indian laborers also returned to Trinidad, though their motivation was different. Many were unable to reintegrate into Indian society and returned to the familiar and accepting environment of Trinidad, where they served as reindentured laborers or as "casuals"—free workers who paid their own transportation fares. Samaroo (1982) indicates that between 1856 and 1901 about 17 percent of 18,966 immigrants who came to Trinidad were returning reindentures.

Anecdotal evidence also supports the belief that many West Indians living abroad return. All of T&T's past prime ministers, more than half of the current members of its parliament, and most of the professors at the country's University of the West Indies campus are return migrants. Accounts in local newspapers indicate that this trend has been confirmed by officials in T&T consulates in the United Kingdom and Canada (*Sunday Guardian* 1993). Figures from T&T's Central Statistical Office also suggest that in recent years an increasing number of Trinidadians, like many of their W.I. counterparts, have been returning to their island homeland.

Yet despite this seemingly mounting evidence of return streams, research has underemphasized them. An indication of this is found in

Brana-Shute's *Bibliography of Caribbean Migration* (1983), which lists only seventy-three different entries on Caribbean return migration out of a total of 2,585 entries. Of these, only nine deal with return migration to the West Indies, and only one, a short article, refers to return migration to T&T. Since then studies of return migration have grown rapidly, but few if any studies specifically address return to T&T. Two factors help to explain this.

First, Trinidadian migration is usually subsumed under a general treatment of Caribbean migrants. This is perhaps due to the fact that, among Caribbean territories, T&T has one of the lowest rates of legal emigration as a percentage of population (Guengant 1985). In addition, as one of the more wealthy countries in the region, T&T has attracted attention as a point of destination rather than a point of departure. In fact, the only significant intra-West Indian migration among civilians during the Second World War was to Trinidad and was due to job opportunities created by the construction of U.S. bases there (Harewood 1985). This trend continued with the opportunities offered by Trinidad's oil refineries (Thomas-Hope 1985). The high numbers of foreign-born residents in T&T confirms this trend (Conway 1994).

Second, T&T's migration statistics, like many of those in the West Indies, are plagued with inaccuracies and do not distinguish between the different patterns of return outlined earlier. The Central Statistical Office defines residents as those residing in T&T for at least one year and those who are abroad for one year or less. The figures in column 2 of table 11.2 therefore include residents who have been abroad for less than a year, citizens who were living abroad and have relocated to T&T, and residents/citizens studying abroad who have returned for a vacation or upon the completion of studies. Given this wide net of return movement, it is impossible to effectively disaggregate these figures to arrive at a meaningful estimate of return migration. The third column is an attempt to gauge the magnitude of the return movement, however, by comparing the total figures for residents departing against the figures for residents returning. Residents departing include emigrants, vacationers, contract workers, and students leaving to initiate or resume studies abroad. It is clear that a strong majority of Trinidadians return to T&T—between 85 and 98 percent of those departing. However, note that these figures do not directly measure long-term return, nor the return of emigrants from any particular time period.

"YUH LEAVE AND YUH COME BACK?" WEST INDIAN MOTIVATIONS FOR RETURN

I always intended to return . . . I was always talking about going back . . . I used to remember hunting. I missed the bush, the countryside.

TABLE 11.2
Departing and Returning Residents of Trinidad & Tobago, 1987–1991

Year	Category	Departing	Returning	2/1
1987	Total[1]	287,746	261,063	.907
	Students	--		
	Emigrants[2]	1,002		
1988	Total	291,272	249,201	.856
	Students	--		
	Emigrants	1,582		
1989	Total	248,143	215, 531	.868
	Students	--		
	Emigrants	1,144		
1990	Total	256,222	233,113	.910
	Students	102		
	Emigrants	2,234		
1991	Total	243,983	238,991	.980
	Students	60		
	Emigrants	2,184		

Source: Compiled from *International Travel Report, 1991.* Trinidad: CSO, 40–42.
[1]This includes departing residents, students, and migrants.
[2]This includes both temporary and permanent emigrants. A temporary emigrant is anyone, except a student, who normally resides in T&T and intends to remain abroad one to three years. A permanent emigrant is anyone, except a student, who normally resides in T&T and intends to remain abroad three years or more; this includes contract workers leaving to return to their homeland.

I wasn't happy. I wasn't free. . . . There I used to gamble, drink, sleep and work. . . . I don't know what kept me in England for eighteen years. It was because of a love for Trinidad that I came back.[2]
—Laurence Bain, Trinidadian returnee[3]

Laurence Bain's sentiments reflect three important factors common to the returnee experience: (1) many West Indians leave the homeland intending to return and work toward meeting that goal; (2) life abroad frequently fuels and reinforces this desire to return; and (3) homeland attachments often weigh most heavily on the decision to return. My sample confirms that these factors are significant. But given the established patterns of emigration and professional discontent with the homeland, why do West Indians hold on to this return desire? Reasons fall into four categories: the homeland milieu, familial reunification, return obligations, and professional fulfillment. These motivations embody location-specific assets that cannot be replicated in the host country or elsewhere in the world (Da Vanzo 1981).

The West Indian Homeland Milieu

The homeland milieu denotes a valued place of origin that affords security and happiness. This comes from a strong identification with the homeland that cannot be denied. Several forces sustain this connection. First, as first-generation migrants, returnees' homeland attachment is vivid and direct. While these ties may diminish the longer the expatriate stays abroad, some migrants nonetheless maintain strong bonds over significant periods abroad of twenty years and more. Despite these long-term returns, it is true that the shorter the time abroad, the fresher the association with the homeland.

A second factor that sustains homeland identification is an inability to fit in and function completely in North Atlantic societies. Even though West Indians adapt to life abroad, they are usually like Simone Farrell who, after thirteen years in Canada, was made to feel that she "did not belong 100 percent." This feeling is engendered by two significant expatriate deficits: sociohistorical roots and cultural baggage.

A lack of roots in the host society leads to a feeling of estrangement. Irma Spicer evokes this impression when she bemoans a lack of community spirit in Canada, where "people were very cold and into themselves. They don't have the pumpkin vine that we have." "Pumpkin vine" connections refer to a tendency among West Indians to associate individuals with members of their family, extended and immediate. This informal social convention of community-based relations and a personalized way of interacting with others emphasizes the individual's roots in the community and serves as a reminder of a recognized place therein.

The inability to relate to cultural norms also weighs heavily on the expatriate's mind. As a contract worker in France, Joanna Pascall missed "West Indianness, interrelationships between people." Irma Spicer similarly notes that in Canada

[people] are very materialistic—they don't give anything for nothing. In T&T if you have no money, you could ask a friend to lend you $10, not in Canada. People were inherently cold. You have to call before you can drop

by so that you can give them time to prepare, to look decent. You could never really get into them.

Images such as these are so prevalent that they have become clichés among expatriates.

Cultural norms are particularly important for retirees who partly derive security from the tendency for families to care for their elderly. Seventy-eight-year-old Mavis Procope notes: "Is not nice to be old in New York. Old people live in old folks' homes like jails. . . . They have no one. Their families hide them as if they are ashamed. I wouldn't like to be old there. . . . I prefer to be here." This convention is perhaps more important than other pull factors such as the pleasant W.I. climate. Retirees are rarely concerned with economic benefits. One local newspaper (*Sunday Mirror*, 8 August 1993, p. 8) cites returned retirees as faring well on a foreign pension: one couple lives on a monthly pension of £280, while another states that life is easier in T&T as "there are no taxes on bank interest, no capital gains tax, and no death duties."

Not having a recognized place in society reinforces this sense of not belonging. Parvatee Chote recounts how uncomfortable it made her feel:

[I] worked with some Guyanese, and some Sri Lankans. The work was real factory style: work, work, work with fifteen minutes break, very regimented. We each had to process four hundred applications in a day. I believe that the Sri Lankans were illegal and they accepted these conditions easily. It was more difficult for me. I felt like an immigrant.

This notion of being a stranger in a foreign land is further reinforced by an inability to materially recreate the cognitive idea of a home (both the homeland and the domicile). Parvatee recalls this sentiment:

There was this W.I. club called Tropics that we used to go to. It was good carrying on [enjoying oneself] in Tropics, it felt like home. But it wasn't. Trinidad was always home. Winter was depressing. I missed family, Carnival, the beach, old friends. I couldn't just take up the car and go as I would in Trinidad. I didn't know where to go in Toronto. I didn't want to just exist. I didn't want to be an immigrant . . . People lived in tall buildings, eighteen stories tall. We lived on the seventh floor. There were odors in the corridors. It was not a house, it wasn't a home. It just wasn't the same.

As Vidia Chen Wing illustrates, return to the homeland quickly reinforces a sense of belonging. She explains, "When I returned, I was surprised to see how much I missed the place. It was then I realized how unhappy I was in London. I felt comfortable. *I felt I belonged.*" This sample demonstrates that this is a persistent and strong motivator for returnee retention in the homeland. One respondent, Bridget Mooteram, sums it up this way, "I wouldn't leave again, meh navel string bury here."[4]

The converse of not belonging, a perception that expatriates are always welcome back, is a third factor that strengthens homeland attachments. Community-based acceptance makes individuals believe that they can rely on others for support. Returnees traditionally harp on this fact. As Kandis Mohammed describes it, "I know that if I go today to buy a roti[5] and I open my wallet and I have no money, (the vendors) will tell me it is all right, that I can pay next time. Or if my car breaks down, that someone would stop to help. Things like that are important." The association in Kandis's mind between sustenance (food) and support is not fortuitous. It suggests that she will never be completely out on a limb in her homeland. Returnees commonly express such sentiments.

This embodies an important motivator of return because it is strongly linked to the idea of a refuge, a place to which one can return in times of trouble. Sixteen percent of the sample returned after a crisis or impelling event led them to believe that they would be better off in T&T. Reasons vary widely. When Marie Aleong's fiancé called off their wedding five weeks prior to the event, she returned to Trinidad, where she found solace among relatives. Similarly, Roxanne Charles returned when her marriage failed. Mathilda Slinger's return was an entirely different experience: "I married an Indian in London. I stole all his money and ran."

A fourth factor that reaffirms the homeland attachment, particularly for migrants with young children, is the manner in which many West Indians have historically been treated abroad. Like most nonwhite immigrants, they have been victims of prejudice, systematic discrimination, legally sanctioned denials of citizenship rights, government policies of segregation, and institutionalized racism.[6] Twenty-eight-year-old Sookdeo Mahabir returned in 1992 with his wife and two children "because we believed that our children would grow up in an outgoing environment, free from racial prejudice in schools and in the street." Fifty-four-year-old Grace Seegobin returned in 1975 due to a lack of black role models for her children in England. Annette Bernard hated having her children grow up "as the only black kids in Colorado." Another could not conceive of raising her children in a society where they would be "third-rate citizens." Fundamentally, West Indians are concerned that such tendencies reflect wider societal values and behavior that are unfamiliar to them and inconsistent with their ideas of childrearing. After twenty-one years in Canada, Horace and Gemma Andrews returned with their four children because they were concerned that the educational system did not instill the values of hard work and perseverance that they grew up with in the West Indies. Similarly, Michelle de Gannes wanted her son "to grow up like a Trinidadian. . . . not to get away with the American way of life . . . with all that leniency, getting away with a lot of crap and being rude to parents."

A final factor that sustains the homeland identification is the maintenance of homeland connections through W.I.-based networks and repetitive return visitation. These connections reflect themselves in a limited interest in the affairs of the host society and in a vivid concern for the parochial affairs of the island homeland. Lima Chin-a-Singh noticed this trend among Trinidadians at her school in Canada: "In my high school there were a few Trinidadians. They would always get together and talk about home. A major train accident could happen in front of them and they wouldn't talk about it because it was Canadian, they only talked about home." Segal alludes to this phenomenon when he notes that "the Caribbean Diaspora has insisted upon full civic, political and economic rights and opportunities (in North Atlantic societies), at the same time that it has resisted assimilation and sought to retain homeland ties and cultural identities" (Chaney 1987, 4; see also chap. 10 here). Apart from helping expatriates confront an inimical reception abroad, it keeps them focused on the homeland and on their eventual reinsertion therein.

Homeland connections are buttressed by frequent repeat visits that keep migrants in touch with local realities and help them determine the timing of return. For some, such as Mavis Procope, it is primarily a way to guard against the depreciation of location-specific assets. In her eleven years abroad, she regularly returned to ensure the upkeep of her house. The income she gained by renting it out in addition to her foreign savings and a regular pension check secures her retirement back home. Similarly, potential returnees ensure a warm welcome in the homeland by maintaining the value of personal relationships and contacts through regular visits, pocket-transfer capital, and remittances (Conway 1984; Richardson 1982). During her eleven years in the United States, Jean McIntyre would visit T&T every other year laden with presents and U.S. dollars for her seven adult children and their children. She also regularly sent money to one of her daughters. When she and her husband returned to T&T, they moved in with this daughter and her family. Attachments to the homeland milieu therefore offer concrete advantages to expatriates—sustaining their identity as West Indians, enabling them to deal with the difficulties of life abroad, and paving the way for eventual return.

Family Reunification

Another significant motivator for West Indians constitutes what Neal Ritchey calls an "affinity hypothesis" whereby mobility is determined by the desire to be in close contact with family members (Harbison 1981). This most commonly denotes a need to be close to elderly parents or children. For many expatriates, like Charmaine Samaroo, the oldest in a family of eleven children, a sudden event necessitates a return. Her father's unexpected death meant that she had to go home to help her mother. Return to be with children left behind is even more significant. Philpott (1968) indicates that the W.I. family, with its loosely defined parental roles and cultural acceptance of foster parentage, encourages a migration ethos. Emigrating West Indians commonly leave their children in the care of others, hoping to send for them at a later date (Ho 1991). Patterson (1968) and Gmelch (1992) suggest, however, that this custom also serves to encourage return, as West Indians feel guilty about having left children behind.

Those who come back to be with children left behind are predominantly women who are single, divorced, or separated. Rookmin Singh, an Indo-Trinidadian who had been ostracized by her family because of her marriage to an Afro-Trinidadian, turned to emigration as a means of maximizing the opportunities for her children. When she arrived in Canada, she tapped into friendship networks for advice and support, and she anticipated their help in securing legal status for her and her children. She thought that all was going well until she heard her friends express negative sentiments about Afro-Trinidadians, and she began to worry about the reception her children would receive:

> When I left, my daughter was about to do her O levels [school leaving exams]. I thought I would go up and send for her later on. I was so worried about her that sometimes I couldn't sleep. I used to wonder if I had done the right thing. I couldn't decide. . . . I think of my daughter and decide that I take a rotten chance. I decide to come back.

Carolyn Sahadeo was similarly concerned about the teenaged sons she left behind:

> I had set up an account for them and I was sending them money regularly. But they were squandering it all. They went to concerts, ate out all the time, and even wrecked the car. They went to stay by parents of friends "rent free," but the parents knew that I was sending them money and they got my sons to pay their TT$12,000 telephone bill.[7] When I found out what was going on, I decided to come back.

Even though Carolyn was able to provide financially for her sons in absentia, she felt the need to return because her sons had become targets due to the remittance money she was sending them. Family members and friends back home therefore symbolize strong personal ties that trigger return. As long as such personal attachments remain in the homeland, they will continue to be an important pull factor of return.

Return Obligations

Emigrating West Indians frequently incur return obligations. The time abroad is meant to fulfill a specific purpose. Once it is achieved, the expatriate comes back home. Return obligations are of two kinds: familial and external.

Familial obligations entail family-based decision making. The family functions as an economic unit attempting to maximize its personnel-resource allocation. Emigration is therefore not a way of leaving the family, but of increasing its resource portfolio. Philip Mayer refers to this as the "morality of kinship" (Harbison 1981) whereby the migrant is taught that the only appropriate goal or motive for migration is maximization of the family's welfare. Robin Carrington explains, "I had my friends, family, and a comfortable situation here. It was an inconvenience that I had to go away. My father had always taught us that whatever knowledge we gained was to be contributed to the betterment of Trinidad." Such desires expressed as patriotic wishes often obfuscate the benefits that families derive from return. Kandis Mohammed notes, "It cost our parents a lot to educate us; it cost them too much for some other country to benefit. Here I rather be a big fish and give something back to my parents." In many instances, a successful return may enable the returnee to make a contribution to the homeland, but it is clear that the individual and the family reap greater rewards.

Kinship debt—traditionally fulfilled through remittances or consumer goods (Philpott 1970; Richardson 1983)—may also be repaid through return migration. Kandis Mohammed explains that her family used their return kinship network to facilitate the emigration of younger siblings. "We each went up there with a purpose. Whoever went up was to come back to pave the way for those after him. We helped each other go up that way." An important component of this process was birth order. Once the obligation to assist parents by paving the way for younger siblings is no longer present, permanent settlement abroad may be entertained.

"*Tied*" return, the return of an expatriate based on another's wishes, is another type of familial return obligation. These are of two kinds. In the first, *tied-spousal return*, the couple decides that the net benefits for the family of joint return exceed the costs. These individuals usually believe that if it were solely up to them, they would come back much later. The second, *tied-parental return*, centers around young children accompanying parents back or students who return at their parents' insistence. Thirty percent of the sample brought children back with them, while 2 percent could not remain abroad without parental support.

External obligations tend to be legal or contractual. Legal obligations sometimes include forced repatriations, but usually signify instances of visa expiration. In such cases, West Indians either overstay or come back home. Wayne Noel wanted to remain abroad but could not because he had "no family abroad, no money to continue at graduate school, no job, no green card, and no visa." Contractual obligations include labor or professional contracts and scholarship stipulations. These obligations, migrants indicate, may be broken, but are usually maintained because the migrant initially has no desire to settle abroad and still maintains very strong homeland attachments. These kinds of obligations will most likely persist in the future as West Indians continue to develop innovative mobility-based survival strategies or to seek extraterritorial contract work.

Professional Fulfillment

Professional difficulties abroad or new opportunities in the homeland prompt return flows. Difficulties abroad encompass a variety of problems and include inability to find a job, racial tokenism, and perceived glass ceilings. In 1990, forty-five-year-old Emile Smith left his minimally paying temporary job in Toronto and took his wife and four children back to T&T because of diminishing financial resources. On the other hand, some migrants, like Colin Warner, fare well professionally, but they leave the North Atlantic because they resent being tokens in a game of racial quotas. He explains:

> I was working in one of the three top companies in America in my field. I had a very high paying job, and I was on managerial track in an accelerated five-year program. I was the token everything. There were only two blacks out of seventy-two people, and I was the only one from the Caribbean.

Others feel a glass ceiling in corporate hierarchies because of their origin. After twenty-five years in Canada, David Joseph came back because "I had reached my peak . . . being Trinidadian, I would not be given the general manager's position." These returnees accept that dollar for dollar the income in T&T would be less than what they earned abroad, but this was weighed against the superior positions that they would hold back home. Davindra Ramlalsingh reiterates this push factor, but attaches equal weight to pull factors. He "decided to come back in 1978, in the boom years. . . . Friends tried to encourage me not to come back, telling me that things were 'ketch arse' (extremely difficult), but a lot of people were coming back then."

As new opportunities emerged in T&T during the 1970s oil boom, skilled personnel were required to fill the posts. Nationals who had acquired training and experience abroad were well positioned to fill these roles. Return to T&T held out the promise of opportunity, prestige, and recognition in the homeland. Richard Chen Wing was one such case. "I came back during the boom years. I went for an interview and one week later I had a job. There were many openings then and the salaries were good. The idea of coming back was greater, more attractive." It was a period when jobs for the foreign educated were abundant. Virtually all those in the sample who returned at that time had little difficulty in securing work.

The situation in T&T with regard to opportunities for specialized skilled expatriate reintegration is somewhat unique among the W.I. islands. Many of the other islands have been unable to provide jobs commensurate with the investment and expectations of well-trained and experienced locals (Anderson 1988; Grasmuck and Pessar 1991). This so-called effective demand drew Trinidadians back to the homeland, and it constitutes an important factor in returnee retention. Bremner's (1983) notion that West Indians refuse to go back because of professional difficulties suggests that current economic hardship and constrained opportunity in most countries may preempt the future influence of professional fulfillment on the decision of whether or not to return home.

Migrants anticipate these problems, and some returnees maintain escape contingency plans. This allows for greater flexibility of movement and decreases the feeling of being trapped in the homeland. Homeland attachments seem to override economic factors in the decision process. Gillian Antoine, a media buyer for an international advertising agency, explains: "The job situation was difficult in both countries, but at least I would be happier in Trinidad, even with less money, because I would be with my family and friends." This recognition, however, is prevalent among locals who have experienced life abroad. Workers with specialized skills who have not lived abroad may still favor effective demand and adequate remuneration over homeland ties.

These four motivations are the most dominant for West Indians, but the effect on the decision to return is seldom easily compartmentalized. The case of Donna Solomon illustrates their interaction:

> I was apprehensive. . . . I didn't want to go back to having to deal with the ol' talk (idle chatter) and gossiping, the inefficiency of the police force, the dust, the dirt, the insects, the lack of ease of shopping, but I thought that the educational system was better for the children, and knowing that changes had taken place and that my husband wanted to come back, I agreed to return.

She returned because of a combination of factors: the benefits of the homeland milieu, tied obligations, and petrodollar funded infrastructural improvements in the country. The influence of these return motivations, independently or combined, establishes the sociocultural framework in which the return decision making takes place. Such a framework suggests that in response to adverse and changing socioeconomic conditions, cultural images and messages sanction emigration and return as a viable individual coping strategy.

SHIFTING SANDS AND LOCAL RESPONSE: TODAY'S ISLAND HOMELANDS AND SOCIOCULTURAL REALITIES UNDERLYING RETURN PERSISTENCE

Today the West Indies are facing some of their greatest challenges. The specter of declining terms of trade, decreasing overseas assistance, constrained professional opportunity, official corruption, and expanding illicit drug activity augur a bleak future for the islands. Traditionally, official response to such problems was misguided or had limited impact. Unpopular austerity measures under structural adjustment, such as the elimination of subsidies, a decrease in public investment, and the containment of public salaries, are not helping to assuage a general sense of despair and discontent. Programs that could potentially increase employment opportunities, such as the Caribbean Basin Economic Recovery Act under the Caribbean Basin Initiative, have made little progress in providing meaningful employment for the majority of the middle classes (Maingot 1994). The collective impact of such problems is changing the context into which returnees must reintegrate. Rhonda Williams, a twenty-seven-year-old who came back in 1992, suggests that these new variables necessitate a reevaluation of the image of return:

> I am careful of assuming that I went away and that I am better for it. That is a certain kind of arrogance. . . . There is a certain resentment of overanxious grads who are coming back. It is naive on their part to expect to impress, they think that foreign is better. . . . [Their attitude is] "I've come for the job." People are wary. . . .

These comments reflect an up-and-coming attitude of "returnee fatigue" that is a backlash from the era when those who returned were favored for top positions over those who remained. Despite these changes, the cultural effect of return migration on the West Indies endures. In a region where long-standing mobility patterns generate their own impetus and collective rationale, return migration will continue to persist as a viable survival strategy because of two key elements: enduring positive images of return and transnational considerations.

POSITIVE IMAGES OF RETURN

Several forces sustain the favorable image of return in T&T. The first constitutes the long-standing association of return with upward mobility. As noted earlier, return historically secured the status quo of French and British Creoles; from the 1960s onward, however, it provided the middle classes with an avenue to upward mobility (Ho 1991). Today, it persists as such. Fifty-five percent of the sample mentioned education as one of the main reasons for emigration. The educational profile of the sample before emigration and on return shown in table 11.3 illustrates that a significant majority (75 percent) had attained education beyond the secondary level at the time of return.

Comma (1980) suggests that given the limited training offered in T&T, an increased number of students emigrate with the intention of returning to benefit from new opportunities. The track record of successful return-ees suggests that people associate foreign accreditation with success. The employment profile of this returning skilled labor pool clearly supports the belief that many returnees enjoy occupational success and prestige. Table 11.4 shows a 45 percent increase in professionals among the sample population. Undoubtedly many students assume professional careers on return. In a way, this pattern reflects a de facto reverse brain drain wherein skilled West Indians are returning for the reasons mentioned earlier.

Another factor perpetuating a positive image is the perception that the returnees enjoyed a privileged lifestyle abroad. To some degree, this is the result of colonial assimilation policies whereby West Indians were made to believe that almost everything foreign was superior and worthy of em-ulation. Initially this manifested itself in the imitation of English values and tastes and in an aspiration to emigrate to England, the "mother coun-try." Today the North American example dominates. This is the result of

TABLE 11.3
Educational Profile of the Sample

Highest Level of Education Completed	Before Emigration	After Return
Primary	5%	4%
Secondary	87%	18%
University	7%	67%
Other tertiary	1%	8%
Vocational	--	3%
Total	100%	100%

Source: Author's survey

TABLE 11.4: Employment Profiles of Returnees to Trinidad & Tobago

Status after Emigration at Time of Interview	Status before Emigration							
	Professional	Nonmanual[1]	Skilled	Unskilled	Unemployed	Student	Retired	None[2]	Row
Professional	9	2	--	1	--	37	--	5	54
Nonmanual	--	10	--	--	--	13	--	5	28
Skilled	--	--	--	1	--	1	--	--	2
Unskilled	--	--	--	3	--	--	--	--	3
Unemployed	--	2	--	--	--	2	--	1	5
Student	--	--	--	1	--	2	--	1	2
Retired	--	3	1	1	--	--	--	--	5
Total	9	17	1	6	--	55	--	12	100

Source: Author's survey
[1]Nonmanual work not requiring highly specialized training.
[2]This refers to emigrants who left Trinidad before they entered the workforce.
[3]The total number of respondents is one hundred.

the proximity to the North American mainland, the global dominance of U.S. culture, and years of exposure to waves of returnees and visiting North American tourists. A local short story captures these migrant dreams:

> Joebell find that he seeing too much hell in Trinidad so he make up his mind to leave and go away. The place he find he should go to is America, where everybody have a motor car and you could ski on snow and where it have seventy-five channels of colour television that never sign off and you could sit down and watch for days, all the boxing and wrestling and basketball, right there as it happening. (Lovelace 1988)

The general nonmigrating population, especially the young, imagine this foreign lifestyle as the dream that the returnee has realized. A recent survey among 914 Trinidadian secondary school students showed that 77 percent said that watching U.S. programs makes them long for the life portrayed on television (Sanka 1994, 19–20). This perception is reinforced throughout the West Indies by streams of consumer goods sent by expatriates for friends and relatives back home. This trend is so prevalent in Jamaica that it has given rise to so-called barrel children—children who subsist, indeed prosper, on barrels of consumer goods sent them by parents residing abroad.

Such goods are one element of a larger cluster of acquired trappings that confer high status on the individual because they reinforce quixotic illusions of foreign opulence. The imitation of North American speech patterns and dress also creates the impression of imported wealth. These widespread images gave rise to a popular term in T&T, *"freshwater Yankee,"* which historically referred to a West Indian who had acquired a U.S. accent by simply visiting the U.S. Embassy or one of the WWII U.S. naval bases (Mendes 1986). Today the term is commonly applied to those who spend a short time in North America and then display conspicuous North American values and mannerisms. This popular image of returnees also resonates as a modern consumption symbol, leaving an indelible impression on the consciousness of many locals and intensifying aspirations for foreign consumption patterns and lifestyles.

The repertoire of ostentatious return is sometimes deliberately upheld by the migrant. Carolyn Sahadeo, an overstayer who worked illegally in the United States, conceals the true motivations of her emigration and the actual conditions of her time abroad. On her return, she presented the image of success abroad. After eighteen months she came back with a video recorder and more than 50 T-shirts, "all these little things that cost so much in Trinidad." Gmelch (1985) also notices this trend among Barbadian returnees. He suggests that those who fare poorly overseas are disinclined to return, as all emigrants are expected to come back with at least enough money to buy a home of their own. Carolyn needed to save face, especially as others knew that she had been remitting money to her sons in T&T. This aura of success, real or imagined, brings an added bonus in the form of respect and awe that she finds empowering:

> People who are familiar with the American lifestyle, and knew you before you left, hold you in awe. They give you more respect. They give you more hearing. They figure that you know a little more. . . . All the girls at work come and ask you for fashion magazines and books. They ask you about the best places to shop in Manhattan. You have information that they want and they seek you out. It's almost a macho feeling. People figure that they can't freeload off you.

For those whose upward mobility is not evident, for retirees or those who maintain their preemigration status, prestige is accorded on the basis of their returnee status.

These kinds of messages, as Gemma Andrews notes, make it difficult to convince others of the difficulties of life abroad. "My friends think that up there is the land of milk and honey. . . . I tell them that it is not (that) easy . . . you have to work hard. . . . They figure that you just go away and you automatically get these things." This is not surprising. Thomas-Hope (1992, 33) notes that "the established image (of life abroad) is bolstered by personal views, hopes, and sometimes information as well. The first impulse is to reject any information that carries a message contrary to the spirit of what is already believed or held by the image." Promising popular images toe the line of these messages.

Local accounts of migrant experiences rarely deal with returnees who experience hardships abroad and come back poor. On the rare occasion when such difficulties are hinted at, they are not accorded much importance or are assumed to be isolated cases. Messages in the press frequently reinforce the prestige of return by including photos, migration histories, achievements (usually educational or professional), and local connections. The favorable image of return is therefore resistant to change because it is firmly entrenched in W.I. culture. Additionally, West Indians want to preserve the accessibility of this outlet in their consciousness, and they do so by bolstering its positive associations.

TRANSNATIONALISM: ONE FOOT IN, ONE FOOT OUT

The very forces that initiated current waves of globalization such as financial liberalization have also generated significant noneconomic effects. One of these, transnationalism—the bidirectional flow of peoples, information, mores, and goods across borders—pervades W.I. societies and performs an important role in enabling West Indians to develop new strategies to overcome homeland difficulties.

Transnational relationships have fostered a freedom of movement that has enabled West Indians to develop double identities: one rooted in the original homeland and the other in the adopted homeland. Hayden Marcelle, a fifty-five-year-old high school teacher who spent eight years in Canada, states, "I never lost touch with T&T. I always felt that I would return. I have dual status. I have one foot in, one foot out. People tell me that I am being smart. I, in fact, have two homes." This swallow movement varies slightly from the definition of long-term circulators (Thomas-Hope 1985). The latter have two homes: a primary one in the Caribbean and a secondary one in the North Atlantic host country to which the migrant travels on work expeditions. Contrary to these circulators, West Indians such as Hayden effectively live in their native country but regularly visit their North Atlantic home in order to legally maintain a double status, not to work. This type of two-home arrangement permits an escape valve for reemigration and a maximization of resources. Christian Farrell explains:

> I remain here essentially for the same reasons that I returned: spiritual, psychological, and social. However, as with many others, this is always held in balance, with the weighing of these considerations versus material, security, and financial ones. The decision to continue living in T&T is a purely voluntary one in my case since I am also a citizen of Canada and therefore can take up residence elsewhere at short notice.

He has found that such a strategy has made returning easier because he can choose either to stay or leave.

This kind of option is attractive to those contemplating the move back home, especially those with children. While 30 percent of the sample returned with children, only 16 percent of those had additional children after returning. Half of those returning with children used their dual status to secure foreign legal status for their T&T offspring. Return is realized when the children are young. The older they are, the more difficult the adaptation to T&T because of host-land attachments. This maximization of benefits for children is illustrated by the case of Marisa Namsoo, who came back before having children, returned to the United States to give birth, then came back to T&T. These strategies suggest that to maximize the benefits to their family, couples wait to give birth abroad and then return to the West Indies to raise their children. Transnationalism therefore not only facilitates return and reintegration by reaffirming homeland attachments and by providing an escape valve but also allows

West Indians to develop innovative strategies for overcoming drawbacks at home.

CONCLUDING OBSERVATIONS AND IMPLICATIONS FOR FUTURE RETURN

Caribbean mobility patterns reflect a growing complexity of interwoven transnational relationships among a people accustomed and historically predisposed to migrate. Today the current political economic realities introduced in chapter 1—especially a globalization of human aspirations and the freer transborder flows of people, information, currencies and goods—influence W.I. international movement and make its control and documentation increasingly difficult and move it beyond government control. Policy responses, particularly the adoption of neoliberal approaches aimed at creating new channels for economic growth, could indirectly help curb W.I. emigration if they were to create employment opportunities in the homeland. In practice, however, these policies fail to affect mobility patterns because they target nontraditional sectors of which many of the migrants have no experience. They involve state actions, whereas much migratory activity is beyond Caribbean state control and they do not account for the self-perpetuating cultural acceptance and prevalence of migration as an option. Despite these policies, and at times in response to them, West Indians leave their homelands in search of greener pastures. The West Indies have experienced a century or more of massive net emigration, but since the eighteenth century, a significant share of Caribbean emigrants have returned home.

The cultural dominance of migration—of which return is just one component—offers a view opposed to the belief that the process behind migration is primarily that migrants temporarily fill short-term increases in foreign labor demands. Evidence in this chapter confirms that return is an enduring cultural feature of W.I. societies. It reflects Ungar's (1988) finding that international migration is a permanent feature of the interdependent economies of the hemisphere (as chap. 10 emphasizes). This cultural dominance is most reflected in homeland attachments, which are the most significant reasons for return. The local legend of the cascadura is one of many images that form and feed the collective image of the benefits of return. These reasons for return suggest that West Indians will continue to move back home despite negative factors, such as decreasing effective demand in the Caribbean.

This chapter has suggested that strategies such as migration and transnational networking have not enhanced the quality of life for the majority of West Indians. Return is primarily an individual and household strategy.

Select household members emigrate to diversify household income or to increase the household resource portfolio. This migration is not an expression of a desire to reside abroad, but rather a strategy for accumulating sufficient savings or upgrading skills so that individuals may ultimately reside comfortably in the homeland. For families and educated professionals, it is principally a strategy to increase their resource portfolio and to take advantage of new opportunities back home afforded by newly acquired skills. For low-skilled returnees, it is an opportunity to benefit from the prestige and increased status that return confers. For others, it is the occasion to remedy an urgent situation back home, to flee unfavorable conditions abroad, or to gain from sociopolitical developments in the island homeland. For all, it is an opportunity to benefit from and to prevent the depreciation of location-specific assets.

Throughout the Caribbean there is a belief that returnees can be driving forces behind progress. Friedland believed that the large number of Puerto Ricans who attended school in the United States were trained in the industrial labor processes, and then returned to their native country would contribute to the development of Puerto Rico. Gonzalez was of the opinion that the same applied to the women who returned to the Dominican Republic from the United States (Stinner and de Albuquerque 1982). Indeed, the Guyana Office for Investment (GO-INVEST) was established in September 1994 to attract and facilitate increased investment in order the fuel the country's economic growth by providing efficient and effective investor services. Along with targeting foreign investors, the office is particularly interested in targeting expatriate Guyanese.

The pursuit of neoliberal development strategies by Caribbean countries offers the prospect of new opportunities in the private sector for highly trained immigrants who wish to return. Some W.I. governments, notably Jamaica's, have embarked on a conscious policy to utilize the vast stock of Caribbean human capital abroad on a temporary as well as permanent basis with the hope that such a policy may stimulate the return flow of more expatriate professionals. In 1993 the government of Jamaica, in cooperation with the Commission of the European Communities and the International Organization for Migration (IOM), embarked on a program called Migration for Development. The intent is to facilitate the return and reintegration, over a two-and-a-half-year period, of forty professional Jamaican nationals residing in industrialized countries "to fill important vacant development positions" such as managers, engineers, and policy analysts. Migration for Development provides several incentives to ease reintegration into the homeland: these include travel expenses for return, an average of $3,000 U.S. reintegration support for housing and living costs, medical and accident insurance for two years, and support for the acquisition of scientific and/or professional equipment and/or literature necessary to perform the job (Casati 1996; Government of Jamaica et al. n.d.).

Additionally, in 1992 the Jamaican government established a returning residents facilitation unit in its Ministry of Foreign Affairs and Foreign Trade. The unit is not engaged in a proactive program to induce Jamaicans resident overseas to return home, but rather facilitates the process of relocation for those who have already made the decision to return. It does so by coordinating with the appropriate ministries to identify potential problem areas, reduce red tape, and work on solutions to common bureaucratic obstacles that returnees may face. Additionally, it works with returning Jamaicans to ensure that they understand the procedures necessary for return and provides them with concessions to facilitate their relocation. These official efforts are buttressed by a number of local "returnee associations" of which there are at least ten (Brice 1996). These associations, run by returnees themselves, fulfill a multiplicity of roles including providing advice and assistance to those contemplating return or to those who have returned and are engaging in philanthropic work in their local communities. The approach that is in place in Jamaica has been successful thus far because it has determined that the strategic opportunity for harnessing the potential of returnees is not in attracting them back per se, but in ensuring that conditions are ripe for their retention.

These observations point to three conclusions with regard to future return flows. First, sociocultural forces suggest that return is a personal decision that will continue regardless of local and global changes. Second, relative to sociocultural forces, government policy will have little effect on emigration flows. Barring rapid transformations, this stream will continue. Governments need not take steps to promote widespread return migration since it will take place anyway, often for noneconomic reasons. Third, the current wave of globalism is facilitating and intensifying return by encouraging flexible mobility and lifestyle patterns across borders.

NOTES

1. The term "West Indies" refers to the Commonwealth Caribbean. While maps will often label all Caribbean islands as the West Indies, its use here (and in the region) largely reflects the membership of the ill-fated West Indies Federation 1958–62 (see chaps. 2, 4).

2. All quotations are reconstructed from interviews and/or survey responses.

3. Respondents' names are fictitious and exemplify names common to T&T.

4. Bridget refers to an old folklore tradition of burying a newborn's umbilical cord at the foot of a tree to inculcate in the child a sense of belonging to the country.

5. A flat wafer bread of East Indian origin in which is folded a thick curry mixture including beef, chicken, goat, shrimp, or any other meat (Mendes 1986).

6. In England the 1962 Commonwealth Immigration Act instituted quotas on nonwhites entering Britain; the 1971 Immigration Act restricted entry to "patrials" (persons with a parent or grandparent born in Britain) and retroactively withdrew residency rights from nonpatrials; the 1981 Nationality Act determined that children born in Britain of W.I. parents would no longer qualify for British citizenship; and "sus laws" in the 1980s allowed the police to stop nonwhite men on suspicion that they might be planning a crime (Sunshine 1988).

7. Roughly the equivalent of U.S. $2,823 then.

SUGGESTIONS FOR FURTHER READING

Gmelch, George. *Double Passage: The Lives of Caribbean Migrants Abroad and Back Home*. Ann Arbor: University of Michigan Press, 1992. Gmelch combines interviews with Barbadian returnees and oral history techniques to examine personal migration histories with the aim of developing a qualitative Caribbean perspective on the double process of emigration and return, providing unique and interesting insights and anecdotes on the region's migration culture and the migrant's relationship to the host country as well as the homeland.

Pastor, Robert A., ed. *Migration and Development in the Caribbean: The Unexplored Connection*. Boulder, Colo.: Westview, 1985. This collection of articles places Caribbean migration in a policy context for development by exploring case studies, migration patterns, host and sending society policy options, and the interaction between migration and development.

Western, John. *A Passage to England: Barbadian Londoners Speak of Home*. Minneapolis: University of Minnesota Press, 1992. A remarkable study that uses detailed questionnaires and intensive interviews to probe Barbadian families in London. It examines the relationship of one set of Caribbean migrants and their children, based in a traditional Caribbean destination, to the Caribbean homeland and the host society. Among the issues it deals with are transnationalism, the notion of home, the identity of Caribbean migrants, and migrant survival strategies and decision making.

V

FUTURE PROSPECTS

12

From Neoliberalism to Sustainable Development?

Thomas Klak and Dennis Conway

The chapter summarizes some of the major issues the Caribbean is facing in the era of globalization and neoliberalism and evaluates their sustainability. For us, sustainability goes beyond long-term employment prospects and environmental management. It includes efforts to shift control and responsibility over development initiatives back to the islands, communities, and people whose lives depend on them. Obviously this requires a shift away from Caribbean development policy dictated by the interests of international capitalists. Our overview has three parts. The first comments on the Caribbean's economic niches (i.e., major export-oriented economic sectors and schemes, as well as various forms of human migration). The second considers how to go about assessing the costs and benefits of neoliberal development involving foreign investment and production for export. The third focuses on issues of sustainability, with priority going to local community interests and nature, in light of an evaluation of the growing importance of various more-or-less benign forms of tourism in the region.

CARIBBEAN RESPONSES TO GLOBALIZATION AND NEOLIBERALISM

The region's development conditions and prospects during the era of globalization and neoliberalism can be gauged by the reactions and roles of people, firms, and governments. In what notable ways has the Caribbean coped with the new exigencies presented by the global economy and the neoliberalism transformation of state and society? Six responses are representative of the region's new roles in the neoliberal era: (1) wage work in the new export-oriented factories, (2) attempts at managing of factories or offices whose products insert into the new international division of labor, (3) export of the traditional primary sector products, (4) export of nontraditional agricultural commodities, (5) the search for a role in off-shore finance, and (6) migration and circulation by Caribbean people. The discussion summarizes much of the evidence from the empirically detailed chapters in this book concerning the Caribbean's international connections under neoliberalism. It also adds other points to arrive at a broad overview of the region.

For a small percentage of the total workforce (although a considerably larger share of young women), one response has been to toil long and hard for the new foreign investors taking advantage of the public subsidies put toward the promotion of nontraditional exports (see chaps. 5, 7). Although Caribbean states are seeking a great range of new exports, described by Wiley in chapter 8 as a "scattershot" approach to filling new export market niches, the investment has gone predominantly into garment assembly operations. This is certainly the case when measured in terms of employment, much of which is located in the new free zone factories. For a sizeable percentage of workers who have taken jobs as assemblers, operators, and keypunchers, one act of defiance has been to challenge the authority of the new factory managers and owners, usually through time-honored forms of passive resistance.

A woefully inadequate but nonetheless significant number of Caribbean entrepreneurs have tried to manage a firm that inserts within the new global commodity chains for garments, tourism souvenirs, fresh fruits and vegetables, information processing, and other nontraditional activities. One young Jamaican woman whom the first author interviewed in 1993 was trying her luck at producing and exporting backpacks and other carrying bags. Her experience offers a window into nascent Caribbean-owned and managed firms in the neoliberal era. She was a local person who obtained business and production skills in the employment of a foreign firm, which she then used to run her own operation called Multi-Kraft. But a search of the island's publically owned industrial parks for other locals running their own operations unearthed little evidence that the neoliberal development model which privileges foreign investors in the immediate term actually yields the promised benefit of local skill transfer in the longer term (see chap. 5). MultiKraft was located on Kingston's far west side, and it was so new that it had yet to settle into a reliable market or cohort of approximately twelve female workers. Workers who proved inadequate were let go. Those who were kept on worked under the pressure of a severely competitive international environment for such common goods. MultiKraft occupied factory space vacated by another Jamaican firm that was one of many failing to succeed at exporting garments to the United States under 807 tariff provisions (see chap. 4). Multi-

Kraft's owner was drawing on (1) two years of experience as a manager for a Hong Kong garment firm called Magma that had shut down, (2) raw materials provided through her Hong Kong connections, (3) workers trained and in her words "stolen" from foreign-owned plants, and (4) recycled sewing equipment from yet another foreign firm that had left the island. MultiKraft survived at least through 1994, although recent attempts to reach the firm by phone for an update have been unsuccessful.

The fact that MultiKraft cannot be reached by phone may be due to the island's notorious shortages of telephone lines. There were less than 4 per 100 population in 1990, the lowest level in Caricom. The British firm Cable and Wireless owns 79 percent of a phone monopoly for which the state guarantees a 17.5–20 percent annual profit rate (Dunn 1995). Such elite-brokered constraints make success even more challenging for newly export oriented firms for which international telecommunications is essential (as chap. 7 emphasizes).

But phone service is just one of many obstacles to nontraditional export development. It would have been difficult for MultiKraft to find adequate markets and meet payroll in recent years. The turnover rates have been high, especially for small, locally owned firms (see chap. 7). The Caribbean Textile and Apparel Institute, located in Kingston, reports that in 1996 alone more the 4,500 textile workers lost their jobs (Rohter 1997a). This is because Jamaica has neither the region's lowest wages nor Mexico's trade advantages through NAFTA. Even the World Bank, neoliberalism's leading advocate in the Caribbean and Central America, predicts that Mexico will soon divert up to a third of their U.S. exports (Passell 1997).

If the Caribbean's new urban-industrial export activities are precarious, there are also attempts at a wide range of export-oriented activities in the rural areas. While the region's traditional primary product exports such as sugar, bananas, bauxite, and petroleum have lost value in recent years, it is premature to deem them irrelevant to the Caribbean's role in the global economy. In 1990, primary products (of traditional and nontraditional types) were still 46.5 percent of the U.S. exports of CBI countries, although manufactured products had by then surpassed them as a share of total (Deere and Melendez 1992). More specifically for Jamaica, as of 1993 traditional primary products were still about 70 percent of its global exports (PIOJ 1994).

Among the Caribbean's traditional commodities, only bananas employs large numbers of small-scale (and until now, reasonably remunerated) farmers, primarily in the southern half of the Lesser Antilles (see map 2 and chap. 8 on Dominican banana farmers). The WTO's ruling in May 1997 that the European Union's market guarantees for ACP banana exports represent discriminatory trade practices is a major blow to the future security and stability of the banana family farm. For the other traditional exports, male-dominated trade unions have over several decades successfully struggled for decent wages and benefits. But they are under serious threat as (1) labor codes are "reformed" under the neoliberal banner (IADB 1996) in order to make investment more attractive to international capital and (2) employment is cut in response to lost revenues (Lewis and Nurse 1994).

Then there is the export of fruits, vegetables, and flowers labeled NTAEs (nontraditional agricultural exports), that by definition have high value by volume and area under cultivation. Compared to Central and South America, the Caribbean has been less successful in meeting the demand for NTAEs in the United States and other northern markets. By 1991 Central America's NTAE earnings exceeded $175 million, while those of the Caribbean were under $90 million. The Caribbean's limited success is especially notable given its more desperate need for new sources of foreign exchange. One indicator of this need is that Caribbean earnings from traditional agricultural exports have fallen faster than those of Central America.[1]

An additional problem is that the image of a small-scale farmer/entrepreneur rising up to meet new export market niches for NTAEs—perhaps substituting snow peas or strawberries for bananas—does not match the reality. Although the experience varies across contexts and products (and therefore leaves hope for greater small-scale sustainable production), the following general characteristics of NTAEs in Latin America and the Caribbean restrict benefits to smaller-scale farmers:

1. Markets are highly competitive, require connections to complex international commodity chains (Gereffi and Korzeniewicz 1994), continually draw new entries from countries worldwide, and risk saturation.
2. Products are highly perishable, require expensive transportation, are subject to wide-ranging price fluctuations, and entail risk for producers.
3. The vast majority of NTAEs are native to temperate rather than tropical climates; this disadvantages Caribbean farmers whose knowledge is of local crops.
4. Crops are usually planted continuously and intensively in monocultures, and buyers demand perfect-looking produce.
5. The above features often lead to the problem of a "pesticide treadmill," and related problems of human and ecological health and unsustainability and residues on crops entering the United States.
6. The above features, combined with the need for large capital invest-

ments, contribute to dominance by large foreign firms, for which local people mainly serve as low-wage labor.

These factors have meant that small-scale farmers have generally not been competitive (Thrupp 1995). The parallels between NTAEs and the data processing industry described in chapter 7 are several and are more than coincidence—for example, dominance by firms from the U.S. and elsewhere in the core triad, inadequate Caribbean state support to develop the sector, shaky performance and low to no growth for small-scale local producers, and poor working conditions for the employees. Core-periphery relations maintain even through regional shifts in economic sectors.

Note that agricultural production serving Caribbean tourists is usually analyzed separately from NTAEs (compare chaps. 6 and 8). The extent to which nontraditional agriculture for Caribbean tourists and for overseas consumers can synergistically complement each other, and thereby overcome some of the problems noted above, would seem to be a worthwhile avenue for research and policy. Another idea that might help overcome the constraints on small scale local participants is to emphasize tropical rather than temperate foods, and thereby seek to exploit the growing interest in creole cuisine while drawing on local crops and local farmer knowledge. A third idea is to focus on processed rather than fresh foods. This would reduce the need for (1) expensive transportation to combat perishability and reach distant markets quickly, and (2) a perfect appearance, which could reduce pesticide abuse. It could also expand forward linkages from agriculture to industry and thus expand employment and foreign exchange.

Another relatively new and globally oriented economic activity that most Caribbean political leaders have eagerly pursued is offshore finance. As usual, Caribbean territories vary tremendously in their success in attracting capital for this venture (see for example the industries and income levels listed in table 2). Further, islands that are winners and losers in the casino capitalism associated with the quest for hypermobile international finance capital have their own set of preexisting attributes and consequent problems. Those islands that have successfully attracted offshore banking and related activities can be viewed as exemplars of neoliberalism. By opening up their economies, tying their development closely to the vagaries of international finance, and adopting social policies designed to maintain political stability, a very few Caribbean territories have managed to ensure their place in the circuits of international finance.

Most successful offshore financial centers are relatively small (even by Caribbean standards) British colonies: the Cayman Islands, the British Virgin Islands, Montserrat, and the Turks and Caicos Islands. Their political status confers the highest level of investor confidence on the territories' political stability. The Bahamas and the Netherlands Antilles have also attracted financial holdings from thousands of foreign firms. In some places such as the Caymans and the British Virgin Islands, offshore finance has become such a major component of the countries' economies that there have been concomitant political and social shifts of great significance (see Roberts 1994; R. Evans 1993; Barry et al. 1984).

But despite government promotions and investment incentives, most islands see little mobile capital or capital of any kind. An island's ability to attract furtive capital into an offshore finance sector is negatively correlated with its need for new sources of foreign exchange earnings. Most islands are now independent countries with many features viewed as unattractive to finance capital, including weak and unstable economies, poverty, high unemployment, and social tensions (chap. 5 explores these contradictions). These and other colonial legacies leave most islands isolated and uninteresting in regard to the offshore financial component of the current round of reordering of the global economy.

Despite the flurry of interest in filling market niches in the global economy, the majority of Caribbean people are not directly involved in such things as producing the various nontraditional exports or in marketing the region as an offshore platform for product assembly or low-surveillance banking. Even if they are, returns have been unsatisfactory for most Caribbean people. In reaction to neoliberalism's harsh creed many Caribbean people have sought entry into the United States or other wealthy North Atlantic countries. As several chapters have stressed, migration has always been a principal way for Caribbean people to make ends meet. The pressure and the impetus to leave are as strong now as ever. As in times past, crises and prolonged hardship at home cause many to seek emigration. The enticing messages from relatives, friends, and the mass media in the north suggest a better life abroad. A recent poll in the Dominican Republic, for example, revealed that half the population now has relatives in the United States, and more than two-thirds would emigrate if given the chance.[2]

As chapters 2 and 11 emphasize, however, not all leave the Caribbean for good. Many see opportunities for employment, education, and making money in North America as part of their strategy (Lowenthal 1972; Richardson 1983). The other part of their livelihood strategy is to utilize their North American sojourn or sojourns to supplement and enrich island existence and to initiate changes in their material circumstances, including meeting basic needs, acquiring a plot of land, building a home, financing the children's education, and even starting new enterprises such as small business ventures (Chevannes and Ricketts 1996; Conway 1993a; Portes and Guarnizo 1991). Migration is not necessarily a one-way ticket, and remittances and return migrants' investments in the Caribbean region are now viewed more positively in the literature (Gmelch 1987, 1992). For Mexico, the weight of evidence on the favorable aspects of "migradollar" impacts and investments is especially persuasive (Durand and Massey 1992; Durand et al. 1996).

A widening Caribbean presence that extends beyond national geographies is suggested by the emergence of overseas enclave communities, their linkages with people back home, and the maintenance of ties between kin on the North American mainland and those remaining in the region. How this plays out in terms of the region's future development in the globalizing world is a subject worthy of much more scrutiny. Indeed, we view the diaspora as an underutilized resource, and we examine it later in this chapter.

GLOBALIZATION AND NEOLIBERALISM: BLESSING OR CURSE?

Does the weight of evidence suggest that development prospects for the Caribbean region are narrowing or expanding in the global and neoliberal era? Many of the chapters have a (justifiably) foreboding tone, but social systems are not deterministic, Caribbean people have always proven their adaptability and creativity, and there are some promising signs and much hope for a better future.

A review of current debates about foreign investment in the Caribbean (and its competitors elsewhere in the South) reinforces one of the important themes of this book: that examinations, evaluations, and progressive reformulations of development policies must be multidimensional. Chapter 1 introduced the notion that this book's political-economy perspective strives to be more self-critical, self-reflective, and open-minded to considering alternative conceptualizations and the weight of evidence than prevailing views based in mainstream economics. The subsequent chapters have provided a wealth of information and analysis concerning the current neoliberal transformation. It is important to examine the impacts across social groups and state coffers, and in terms of economic linkages (Klak 1995, 1996).

Chapter 1 also discussed how the discourse of mainstream economics has infiltrated popular and (unfortunately) even scholarly understandings of globalization and neoliberalism. One manifestation of this infiltration relates to current governmental efforts to attract foreign investment. The debate and criteria used to evaluate the merits of foreign investment in export agriculture or manufacturing in the Third World are often remarkably narrow. Debate centers on how many jobs are "created" and at what wage levels (Goldberg 1995). At issue is the question of whether the wage and working condition standards of the United States or the host country should apply. That dichotomous choice in turn leads to an implicit assessment, if not a firm judgment, of whether the investment is good or bad for the host country.

On one side, critics who ideologically favor a deep redistribution of wealth and power instead focus on commonsensical issues such as the appallingly meager wages and poor working conditions suffered by young female workers. Wage rates are a recurrent and simple theme in public economics discourse (Giddens 1990, 40) and therefore make good sound bites for liberal reporters (e.g., Herbert 1995; Falk 1996). For example, recent calculations show that sewers of clothing for the Gap in El Salvador or for Disney's Pocohantas line in Haiti are paid less than one percent of the price consumers pay. Those same Disney workers are paid between twenty-eight to forty-two cents an hour, while a Honduran worker sewing the Kathie Lee Gifford pants sold at Wal-Mart reports pay of thirty-one cents an hour (NLC 1995, 1996a,b).

On the other side, defenders react by noting that wages in export processing industries are at and above the going rates in the host countries. Since young women have the highest levels of unemployment, factories offer much needed and often the first source of steady income.[3]

The constricted nature of the debate is suggested by the fact that both sides are largely correct. The pay levels are extremely low by First World standards, and at the same time the jobs and wages are generally highly desired by the mostly young women who have few alternatives (Klak 1996). Foreign industrialists do not create the poverty and desperation surrounding the free zones to which workers return after a long day at the factory. Foreign firms insert into and in fact are attracted to the conditions of squalor that for them mean a wage-saving bargain.

The debate's status quo-reinforcing nature is revealed in the solutions that logically extend from the criticisms. These heavily favor the defenders. The issues in the debate can lock critics into advocating simple solutions such as higher wages and improved working conditions. The recent proposal in Haiti, for example, is for Disney to pay sixty cents a hour, which workers say is a liveable wage (NLC 1996a). This undoubtedly would provide workers with some immediate relief. But it would hardly lift them out of poverty, marginality, and subordination, nor more broadly improve the host country's development prospects. This should not be construed as a difference between being "realistic" (higher wages) and "idealistic" (local empowerment). If demands for higher wages are but a first step in a series aimed at local empowerment through such things as productivity increases other than through flexible Taylorism (see chap. 7) and expanded economic linkages, then they hold more promise. But they are unlikely to proceed in this way.

The immediate problem with the narrow focus on wage increases is that workers are unlikely to benefit within the prevailing organization of production. Wage demands encourage direct employers or contractors such as Disney to (1) pressure sewers for more production per unit time, usually by increasing quotas in the piece-rate system, and/or (2) stop producing. The latter can be done by halting orders from a factory or by fleeing (or threatening to flee) to countries offering cheaper labor, a better public relations image, and/or trade policy advantages. Most states promoting their EPZs do so by effectively trying to underprice their competitors' wage rates, a process that has been labeled a "race to the bottom" (chap. 5 describes this competition).[4]

The essential problem with the pragmatic campaign for higher wages is that it fails to situate EPZs within their broader context of social, economic, and political relations. By ignoring the surrounding nexus of social relations, well-meaning critics inadvertently reproduce them through their solutions (Yapa 1996). To evaluate the extent to which host countries can and sometimes do benefit from foreign investment for export production, the jobs and wages debate must be expanded to consider this broader political and economic context. This broadening can be illustrated by the export processing zones that so many Caribbean governments now provide (see chap. 5). A definitive judgment as to whether the "blessing" or "curse" interpretation is more compelling awaits considerably more detailed empirical research. We can make progress toward such an evaluation, however, by identifying the criteria and providing a preliminary general assessment.

A "blessing" reading is supported to the extent that the international exposure associated with economic opening in general, including EPZs in particular, serves as a force for positive change. Such exposure can help to dislodge traditional internal constraints on social mobility, which modernization theorists attribute to local culture (Harrison 1985) and dependency theorists blame on comprador elite and other local expressions of international core-periphery relations (see chap. 2; Cardoso and Faletto 1979). Economic opening also presents new opportunities for benefiting from international trade. Integration into global commodity chains can be positive if it forces the host country to confront a wide range of internal problems. These include bringing jobs to economies stagnant under the weight of local mercantilist capital, and challenges to local production methods that have only narrow beneficiaries. This reasoning underlies some of the current enthusiasm in the Caribbean for NAFTA parity: to bring economic dynamism to stagnant economies. Such an evaluation is not unequivocal, however. International exposure can be negative because the unequal competition posed by large foreign firms can swiftly annihilate both old and new local producers (chap. 4 discusses this dilemma).

Global integration can also help to expose government mismanagement, graft, and nepotism that has long plagued many Caribbean countries (see chap. 2). As Jamaica's ambassador to the United States recently argued, "Stronger trade links will inevitably lead to better cooperation in . . . anticorruption activities" (Bernal 1996, A13). Suddenly there are many more external interests connected to the host countries that can expose (but also potentially benefit themselves from) such illegal practices. Issues of human rights can also be brought to international attention through greater global connections. The publicity campaigns in recent years against Nike, Reebok, Kathie Lee Gifford, and Disney (or their subcontractors) for their Third World employment practices demonstrate this (NLC 1997). However narrowly defined the criticisms sometimes are with respect to issues of human development, the campaigns are making internationally known the working conditions that have long been sequestered by distance, foreign culture, and more closed societies.

Real, sustained local benefits from export processing will have positive impacts on a range of domestic social groups. A full assessment of local benefits would need to measure impacts in terms of the following criteria:

1. Employment, in terms of both quantity (EPZ workers as a percentage of the work force) and quality (the percentage of jobs paying above a livable minimum-wage)
2. Domestic industrial exporters, in terms of both quantity (percentage of total exporters) and quality (firm size, output value, technological level, market access, stability)
3. Product diversification beyond garments (including electronics, data processing or other sectors)
4. Net foreign-exchange earnings (over the public costs of subsidies to service the EPZs)
5. Backward linkages (subcontracting for EPZ firms and local inputs such as raw materials, cardboard, printing, and services; see Klak 1995, 1996)

How is the Caribbean doing in these terms? The vignettes concerning St. Lucia and Jamaica in chapter 5 showed that neither has performed well across these criteria. More broadly, it is difficult to find strong evidence in this book or elsewhere for success according to these criteria anywhere in the Caribbean region. As Conway suggests in chapter 2, Barbados comes closest, but it too has had extreme difficulty in maintaining foreign investment and quality employment in nontraditional export sectors (Freeman 1993).

For a better example of a small, dependent country for which development based on foreign investment for export has yielded dramatic gains (a "blessing" interpretation), one needs to look well outside the Caribbean region to the island of Mauritius off the east coast of Africa (Klak and Myers 1997; Myers and Klak 1998). That a real success story only exists outside the Caribbean has meaning in itself. U.S. dominance of and intervention in the Caribbean makes developing a diversified set of investors, export sectors, markets, local interpretations of "democracy," and foreign-policy relations extremely difficult there (see chaps. 2, 9; Deere et al. 1990; Kenworthy 1995).

TOWARD A SUSTAINABLE, PEOPLE-ORIENTED, ENVIRONMENTALLY SOUND FUTURE?

This book has focused attention on the range of Caribbean development policies being pursued under the neoliberal banner. These are obviously top-down arrangements, while the vast majority of Caribbean people are left to fend for themselves within institutional constraints. Nature too is usually left as a residual category. We would like to conclude focusing on the creative energies of Caribbean people and on nature as the center of any future plans for resource use and investment. We also include a reformulation of the region's largest economic sector, tourism, within a sustainable approach to regional development.

In Caribbean societies, where smallness is the rule, not the exception, there is openness and interrelatedness of the social, economic, political, and cultural spheres with the outside world (Conway 1990). Intraregional, transnational, international, multinational, even virtual linkages within networks characterize the geographies of Caribbean people via movements of people, capital, material things, ideas, commitments, obligations, and facilitated in ways never before envisaged by today's transportation and communication infrastructure. For Caribbean people, the global/local linkages are more influential than ever. In this context, neglect of local, person-to-person interactions, family networks, and presences and absences leaves any analysis short on applied content, if not conclusions. Smallness in societal interactions and a ubiquitous openness of Caribbean society should not be construed to mean that island, national, and regional identities are lost, diminished, or devalued. Indeed, we do not need to question the consensus that Caribbean island people retain their identity despite absences, transnational experiences, and even transnational lives.

In this context, are there signs for optimism? We believe so, despite persuasive arguments to the contrary: the region's structural constraints; the catalog of pain and suffering imposed by neoliberal regimes, restructuring, and IMF and World Bank "conditionalities"; predictions of growing dominance by the core economies, growing inequalities between core and periphery, and greater concentration of capital and therefore power in the hands of fewer and fewer corporate elites and technocrats: the international capitalist class no less. But the region is not bereft of human resources, the experiences of the people have not been totally without positive returns, and island-specific examples may point the way to an agenda for the future that is not hopeless or helpless. There is evidence of communal collective action at local and regional scales, of self-help activism, of entrepreneurship, of innovation and creativity, all of which counter the notion that powerlessness reigns. Experiments with social democratic regimes were built on firmly held socialist principals among the masses. This legacy has not vanished, even though it has waned. The region's anticolonial traditions certainly fostered nationalism, as well as searches for new identities among Caribbean people. This has largely been a progressive movement of considerable merit. Long-standing traditions of labor union movements characterize these islands' societal orders. Many an island's lack of infrastructure and (under)development helped foster self-help initiatives like credit union associations, home self-building, and community activities (Potter and Conway 1997).

Today, local environmental activism in Puerto Rico, Barbados, and other islands has spurred resistance to thoughtless development projects (Conway and Lorah 1995). The successful achievements of Cuba's "microbrigades" and recent "green revolution" are better respected in the Caribbean than in North America. The region's educated have always been at the forefront of opposition to the "forces of imperialism," whatever their guise. The educational systems of many of the excolonial islands have remained their treasured asset, and this reservoir of human capital certainly offers hope and potential for the future. Most significantly in today's globalizing world, the numerous diasporas constitute an enlarged resource reservoir that the Caribbean can little afford to ignore. There are progressive legacies on which to build an alternative path to one that is fashioned (or agreed to by default) by resigned acquiescence to neoliberalism and free-market triumphalism.

We now want to draw on observations from Caribbean reality to frame a set of alternative paths with potential for a progressive transformation of peoples' life courses and life politics: nothing less than a vision of a sustainable future for Caribbean people (Nettleford 1993). Included among the issues taken into account are (1) gender divisions and relations, (2) the strengths and weaknesses of local, informal economies, (3) pressing needs for appropriately managed tourism policies, (4) a regionwide need for innovation and aggressive transformations in the private sectors of micro states to meet today's challenges in more diversified economies capable of competing for niches in the globalizing markets of the Caribbean region and the American hemisphere, (5) the unrealized potential of the region's diasporas, (6) progressive use and empowerment of existing local (and regional) communal agencies and institutional bases, and (7) the need for environmental policies that mesh with the promotion of industrial and agricultural diversification, better meet the plurality of local needs, and draw on local and regional comanagement and stakeholder, self-management initiatives (see Conway and Lorah 1995).

If the societies of the Caribbean region are to muster their collective agency to address the problems they face, then women as well as men must be given the responsibility and must be afforded the chance to fully participate in the endeavor. Some might argue that women's participation is the essential ingredient that has been missing in the development project to date (Carmen 1996). Nor should we embrace simplistic notions that women's domestic roles prohibit their participation in labor markets or that within Caribbean family contexts, matrifocality, extraresidential unions, and alternative patterns of parental responsibilities are anything but flexible family forms that are appropriate and viable in the prevailing societal conditions (Barrow 1996). Women participate, contribute, and undertake progressive communal activities, notwithstanding the fact that many are vulnerable groups among the "poorest of the poor" (Massiah 1983).

The involvement of increasing numbers of Caribbean people in a whole range of casual, temporary, small-scale economic activities that are classified as informal or underground might be dismissed as ephemeral, merely survival or subsistence, or "disguised unemployment" because they appear to lack the long-term continuities of formal employment. Such a prejudiced view of this complementary "real-life economic" sector (Wheelock 1992) belies its central role in the day-to-day struggle of the Caribbean poor and not so poor. Self-help work serves to make ends meet, put food on the table, acquire some modest savings, and provide for children's schooling needs, among other household basic needs (Roberts 1994). Local activities have long traditions, often built on church affiliations, community self-reliance, and village community endeavors (Gomes 1985; Riviere 1981). The "higglers" of rural Jamaica have been highlighted as successful female entrepreneurs in the trading business (Durant-Gonzalez 1985). Trinidadian (and other Commonwealth Caribbean) poor maintain deeply entrenched traditions and practices of rural-urban interactions in informal transfers of goods, people (labor), services, favors, reciprocal activities, obligations, financial, and communal support (Lloyd-Evans and Potter 1991; Potter 1993). Thus self-help networks are in place and are effectively operating in many parts of the region.

On the other hand, peoples' reliance on "informal sector" activities should not be heralded carte blanche as salvation. Some underground eco-

nomic activities are criminal, by intent and purpose, some embroil participants in dubious and illegal ventures, and some snare relatively innocent
(if desperate) people in their vice, prostitution, gambling, and criminal
rings (Richardson 1992). The extent of the penetration of international
drug-running cartels in many Caribbean countries' underground economy is a very real threat as well as a serious problem, serving as a somber
counter to more positive characterizations of such "internationalized"
systems of informal enterprises (Cumberbatch and Duncan 1990; Griffith
1995; Maingot 1994). That drug smuggling is also embedded in the neoliberal "marketscape of opportunities" that is the North American hemisphere's commercial domain has been noted (de Albuquerque 1997). If
we are to characterize informal-sector activities in terms of their potential
to foster positive returns for Caribbean people, then it is worth stressing
that it must be at the local and community levels that such activities contribute to livelihood. Beware of international influences and be wary of
the international patrons and financiers (money launderers) who offer
get-rich-quick schemes (Conway 1996b).

Where does tourism fit in this equation? The governments in the Caribbean, one by one, sooner or later, have come to rely on this complex,
multifaceted "global" industry. The growth of this twentieth-century industrial ensemble as a worldwide phenomenon has been nothing short of
spectacular, outgrowing all other more conventional commercial sectors.
Yet tourism provides plenty of evidence for its critics, who have been
especially troubled by the social costs incurred (Karch and Dann 1981;
McAfee 1991; Pattullo 1996). On the positive side, however, there is Auli-
ana Poon's (1993) enthusiastic, and persuasive, propositions on how the
Caribbean can plan for and benefit from "new tourism" (Conway 1995).
We can offer up several unresolved issues here, as much to test the robust-
ness of Poon's positive views as to critically challenge her main arguments
about new tourism and what it means for Caribbean development. We
generally concur with Poon's (1993) positive perspective on developing a
sustainable tourist industrial sector: putting the environment first; making
tourism a leading sector; strengthening marketing and distribution channels; building a dynamic private sector; seeking to be competitive globally
rather than intraregionally. These issues require more scrutiny, and research by Dimitri Ionnades on Cyprus's tourism (Ionnades 1995a,b) provides further insights for the Caribbean.

"New tourists" are certainly a welcomed differentiation, with their
higher multiplier effects and their niche markets providing wider opportunities and incentives for a differentiated and more culturally rich Caribbean tourism product (as argued elsewhere; see Conway 1993b). Weaver's
(1991, 1993) advocacy of "alternative ecotourism" strategies for some
venues is also appropriate. We should add that other low-density variants

are equally socially conformable and appropriate: sport tourism, nature tourism, heritage/culture tourism, and even retirement tourism. However, whether new tourism's emergence heralds the industry's transformation to a flexible, restructured ensemble replacing "mass tourism," as "flexi-bilism" has been thought to restructure Fordism/Taylorism manufacturing systems, is still in considerable doubt. Caribbean venues such as St. Croix, Puerto Rico, and Barbados, already in stage 3 of what McElroy and de Albuquerque (1991) call "high density tourism styles," are so dependent on mass tourism that they may not have the flexibility to diversify in socially appropriate and environmentally sustainable ways (see the discussion around table 6.1). The major external airlines that dominate the travel scene have the delivery of masses of tourists at the heart of their interests in serving the Caribbean. The contemporary cruise-line invasion of the Caribbean is scarcely a trend in tourism with the dimensions of flexibility that those of us advocating the maintenance of low-density styles would like to see encouraged. Indeed, the threat posed by unplanned and unmanaged cruise-line tourism is considerable, and it may constitute a fast-looming crisis that should merit the progressive, even aggressive, intervention of Caribbean states to ward off this assault or at least neutralize its overwhelming effects.

In light of these considerations of trends in tourism, Poon's (1993) unbridled enthusiasm for tourism in the global and neoliberal era must be questioned. Caribbean people, as well as decision makers in the public and private sectors alike, must retain a healthy skepticism of the effects of such global external forces. Most crucial in this respect must be the progressive and proactive involvement of the state in its "stewardship role" of maintaining each country's landscapes, coastal zones, marine habitats, and cultural heritages. There must be progressive "comanagement," in which authority and decision making are shared among several organizations, often operating at different geographical scales. Of even higher priority is local democratic decision making on economic matters, involving not only those within the tourist sector, broadly defined, but local communities, public-private coalitions of local authorities, NGOs, artisans, citizens, and even children (see Conway and Lorah 1995). We advocate being "flexible" and creative, embracing visionary plans for island bundles to be at the forefront of new tourism, and taking advantage of appropriate information and communication technologies. Caribbean self-interest and territorial sovereignty must not be compromised or subverted to international and transnational capital profiteering. If "capital by invitation" is nothing more than today's variant of the failed "industry by invitation" that haunted Caribbean industrialization experiences, then *skepticism* should be the watchword.

Furthermore, the unknown, underexplored, and undervalued dimensions of sustainable tourism may well be the industry's capacity to incubate and spawn wider multiplier effects than previously envisioned. These need to go beyond the essential linkages that tourism *must* engender between local agriculture, microbusinesses (formal and informal), and producer services. They also include local manufacturing of what are now imported commodities and technologies; these need customizing for tropical/Caribbean island uses. The wider multipliers also include tourism's place in transnational systems, interregional associations and cooperative ventures (rather than competitive scenarios), and tourism's partnership with other sectoral expansions, especially communication services development and customizing. Long-term success hinges on the state's role in aiding and facilitating comanagement initiatives, where tourism planning, environmental conservation and marine resources management, and local, democratic economic decision making are joint undertakings and are treated as a merged bundle of policy mandates and practices.

Long-held traditions of international mobility, emigration, and circulation are highly interrelated with the region's development and underdevelopment. They have led to today's well-developed diasporas, with enclave populations in multilocal networks spread between locales within the Caribbean region, the northern hemisphere, and the trans-Atlantic (Europe). Family networks, wider kin networks, ethnic networks, and Internet transfers all facilitate the movement of people, goods, information, technology, and capital. Caribbean residents are linked to overseas relatives, friends, business acquaintances, and a wealth of opportunities far wider than the geographically constrained fields of the island home. The potential for better use of these already existing circuits is obvious and potentially progressive. Overseas Caribbean enclave populations constitute political, social, cultural, and economic forces that are presently undervalued and underutilized. Remittances constitute a flow of capital and goods in kind that have progressive impacts on recipients' livelihoods (Conway 1992). Return migrants are a pool of undervalued resources too easily dismissed as ineffective agents of change (Gmelch 1992). The future of every Caribbean society is inextricably tied to the wider world, which would include overseas enclave sojourners, emigrant relatives, and expatriates as essential functionaries, not lost emigres.

Last but not least we need to bring the environment explicitly into the equation. The long-term survival of Caribbean tourism is dependent on environmentally conscious plans of action. The responsible "stewards" must be us—Caribbeanists, advocates of Caribbean democratic processes, and the Caribbean people—who contribute to forging a "globalization from below." We can no more leave it to the international community of nation-states than we can to international business, commerce, and financial capital. We certainly must resist the threatening influences of global crime, drug running, money laundering, toxic waste dumping, and the like. Profiteering interests are hardly to be taken into account when it comes to Caribbean regional and local self-interests. The destructive tendencies of globalization and neoliberalism deserve our determined opposition.

The optimistic message in John Cox and C. Sid Embree's (1990) report entitled *Sustainable Development in the Caribbean* is worth summarizing here. The conference on which the report is based concentrated on the types of policy shifts that would be needed, regionally, nationally, and internationally, to bring about sustainable development in a natural-resource-dependent area like the Caribbean. Though the last two decades had witnessed a drop in the standard of living and rapid population growth in a number of countries, the nearly 6 percent per annum increase in economic growth that was considered necessary to meet peoples' basic needs is possible without destroying the natural environment. But it has to be a new kind of growth. Under this new growth regime, the region must begin living off the interest on its stock of ecological capital instead of running down its stock of natural resources. National development policies and projects must emanate from ecologically sound analyses of the natural resource base. Projects not meeting "sustainability" criteria must be rejected, even those that promise immediate foreign-exchange earnings, are offered by international donors, or are promoted by international financial institutions.

Most important, sustainable development goals can only be reached when development policies integrate economic and natural resources management planning. This new sustainable-development regime must embrace a strategic imperative to involve people in the development process, as well as the recognition that culture is a precondition of development and progress. In this regard special attention must be given to involving women, youth, and the labor force in decisions affecting their lives, livelihoods, local environments, and living spaces. The conferees saw signs for optimism in the new priorities emerging at the international level, where environmental project support has been thrust to the forefront of global consciousness (Cox and Embree 1990). It has been further pushed into the spotlight by such U.N. efforts as the Rio Environmental Conference of 1992, its accompanying NGO Forum, and the recently concluded Barbados Conference. Recent examinations of the extent of environmental action and of the growth and success of regional comanagement efforts by NGOs such as the Caribbean Natural Resources Institute (CANARI) and the Caribbean Conservation Association (CCA), suggest some progress (see Conway and Lorah 1995; Renard 1992; Smith and Berkes 1991; Smith 1994). Among many analysts, intellectuals, scien-

tists, practitioners, and NGOs the "will" is there, but does the government have the necessary "political will"? Will the peoples' strengths be
drawn on, will their innovativeness be allowed to flourish, or will "market
forces" be allowed to frustrate and constrain the peoples' opportunities,
whether in the Caribbean region or in the enlarged, hemispheric pan-
Caribbean community of peoples? Past experience suggests we need to be
cautious in acclaiming that the future offers hope. Certainly the twenty-
first century is anything but certain.

We conclude by turning to the global implications of the trends reviewed in this book. Neoliberal ideas with respect to the Caribbean setting have been explored, but these ideas are simultaneously being
confronted in regional contexts worldwide. On this front, Caribbean peoples and researchers are united with many others in the world community
who are concerned about the human and ecological impacts and future
viability of a political economy based on neoliberalism and globalization.
Understanding the current economic dilemmas and the many ways in
which states and peoples worldwide are responding to them is essential
for shaping a humanly and ecologically just and sustainable path into the
future. We hope to have contributed to that task.

NOTES

1. For this comparison Central America includes Guatemala, Honduras, Costa
Rica, El Salvador, and Panama. The Caribbean includes the Dominican Republic,
Jamaica, Haiti, and Belize (Thrupp 1995, 59).

2. As a result of growing interest in economic opportunities abroad, the U.S.
consulate in Santo Domingo was the third-busiest for immigration visa applications in 1996. Only the consulates in capital cities of countries with far larger
populations, Manila and Mexico City, had more requests (Rohter 1997b).

3. Tom Austin, the president of Disney's largest subcontractor in Haiti, articu-
lates this viewpoint: "We live in a market economy and the market determines
what the wages are, and it's the most effective allocator of resources. . . . It [our
rate of pay in Haiti] is a living wage. While it's not a wage that you or I or anyone
else would want to live on, there's a whole bunch of people who are [otherwise]
unemployed and those people are living" (NLC 1997, 6). Disney spokesperson
John Dreyer further explains that by providing Haitians with jobs, "Disney is
helping to develop Haiti's economy, the poorest in the Western Hemisphere"
(NLC 1997, 6).

4. The threat in the case of Disney is that it will respond by leaving Haiti,
further consolidate operations in countries such as China, and leave Haitian workers worse off. In 1996 Wal-Mart stopped buying Kathie Lee Gifford clothing from
a Honduras plant and Disney stopped buying clothing from contractors in
Burma. These moves, of course, mean workers go from having jobs with inadequate pay to having no pay at all. The production manager of one of Disney's

suppliers in Haiti recently told workers that if they ask for higher pay, "the Americans will come and take the jobs to the Dominican Republic" (NLC 1996b, 17). In response to these threats the Haitian workers' principal request is even more modest than a pay increase; they simply ask Disney to stay and send more work orders (NLC 1996a).

SUGGESTIONS FOR FURTHER READING

Carmen, Raff. *Autonomous Development: Humanizing the Landscape.* Atlantic Heights, N.J.: Zed, 1996. Written by a practitioner-turned-skeptical-scholar with many years of village-level work experience in Africa, this book seeks to disrobe the whole gamut of conventional ideas and practices concerning development, progress, growth, poverty, and backwardness. The writing is accessible and humorous, but the volume addresses crucial issues affecting the lives of the oppressed people of the world.

Escobar, A. *Encountering Development: The Making and Unmaking of the Third World.* Princeton: Princeton University Press, 1995. Escobar is a major figure in the Latin American movement to find "alternatives to development," often termed the "antidevelopment" school of thought.

Lalta, Stanley, and Marie Freckleton, eds. *Caribbean Economic Development: The First Generation.* Kingston, Jamaica: Ian Randle, 1993. This a collection of twenty-seven short essays on an array of issues related to economic conditions and policies. Sections of the book treat the historical context, international relations, economic sectors and policies, and the path forward. It includes both republished and new material from a wide range of regional scholars.

Bibliography

Acosta, D. *Employment-Cuba.* InterPress Service [IPS], Third World News Agency, Montevideo/Cuba, 4 May 1995.

ACP-EEC. Convention of Lomé (Lomé IV). Signed 15 December 1989 in Lomé, Togo.

Alavi, H. "State and Class under Peripheral Capitalism." In *Introduction to the Sociology of Developing Societies,* edited by H. Alavi and T. Shanin, 289–307. London: Macmillan, 1982.

Alleyne, F. "The Expansion of Tourism and Its Concomitant Unrealised Potential for Agricultural Development in the Barbadian Economy." In *Proceedings of the Ninth West Indian Agricultural Economics Conference.* St. Augustine, Trinidad: University of the West Indies Press, 1974.

Altimir, O. *The Challenge of Strengthening Development.* San Jose, Costa Rica: ECLAC, 1996. http://www.eclac.cl/ps26/ialtimir.html.

Altvater, E. *The Future of the Market.* Translated by Patrick Camillan. New York: Verso, 1993.

Alvarez, E. "El ajuste importador en la economia cubana: apuntes para una evaluacion." *Economia Cubana* 14 (January 1994): 3–16.

Alvarez, J. H. "Return Migration to Puerto Rico." Population Monograph Series, no. 1. Berkeley: University of California Press, 1967.

Ambursley, F. "Grenada: The New Jewel Revolution." In *Crisis in the Caribbean,* edited by F. Ambursley and R. Cohen, 191–222. London: Heineman, 1983.

———. "Jamaica: From Michael Manley to Edward Seaga." In *Crisis in the Caribbean,* edited by F. Ambursley and R. Cohen, 72–104. London: Heineman, 1983.

Ambursley, F., and R. Cohen. *Crisis in the Caribbean.* London: Heineman, 1983.

Analco, G. "A Dual Economy Creates a Mess." *Latin America News Update,* April 1995, pp. 22–23.

Anderson, P., and M. Witter. *Crisis, Adjustment, and Social Change: A Case-study of Jamaica.* Report for the project Crisis, Adjustment and Social Change for the UN Research Institute for Social Development and the Consortium Graduate School of the Social Sciences, University of the West Indies, 1992.

Anderson, P. "Manpower Losses and Employment Adequacy among Skilled Workers in Jamaica, 1976–1985." In *When Borders Don't Divide: Labor Migra-*

tion and Refugee Movements in the Americas, edited by P. Pessar, 96–128. New York: Center for Migration Studies, 1988.

Anderson, S., J. Cavanagh, D. Ranney, and P. Schwalb, eds. *Nafta's First Year: Lessons for the Hemisphere.* Washington, D.C.: Institute for Policy Studies, 1994.

Anglo-American Caribbean Commission. *Caribbean Tourist Trade: A Regional Approach.* Washington, D.C., 1945.

Annual Statistical Digest, 1992. Castries, St. Lucia: Government Statistics Office.

Appadurai, A. "Disjuncture and Difference in the Global Cultural Economy." *Public Culture* 2 (1990): 1–24.

Arthur, O. Address delivered at the 1996 lecture series of the Institute of International Relations, University of the West Indies, St. Augustine, Trinidad, 16 April 1996. Owen is prime minister of Barbados.

Aslanbeigui, N., S. Pressman, and G. Summerfield, eds. *Women in the Age of Economic Transformation.* New York: Routledge, 1994.

Asociacion Nacional de Economistas Independientes de Cuba [ANEIC]. Documento numero 1, 1994. http://www.unipr.it/davide/cuba/economy/aneicDB/aneic.html.

Asociacion Nacional de Economistas Independientes de Cuba [ANEIC 11]. *Ingresos y gastos de la poblacion cubana,* 1995. http://www.unipr.it/davide/cuba/economy/aneicDB/aneic.html.

Association for Work Process Improvement. "Recap of DEMA Surveys, 1986–1992." *Work Process Improvement TODAY* 16, no. 1 (1993): 45–54.

Atkinson, J., and D. Gregory. "A Flexible Future: Britain's Dual Labour Force." *Marxism Today* 30, no. 4 (1985): 12–17.

Bakan, A., D. Cox, and C. Leys. *Imperial Power and Regional Trade: The Caribbean Basin Initiative.* Waterloo, Ontario: Wilfred Laurier University Press, 1993.

Baker, R. *Public Administration in Small and Island States.* West Hartford, Conn.: Kumarian, 1992.

Barasorda, M. "Tourism in Development Planning." In *Planning for Economic Development in the Caribbean.* Hato Rey, Puerto Rico: Caribbean Organization, 1963.

Barbados Statistical Service. *Digest of Tourism Statistics.* Barbados: Government Printing Department, 1996.

Barnes, T. "Political Economy I: 'The Culture, Stupid.'" *Progress in Human Geography* 19, no. 3 (1995): 423–31.

Barnet, R., and J. Cavanaugh. *Global Dreams: Imperial Corporations and the New World Order.* New York: Touchstone, 1994.

Barrow, C. *Family in the Caribbean: Themes and Perspectives.* Oxford: James Currey; Kingston, Jamaica: Ian Randle, 1996.

Barry, T., B. Wood, and D. Preusch. *The Other Side of Paradise: Foreign Control in the Caribbean.* New York: Grove, 1984.

Basch, L., N. Glick Schiller, and C. Szanton Blanc. *Nations Unbound: Transnational Projects, Postcolonial Predicaments, and Deterritorialized Nation States.* Langhorne, Pa.: Gordon and Breach, 1994.

Bascom, W. "Remittance Inflows and Economic Development in Selected Anglophone Caribbean Countries." Commission for the Study of International Migration and Co-operative Economic Development, Working Paper no. 58. Washington, D.C., 1990.

Bass, J. *Agricultural Development Plan for Montserrat.* Montserrat: Ministry of Agriculture, Trade, Lands and Housing, 1984.

Beckford, G., and N. Girvan. *Development in Suspense.* Kingston, Jamaica: Friedrich Ebert Stiftung/Association of Caribbean Economists, 1989.

Beckles, H. *A History of Barbados: From Amerindian Settlement to Nation State.* Cambridge: Cambridge University Press, 1990.

———. "Where Will All the Garbage Go? Tourism, Politics, and the Environment in Barbados." In *Green Guerrillas: Environmental Conflicts and Initiatives in Latin America and the Caribbean: A Reader,* edited by H. Collinson, 187–93. London: Latin American Bureau, 1996.

Beckles, H., and B. Stoddart. *Liberation Cricket: West Indies Cricket Culture.* Kingston, Jamaica: Ian Randle, 1995.

Belisle, F. "Tourism and Food Production in the Caribbean." *Annals of Tourism Research* 10 (1983): 497–513.

———. "The Significance and Structure of Hotel Food Supply in Jamaica." *Caribbean Geography* 1, no. 4 (1984): 219–33.

———. "Tourism and Food Imports: The Case of Jamaica." *Economic Development and Cultural Change* 32, no. 4 (1984): 819–42.

Beller, W., ed. *Proceedings of the Interoceanic Workshop on Sustainable Development and Environmental Management of Small Islands.* Humacao, Puerto Rico: U.S. Man in the Biosphere Program, 1986.

Benedict, B. *Problems of Smaller Territories.* London: Athlone Press/Institute of Commonwealth Studies, University of London, 1967.

———. Introduction. In *Problems of Smaller Territories,* edited by B. Benedict. London: Athlone Press/Institute of Commonwealth Studies, University of London, 1967.

Bengelsdorf, C. *The Problem of Democracy in Cuba.* New York: Oxford University Press, 1994.

Benjamin, M. "On Its Own: Cuba in the Post-Cold War Era." In *Cuba: A Current Issues Reader 1995,* edited by D. Downton, 2. San Francisco: Global Exchange, 1995.

Bernal, R. "A Jamaican's Case for Trade Parity with NAFTA." *The Wall Street Journal,* 22 March 1996.

Bernal, R., M. Figueroa, and M. Witter. "Caribbean Economic Thought: The Critical Tradition." *Social and Economic Studies* 33, no. 2 (1984): 5–96.

Bertram, I. "Sustainable Development in Pacific Micro-Economies." *World Development* 14, no. 7 (1986): 889–992.

Best, L. "Size and Survival." *New World Quarterly* 2, no. 3 (1966): 58–63.

Bibly, K. "The Caribbean as a Musical Region." In *Caribbean Contours,* edited by S. Mintz and S. Price, 181–218. Baltimore: Johns Hopkins University Press, 1985.

Blackman, C. "The Economic Management of Small Island Developing Countries." *Caribbean Affairs* 4, no. 4 (1991): 1–12.

———. *The Practice of Persuasion.* Bridgetown, Barbados: Cedar, 1982.

Blanco, J., and M. Benjamin. *Cuba: Talking about Revolution.* Melbourne, Australia: Ocean, 1994.

Blasier, C. "The End of the Soviet-Cuban Partnership." In *Cuba after the Cold War,* edited by C. Mesa-Lago, 148. Pittsburgh: University of Pittsburgh Press, 1993.

Blood, Sir H. *The Smaller Territories: Problems and Future.* London: Conservative Political Centre, 1958.

Boswell, T. "An Inventory of Migration Research Dealing with Caribbean Topics." In *Geographic Research on Latin America: Benchmark 1980,* edited by T. Martinson and G. Elbow, 8:100–118. Muncie, Ind.: Ball State University Press/ CLAG, 1981.

Boswell, T., and D. Conway. *The Caribbean Islands: Endless Geographical Diversity.* New Brunswick, N.J.: Rutgers University Press, 1992.

Boswell, T., and J. Curtis. *The Cuban-American Experience.* Totowa, N.J.: Rowman and Allenheld, 1984.

Bouvier, L., and D. Simcox. *Many Hands, Few Jobs: Population, Unemployment and Emigration in Mexico and the Caribbean.* CIS Paper no. 2. Washington, D.C.: Center for Immigration Studies, 1986.

Bowen, R., L. Cox, and M. Fox. "The Interface between Tourism and Agriculture." *Journal of Tourism Studies* 2 (1991): 43–54.

Brana-Shute, R., and G. Brana-Shute. "The Magnitude and Impact of Remittances in the Eastern Caribbean." In *Return Migration and Remittances: Developing a Caribbean Perspective,* edited by W. Stinner et al., 267–89. Research Institute on Immigration and Ethnic Studies, Occasional Paper no. 3. Washington, D.C.: Smithsonian Institution, 1982.

Brana-Shute, R. *A Bibliography of Caribbean Migration and Caribbean Immigrant Communities.* Gainesville, Fla.: University of Florida Libraries/The Center for Latin American Studies, University of Florida, 1983.

Brautigam, D. "State Capacity and Effective Governance." In *Agenda for Africa's Economic Renewal,* edited by B. Ndulu and N. van de Walle. Washington, D.C.: Overseas Development Council, 1996.

Bray, M. Review of "Small Countries in International Development." *The Journal of Development Studies* (1986): 295–300.

Bremner, T. "The Caribbean Expatriate: Barriers to Returning, Perspectives of the Natural Scientist." In *Caribbean Immigration to the United States,* edited by R. Bryce-Laporte and D. Mortimer, 149–57. RIIES Occasional Papers no. 1. Washington, D.C.: Smithsonian Institution, 1983.

Brereton, B. *A History of Modern Trinidad.* Port-of-Spain, Trinidad: Heineman, 1981.

Bresser Pereira, L., J. Maravall, and A. Przeworski. *Economic Reforms in New Democracies.* Cambridge: Cambridge University Press, 1993.

Brice, D. Correspondence with Roger-Mark De Souza, 10 October 1996. Brice is head of the Returning Residents Facilitation Unit, Ministry of Foreign Affairs and Foreign Trade, Kingston, Jamaica.

Britton, S. "Tourism, Capital, and Place: Towards a Critical Geography of Tourism." *Environment and Planning D. Society and Space* 9 (1991): 451–78.

Broad, D. "Globalization versus Labor." *Monthly Review*, December 1995, 20–31.

Brohman, J. "New Directions in Tourism for Third World Development." *Annals of Tourism Research* 23 (1996): 48–70.

———. *Popular Development: Rethinking the Theory and Practice of Development.* Oxford: Blackwell, 1996.

Bromley, R. "Small May Be Beautiful, but It Takes More Than Beauty to Ensure Success." In *Planning for Small Enterprises in Third World Cities,* edited by R. Bromley, 321–41. New York: Pergamon, 1985.

Brown, H. "The Impact of the Tourist Industries on the Agricultural Sector." In *Proceedings of the Ninth West Indian Agricultural Economics Conference,* 129–42. St Augustine, Trinidad: University of the West Indies Press, 1974.

Bryan, A., E. Greene, and T. Shaw, eds. *Peace, Development and Security in the Caribbean.* New York: St. Martin's Press, 1990.

Bryan, A., ed. *The Caribbean: New Dynamics in Trade and Political Economy.* New Brunswick, N.J.: Transaction Books, 1995.

Bryce-Laporte, R., and D. Mortimer, eds. *Caribbean Immigration to the United States.* RIIES Occasional Papers, no. 1. Washington, D.C.: Smithsonian Institution, 1983.

Bryce-Laporte, R. "New York City and the New Caribbean Immigration." In *Caribbean Life in New York City: Sociocultural Dimensions,* edited by C. Sutton and E. Chaney, 54–73. New York: Center for Migration Studies, 1987.

Bryden, J. *Tourism and Development: A Case Study of the Commonwealth Caribbean.* London: Cambridge University Press, 1973.

———. "The Impact of the Tourist Industries on the Agricultural Sectors." In *Proceedings of the Ninth West Indian Agricultural Economics Conference,* 153–62. St Augustine, Trinidad: University of the West Indies Press, 1974.

Bussey, J. "Clinton Aide: Free Trade Is Still a Priority." *Miami Herald,* 13 December 1996.

Butler, R. "The Concept of a Tourist Area Cycle of Evolution: Implications for the Management of Resources." *Canadian Geographer* 24 (1980): 5–12.

Buttel, F., and D. Goodman. "Class, State, Technology, and International Food Regimes." *Sociologia Ruralis* 29, no. 2 (1989): 87–89.

Cabort-Masson, G. *Les Puissances d'Argent en Martinique: L'Etat Francais, La Caste Bekee et les Autres.* Martinique, DOM: Laboratoire de Recherches de L'A.M.E.P., 1984.

Caivano, J. "Dollars, Darkness and Diplomacy: Three Perspectives on Cuba." Cuba Briefing Paper Series, no. 6. Washington, D.C.: Cuba Project, Center for Latin American Studies, Georgetown University, 1994.

Caldwell, J., et al. "The Demography of Micro-States." *World Development* 8, no. 12 (1980): 953–67.

Campbell, J. "Layoffs Crippling Job Market." *The Jamaica Weekly Gleaner,* 8–14 March 1996.

Cardoso, F., and E. Faletto. *Dependency and Development in Latin America.* Berkeley: University of California Press, 1979.

Caribbean Insight. London: West Indies Committee, 1997.

Caribbean Tourism Organization [CTO]. *Dominica Visitor Survey: Summer 1993.* Barbados: CTO, 1994.

————. *Montserrat Visitor Survey 1993/94.* Barbados: CTO, 1994.

————. Press release. Bridgetown, Barbados, 1995.

————. *Statistical News, Quarterly Review of Caribbean Tourism Trends.* Christ Church, Barbados: CTO, 1995.

————. *Quarterly Reports.* St. Michael, Barbados: CTO, 1996.

Caribbean Tourism Research and Development Centre [CTRC]. *Study of Linkages between Tourism and Local Agriculture.* Christ Church, Barbados: CTRC, 1984.

————. *An Overview of Tourism as a Major Positive Force in Caribbean Economic Growth and Development.* Christ Church, Barbados: CTRC, 1986.

CARICOM. "The Caribbean Community in the 1980s: Report by a Group of Experts to the Caribbean Common Market Council of Ministers." Georgetown, Guyana: The Caribbean Community Secretariat, 1981.

Carlson, A. "Caribbean Immigration to the US, 1965–1989." *Caribbean Affairs* 7, no. 1 (March/April 1994).

Carnegie, C. "Strategic Flexibility in the West Indies." *Caribbean Review* 11, no. 1 (1982): 11–13, 54.

Casati, N. Interview with Roger-Mark De Souza, 12 September 1996. Casati is program officer with the International Organization for Migration, Washington, D.C.

Castro, F. Speech delivered at the closing session of Seventeenth Congress of the Central Organization of Cuban Trade Unions (UTC), 30 April 1996. In *Granma,* Internet edition. http://www.cubaweb.cu/granma/mayo/fideli.html.

Caufield, C. *Masters of Illusion: The World Bank and the Poverty of Nations.* New York: Henry Holt, 1996.

Cazes, G. "Le rôle du tourisme dans la croissance économique: Réflexions à partir de trois examples antillais." *Revue de Tourisme* 27, no. 3 (1972): 93–98, 144–48.

Center for Asian Research, Economics Department. *China Economic Bulletin.* Japan Research Institute, 1995.

Central Statistical Office [CSO]. *Population and Housing Census, 1991.* Roseau, Dominica: Commonwealth of Dominica, 1994.

————. *Statistical Digest no. 8.* Roseau, Dominica: Commonwealth of Dominica, 1995.

————. *Travel Report for 1994.* Roseau, Dominica: Commonwealth of Dominica, 1995.

Central Statistical Office of the Republic of Trinidad and Tobago. *International Travel Report, 1991.* Trinidad: CSO, 1992.

Chandra, R. *Industrialization and Development in the Third World.* New York: Routledge, 1992.

Chaney, E. "The Context of Caribbean Migration." In *Caribbean Life in New York City: Sociocultural Dimensions,* edited by C. Sutton and E. Chaney, 3–14. New York: Center for Migration Studies, 1987.

Chaney, E., and C. Sutton. *Caribbean Life in New York City.* New York: Center for Migration Studies, 1987.

Charles, K. "Total Quality Management and Caribbean Competitiveness in a Global Economy." Paper presented at the Caribbean Studies Association's eighteenth annual conference, Grenada, 26–29 May 1992.

Chernick, S. *The Commonwealth Caribbean: The Integration Experience.* Baltimore: World Bank/Johns Hopkins University Press, 1978.

Chevannes, B., and H. Ricketts. "Return Migration and Small Business Development in Jamaica." In *Caribbean Circuits: New Directions in the Study of Migration,* edited by P. Pessar. New York: Center for Migration Studies, 1997.

Chevigny, P. "Law and Order? Policing in Mexico City and Kingston, Jamaica." *NACLA Report on the Americas* 30, no. 2 (1996): 24–30.

CIA. *Cuba Country Report.* Washington, D.C.: CIA, 1995.

Clarendon, H. Interview with James Wiley, 26 May 1995. Clarendon is general manager of DEXIA, Roseau, Dominica.

Clark, S. "The Second Assassination of Maurice Bishop." *New International* 6 (1987): 11–96.

Clarke, C., and A. Payne, eds. *Politics, Security, and Development in Small States.* Winchester, Mass.: Unwin Hyman, 1988.

Cleland, J., and S. Singh. "Islands and the Demographic Transition." *World Development* 8, no. 12 (1980): 969–93.

Clifford, J. "Diasporas." *Cultural Anthropology* 9 (1994): 302–38.

Cole, J. *Geography of the World's Major Regions.* New York: Routledge, 1996.

Cole, W., and J. Mogab. *The Economics of Total Quality Management.* Oxford: Blackwell, 1995.

Collins, J. "Hemispheric Trade Role for Puerto Rico." *Caribbean Week,* 28 September–11 October 1996.

Comma, J. "Trinidadian Adjustment." Ph.D. diss., George Washington University, 1980.

Commonwealth of Dominica. *Population and Housing Census, 1991.* Roseau, Dominica: Central Statistical Office, 1991.

Commonwealth Secretariat. *Vulnerability: Small States in the Global Society.* London: Commonwealth Secretariat, 1985.

Communist Party Politburo. *Politburo Report.* Fifth Plenum of the Central Committee of the Communist Party of Cuba, 23 March 1996. In *Granma on Line, April 1996.* No. 2. Cubaweb, 1996.

Connell, J. "Island Microstates: Development, Autonomy, and the Ties That Bind." In *The Development Process in Small Island States,* edited by D. Lockhart et al., 117–47. New York: Routledge, 1993.

Conway, D. "Tourism and Caribbean Development." University Field Staff International Reports, no. 27. Hanover, N.H: Universities Field Staff International, Inc., 1983.

———. "Grenada–United States Relations Part I, 1979–1983: A Prelude to Invasion." University Field Staff International Reports, no. 39. Hanover, N.H.: Universities Field Staff International, Inc., 1983.

———. "Grenada–United States Relations Part II, October 12–27, 1983: Sixteen Days That Shook the Caribbean." University Field Staff International Reports, no. 40. Hanover, N.H.: Universities Field Staff International, Inc., 1983.

———. "Caribbean International Mobility Traditions." *Boletin Latino-Americanos y del Caribe* 46, no. 2 (1989): 17–47.

———. "Small May Be Beautiful, But Is Caribbean Development Possible?" UFSI Field Staff Reports: Latin America, no. 13. Indianapolis: Universities Field Staff International, 1990–91.

———. "Migration in the Caribbean." *Conference of Latin Americanist Geographers.* Vol. 17/18. Baton Rouge, La.: Conference of Latin Americanist Geographers, 1992.

———. "Rethinking the Consequences of Remittances for Eastern Caribbean Development." *Caribbean Geography* 4, no. 2 (1993): 116–30.

———. "The New Tourism in the Caribbean: Reappraising Market Segmentation." In *Tourism Marketing and Management in the Caribbean,* edited by D. Gayle and J. Goodrich, 167–77. London: Routledge, 1993.

———. "The Complexity of Caribbean Migration." *Caribbean Affairs* 7, no. 4 (1994).

———. "The 'New Tourism' and Caribbean Development Imperatives." *Caribbean Studies Association Newsletter* 22, no. 3 (1995): 4–5.

———. "What about the Underside of Paradise?" *Caribbean Studies Association Newsletter* 23, no. 2 (1996): 3–4.

———. "The Complexity of Caribbean Migration." *Caribbean Affairs* 7, no. 4 (September/October 1997).

Conway, D., and P. Lorah. "Environmental Protection Policies in Caribbean Small Islands: Some St. Lucia Examples." *Caribbean Geography* 6, no. 1 (1995): 16–27.

Conway, D., and C. Glesne. "Rural Livelihood, Return Migration, and Remittances in St. Vincent." *Conference of Latin Americanist Geographers.* Vol. 12. Baton Rouge, La.: Conference of Latin Americanist Geographers, 1986.

Corbridge, S. *Development Studies: A Reader.* London: Edward Arnold, 1995.

Council Regulation 404/93. Brussels, Belgium: E.U. Council of Ministers, 1993.

Cowell, N., and I. Boxill., eds. *Human Resource Management: A Caribbean Perspective.* Kingston, Jamaica: Canoe Press, 1995.

Cox, J., and C. Embree. *Sustainable Development in the Caribbean.* South Halifax, N.S.: Institute for Research on Public Policy, 1990.

Cox, K. "Globalization and Geographies of Workers' Struggle in the Late Twentieth Century." In *Society, Place, Economy.* Edited by R. Lee and J. Wills. London: Edward Arnold, 1997.

Cox, R. "A Perspective on Globalization." In *Globalization: Critical Reflections,* edited by J. Mittelman, 21–30. Boulder, Colo.: Lynne Rienner, 1996.

Crane, J. *Educated to Emigrate: The Social Organization of Saba.* Assen, Netherlands: Van Gorcum, 1971.

———. *Saba Silhouettes: Life Stories from a Caribbean Island.* New York: Vantage, 1987.

Crick, M. "Representations of International Tourism in the Social Sciences: Sun, Sex, Sights, Savings, and Servility." *Annual Review of Anthropology* 18 (1989): 307–44.

Cross, M. *Urbanization in the Caribbean.* London: Cambridge University Press, 1965.

Crusol, J. "An Economic Policy for Martinique." In *Dual Legacies in the Contemporary Caribbean*, edited by P. Sutton, 188–200. London: Frank Cass, 1986.

Cruz, M., et al. "The Demographic Dynamics of Small Island Societies." *Ekistics* 54 (1987): 110–15, 323–24.

CSA [Caribbean Studies Association]. Panel and papers on immigration to St. Martin. Curacao meeting, 1995.

———. Panel and papers on swallows migration. San Juan, Puerto Rico, 1996.

CTRC. *The Contribution of Tourism to Economic Growth and Development in the Caribbean*. Barbados: Caribbean Tourism Research and Development Centre, 1987.

Cuban Ministry of Economy and Planning. "Cuba Economic Report: First Semester 1996." *Prensa Latina* Special Report. http:www.prensa-latina.org/econ-696.html.

"Cuba: Adapting to a Post-Soviet World." *NACLA Report on the Americas* 29, no. 2 (September/October 1995).

Cubaweb. "Growth in Exports." In *Business Tips on Cuba, May 1996*. http://www.cubaweb.cu/tips/mayo/not-in.html.

Cubitt, T. *Latin American Society*. 2nd ed. New York: John Wiley, 1995.

Culpepper, R. *Growth and Adjustment in Smaller Highly Indebted Countries*. Ottawa, Canada: North-South Institute, 1991.

Cumberbatch, J., and N. Duncan. "Illegal Drugs, USA Policies, and Caribbean Responses: The Road to Disaster." *Caribbean Affairs* 3, no. 1 (1990): 150–81.

Da Vans, J. "Microeconomic Approaches to Studying Migration Decisions." In *Migration Decision Making*, edited by G. De Jong and R. Gardner, 90–130. New York: Pergamon, 1981.

Dalby, S. "Reading Rio, Writing the World: The *New York Times* and the 'Earth Summit.' " *Political Geography* 15, nos. 6–7 (1996): 593–613.

Dalley, G. "Preserving the Benefits of the CBI: The Case for NAFTA Parity." *Nueva Cuenca del Caribe* 12, no. 2 (1996).

Danaher, K. *Fifty Years Is Enough: The Case against the World Bank and the International Monetary Fund*. Boston: South End, 1994.

Daniel, E. "Perspectives on the Total Utilization of Manpower and the Caribbean Expatriate: Barriers to Returning." In *Caribbean Immigration to the United States*, edited by R. Bryce-Laporte and D. Mortimer, 158–68. RIIES Occasional Papers, no. 1. Washington, D.C.: Smithsonian Institution, 1983.

Davidson, B. "No Place Back Home: A Study of Jamaicans Returning to Kingston, Jamaica." *Race* 9, no. 4 (1969): 449–509.

Davis, K. *Mission for Caribbean Change*. Frankfurt am Main: Verlag Peter Lang, 1982.

Davis, S., and P. Simon. *Reggae International*. New York: Knopf, 1983.

DBMC. *Annual Report 1993*. Roseau, Dominica: Dominica Banana Marketing Corporation, 1994.

———. *Annual Report 1995*. Roseau, Dominica: Dominica Banana Marketing Corporation, 1996.

de Albuquerque, K. "How Bad Is Crime in the Caribbean?" *Caribbean Week* 6, no. 19 (1995): 1–8.

de Kadt, E. *Tourism: Passport to Development?* Washington, D.C.: World Bank, 1979.

Deere, C. "The New Agrarian Reforms." *NACLA Report on the Americas* 29, no. 2 (September/October 1995): 13–17.

Deere, C., et al. *In the Shadows of the Sun: Caribbean Development Alternatives and U.S. Policy.* Boulder, Colo.: Westview, 1990.

Deere, C., and E. Melendez. "When Export Growth Isn't Enough: U.S. Trade Policy and Caribbean Basin Economic Recovery." *Caribbean Affairs* 5 (1992): 61–70.

De la Osa, J. "7.9 in the top 20." *GI. Granma International,* 2 January 1997.

Demas, W. *The Economics of Development in Small Countries with Special Reference to the Caribbean.* Montreal: McGill University Press, 1965.

Demko, G., and W. Wood, eds. *Reordering the World: Geopolitical Perspectives on the 21st Century.* Boulder, Colo.: Westview, 1994.

Department of State. *Caribbean Basin Maps.* Washington, D.C., 1984.

Dicken, P. *Global Shift: The Internationalization of Economic Activity.* New York: Guilford, 1992.

Dommen, E., and P. Hein, eds. *States, Microstates, and Islands.* London: Croom Helm, 1985.

Duany, J. *Los Dominicanos en Puerto Rico: Migración en la Semi-periferia.* Rio Piedras: Huaracan, 1990.

———. "Beyond the Safety Valve: Recent Trends in Caribbean Migration." *Social and Economic Studies* 43, no. 1 (1994): 95–122.

Duncan, N. "The Future of Mini-States in the Caribbean." *Bulletin of Eastern Caribbean Affairs* 3, nos. 3–4 (1977): 1–6.

Dunn, H. "Caribbean Telecommunications Policy: Fashioned by Debt, Dependency, and Underdevelopment." *Media, Culture and Society* 17 (1995): 201–22.

Dupuy, A. *Haiti in the World Economy: Class, Race, and Underdevelopment since 1700.* Boulder, Colo.: Westview, 1989.

———. *Haiti in the New World Order: The Limits of the Democratic Revolution.* Boulder, Colo.: Westview, 1997.

Durand, J., and D. Massey. "Mexican Migration to the United States: A Critical Review." *Latin American Research Review* 27, no. 2 (1992): 3–42.

Durand, J., E. Parrado, and D. Massey. "Migradollars and Development: A Reconsideration of the Mexican Case." *International Migration Review* 30, no. 2 (1996): 423–44.

Durand, T. Interview with James Wiley, 15 March 1996. Durand is public/grower relations officer, Dominica Banana Marketing Corporation, Roseau, Dominica.

Durant-Gonzalez, V. "Higglering: Rural Women and the Internal Market System in Jamaica." In *Rural Development in the Caribbean,* edited by P. Gomes, 103–22. Kingston, Jamaica: Heineman Caribbean, 1985.

East Database. Table 2. Eastern Europe: GDP, Real Growth, 1990–1995.

Eckstein, S. *Back from the Future: Cuba under Castro.* Princeton: Princeton University Press, 1994.

ECLAC [CEPAL]. Secretariat. "Strengthening Development." Report presented at conference in San Jose, Costa Rica, 15–20 April 1996. http://www.eclac.cl/ps26/forti.html.

ECLAC [CEPAL]. "Poverty in Latin America and the Caribbean Is Greater Now Than in the 1980s." Press conference report, San Jose, Costa Rica, 15–20 April 1996. http://www.eclac.cl/ps26/pr7.html.

Economist Intelligence Unit. *Tourism in the Caribbean: Special Report.* London: Economist, 1993.

Edwards, M. Interview with James Wiley, 24 May 1995. Edwards is director of the Division of Tourism, Dominica National Development Corporation, Roseau, Dominica.

Ehret, P. Interview with James Wiley, 1 June 1995. Ehret is an agricultural economist with the French Agricultural Cooperation Project, Roseau, Dominica.

Elkan, R., and R. Morley. *Employment in a Tourist Economy: The British Virgin Islands.* Durham, England: Department of Economics, University of Durham, 1971.

Escobar, A. *Encountering Development.* Princeton: Princeton University Press, 1995.

Esteva, G. "Development." In *The Development Dictionary: A Guide to Knowledge and Power,* edited by W. Sachs, 6–25. London: Zed Books, 1992.

"Europe's Cuban Interest." *Wall Street Journal,* 5 August 1996, p. A18.

Evans, P. "After Dependency: Recent Studies of Class, State, and Industrialization." *Latin American Research Review* 20, no. 2 (1985): 149–60.

———. *Embedded Autonomy: States and Industrial Transformation.* Princeton: Princeton University Press, 1995.

Evans, R. "Banking on the Black Economy." *The Economist,* September 1993, 40–2.

Everleny, O. Interview with O. Everleny, Subdirector of the Centre for Studies of the Cuban Economy (CEEC). Interview with Janet Henshall Momsen, June 1995.

Exporters of Information Group. "Going for the Iceberg: A Blueprint for Growth and Development of the Export of Information Services." Report for the Jamaica Exporters of Information Services Group, Kingston, Jamaica, 1989.

Eyre, A. "The Effects of Political Terrorism on the Residential Location of the Poor in the Kingston Urban Region, Jamaica, West Indies." *Urban Geography* 7, no. 3 (1986): 227–42.

Fact publications on Caricom countries, 1995. http://www.odci.gov/cia/publications/95 fact/html.

Fadelle, M. Interview with James Wiley, 12 March 1996. Fadelle is senior investment promotion officer in Roseau, Dominica.

Fagin, V. Interview with James Wiley, 13 March 1996. Fagin is owner of Bello, Ltd., Roseau, Dominica.

Falk, W. "Twenty-eight Cents an Hour: Poverty-level Pay for Some Garment Workers Making Clothes for U.S. Apparel Giants." *Newsday: The Long Island Newspaper,* 16 June 1996, pp. A4, A5, A31, A43.

Fanon, F. *Black Skins, White Masks.* Harmondsworth, England: Penguin Books, 1968.

———. *Wretched of the Earth.* Harmondsworth, England: Penguin Books, 1967.

Farrell, T. "Some Notes towards a Strategy for Economic Transformation." In

Caribbean Economic Development: The First Generation, edited by S. Lalta and M. Freckleton, 330–42. Kingston, Jamaica: Ian Randle, 1993.

Fass, S. *Political Economy in Haiti: The Drama of Survival.* New Brunswick, N.J.: Transaction, 1990.

Fernandez, R. *New Foreign-Investment Law.* CubaWeb, Government Information, 1996.

Fevrier, W. Interview with James Wiley, 23 May 1995. Fevrier is director of the Dominica Planned Parenthood Federation, Roseau, Dominica.

Fitzpatrick, J. *Puerto Rican Americans: The Meaning of Migration to the Mainland.* Englewood Cliffs, N.J.: Prentice-Hall, 1987.

Floyd, B. "The Two Faces of Jamaica." *Geographical Magazine* 46 (1974): 424–31.

Foner, N. *Jamaica Farewell.* London: Routledge, 1979.

Frank, A. "The Development of Underdevelopment." *Monthly Review* 18, no. 4 (1966). Reprinted in *Development Studies: A Reader,* edited by S. Corbridge, 27–37. London: Edward Arnold, 1995.

Freeman, C. "Designing Women: Corporate Discipline and Barbados's Off-Shore Pink-Collar Sector." *Cultural-Anthropology* 8, no. 2 (1993): 169–86.

Friedland, J. "Latin America Stays the Course on Reform." *Wall Street Journal,* 5 August 1996, p. A15.

Friedmann, H. "The Political Economy of Food." *New Left Review* 197 (1993): 29–57.

Frisby, M. "White House Is Divided over Politics of Trade." *Wall Street Journal,* 19 March 1996.

Frucht, R. "Emigration, Remittances, and Social Change: Aspects of the Social Field in Nevis, West Indies." *Anthropologica* 10 (1968): 193–208.

Fukuyama, F. *The End of History and the Last Man.* New York: Free Press, 1991.

Gayle, D. "The Caribbean Basin Initiative: Retrospect and Prospect." Paper presented at the International Studies Association, 27th annual convention, Anaheim, California, 1986.

———. "Message from the Managing Editor." *Caribbean Studies Newsletter* 23, no. 3 (Fall 1996).

Gayle, D., and B. Tewarie. "The International Business Environment and Its Implications for Caribbean Business Organizations." Paper presented at the annual conference of the International Association for Business and Society, Vienna, Austria, 1995.

Gayle, D., and J. Goodrich. *Tourism Marketing and Management in the Caribbean.* London: Routledge, 1993.

Gale, M. Presentation to the Conference on the Caribbean and Latin America, Miami, Florida, 11 December 1996.

Gereffi, G., and M. Korzeniewicz, eds. *Commodity Chains and Global Capitalism.* Westport, Conn.: Praeger, 1994.

Giddens, A. *The Consequences of Modernity.* Stanford, Calif.: Stanford University Press, 1990.

Gill, H. "NAFTA: Challenges for the Caribbean Community." In *The Caribbean: New Dynamics in Trade and Political Economy.* Edited by A. Bryan. New Brunswick, N.J.: Transaction Books, 1995.

Gill, S. "Economic Globalization and the Internationalization of Authority: Limits and Contradictions." *Geoforum* 23, no. 3 (1992): 269–83.

Giraud, M. "Personal Communication: Observations Made at the Seminar in Comparative History of Migration within the Caribbean and to Europe." Oxford University, Oxford, England, 23 September 1995.

Girvan, N., and G. Marcelle. "Overcoming Technological Dependency: The Case of Electric Arc (Jamaica) Ltd., A Small Firm in a Small Developing Country." *World Development* 18, no. 1 (1990): 91–107.

Glasgow, R., and W. Langley. *The Troubled and the Troubling Caribbean.* New York: Edwin Mellon, 1989.

Gmelch, G. "Work, Innovation, and Investment: The Impact of Return Migrants in Barbados." *Human Organization* 46, no. 2 (1987): 131–40.

———. *Double Passage: The Lives of Caribbean Migrants Abroad and Back Home.* Ann Arbor: University of Michigan Press, 1992.

GNN News. Reuters News Media. *ILO: Work Accidents Kill 220,000 Annually.* 22 April 1996.

Goldberg, R. "We're Creating Jobs in the Third World." *New York Times,* 1 August 1995, p. A10. Goldberg is president of New Age Intimates.

Gomes, P. *Rural Development in the Caribbean.* Kingston, Jamaica: Heineman Caribbean, 1985.

Gomes, A. "Integrating Tourism and Agricultural Development." In *Tourism Marketing and Management in the Caribbean,* edited by D. Gayle and J. Goodrich, 155–66. London: Routledge, 1993.

Gonzáles, A. "Europe and the Caribbean: Toward a Post-Lomé Strategy." In *The Caribbean: New Dynamics in Trade and Political Economy.* Edited by Anthony Bryan. Miami: North-South Center, 1995.

Gonzalez, N. *Black Caribs, Household Structures.* Seattle: University of Washington Press, 1969.

Gooding, E. "Food Production in Barbados with Particular Reference to Tourism." Appendix 1 in *The Tourist Industry in Barbados: A Socioeconomic Assessment,* edited by G. V. Doexy. Kitchener, Ont.: Ruseo Graphics, 1971.

Goodman, D., and M. Watts. "Reconfiguring the Rural or Fording the Divide? Capitalist Restructuring and the Global Agro-Food System." *Journal of Peasant Studies* 22, no. 1 (1994): 1–49.

Goodrich, J. "Health-care Tourism in the Caribbean." In *Tourism Marketing and Management in the Caribbean,* edited by D. Gayle and J. Goodrich. London: Routledge, 1990.

Gordon, D. "Race, Class, and Social Mobility in Jamaica." In *Garvey: His Work and His Impact,* edited by R. Lewis and P. Bryan, 265–82. New Jersey: Africa World Press, 1991.

Goss, B., and D. Conway. "Sustainable Development and Foreign Direct Investment in the Eastern Caribbean: A Strategy for the 1990s and Beyond?" *Bulletin of Latin American Research* 11 (1992): 307–26.

Goss, B., and D. Knudsen. "Flexibility in Offshore Assembly Operations in the Commonwealth Caribbean." *The Developing Economies* 32 (1994): 210–27.

Gourou, P. "Pressure on Island Environment." In *Man's Place in the Island Ecosystem,* edited by E. Fosberg. Honolulu: Bishop Museum Press, 1970.

Government of Jamaica, Commission of the European Communities, and International Organization for Migration. *Return and Reintegration Programme of Qualified Jamaican Nationals for Development.* N.d.

Grasmuck, S., and P. Pessar. *Between Two Islands: Dominican International Migration.* Berkeley: University of California Press, 1991.

Green, D. *Silent Revolution: The Rise of Market Economics in Latin America.* London: Cassell, 1995.

Gregoire, S. Interview with James Wiley, 12 March 1996. Gregoire is general manager of the National Development Corporation, Roseau, Dominica.

Grell, O. Interview with James Wiley, 23 May 1995. Grell is director of the agriculture diversification program, Ministry of Agriculture, Roseau, Dominica.

Grewal, I., and C. Kaplan, eds. *Scattered Hegemonies: Postmodernity and Transnational Feminist Practices.* Minneapolis: University of Minnesota Press, 1994.

Griffin, K., and A. Khan. "The Transition to Market-Guided Economies." In *Whither Marxism,* edited by B. Magnus and S. Cullenberg, 153–89. New York: Routledge, 1995.

Griffith, I. "Drugs in the Caribbean: An Economic Balance Sheet." *Caribbean Studies* 28, no. 2 (1995): 285–303.

Grindle, M., and F. Thoumi. "Muddling towards Adjustment." In *The Political Economy of Structural Adjustment,* edited by A. Krueger and R. Bates, 123–78. London: Basil Blackwell, 1993.

Guengant, J.-P. *Population and Development in the Caribbean: A Demographic Survey.* New York: Inter-American Parliamentary Group on Population and Development, 1985.

Gunn, G. "Cuba's NGOs: Government Puppets or Seeds of Civil Society?" Cuba Briefing Paper Series, no. 7. Washington, D.C.: Cuba Project, Center for Latin American Studies, Georgetown University, 1995.

Hach, J. "The Island Question: Problems and Prospects." *Ekistics* 54 (1987): 88–92, 323–24.

Haggard, S., and S. Webb. *Voting for Reform: Democracy, Political Liberalization, and Economic Adjustment.* New York: Oxford University Press, 1994.

Halebsky, S., and J. Kirk, eds. *Cuba: Twenty-Five Years of Revolution, 1959–1984.* New York: Praeger, 1985.

———. *Cuba in Transition: Crisis and Transformation.* Boulder, Colo.: Westview, 1992.

Harbison, S. "Family Structure and Family Strategy in Migration Decision Making." In *Migration Decision Making,* edited by G. De Jong and R. Gardner, 225–51. New York: Pergamon, 1981.

"Hard Times Abroad Hurting Emigrants: Trinis Coming Home." *Sunday Guardian* [Port-of-Spain], 13 June 1993.

Harden, S. *Small Is Dangerous: Micro States in a Macro World.* London: Frances Pinter, 1985.

Hardy, C. *The Caribbean Development Bank.* Boulder, Colo.: Lynne Rienner; Ottawa, Canada: The North-South Institute, 1995.

Harewood, J. *Population and Employment in the Caribbean.* New York: Inter-American Parliamentary Group on Population and Development, 1985.

Harris, C. Interview with James Wiley, 2 June 1995 and 11 March 1996. Harris is director of the implementation unit of the Ministry of Finance and Development, Roseau, Dominica.

Harris, D. "Market Size, Industrialization, and Regional Integration." *Social and Economic Studies* 29, no. 4 (1980): 76–84.

Harrison, L. *Underdevelopment Is a State of Mind: The Latin American Case.* Lanham, Md.: Madison Books, 1985.

Harvey, D. "Money, Time, Space, and the City." Chap. 6 in *The Urban Experience.* Baltimore: Johns Hopkins University Press, 1985.

———. "Globalization in Question." *Rethinking Marxism* 8, no. 4 (1995): 1–17.

Health, K., D. Costa-Martinez, and A. Sheon. *Trinidad and Tobago Demographic and Health Survey, 1987.* Columbia, MD: Institute for Resource Development/ Westinghouse, 1988.

Hendricks, G. *The Dominican Diaspora.* New York: Teachers College Press, 1974.

Henke, H., and I. Boxill, eds. *The Rise of Industrial Asia and Its Implications for Small Developing States.* Forthcoming.

Henry, F. *The Caribbean Diaspora in Toronto: Learning to Live with Racism.* Toronto: University of Toronto Press, 1994.

Henry, R. "A Reinterpretation of Labor Services of the Commonwealth Caribbean." Commission for the Study of International Migration and Cooperative Economic Development, Working Paper no. 61, 1990.

Henshall, J. "Gender versus Ethnic Pluralism in Caribbean Agriculture." In *Geography and Ethnic Pluralism,* edited by C. Clarke, D. Ley, and C. Peach, 173–90. London: George Allen and Unwin, 1984.

Henwood, D. "The Free Flow of Money." *NACLA Report on the Americas* 29, no. 4 (January/February 1996): 11–17.

Herbert, B. "Not a Living Wage." *New York Times,* December 1995, op-ed page.

Hernandez, D., and J. Scheff. "Rethinking Migration: Having Roots in Two Worlds." Paper presented at 1994 Caribbean Studies Association meeting, Merida, Mexico, 1994.

Hersh, S. "Operation Urgent Fury." *Frontline,* aired 29 January 1991. Television documentary produced by the Corporation for Public Broadcasting.

Hey, J., and T. Klak. "From Protectionism to Neoliberalism: Tracing the Transition to Ecuador, 1981–1995." Discussion paper, Miami University, 1997.

Hintjens, H., and M. Newitt, eds. *The Political Economy of Small Tropical Islands: The Importance of Being Small.* Exeter: Exeter University Press, 1992.

Hirst, P., and G. Thompson. *Globalization in Question: The International Economy and the Possibilities of Governance.* Cambridge: Polity, 1996.

Ho, C. "The Internationalization of Kinship and the Feminization of Caribbean Migration: The Case of Afro-Trinidadian Immigrants in Los Angeles." *Human Organization* 52, no. 1 (1993): 32–40.

———. *Salt-water Trinnies: Afro-Trinidadian Immigrant Networks and Non-assimilation in Los Angeles.* New York: AMS Press, 1991.

Homiak, J. "The Hucksters of Dominica." *Grassroots Development* 10, no. 1 (1986): 28–37.

Honychurch, L. *The Dominica Story: A History of the Island.* London: Macmillan Caribbean Publishers, 1995.

IADB [Inter-American Development Bank]. *Economic and Social Progress in Latin America: 1992 Report.* Washington, D.C.: IADB, 1992.

———. *Economic and Social Progress in Latin America. 1995 Report: Overcoming Volatility.* Washington, D.C.: IADB, 1995.

———. "Labor Reform." In *Economic and Social Progress in Latin America: 1992 Report,* 185–206. Washington, D.C.: IADB, 1996.

Ince, B. "Decolonization and Self-Determination in the United Nations: A Third World Perspective." In *Essays on Race, Economics, and Politics in the Caribbean,* edited by B. Ince, 91–131. Puerto Rico: Universidad de Puerto Rico en Mayaguez/Cuadernas de Arts y Ciencas, 1972.

"Information Services: Way Forward for the Caribbean." *Caribbean Week,* 13–26 November 1996.

INSED [Institute of Demographic Studies], Paris. Series of monographs on French Antilleans in metropolitan France, 1990.

Instituto del Tercer Mundo. *Third World Guide, 91/92.* Section on Trinidad and Tobago, 537–39. Uruguay: Instituto del Tercer Mundo, 1990.

International Labour Organization. *Labour Uncertainty Reigns in All Industrialized Nations: Lowest-Paid Workers Hit the Hardest.* ILO Press Release. 1 April 1996.

International Monetary Fund. *Balance of Payments Statistics Yearbook.* Washington, D.C.: IMF, 1993.

Ionnades, D. "Strengthening the Ties between Tourism and Economic Geography: A Theoretical Agenda." *Professional Geographer* 47, no. 1 (1995): 49–60.

———. "Planning for International Tourism in Less Developed Countries: Towards Sustainability?" *Journal of Planning Literature* 9, no. 3 (1995).

IRELA [Instituto de Relaciones Europeo-Latinoamericanos]. *Brazil under Cardoso: Returning to the World Stage.* Dossier no. 52. Madrid, Spain: IRELA, 1995.

Jacobs, W., and B. Jacobs. *Grenada: The Route to Revolution.* Havana, Cuba: Casa de las Americas, 1980.

Jainarain, C. *The Caribbean in 1993: Special Report on International Business.* Miami: The Beacon Council, 1993.

———. *Annual Report on Trade, 1995–1996: U.S., Florida, Latin America and the Caribbean.* Miami: Summit of the Americas Center, 1996.

Jalan, B., ed. *Problems and Policies in Small Economies.* London: Croom Helm, 1982.

James, A. Interview with James Wiley, 30 May 1995. James is director of Division of Forestry, Ministry of Agriculture, Roseau, Dominica.

James, C. *State Capitalism and World Revolution.* Detroit: Facing Reality, 1969.

James, H. Interview with James Wiley, 6 June 1995 and 12 March 1996. James is chief technical officer, Ministry (1995), and permanent secretary, Ministry of Trade, Industry, and Tourism (1996), Roseau, Dominica.

James, W., and C. Harris. *Inside Babylon: The Caribbean Diaspora in Britain.* London: Verso, 1993.

JAMPRO. "Background Report into Export Processing Zones in Jamaica." Paper prepared by the Information Processing Unit, Kingston, Jamaica, 1995.

————. "Framework Paper of Determining Guidelines for Industrial Policy in the Jamaican Information Processing Industry." Draft document by the Jamaican Promotions Organization Information Processing Unit, 1993.

Johnson, T. "Clinton Aide Urges New Hemispheric Trade Summit." *Miami Herald,* 20 March 1996.

Kahn, J. "Shanghai Campaigns to Attract the Rich." *Wall Street Journal,* 13 August 1996, p. A9.

Kaplinsky, R. "A Reply to Willmore." *World Development* 23, no. 3 (1995): 537–40.

Karch, C., and G. Dann. "Close Encounters of the Third World." *Human Relations* 34, no. 4 (1981).

Kasinitz, P. *Caribbean New York: Black Immigrants and the Politics of Race.* Ithaca, N.Y.: Cornell University Press, 1992.

Kay, C. *Latin American Theories of Development and Underdevelopment.* New York: Routledge, 1989.

Kearney, M. "The Local and the Global: The Anthropology of Globalization and Transnationalism." *Annual Review of Anthropology* 24 (1995): 547–65.

Kelly, D. *Report of Board of Inquiry into the Garment Industry.* Report for Jamaica's Ministry of Labour, Kingston, Jamaica, February 1989.

Kenworthy, E. *America/Américas: Myth in the Making of U.S. Policy toward Latin America.* University Park: Pennsylvania State University Press, 1995.

King, R. "Return Migration and Regional Economic Development: An Overview." *Return Migration and Regional Economic Problems,* edited by R. King, 1–37. New Hampshire: Croom Helm, 1986.

Klak, T. "Havana and Kingston: Mass Media Images and Empirical Observations of Two Caribbean Cities in Crisis." *Urban Geography* 15, no. 4 (1994): 318–44.

————. "Maidenforming the Caribbean: Concerns about Jamaica's Industrial Export Promotion Policy." *Caribbean Geography* 5, no. 2 (1994).

————. "A Framework for Studying Caribbean Industrial Policy." *Economic Geography* 71, no. 2 (1995): 297–316.

———— "Squandering Development Possibilities from Within or Without? Problems with Neoliberal Industrial Export Policy in Jamaica." Paper presented at the Association of American Geographers annual meeting, Chicago, 14–18 March 1995.

————. "Distributional Impacts of the 'Free Zone' Component of Structural Adjustment: The Jamaican Experience." *Growth and Change* 27 (Summer 1996): 352–87.

Klak, T., and G. Myers. "The Discursive Tactics of Neoliberal Development in Small Third World Countries." In *Geoforum.* Forthcoming.

Klak, T., and J. Rulli. "Regimes of Accumulation, the Caribbean Basin Initiative, and Export-Processing Zones: Scales of Influence on Caribbean Development." In *The New Localism,* edited by E. Goetz and S. Clarke, 117–50. Beverly Hills: Sage, 1993.

Koechlin, T. "The Globalization of Investment." *Contemporary Economic Policy* 13 (January 1995): 92–100.

Kopinak, K. *Desert Capitalism: Maquiladoras in North America's Western Industrial Corridor.* Tucson: University of Arizona Press, 1996.

Krueger, A. *Political Economy of Policy Reform in Developing Countries.* Cambridge, Mass.: MIT Press, 1993.

Kurlansky, M. *A Continent of Islands.* Reading, MA: Addison-Wesley, 1992.

Kuznets, S. "Economic Growth of Small Nations." In *Economic Consequences of the Size of Nations,* edited by E. Robinson, 14–32. London: Macmillan, 1960.

La Riva, G. "Rising Harvest: Cubans Mobilize to Bring in the Sugar." Workers World News Service. http://www.workers.org/cuba/sugar.html, reprinted from May 23, 1996.

Laird, C., and A. Hall. *And the Dish Ran Away with the Spoon.* Film documentary (1993) distributed by Bullfrog Films, P.O. Box 149, Oley, Pa. 19547.

Lalta, S., and M. Freckleton, eds. *Caribbean Economic Development: The First Generation.* Kingston, Jamaica: Ian Randle, 1993.

Lande, S. *The FTAA Process: Maintaining the Miami Summit Momentum.* Coral Gables, Fla.: North-South Center, University of Miami, 1996.

Lange, O. "On the Economic Theory of Socialism." In *On the Economic Theory of Socialism,* edited by B. Linnicott, 57–143. Minneapolis: University of Minnesota Press, 1938.

Latimer, H. "Developing Island Economies . . . Tourism v. Agriculture." *Tourism Management* 6 (1985): 32–42.

———. "Urban Violence." *Latin American Press* 29, no. 13 (1997): 7.

Latin American Bureau. *The Poverty Brokers: The IMF and Latin America.* London: Latin American Bureau, 1983.

Laurence, K. *Immigration into the West Indies in the 19th Century.* Barbados: Caribbean Universities Press, 1971.

Lavoie, D. "The Market as a Procedure for Discovery and Conveyance of Inarticulate Knowledge." *Comparative Economic Studies* 28, no. 1 (1986): 1–19.

"Leather Goods Factory Aids Employment in St. Thomas." *Jamaican Weekly Gleaner* [Kingston], 3 February 1986, p. 27.

Lee, J. "Confessions of an Intellectual Musketeer." *St. Lucia Mirror,* 4 October 1996, pp. 14–15.

Lee, S. "Maximizing the Export of Goods and Services." *Granma International,* 2 October 1996.

———. "The State Can Achieve More through Better Organization and Efficiency." *Granma International,* 27 December 1996.

Leslie, D. "Global Scan: The Globalization of Advertising Agencies, Concepts, and Campaigns." *Economic Geography* 71 (1995): 402–26.

Lestrade, S. *CARICOM's Less Developed Countries: A Review of the Progress of the LDCs under the CARICOM Arrangements.* Occasional Paper no. 16. Cave Hill, Barbados: ISER, University of the West Indies, 1981.

Levine, B., ed. *The Caribbean Exodus.* New York: Praeger, 1987.

Levine, D. Remarks at forum on migration from the Caribbean: Issues for the 1990s. Program on Latin American and Caribbean Studies, University of Michigan, Ann Arbor, 3 April 1995.

Levitt, K. *The Origins and Consequences of Jamaica's Debt Crisis, 1970–1990.* Kingston, Jamaica: Consortium Graduate School of Social Sciences, 1991.

Lewis, G. *The Growth of the Modern West Indies.* London: MacGibbon and Kee, 1968.

————. "The Contemporary Caribbean: A General Overview." In *Caribbean Contours*, edited by S. Mintz and S. Price, 219–50. Baltimore: Johns Hopkins University Press, 1985.

Lewis, L., and L. Nurse. "Caribbean Trade Unionism and Global Restructuring." In *The Caribbean in the Global Political Economy*, edited by H. Watson, 191–206. Boulder, Colo.: Lynne Rienner; Kingston, Jamaica: Ian Randle, 1994.

Lewis, V. *Size, Self Determination, and International Relations: The Caribbean.* Mona, Jamaica: Institute for Social and Economic Research, University of the West Indies Press, 1976.

Lewis, W. "The Industrialization of the West Indies." *Caribbean Economic Review* 2, no. 1 (1950): 1–61.

Leymarie, I. "Salsa and Migration." In *The Commuter Nation: Perspectives on Puerto Rican Migration*, edited by C. Torre, H. Vecchini, and W. Burgos. Rio Pedras, PR: Editorial de la Universidad de Puerto Rico, 1994.

Leyshon, A. "True Stories: Global Nightmares, Global Dreams, and Writing Globalization." In *Society, Place, Economy: States of the Art in Economic Geography*, edited by R. Lee and J. Wills. London: Edward Arnold, 1997.

Linnicott, B. Introduction. In *On the Economic Theory of Socialism*, edited by Benjamin E. Linnicott. Minneapolis: University of Minnesota Press, 1938.

Lloyd-Evans, S., and R. Potter. "The Informal Sector of the Economy in the Commonwealth Caribbean." *Papers on Geography*, no. 8. London: Royal Holloway/Bedford New College, University of London, 1991.

————. "Government Response to Informal Sector Retail Trading: The Peoples' Mall, Port of Spain, Trinidad." *Geography* 78, no. 3 (1993): 315–18.

Locher, U. *Haitian Migration Networks.* Paper presented at 1979 Caribbean Studies Association Meeting, Martinique, 1979.

Lockhart, D., D. Drakakis-Smith, and J. Schembri. *The Development Process in Small Island States.* London: Routledge, 1993.

Lorah, P. "An Unsustainable Path: Tourism's Vulnerability to Environmental Decline in Antigua." *Caribbean Geography* 6, no. 1 (1995): 28–39.

Lovelace, E. *A Brief Conversion and Other Stories.* Great Britain: Heineman International, 1988.

Lowenthal, D. *West Indian Societies.* New York: Oxford University Press, 1972.

Lowenthal, D., and C. Clarke. "Caribbean Small Island Sovereignty: Chimera or Convention?" In *Problems of Caribbean Development*, edited by U. Fanger et al. Munich: Wilhelm Fink Verlag, 1982.

————. "Island Orphans: Barbuda and the Rest." *Journal of Commonwealth and Comparative Politics* 18, no. 3 (1980): 293–307.

Lowenthal, D., and L. Comitas. "Emigration and Depopulation: Some Neglected Aspects of Population Geography." *Geographical Review* 52 (1962): 195–210.

Lundahl, M. *Peasants and Poverty: A Study of Haiti.* New York: St. Martin's Press, 1979.

————. "A Note on Haitian Migration to Cuba, 1890–1938." *Cuban Studies* 12, no. 2 (1982): 21–36.

————. *The Haitian Economy.* New York: St. Martin's Press, 1983.

————. *Politics or Markets: Essays on Haitian Underdevelopment.* London: Routledge, 1992.

Lundgren, J. "Agricultural Marketing and Distribution Arrangements with Respect to the Resort Hotel in the Caribbean." Paper presented at the Sixth West Indies Agricultural Economics Conference, Georgetown, Guyana, 1971.

Lyon, P. *Small States and the Commonwealth.* London: Butterworth, 1985.

MacMillan, A. "Land of the Hummingbird." In *Parang: A Poetry Anthology for Caribbean Primary Schools, Book 2,* edited by Cecil Gray. Kingston, Jamaica: Nelson Caribbean, 1977.

Magloire, W. Interview with James Wiley, 1995. Magloire is field coordinator of the Ministry of Agriculture, Roseau, Dominica.

Maingot, A. *The United States and the Caribbean: Challenges of an Asymmetrical Relationship.* Boulder, Colo.: Westview, 1994.

Maingot, A., ed. *Small Country Development and International Labor Flows: Experiences in the Caribbean.* Vol. 5. Series on Development and International Migration in Mexico, Central America, and the Caribbean Basin. Boulder, Colo.: Westview, 1991.

———. *The United States and the Caribbean.* Warwick University Caribbean Studies. London: Macmillian Caribbean Publishers, 1994.

Manley, M. *The Politics of Change: A Jamaican Testament.* London: Andre Deutsch, 1974.

———. *A Voice at the Workplace: Reflections on Colonialism and the Jamaican Worker.* London: Andre Deutsch, 1975.

———. *Jamaica: Struggle in the Periphery.* London: Third World, 1982.

———. Forward to *Last Resorts: The Cost of Tourism in the Caribbean,* by P. Pattullo. New York: Monthly Review Press, 1996, ix–x.

Manning, F. *Black Clubs in Bermuda: Ethnography of a Play World.* Ithaca, N.Y.: Cornell University Press, 1973.

Manuel, P. *Caribbean Currents.* New York: HarperCollins, 1995.

Marsden, T., and A. Arce. "Constructing Quality: Emerging Food Networks in the Rural Transition." *Environment and Planning* 27 (1995): 1261–79.

Marshall, Dawn. "The International Politics of Caribbean Migration." In *The Restless Caribbean: Changing Patterns of International Relations,* edited by R. Millet and W. Will. New York: Praeger, 1979.

———. *Haitians in the Bahamas.* Barbados: University of the West Indies Press, 1980.

———. "The History of Caribbean Migrations." *Caribbean Review* 11, no. 1 (1982): 6–9, 52–53.

———. "A History of West Indian Migration: Overseas Opportunities and 'Safety Valve' Policies." In *The Caribbean Exodus,* edited by B. Levine, 15–31. New York: Praeger, 1987.

Marshall, Don. "From the Triangular Trade to (N)AFTA: A Neostructuralist Insight into Missed Caribbean Opportunities." *Third World Quarterly* 17, no. 3 (1996): 427–53.

Martin, A. Interview with James Wiley, 1995. Martin is chair of the Dominica Conservation Association, Roseau, Dominica.

Martin, U. Interview with James Wiley, 22 May 1995. Martin is IICA coordinator for Dominica (OAS), Roseau, Dominica.

Marx, K. *Capital.* Vol. 1. New York: Vintage, 1976.

Marx, K., and F. Engels. "The Communist Manifesto." In *Selected Works.* New York: International Publishers, 1980.

Massiah, J. *Women as Heads of Households in the Caribbean: Family Structure and Feminine Status.* Paris: UNESCO, 1983.

Masud-Piloto, F. *With Open Arms: Cuban Migration to the U.S.* Totowa: Rowman and Allenheld, 1988.

Mather, S., and G. Todd. *Tourism in the Caribbean.* Special Report no. 455. London: The Economist Intelligence Unit, 1993.

Mathey, K. "Self-Help Housing Strategies in Cuba." In *Self-Help Housing, the Poor, and the State in the Caribbean,* edited by R. Potter and D. Conway, 164–87. Knoxville: University of Tennessee Press; Kingston, Jamaica: University of the West Indies Press, 1997.

Mayn, M. "Puerto Rico's Energy Fix." In *Green Guerrillas: Environmental Conflicts and Initiatives in Latin America and the Caribbean,* edited by H. Collinson. London: Latin American Bureau, 1996.

McAfee, K. "Grenada: The Revo in Reverse." *NACLA Report on the Americas* 23, no. 5 (February 1990), 27–32.

———. *Storm Signals: Structural Adjustment and Development Alternatives in the Caribbean.* Boston: South End/Oxfam America, 1991.

McElroy, J., K. de Albuquerque, and E. Towle. "Old Problems and New Directions for Planning Sustainable Development in Small Islands." *Ekistics* 54 (1987): 93–99, 323–24.

McElroy, J., and K. de Albuquerque. "Migration Transition in Small Northern and Eastern Caribbean States." *International Migration Review* 22, no. 8 (1988): 30–58.

———. *An Integrated Sustainable Ecotourism for Small Caribbean Islands.* Occasional Paper no. 8. Bloomington: Indiana Center on Global Change and World Peace, 1992.

———. "Tourism Styles and Policy Responses in the Open Economy-Closed Environment Context." In *Caribbean Ecology and Economics,* edited by N. Girvan and D. Simmons, 143–64. Barbados: Caribbean Conservation Association, 1994.

———. "The Social and Economic Propensity for Political Dependence in the Insular Caribbean." *Social and Economic Studies* 44, nos. 2–3 (1996): 167–93.

McGowan, L. "Structural Adjustment and the Aid Juggernaut in Haiti." Report prepared for the Development Group for Alternative Policies, Inc. (the Development GAP), 1997.

McIntyre, A. "Adjustments of Caribbean Economies to Changing International Economic Relations." *CARICOM Bulletin* 3 (1982): 1–9.

McKee, D., and C. Tisdell. "The Development Implications of Migration from and between Small Island Nations." *International Migration (Geneva)* 26, no. 4 (1988): 417–25.

McMichael, P. "Incorporating Comparison within a World-Historical Perspective: An Alternative Comparative Method." *American Sociological Review* 55 (June 1990): 385–97.

————. "Globalization: Myths and Realities." *Rural Sociology* 61, no. 1 (1996): 25–55.

Meidner, R. "Why Did the Swedish Model Fail?" In *Socialist Register 1993,* edited by R. Miliband and L. Panitch, 211–28. London: Merlin, 1993.

Mendes, J. *Cote ci, cote la: Trinidad and Tobago Dictionary.* Port-of-Spain, Trinidad, 1986.

Mesa-Lago, C. "Cuba and the Downfall of Soviet and Eastern European Socialism." In *Cuba after the Cold War,* edited by C. Mesa-Lago, 133–96. Pittsburgh: University of Pittsburgh Press, 1993.

————. "Cuba's Economic Policies and Strategies for Confronting the Crisis." In *Cuba After the Cold War,* edited by C. Mesa-Lago, 197–257. Pittsburgh: University of Pittsburgh Press, 1993.

Millett, T. *The Chinese in Trinidad.* Port-of-Spain: Caribbean Limited, 1993.

Ministry of Agriculture. *Crop Development Plans, 1993–1995.* Roseau, Dominica: Commonwealth of Dominica, 1992.

Mintz, S. "Enduring Substances, Trying Theories: The Caribbean region as *oikoumene.*" *Journal of the Royal Anthropological Society* 2, no. 2 (1996): 289–311.

Mintz, S., and S. Price, eds. *Caribbean Contours.* Baltimore: Johns Hopkins University Press, 1985.

Mody, A., and D. Wheeler. "Towards a Vanishing Middle: Competition in the World Garment Industry." *World Development* 15 (1987): 1269–84.

Mohammed, P., and C. Shepherd. *Gender in Caribbean Development.* Trinidad and Tobago: Women and Development Studies Project, University of the West Indies, 1988.

Momsen, J. D. *Report on Vegetable Production and the Tourist Industry in St. Lucia.* Alberta, Canada: Department of Geography, University of Calgary, 1972.

————. *Report on Vegetable Production and the Tourist Industry in Montserrat.* Alberta, Canada: Department of Geography, University of Calgary, Alberta, 1974.

Momsen, J. H. "Recent Changes in Caribbean Tourism with Special Reference to St. Lucia and Montserrat." In *Canadian Studies of Parks, Recreation and Tourism in Foreign Lands,* edited by J. Marsh. Occasional Paper 11. Ontario: Department of Geography, Trent University, 1986.

————. Survey of Hotel Food Use in Barbados. Department of Geography, University of Newcastle upon Tyne, 1990.

————. "Tourism, Gender, and Development in the Caribbean." In *Tourism: A Gender Analysis,* edited by D. Hall and V. Kinnaird, 106–20. Chichester: Wiley and Sons, 1994.

Morrison, T., and R. Sinkin. "International Migration in the Dominican Republic: Implications for Development Planning." *International Migration Review* 16, no. 4 (1982).

Mullings, B. "Telecommunications Restructuring and the Development of Export Information Processing Services in Jamaica." In *Globalization, Communications, and Caribbean Identity,* edited by H. Dunn, 174–91. Kingston, Jamaica: Ian Randle, 1995.

Myers, G., and T. Klak. "Export-Processing as Development Policy in the Caribbean and Africa: Liberalism Distinct from the East Asian Model." In *The Rise of Industrial Asia and Its Implications for Small Developing States,* edited by H. Henke and I. Boxill. Forthcoming. (1998).

Nanton, P. "The Caribbean Diaspora in Question: The United Kingdom Context." Paper presented at the 1995 annual meeting of the Caribbean Studies Association, Curacão, 1995.

Navarro, M. "Cuba Passes Law to Attract Greater Foreign Investment." *New York Times,* 7 September 1995.

Nelson, J., ed. *Economic Crisis and Policy Choice.* Princeton: Princeton University Press, 1990.

Nettleford, R. "Caribbean Crisis and Challenges to Year 2000." *Caribbean Quarterly* 35, nos. 1–2 (1989): 6–16.

———. *Inward Stretch, Outward Reach: A Voice from the Caribbean.* London: Macmillan, 1993.

News in Brief. *Prensa Latina,* 6 July 1996. http//:www.prensa-latina.org/Samples/CubaNewsinBrief/96–0 706

Nietschmann, B. "Ecological Change, Inflation, and Migration in the Far Western Caribbean." *Geographical Review* 69, no. 1 (1979): 1–24.

NLC [National Labor Committee]. "Zoned for Slavery: The Child behind the Label." NLC video documentary, 1995. Available from the NLC (275 Seventh Avenue, New York, N.Y. 10001; tel. 212–242–0986).

———. "Mickey Mouse Goes to Haiti: Walt Disney and the Science of Exploitation." NLC video documentary, 1996.

———. "An Open Letter to Walt Disney." 29 May 1996.

———. "Setting the Record Straight: The Real Disney in Burma, Haiti, Indonesia, China." 17 January 1997.

Nove, A. *The Economics of Feasible Socialism.* Boston: George Allen and Unwin, 1983.

New York Times News Service. *Cuban A-Plant Project Worries,* 24 February 1996. http://www.nandotimes.com/newsroom/ntn/world/022496/world 424967.h tml.

Nyerere, J. *Freedom and Socialism.* Dar es Salaam, Tanzania: Oxford University Press, 1969.

OAS. *Final Report: OAS/CRTC Workshop on Tourism and Agricultural Linkages in the Caribbean.* OAS: Washington, D.C., 1984. The workshop convened in Barbados in July 1984.

OECD. *European Business Directory, 1995.* Paris, 1995.

"OECS Manufacturers Struggle for Survival." *Caribbean Week,* 25 May–7 June 1996.

OECS. *Information Industry Market Place: Opportunities for Eastern Caribbean Countries.* Unpublished study produced in cooperation with the World Bank, 1995.

OECS/ADCU. *Fresh Produce Exporter.* Issue no. 8. Roseau, Dominica: Agricultural Diversification Coordination Unit, 1994.

———. *Fresh Produce Exporter.* Issue no. 10. Roseau, Dominica: Agricultural Diversification Coordination Unit, 1994.

O'Loughlin, C. "Economic Problems of the Smaller West Indian Islands." *Social and Economic Studies* 11, no. 1 (1962): 44–56.

————. *Economic and Political Change in the Leeward and Windward Islands.* New Haven: Yale University Press, 1968.

Olwig, K. *Global Culture, Island Identity: Continuity and Change in the Afro-Caribbean Community of Nevis.* Philadelphia: Harwood, 1993.

Oostindie, G. *Ethnicity, Nationalism and the Exodus: The Dutch Caribbean Predicament.* Paper presented at the 1995 meeting of the Caribbean Studies Association, Curacão, 1995.

Oppenheimer, A. "U.S.-Mexico Job Shift Not Detected." *Miami Herald,* 13 January 1997.

O Tuathail, G., and T. Luke. "Present at the (Dis)integration." *Annals of the Association of American Geographers* 84, no. 3 (1994): 351–80.

Palmer, R. "Development with Dependence: The Problem of the Caribbean States." *Caribbean Educational Bulletin* 8, no. 2 (1981): 23–32.

————. *Problems of Development in Beautiful Countries: Perspectives on the Caribbean.* Lanham, Md.: North-South Publications, 1984.

Palmer, R., ed. "A Decade of West Indian Migration to the U.S.A., 1962–72." *Social and Economic Studies* 23, no. 4 (1974): 571–87.

————. *In Search of a Better Life: Perspectives on Migration from the Caribbean.* New York: Praeger, 1990.

————. *Pilgrims from the Sun: West Indian Migration to America.* New York: Twayne Publishers, 1995.

Pantin, D. "Export-Based Information Processing in the Caribbean with Particular Respect to Offshore Data-Entry/Processing." Report for the International Federation of Commercial, Clerical, Professional and Technical Employers, Geneva, Switzerland, 1995.

————. "Long Waves and Caribbean Development." *Social and Economic Studies* 36, no. 2 (1987): 1–20.

Pantojas-García, E. *Development Strategies as Ideology: Puerto Rico's Export-Led Industrialization Experience.* Boulder, Colo.: Lynne Rienner, 1990.

Pantojas-García, E., and J. Dietz. "North American Free Trade, Economic Restructuring and Export-led Industrialization in the Caribbean." *Caribbean Studies* 29, no. 1 (1996): 49–66.

Passell, P. "Trade Pacts by Regions: Not the Elixir as Advertised." *New York Times,* 4 February 1997, p. D1.

Pastor, Jr., M., and A. Zimbalist. "Cuba's Economic Conundrum." *NACLA Report on the Americas* 29, no. 2 (September/October 1995): 10.

Pastor, R. *Whirlpool: U.S. Foreign Policy toward Latin America and the Caribbean.* Princeton: Princeton University Press, 1992.

Pastor, R., ed. *Migration and Development in the Caribbean: The Unexplored Connection.* Boulder, Colo.: Westview, 1985.

————. "Migration and Development: Implications and Recommendations for Policy." *Studies in Comparative International Development* 24, no. 1 (1989).

Patterson, O. "West Indian Migrants Returning Home: Some Observations." *Race* 10, no. 1 (1968): 69–77.

———. "The Emerging West Atlantic System." In *Population in an Interacting World,* edited by W. Alonso, 227–60. Cambridge: Harvard University Press, 1987.

———-. "Ecumenical America: Global Culture and the American Cosmos." *World Policy Journal* 11, no. 2 (1994): 103–17.

Pattullo, P. *Last Resorts: The Cost of Tourism in the Caribbean.* New York: Monthly Review Press, 1996.

———-. "Green Crime, Green Redemption." In *Green Guerrillas: Environmental Conflicts and Initiatives in Latin America and the Caribbean,* edited by H. Collinson, 187–93. London: Latin American Bureau, 1996.

Pearson, R. "Gender and New Technology in the Caribbean: New Work for Women." In *Women and Change in the Caribbean,* edited by J. Momsen, 287–95. Kingston, Jamaica: Ian Randle, 1993.

Peck, J. *Work Place: The Social Regulation of Labor Markets.* New York: Guilford, 1996.

Perez, L. "Implications and Consequences of Possible Future Cuban Emigration to the U.S." Miami: Cuban Research Institute, Florida International University, 1994. Paper commissioned by the U.S. Department of State.

Pérez Jr., L. "Aspects of Underdevelopment: Tourism in the West Indies." *Science and Society* 37 (1973–74): 473–80.

Persaud, B. "Small States: Economic Problems and Prospects." *Bulletin of Eastern Caribbean Affairs* 12, no. 5 (1986): 1–11.

Pessar, P., and S. Grasmuck. *Between Two Islands: Dominican International Migration.* Berkeley: University of California Press, 1991.

Philpott, S. "Remittance Obligations, Social Networks, and Choice among Montserratian Migrants in Britain." *Man* 3, no. 3 (1968): 465–76.

PIOJ. *Economic and Social Survey of Jamaica.* Annual publication. Kingston: Planning Institute of Jamaica, 1987, 1994–96.

———. *Jamaica Five-Year Development Plan.* Kingston: Planning Institute of Jamaica, 1990.

Piore, M. *Birds of Passage: Migrant Labor and Industrial Societies.* New York: Cambridge University Press, 1979.

Plischke, E. *Microstates in World Affairs: Policy Problems and Options.* Washington, D.C.: American Enterprise Institute, 1977.

Pocket World in Figures. 1997 edition. London: The Economist, 1996.

Poon, A. *Tourism, Technology, and Competitive Strategies.* Wallingford, Oxford: C.A.B. International, 1993.

Population Reference Bureau [PRB]. *1995 World Population Data Sheet.* Washington, D.C.: PRB, 1995.

———. *World Population Data Sheet.* Washington, D.C.: PRB, 1996.

Porter, M. *The Competitive Advantage of Nations.* New York: Free Press, 1990.

Portes, A., and L. Guarnizo. "Tropical Capitalists." In *Migration, Remittances, and Small Business Development: Mexico and Caribbean Basin Countries,* edited by S. Diaz-Briquets and S. Weintraub, 101–31. Boulder, Colo.: Westview, 1991.

Potter, R. "Basic Needs and Development in the Small Island States of the Eastern

Caribbean." In *The Development Process in Small Island States*, edited by D. Lockhart et al., 92–116. New York: Routledge, 1994.

Potter, R., and D. Conway, eds. *Self-Help Housing, the Poor, and the State in the Caribbean*. Knoxville: University of Tennessee Press; Kingston, Jamaica: University of the West Indies Press, 1997.

Prada, P. *Island under Siege: The U.S. Blockade of Cuba*. Melbourne, Australia: Ocean, 1995.

Premdas, R. "Politics of Preference in the Caribbean." In *Ethnic Preference and Public Policy in Developing States*, edited by N. Nevitte and C. Kennedy, 160–69. Boulder, Colo.: Lynne Rienner, 1986.

Qureshi, Z. "Globalization: New Opportunities, Tough Challenges." *Finance and Development*. March 1996, pp. 30–33. This article summarizes the main points from *Global Economic Prospects and the Developing Countries*, published by the World Bank, Washington, D.C., 1996.

Rakowski, C., ed. *Contrapunto: The Informal Sector Debate in Latin America*. Albany: State University of New York Press, 1994.

Ramirez de la O, R. *North American Investment under NAFTA*. The NAFTA Effects Working Paper Series. Montreal, Quebec: Commission for Environmental Cooperation, 1996.

Rampersad, F. "Is Trinidad and Tobago Ready for NAFTA?" *Caribbean Affairs* 7, no. 5 (1995).

Ramphall, D. "Caribbean Industrialization as Sustainable Development: Exploring the Contradictions." *Caribbean Geography* 5, no. 2 (1995): 81–91.

Ramphal, S. "Small Is Beautiful but Vulnerable." Address by the Secretary-General at the meeting of Commonwealth ministers, New Delhi, India, November 1983. Marlborough House, London: Commonwealth Secretariat, 1984.

Ramsaran, R. *The Challenge of Structural Adjustment in the Commonwealth Caribbean*. New York: Praeger, 1992.

Raymond, M. "Jamaica Goes Global." *Forbes*. Special Advertising Supplement, 8 June 1996.

Reynolds, L. "The Restructuring of Third World Agro-exports: Changing Production Relations in the Dominican Republic." In *The Global Restructuring of Agro-food Systems*, edited by P. McMichael, 214–38. Ithaca, N.Y.: Cornell University Press, 1994.

Regueiro, L. "Cuba: dilemas de la integracion." *Economia Cubana/Boletin Informativo* 24 (November/December 1995): 3–17.

Reich, R. *The Work of Nations: Preparing Ourselves for 21st Century Capitalism*. New York: Vintage, 1991.

Reid, S. "An Introductory Approach to the Concentration of Power in the Jamaican Corporate Economy and Notes on its Origin." In *Essays on Power and Change in Jamaica*, edited by C. Stone and A. Brown, 15–43. Kingston: Jamaica Publishing House, 1977.

"Remapping South America: A Survey of Mercosur." *The Economist*, 12–18 October 1996.

Renard, Y. *Popular Participation and Community Responsibility in Natural Resource Management: A Case from St. Lucia, West Indies*. Castries, St. Lucia: CANARI and World Wild Life Fund, 1992.

Rice, J. "Cuba Expects Rebound in 1996 for Economy; Sugar Harvest Weak." *Naples Daily News,* 28 December 1995, p. 3D.

Richardson, B. "The Overdevelopment of Carriacou." *The Geographical Review* 65, no. 3 (1975): 390–99.

———. "The Origins and Continuity of Return Migration in the Leeward Caribbean." In *Return Migration and Remittances: Developing a Caribbean Perspective,* 35–44. RIIES Occasional Papers, no. 3. Washington, D.C.: Smithsonian Institution, 1982.

———. *Caribbean Migrants: Environment and Human Survival on St. Kitts and Nevis.* Knoxville: University of Tennessee Press, 1983.

———. *Panama Money in Barbados, 1900–1920.* Knoxville: University of Tennessee Press, 1985.

———. "Caribbean Migrations, 1838–1995." In *The Modern Caribbean,* edited by Franklin Knight and Colin Palmer, 203–28. Chapel Hill: University of North Carolina Press, 1989.

———. *The Caribbean in the Wider World Economy, 1492–1992.* Cambridge: Cambridge University Press, 1992.

Rickard, T., and B. Carmichael. "Linkages between the Agricultural and Tourism System in Sustaining Rural Development in Jamaica." In *The Sustainability of Rural Systems,* edited by C. Bryant and C. Marois, 345. Montreal: Département de géographie, Université de Montreal, 1995.

Riviere, B. "Contemporary Class Struggles and the Revolutionary Potential of Social Classes in Dominica." In *Contemporary Caribbean: A Sociological Reader,* edited by S. Craig, 2:365–83. Port-of-Spain, Trinidad: College Press, 1981.

———. *State Systems in the Eastern Caribbean.* Mona, Jamaica: ISER, University of the West Indies, 1990.

Roberts, B. "Informal Economy and Family Strategies." *International Journal of Urban and Regional Research* 18, no. 1 (1994): 6–23.

Roberts, S. "Fictitious Capital, Fictitious Spaces? The Geography of Off-shore Financial Flows." In *Money, Power, and Space,* edited by S. Corbridge, R. Martin, and N. Thrift, 88–120. Oxford: Blackwell, 1994.

Robinson, D., Dr. Interview with James Wiley, 23 May 1995. Robinson is chief technical officer in the Ministry of Agriculture, Roseau, Dominica.

Rodriguez, E. "Duty-free Zones: New Attraction for Investment in Cuba." *Granma International,* 2 June 1996. http://www.cubawebcu/granma/2junio/5jun8i.html.

———. "Economic Opening Makes Insurance Legislation Indispensable." *Granma International,* 2 September 1996.

Rodriguez, J. "Report on 1996 Economic Results and 1997 Economic and Social Plan." *Granma International,* 2 January 1997.

Roemer, J. "Market Socialism, a Blueprint: How Such an Economy Might Work." In *Why Market Socialism? Voices from Dissent,* edited by F. Roosevelt and D. Belkin, 269–81. New York: M. E. Sharpe, 1994.

Rohter, L. "Cuban Rights Group Cancels Conference." New York Times News Service, 21 February 1996. http:www.latinolink.com/news/cuba0221.html.

———. "Impact of NAFTA Pounds Economies of the Caribbean." *New York Times,* 30 January 1997.

———. "Flood of Dominicans Lets Some Enter U.S. by Fraud." *New York Times,* 19 February 1997, p. A4.

Roque, C., and M. Beatriz. *Una opinion sobre las reformas economicas en Cuba.* Habana (gopher.gate.net). Distributed by CubaNet, ANEIC, 17 May 1995.

Rosenberg, M., and J. Hiskey. "Interdependence between Florida and the Caribbean." *Caribbean Affairs* 6, no. 1 (January/March 1993).

Rosset, P., and M. Benjamin. "Cuba's Nationwide Conversion to Organic Agriculture." *Capitalism, Nature, Society* 5, no. 3 (September 1994): 79–97.

Rosset, P., and M. Benjamin, eds. *The Greening of the Revolution: Cuba's Experiment with Organic Agriculture.* San Francisco: Global Exchange, 1996.

Rubenstein, H. "Return Migration to the English-Speaking Caribbean: Review and Commentary." In *Return Migration and Remittances: Developing a Caribbean Perspective,* edited by William F. Stinner et al., 3–34. RIIES Occasional Papers, no. 3. Washington, D.C.: Smithsonian Institution, 1982.

———. "Remittances and Rural Underdevelopment in the English-Speaking Caribbean." *Human Organization* 42, no. 2 (1983): 295–306.

Rubio, L. "Gobierno y corresponsales extranjeros." *La Jornada Semana,* 25 June 1995, p. 4.

Ryan, S. *Social and Occupational Stratification in Contemporary Trinidad and Tobago.* St. Augustine, Trinidad: Institute of Social and Economic Research, University of the West Indies, 1991.

Sachs, W., ed. *The Development Dictionary: A Guide to Knowledge as Power.* Atlantic Highlands, N.J.: Zed Books, 1992.

Safa, H. *The Myth of the Male Breadwinner: Women and Industrialization in the Caribbean.* Boulder, Colo.: Westview, 1995.

Samaroo, B. "In Sick Longing for the Further Shore: Return Migration by Caribbean East Indians during the Nineteenth and Twentieth Centuries." In *Return Migration and Remittances: Developing a Caribbean Perspective,* edited by W. Stinner et al., 45–72. RIIES Occasional Papers, no. 3. Washington, D.C.: Smithsonian Institution, 1982.

Samuel, W. "Regional Cooperation as an Element of Caribbean Development Strategy." In *Integration and Participatory Development,* edited by J. Wedderburn, 7–65. Kingston, Jamaica: Friedrich Ebert Stiftung/Association of Caribbean Economists, 1990.

Sandoval, J. "State Capitalism in a Petroleum-based Economy: The Case of Trinidad and Tobago." In *Crisis in the Caribbean,* edited by F. Ambursley and R. Cohen, 247–68. London: Heineman, 1983.

Sanka, C. "T&T Raising Young Americans: Survey—U.S. TV a Bad Influence." *Sunday Express,* 12 June 1994, pp. 19–20.

Satney, A. Interview with James Wiley, 25 May 1995. Satney is marketing intelligence officer, OECS Agricultural Diversification Co-ordinating Unit, Roseau, Dominica.

Sawyer, F. *Nightline—Cuba Incorporated.* ABC Television, 2 July 1996.

Sayer, A. *Radical Political Economy: A Critique.* Cambridge, Mass.: Blackwell, 1995.

Sayer, A., and R. Walker. *The New Social Economy: Reworking the Division of Labor.* Cambridge, Mass.: Blackwell, 1992.

Schmitter, P. "Still the Century of Corporatism?" In *The New Corporatism: Social-Political Structures in the Iberian World,* edited by F. Pike and T. Stritch. South Bend, Ind.: University of Notre Dame Press, 1974.

Schoepfle, G., and J. Perez-Lopez. "Export Assembly Operations in Mexico and the Caribbean." *Journal of Interamerican Studies* 31, no. 4 (Winter 1989): 131–61.

Schrieberg, D. "Dateline Latin America: The Growing Fury." *Foreign Policy* 106 (Spring 1997): 161–75.

Schumaker, E. *Independence and Economic Development.* Sir Winston Scott Memorial Lecture. Bridgetown, Barbados: Central Bank of Barbados, 1976.

———. "Issues of Size and Technology." In *Planning for Small Enterprises in Third World Cities,* edited by R. Bromley, 7–14. New York: Pergamon, 1985.

Schware, R., and S. Hume. *The Global Information Industry and the Eastern Caribbean.* Finance and Private Sector Development Note, no. 17. Washington, D.C.: World Bank, 1994.

Scott, A., and M. Storper. "Work Organization and Local Labour Markets in an Era of Flexible Production." *International Labour Review* 129 (1990): 573–91.

Seager, J. *The State of Women in the World Atlas.* 2nd ed. New York: Penguin, 1997.

Segal, A. "Collecting the Caribbean." *Caribbean Review.* Spring 1984, 29–31, 50–51.

———. *An Atlas of International Migration.* London: Bowker, 1993.

Segal, A., and B. Weinstein. *Haiti: The Failure of Politics.* New York: Praeger, 1992.

Selwyn, P. *Development Policy in Small Countries.* London: Croom Helm, 1975.

———. "Smallness and Islandness." *World Development* 8, no. 12 (1980): 945–51.

Sergent, J. *Report of the Tripartite Economic Survey of the Eastern Caribbean.* London: Ministry of Overseas Development, HMSO, 1967.

Shand, R. *The Island States of the Pacific and Indian Oceans.* Canberra: Australian National University, 1980.

Sharkey, D. "Alternative Tourism in Dominica, West Indies: Problems and Prospects." Masters thesis, University of California-Davis, 1994.

Sharkey, D., and J. Momsen. "Tourism in Dominica: Problems and Prospects." *Caribbean Geography* 6, no. 1 (1995): 40–51.

Shaw, B. "Smallness, Islandness, Remoteness, and Resources: An Analytical Framework." *Regional Development Dialogue,* Special Issue (1982): 95–109.

Sherwood, R., and C. Primo Braga. *Intellectual Property, Trade, and Economic Development: A Road Map for the FTAA Negotiations.* Coral Gables, Fla.: North-South Center, University of Miami, 1996.

Shorrock, T. "Drop Seen in Real Wages in All Three NAFTA Countries." *The Daily Item* [Sunbury, Pa.], 29 May 1996, p. A6.

"Show time." *Latin American Press* 28, no. 34 (1996): 7.

Simmons, A., and J. Guengant. "Caribbean Exodus and the World System." In *International Migration Systems: A Global Guide,* edited by M. Kritz, L. Lim, and H. Zlotnik. Oxford: Clarendon, 1992.

Smith, A. "Community Involvement in Coral Reef Monitoring for Management in the Eastern Caribbean." In *Collaborative and Community-based Management of Coral Reefs,* edited by A. White et al., 59–67. West Hartford, Conn.: Kumarian, 1994.

Smith, A., and F. Berkes. "Solutions to the 'Tragedy of the Commons': Sea Urchin Management in St. Lucia." *Environmental Conservation* 18, no. 2 (1991): 131–36.

Smith, L., and A. Padula. *Sex and Revolution: Women in Socialist Cuba.* New York: Oxford University Press, 1996.

Smith, M. *Culture, Race and Class in the Commonwealth Caribbean.* Mona, Jamaica: Department of Extra-Mural Studies, University of the West Indies, 1984.

Smith, R. *Kinship and Class in the West Indies.* New York: Cambridge University Press, 1988.

Soares, A. "Work Organization in Brazilian Data Processing Centres: Consent and Resistance." *Labour, Capital and Society* 24, no. 2 (1991): 154–83.

"Special Economic Bulletin." *Prensa Latina,* 10 December 1996.

St. Cyr, E. "The Theory of Caribbean-type Economy." In *Caribbean Economic Development: The First Generation,* edited by S. Lalta and M. Freckleton, 8–16. Kingston, Jamaica: Ian Randle, 1993.

Stewart, T. "The Marrakesh Agreement on Trade-Related Intellectual Property Rights: Implications for CARICOM Countries." Paper presented at the conference of the Caribbean Studies Association, San Juan, Puerto Rico, 1996.

Stone, C. *Democracy and Clientelism in Jamaica.* New Brunswick, N.J.: Transaction Books, 1980.

———. *Work Attitudes Survey: A Report to the Jamaican Government.* St. Ann, Jamaica: Earle Publishers, 1986.

———. "Race and Economic Power in Jamaica." In *Garvey: His Work and His Impact,* edited by R. Lewis and P. Bryan, 243–64. Trenton, N.J.: Africa World Press, 1991.

Stubbs, J. *Cuba: The Test of Time.* London: Latin American Bureau, 1989.

Sunshine, C. *The Caribbean: Survival, Struggle and Sovereignty.* Washington, D.C.: Ecumenical Program on Central America and the Caribbean, 1988.

Susman, P. "Spatial Equality in Cuba." *International Journal of Urban and Regional Research* 11, no. 2 (1987).

Sutton, C. "The Caribbeanization of New York City and the Emergence of a Transnational Socio-Cultural System." In *Caribbean Life in New York City: Sociocultural Dimensions,* edited by C. Sutton and E. Chaney, 15–30. New York: Center for Migration Studies, 1987.

Sutton, P. "The 'New Europe' and the Caribbean." *European Review of Latin American and Caribbean Studies* 59 (December 1995): 37–57.

Szulc, T. "Castro's China Model." *New York Times,* 29 February 1996.

Taylor, B., J. Morison, and E. Fleming. "The Economic Impact of Food Import Substitution in the Bahamas." *Social and Economic Studies* 40 (1991): 45–62.

Teague, P. "The Political Economy of the Regulation School and the Flexible Specialization Scenario." *Journal of Economic Studies* 17, no. 5 (1990): 32–54.

Telfer, D., and G. Wall. "Linkages between Tourism and Food Production." *Annals of Tourism Research* 23, no. 3 (1996): 635–53.

Thomas, C. "State Capitalism in Guyana: An Assessment of Burnham's Co-operative Socialist Republic." In *Crisis in the Caribbean,* ed. F. Ambursley and R. Cohen, 27–48. London: Heineman, 1983.

————. *The Poor and Powerless: Economic Policy and Change in the Caribbean.* London: Latin American Bureau, 1988.

————. "Restructuring the World Economy and Its Political Implications for the Third World." In *Instability and Change in the World Economy,* edited by A. MacEwan and W. Tabb, 331–61. New York: Monthly Review Press, 1989.

————. "Alternative Development Model for the Caribbean." In *Caribbean Economic Development: The First Generation,* edited by S. Lalta and M. Freckleton, 314–29. Kingston, Jamaica: Ian Randle, 1993.

Thomas-Hope, E. "Return Migration and Its Implications for Caribbean Development." *Migration and Development in the Caribbean: The Unexplored Connection,* edited by R. Pastor, 157–77. Boulder, Colo.: Westview, 1985.

————. "Transients and Settlers: Varieties of Caribbean Migrants and the Socio-Economic Implications of Their Return." *International Migration Review* 24, no. 3 (1986): 559–627.

————. *Explanation in Caribbean Migration—Perception of the Image: Jamaica, Barbados, St. Vincent.* Warwick University Caribbean Studies. London: Macmillan, 1992.

Thompson, E. *The Making of the English Working Class.* New York: Pantheon Books, 1963.

Thompson, G., et al., eds. *Markets, Hierarchies, and Networks: The Co-ordination of Social Life.* London: Sage, 1991.

Thomson, R. *Green Gold: Bananas and Dependency in the Eastern Caribbean.* London: Latin American Bureau, 1987.

Thorndike, T. *No End to Empire.* London: Department of International Relations and Politics, Stafford Polytechnic and Foreign and Commonwealth Office, 1988.

Thrupp, L. *Bittersweet Harvests for Global Supermarkets: Challenges in Latin America's Agricultural Export Boom.* Washington, D.C.: World Resources Institute, 1995.

Tirado de Alonso, I. *Trade Issues in the Caribbean.* Philadelphia: Gordon and Breach, 1992.

Tolkacheva, J. *Russian Economy Shrank by Four Percent in 1995.* ZHI Press, Reuters. 16 January 1996. http://www.nd.edu/astrouni/zhiwriter/ spool/ 96022609.htm and EAST database.

"Trade Barriers Cost America $19 Billion a Year, Study Says." *Miami Herald,* 27 November 1993.

Trejos, A., and R. Galles. *Industrialization and Trade in the Caribbean Basin.* San Jose, Costa Rica: Institute for Economic and Social Research on the Caribbean Basin [IESCARIBE], 1987.

Trouillot, M. *Peasants and Capital: Dominica in the World Economy.* Baltimore: Johns Hopkins University Press, 1988.

"UNICEF and UNDP Outline Negative Consequences of Blockade against Cuba." *GI Granma International,* 17 November 1997.

United Nations. Secretariat. *The World Economy at the Beginning of 1996.* http://www.unicc.org/html.

United Nations. Population Division. *World Migrant Populations: The Foreign-Born.* New York: United Nations, 1989.

United Nations. *Human Development Report.* New York: United Nations, 1996.

Urry, J. *The Tourist Gaze: Leisure and Travel in Contemporary Societies.* London: Sage, 1990.

U.S. Department of State. Bureau of Public Affairs. *Russian Economy,* 1995. http://dosfan.lib.uic.edu/www/regions/nis/4rusecon.html.

U.S. Department of State. Bureau of Public Affairs. Figures calculated from data presented in *Russian Economy,* 1995. http://dosfan.lib.uic.edu/www/regions/nis/4rusecon.html

Vakil, C., and P. Brahmananda. "The Problems of Developing Countries." In *Economic Consequences of the Size of Nations,* edited by E. Robinson, 133–50. London: Macmillan, 1960.

Vanderbush, W., and T. Klak. "'Covering' Latin America: The Exclusive Discourse of the Summit of the Americas as Viewed through the *New York Times.*" *Third World Quarterly* 17 (1996): 537–56.

Villamil, J. "Size and Survival: Planning in Small Island Systems." *Micro State Studies,* no 1. Charlotte Amalie, U.S.V.I.: Caribbean Research Institute, College of the Virgin Islands, 1977.

Vitalis, D. "Dr. Lewis: Nothing's Changed." *St. Lucia Mirror,* 4 October 1996, p. 2.

Wagenheim, K. *Caribbean Update* 9, no. 10 (November 1993).

———. *Caribbean Update* 12, no. 4 (May 1996).

———. *Caribbean Update* 12, no. 12 (January 1997).

Watson, H. "Theoretical and Methodological Problems in Commonwealth Caribbean Migration Research: Conditions and Causality." *Social and Economic Studies* 31, no. 1 (1982): 165–205.

———. "The Internationalization of Capital, Development, and Labor Migration from the Caribbean." In *The Troubled and the Troubling Caribbean,* edited by R. Glasgow and W. Langley, 168–200. Lewiston, N.Y.: Edwin Mellon, 1989.

Watson, H., ed. *The Caribbean in the Global Political Economy.* Boulder, Colo.: Lynne Rienner, 1994.

Watson, H. "Global Powershift and the Techno-Paradigm Shift: The End of Geography, World Market Blocs, and the Caribbean." In *Postintegration Development in the Caribbean,* edited by M. Aponte Garcia and C. Gautier Mayoral, 74–146. Rio Pedras, Puerto Rico: Social Science Research Center, 1995.

Watts, D. *The West Indies: Patterns of Development, Culture, and Environmental Change since 1492.* Cambridge: Cambridge University Press, 1987.

Watts, M. "Mapping Identities: Place, Space, and Community in an African City." In *The Geography of Identity,* edited by P. Yeager, 59–97. Ann Arbor: University of Michigan Press, 1996.

Weaver, D. "The Evolution of a 'Plantation': Tourism Landscape on the Caribbean Island of Antigua." *Tijdschrift voor Economische en Sociale Geographie* 79 (1988): 319–31.

———. "Alternative to Mass Tourism in Dominica." *Annals of Tourism Research* 18, no. 3 (1991): 414–32.

———. "Ecotourism in the Small Island Caribbean." *Geojournal* 31, no. 4 (1993): 457–65.

Wedderburn, J. *Integration and Participatory Development.* Kingston, Jamaica: Friedrich Ebert Stiftung/Association of Caribbean Economists, 1990.

Weintraub, S., and J. Gilbreath. *North American Trade under NAFTA.* The NAFTA Effects Working Paper Series. Montreal, Quebec: Commission for Environmental Cooperation, 1996.

West Indies Commission. *Time for Action: Overview of the Report of the West Indian Commission.* Barbados, 1992.

Western, J. *A Passage to England: Barbadian Londoners Speak of Home.* Minneapolis: University of Minnesota Press, 1992.

Wheelock, J. "The Household in the Total Economy." In *Real-Life Economics: Understanding Wealth Creation,* edited by P. Ekins and M. Max-Neef, 123–36. London: Routledge, 1992.

Wiarda, H., and M. Kryzanek. *The Dominican Republic: A Caribbean Crucible.* 2nd ed. Boulder, Colo.: Westview, 1992.

Wilentz, A. *In the Rainy Season: Haiti since Duvalier.* New York: Touchstone, 1989.

Wiley, J. "The European Union's Single Market and Latin America's Banana Exporting Countries." In *CLAG Yearbook 1996. CLAG* is the journal of the Conference of Latin Americanist Geographers.

———. "The NTAE Imperative: Neoliberalism and Agricultural Diversification in the Eastern Caribbean." Paper presented at the annual meeting of the Association of American Geographers (AAG), Ft. Worth, 1–5 April 1997.

Wilkinson, A. *Big Sugar: Seasons in the Cane Fields of Florida.* New York: Vintage Books, 1989.

Williams, E. Interview with James Wiley, 1995. Williams holds the position of permanent secretary, Ministry of Health, Dominica.

Williamson, J. "The Progress of Policy Reform in Latin America." In *Latin American Adjustment: How Much Has Happened?* edited by J. Williamson, 353–420. Washington, D.C.: Institute for International Economics, 1990.

Willmore, L. "Export Processing in the Caribbean: The Jamaican Experience." *CEPAL Review* 52 (1994): 91-104.

World Bank. *Export Processing Zones.* Policy and Research Series, no. 20. Washington, D.C.: World Bank, 1992.

———. *The East Asian Miracle: Economic Growth and Public Policy.* Washington, D.C.: World Bank, 1993.

———. *Global Economic Prospects and the Developing Countries.* Annual report. Washington, D.C.: World Bank, 1995.

———. *World Development Report, 1992–1996.* Washington, D.C.: World Bank.

Worrell, D. *The Caribbean Economy in the Nineties: Challenge and Response.* Central Bank of Barbados: Sir Winston Scott Memorial Lectures, December 1986.

———. *Small Island Economies: Structure and Performance in the English-Speaking Caribbean since 1970.* New York: Praeger, 1987.

Yapa, L. "What Causes Poverty? A Post-modern View." *Annals of the Association of American Geographers* 86, no. 4 (1996): 707–28.

Yeats, A. *Trade Creation versus Trade Diversion in Mercosur.* Washington, D.C.: World Bank, 1996.

Yelvington, K., ed. *Trinidad Ethnicity.* Knoxville: University of Tennessee Press, 1993.

Yunker, J. "A New Perspective on Market Socialism." *Comparative Economic Studies* 32, no. 2 (1990): 69–116.

Zalesova, O. "Labour Market: Development Trends." In *Russian Economy: Trends and Perspectives.* Moscow: Institute for the Economy in Transition, 1996. http://www.online.ru/sp/iet/trends/apr96/apr96e.11.html.

Zapata, F. *Labor Perspectives on the NAFTA Agreement.* Sponsored by the Center for the Study of Global Change. Indianapolis: Indiana University/Purdue University, 1996.

Zelinsky, W. "The Race between Population and Resource Development in Central America and the West Indies." In *Geography and a Crowded World,* edited by W. Zelinsky et al., 511–34. New York: Oxford University Press, 1970.

Zimbalist, A. "Teetering on the Brink: Cuba's Current Economic and Political Crisis." *Journal of Latin American Studies* 24, no. 2 (1992): 407–18.

Index

ABC Islands (Aruba, Bonaire, and Curacao), 30, 55, 75
Andean Community, 67, 84
Anguilla, 30, 45, 55, 78
Antigua, 35, 41, 45, 55
Association of Caribbean States, 47, 72, 84, 187

Bahamas, 78; agriculture and tourism in the, 118
Bailey, Donovan, 58
backward linkages, 107, 124–25, 261
banana exports, 158–61
Barbados, 35, 43, 45; characteristics of and progress in, 40–41; compared to EPNDP in St. Lucia and Jamaica, 104–105; data processing in, 78, 146; industrial exports in, 99–101; investment promotion in, 92–97, 101, 103; NAFTA and, 84; political parties and leaders of, 40; pursuance of neoliberal policies in, 88–89; tourism and agriculture in, 125–32
Barbuda, 45, 55
Bermuda, 29, 30, 41, 57
Bishop, Maurice, 39, 87
brain drain, 230–31
Bretton Woods Agreement, 35
Britain, 30, 57; British Royal Commission of 1897, 45; Commonwealth Immigration Act of, 253n6; Nationality Act of, 253n6

British Virgin Islands, 30, 128
Burnham, Forbes. *see* Guyana
Bustemante, Sir Alexander, 45

Cable and Wireless, 80, 82, 140, 173, 259
Canada, 44; immigration quotas of, 222. *See also* NAFTA
Caribbean Basin Initiative (CBI), 26–27, 31, 47, 65, 94, 244; described, 74–75; members of the, 85n11; NAFTA and the, 69, 70, 71, 74; Reagan Administration and the, 74, 76
Caribbean-Canadian trade agreement (Caribcan), 47
Caribbean Development Bank, 47
Caribbean Integration and Free Trade Agreement (Carifta), 46
Caribbean region: Caribbean Labour Congress of 1938, 45; corporate takeovers and mergers in the, 80–81, 161; defined, 3, 213; demographic trends in the, 215–17; economic characteristics of the, 32–33; emigration from the, 11, 52, 57–58, 212–13, 221–24; fragmented island nations of the, 55; gaps between income and cost of living in the, 7; languages spoken in the, 214; manufacturing in the, 81–82; migrations to the, 31, 211–12, 220–21, 224–26;

About the Contributors

Dennis Conway has a Ph.D. in Geography from the University of Texas at Austin. He is currently professor of geography at Indiana University. He has lived and studied at length in the Caribbean, Britain, and the United States and has written extensively on issues of Caribbean development, migration, and sustainability. His books include *The Caribbean Islands: Endless Geographical Diversity* (Rutgers University Press, 1992, with Thomas Boswell) and *Self-Help Housing, the Poor and the State: Pan-Caribbean Perspectives* (University of the West Indies Press and University of Tennessee Press, 1996, with Robert Potter).

Roger-Mark De Souza has lived most of his life in Trinidad and took a B.A. and a Post Graduate Diploma in International Relations at the University of the West Indies, St. Augustine. He also holds an M.A. degree in International Affairs and Development from George Washington University. He now works as a research assistant at the World Resources Institute, a Washington-based center that provides information and proposals for policy change relating to sustainable development. De Souza has conducted field work in Jamaica and Trinidad on population and environmental issues.

Dennis Gayle is professor of international business environment and chair of the Asian Studies Program at Florida International University in Miami. Born and raised in Jamaica, he has since conducted research on economic development issues throughout the Caribbean region. He has served as the managing editor of the *Caribbean Studies Newsletter* and is the co-author of *Tourism Marketing and Management in the Caribbean* (with Jonathan Goodrich, 1993, Routledge).

Thomas Klak obtained his Ph.D. in Geography at the University of Wisconsin–Madison. He is currently associate professor of geography and director of the Latin American Studies Program at Miami University in Oxford, Ohio, and adjunct faculty in the geography department at Ohio

State University. His research interests include the critical analysis and deconstruction of development discourse in government policy and in the news media and the assessment of the distributional impacts of structural adjustment and neoliberalism in countries of the South. His work has appeared in development- and planning-oriented journals such as *World Development, Third World Quarterly, Geoforum, Antipode, Political Geography, Economic Geography, Tijdschrift Voor Economische en Sociale Geografie, the Journal of the American Planning Association,* and *Caribbean Geography.*

Janet Henshall Momsen obtained a Ph.D. in Geography from King's College and the London School of Economic and Political Science of the University of London. She is professor in the human and community development department at the University of California–Davis. She has conducted research throughout the Caribbean on issues of agriculture, tourism, gender, and development. Her recent books include *Different Places, Different Voices: Gender and Development in Africa, Asia and Latin America* (Routledge, 1993, with Vivian Kinnaird) and *Women and Change in the Caribbean: A Pan-Caribbean Perspective* (co-published by Ian Randle in Jamaica, Indiana University Press in the United States, and James Currey in Britain, 1993).

Beverley Mullings holds a Ph.D. in Geography from McGill University and is currently assistant professor of geography at Syracuse University. She has lived for extended periods and holds degrees from universities in Jamaica, Britain, and Canada. Her research interests include international divisions of labor, state policies, and gender relations.

Garth Myers holds a Ph.D. in Geography from the University of California, Los Angeles, and is currently assistant professor of geography and African/African American studies at the University of Kansas. He has published widely on issues of Third World urban and development planning and on the way that images of Third World peoples and places, from colonial times to the present in the news media, shape interactions from the individual to the international levels. He has engaged in extensive research in Eastern Africa, particularly in Zanzibar. He is interested most broadly in the roles of peoples and places in the global political economy.

Until his death in April 1997, **Aaron Segal** was professor of political science at the University of Texas at El Paso. He conducted extensive comparative research on the development prospects, population characteristics, and migration features of countries of the Caribbean region. His books include the classic work *Population Policies in the Carib-*

bean (Lexington Books, 1975) and more recently *An Atlas of International Migration* (Hanzell Publishers, 1993).

Paul Susman has a Ph.D. in Geography from Clark University. He is presently associate professor and chair of the geography department at Bucknell University. His research interests include the development and industrialization of Caribbean territories within the global political economy.

James Wiley holds a Ph.D. in Geography from Rutgers University and is presently an associate professor in the economics and geography department at Hofstra University. He has travelled and conducted research in many parts of the Caribbean, Central America, and South America. His interests include international trade and trade alliances, rural development, and the prospects of small states in the global economy.